Sublime Understanding

Studies in Contemporary German Social Thought (a selection)
Thomas McCarthy, general editor

Sublime Understanding

Aesthetic Reflection in Kant and Hegel

Kirk Pillow

The MIT Press
Cambridge, Massachusetts
London, England

First MIT Press paperback edition, 2003

This book was set in New Baskerville by The MIT Press and printed and bound in the United States of America.

Library of Congress Cataloging-in-Publication Data

Pillow, Kirk.
  Sublime understanding : aesthetic reflection in Kant and Hegel / Kirk Pillow.
    p.   cm. — (Studies in contemporary German social thought)
  Includes bibliographical references and index.
  ISBN 0-262-16192-3 (hc : alk. paper), 0-262-66136-5 (pb)
  1. Kant, Immanuel, 1724–1804—Aesthetics. 2. Hegel, Georg Wilhelm Friedrich, 1770–1831—Aesthetics. 3. Kant, Immanuel, 1724–1804—Contributions in the concept of the sublime. 4. Aesthetics. 5. Sublime, The I. Title. II. Series.
  B2799.A4 P55   2000
  111'.85'092243—dc21   00-021975

10 9 8 7 6 5 4 3 2

Contents

Contents

Acknowledgments

This book has been a long time in the making, and a number of people have provided assistance and inspiration along the way. Let me thank all of the following for their varied parts in helping this project happen: Peter Fenves, Pauline Kleingeld, David Kolb, Tom McCarthy, John McCumber, Terry Pinkard, Robert Pippin, the late Sam Todes, and the anonymous readers for MIT Press.

Everyone familiar with Rudolf Makkreel's work on Kant's third *Critique* will see his wide influence on this study, despite some disagreements. I thank him for his ongoing stimulation and encouragement of my views.

The philosophy departments at Northwestern University and at Hamilton College provided the friendly confines in which this work was gestated, written, rewritten, and rewritten again. I salute my graduate colleagues at Northwestern who played such a formative role in my becoming the person who could produce this, especially Joel Anderson, Barbara Fultner, Bill Hohengarten, and Diane Rothschild. At Hamilton I thank Katheryn Doran for all of her support, and Jamie McKee and Brandon Sornberger for their help with the last stages of the project.

Portions of the argument have appeared elsewhere in substantially different form. Parts of chapters 2 and 3 correspond to "Form and Content in Kant's Aesthetics: Situating Beauty and the Sublime in the Work of Art," in *Journal of the History of Philosophy* 32 (1994): 443–459; parts of chapters 5 and 6 to "Habituating Madness and

Phantasying Art in Hegel's *Encyclopedia,*" in *The Owl of Minerva* 28 (1997): 183–215. I gratefully acknowledge permission to reprint these materials.

I dedicate this book to Mitchell Stevens for his patience, his caring, and his confidence in me, not to mention his willingness to read with improving pen in hand.

Introduction: Facing the Sublime

Interest in Immanuel Kant's aesthetic theory has grown exponentially in recent years, and no aspect of it has received wider attention lately than his treatment of the sublime. Both these features of the way in which the *Critique of Judgment* is currently received are rather curious. Kant wanted his "Analytic of Aesthetic Judgment" to serve as a preparation for the reflections on teleology that he thought would secure the unity of theoretical and practical cognition. This preparatory part of the third *Critique* now occupies the center of attention. Within his Analytic, the sublime especially fascinates us today, despite Kant's indications that his treatment of it forms a "mere appendix" to the analysis of that purest form of aesthetic reflection, the judgment of taste.

A primary aim of this study will be to show why Kant's aesthetics generally, and his judgment of sublimity in particular, enjoy such a following today. The answer is surely in part that Kant's aesthetic theory, and especially its take on the sublime, explores the limits of determinately conceptual or representational thinking. Kant's aesthetics of the sublime marks the border zone where our efforts at comprehension fail, where the unity of understanding crumbles. Yet at the same time it articulates those moments when the displeasure of this crumbling gives way to an *indeterminate* felt sense for and orientation toward the whole that supercedes a discursively conceptual cognition. As such the Kantian sublime appeals to all those tendencies in contemporary thought that would valorize indeterminacy, suspect conceptual unities, and bind all understanding to prediscursive felt

contexts of intelligibility. However much the sublime performs a limiting function on our presentational powers, though, it will have a
positive role in my account in structuring an interpretive activity that
is broadly exemplified in our everyday engagements. Hence this project joins recent scholarship in reviving interest in the sublime, while
bringing judgments of sublimity into the fold of an alternative conception of aesthetic reflection. My focus will draw an aesthetics of
sublimity from Kant's third *Critique,* bolster it with help from Hegel,
and establish its place in a broadened conception of human understanding. Sublime reflection can provide, I will argue, a model for a
kind of *interpretive response* to the uncanny Other "outside" our conceptual grasp. It thereby advances our sense-making pursuits even
while eschewing unified, conceptual determination.

Kant's account of aesthetic judgment locates it as a species of what
he calls reflective judgment—the process of seeking a universal under
which to think an unfamiliar particular. This feature of Kant's
thought has received great attention of late, but much of that attention has not adequately surmised the nature of reflective judgment
nor addressed the specific character of aesthetic reflection as a
species of it. The contrast with determinative judgment—the conceptual cognition that is the purview of Kant's first *Critique*—has led
some commentators to regard reflective judgment as a supplement to
conceptual determination. On this view, reflective judgment forms
new empirical concepts under which the uncanny particular can be
subsumed and "normalized"; reflection brings what had exceeded
our conceptual grasp into the fold of an expanded repertoire of determining concepts. But as we will see, Kant insists that *aesthetic* reflection produces no concepts at all, so the question will be what
other pre- or nonconceptual means of "understanding" a properly
felt, aesthetic response provides. This study will present Kant's instances of aesthetic reflection, the judgments of taste and of sublimity, as moments in a larger process of interpretive response that can
be extrapolated from his account of them.

By pursuing Kant's occasional indications that reflective judgment
involves comparing and relating presentations, or features of presentations, I will locate the kinds of Kantian aesthetic judgment in a *connecting* or *relational* reflective activity. In contrast to the subsumptive

unity of determinate concepts, in which difference is ignored for the sake of identifying sameness, imagination produces in aesthetic play a distinctive sort of *aesthetic unity* other than the conceptual unity of the understanding or the systematic unity demanded by Kantian reason. Aesthetic unities relate diverse materials into indeterminate yet apparently purposive "un-wholes" in which a balance of difference and affinity is preserved. The judgment of taste, for example, in its response to natural beauty or to works of art, has the task of relating the various elements of a spatio-temporal manifold into a purposive *formal* unity, yet without appeal to any concept. We find something beautiful, according to Kant, when its form invites a play of imaginative responses in which we explore ways to connect and relate its parts as a conceptually undetermined yet seemingly designed "whole." And on standard readings, Kant's judgment of (mathematical) sublimity involves attempting and failing to comprehend all the components of an overwhelming object as a related whole. Now, Kant's judgment of taste, as I will claim, demands a formalistic apprehension of aesthetic objects. The representational, expressive, or thematic material of works of art lies beyond the reflective purview of this judgment. I will make a case that the judgment of sublimity, conversely, when applied to works of art, seeks to make sense of a *meaningfully expressive* whole. It seeks to weave features of a work into a web of meaningful relations, though as a response to sublimity, and as an instance of aesthetic reflection per se, it always falls short of determining a work's theme in any unified conceptual form.

Kant has a reputation as a formalist aesthetician, and although students of his aesthetics frequently see the judgment of taste as limited to a reflection on form, construing the judgment of sublimity as a response to art's expressive content is an unorthodox position to take. It is a position that confirms the formalism of taste while denying that Kant's aesthetic theory as a whole need be considered formalistic. It will turn out that viewing interpretation of a work's meaning as a matter of judging the sublime rather than as a matter of taste resolves a longstanding dispute over the roles of form and expression in Kant's theory. But more importantly, it reveals the work of a sublime understanding in the production of networked webs of meaningful relation that, on my view, will shape not only interpretations of works of art but also the contexts of shared sense in which we live and act. That is, I interpret reflective judgment as the Kantian subject's means of situating and orienting itself in webs of meaning, in networks that make possible an interpretive sense for the whole, an understanding approach to living out a context. I privilege sublime reflection in particular because it best models our interpretive search for meanings in things, something Kant's formalist judgment of taste cannot manage. Furthermore, this reflection acknowledges the constitutive limitations of context-dependent understanding, its incapacity to determine fully the sense-making wholes it reaches to comprehend.

Articulating a broad interpretive practice of sublime reflection requires developing a key notion of Kant's aesthetic theory more thoroughly than he himself does. If the judgment of taste responds to the pleasing bounds of an object's form, the sublimity of a work of art lies in its richness as a focal site of unbounded meanings and possible interpretive elaborations. In Kant's theory, something he calls *aesthetic ideas* give content and expressive power to works of art. An aesthetic idea will be formed from the differential affinity of a "multitude of kindred presentations" a work suggests to its audience, and which that audience seeks but fails to make sense of as a whole. Hence on my view the aesthetic idea will be as much a product of interpretation, which will come together differently for various interpreters, as a "meaning" given in advance by artistic genius. Unfortunately, though, Kant's discussion of aesthetic ideas is brief and vague; he does not fully explain how the interpretive response to them proceeds. A primary aim of this book will be to develop the doctrine of aesthetic ideas well beyond Kant's brief comments. In particular, I will make a case that we interpret aesthetic ideas, and hence ascribe meanings to works of art, by means of a judgment of sublimity. My interpretation specifically of Kant's "mathematical" sublime will emphasize a productive imagination that freely emulates a rational demand for totality by striving to encompass the meaning of a work, only to fail at that task and instead produce the loose relational unity of aesthetic ideas. On this view, aesthetic ideas will constitute proposed interpretations of works of art. By arguing, then, that a sublime understanding, over and above its responses to art, adds to our interpretive immersion in worlds of shared meaning, I will effectively be claiming that those webs of connection take the form of Kantian aesthetic ideas. To be sure, this will have its implications.

Kant's aesthetic theory, like any other, is concerned with our responses to certain kinds of objects and situations, natural scenes or entities and works of art. I maintain, though, that the *indeterminate sense for the whole* that the *Critique of Judgment* articulates informs our broadly lived condition as interpreting beings. This aesthetic sense is not an isolated talent that we use only in museums or on camping trips, but rather orients all our encounters with the sublime, that is, with the limits of current comprehension. So what I will call *sublime understanding* is that always partial, indeterminate grasping of contextual wholes through which we make sense of the uncanny particular. As a special construal of Kantian reflective judgment, sublime understanding helps weave and reweave the networks of meaning-relations that lay down current pathways of intelligibility. Because facing the sublime means confronting the Other of conceptual understanding, the encounter will have a disrupting and a *dehabituating* effect on current categories, current ways of slicing up and threading together worlds. Sublime understanding, as a disclosive power of imagination, illuminates our sedimented sense-making networks. But as an "ingenious" inventive power, sublime reflection also forges into the unpresentable Other of our conceptual store, in search of how else we might make sense of our shared worlds. In this sense, aesthetic experience has the potential to challenge "natural" seeming habits of thought, to destabilize taken-for-granted patterns of judgment. My account of sublime reflection will thus implicitly position Kant in relation to the tradition of aesthetic dehabituation which follows him, at least from Nietzsche onward (I will argue that art has a special dehabituating function for Hegel as well). But at the same time, sublime reflection will produce an understanding of its own, distinct from conceptual determination: an holistic but always partial understanding of the webs of significance that make our more determinate acts of conceptual cognition possible.

Contemporary treatments of the sublime tend to emphasize its profound alterity and unpresentability. For many "Continental" writers on the subject, including Adorno and Lyotard in rather different ways, the sublime would be that unpresentable Beyond that gives the lie to the totalizing claims of rational cognition. My formulation of sublime reflection grants the limits of conceptualization, the perpetual absence of complete (self-) understanding that the sublime assures. But in addition it discerns a more positive role imagination plays in the (partial) comprehension of aesthetic unities that defy conceptual unification. Hence this study will take some issue with "postmodern" treatments of the sublime that proclaim its ineluctable alterity, violence, and negativity. My approach appreciates the disruption caused by the *unattainable demand for unity* that induces the feeling of sublimity, while emphasizing the positive role of a sublime understanding in the interpretive manufacture of always partial, never finished shared worlds. As much as the pursuit of an aesthetics of sublimity works to undermine conventional conceptuality, it does not only destroy. Facing the sublime also propels us to cut new paths of sense that, in their relating of the (as yet) unrelated, defy given conceptual rules.

In particular, by formulating a notion of aesthetic reflection that involves producing revealing connections among disparate phenomena, I thematize *metaphor* as a paradigmatic product of sublime understanding. I consider the common view that Kant's doctrine of aesthetic ideas embodies something like a theory of metaphor, and I demonstrate that the metaphoricity of aesthetic ideas in fact prefigures the most satisfying contemporary account of metaphor, known across variations as the "interactionist" theory. As a form of aesthetic reflection, metaphorical expression will make the *validity claims* that such reflection generally makes for Kant, and as such a positive notion of "metaphorical truth" will be secured. So to the extent that products of sublime understanding receive validation through intersubjective agreement, as will be the claim, the sublime will not have merely the "humbling" function recent theorists have emphasized. Metaphor and other imaginative inventions that issue from facing the sublime will contribute as much to our ongoing sense-making efforts as do more conventional forms of claims-making.

Part III will suggest that the validated contributions that metaphors—and aesthetic reflection more broadly—make to our interpretive engagements warrants rethinking the hierarchy of literal concept over metaphorical figure, of cognitive determinacy over aesthetic play. The sublime understanding of indeterminate felt wholes is deeply involved in the combinatory processes by means of which we haphazardly design the webs of meaning in which we live and judge. It contributes as much to a lived understanding as determinate conceptual construals of things. Insofar as a decidedly *aesthetic* form of reflective judgment helps us to clarify and transform the worlds we inhabit, this study contributes to current efforts to rethink the status of "reality" in relation to our takes on it. Insofar as intersubjective processes of meaning construction constitute the worlds we inhabit, those constructions bear the mark of works of art. So, ultimately, bringing Kant's aesthetic theory "up to date" in the way I do—by unfolding its prescience of current concerns about metaphor, interpretation, and conceptual indeterminacy—will reveal that the traditional category of the "aesthetic" is deeply implicated in a broadened conception of human understanding. Because sublime understanding contributes an aesthetic dimension to our broad sense-making practices, I want to explore what implications the intersubjective validity of metaphorical "world-making" may have for current debates about the function of aesthetic experience in relation to conceptual cognition. One contribution of this book will be the opportunity which such discussion provides for relating Kantian and "Continental" approaches to aesthetics to current "analytic" and neopragmatist aesthetic theory.

This book is about Hegel as well as Kant, although Kant provides the general account of aesthetic reflection that remains the theoretical orientation of the entire argument. Even so, Kant offers little more than an outline of the sort of sublime reflection and the sort of response to aesthetic ideas of interest here. Hegel's massive philosophy of art will offer theoretical equipment essential to the full articulation of these interpretive activities. For example, treatment of Kant's theory will establish the fundamental role of a productive imagination in aesthetic reflection, but just what this imagination reflects on, and just what it produces under the heading of aesthetic ideas, Kant leaves rather vague. By studying Hegel's theory of imagination in detail, it will be possible to develop in specifics the range of imaginative capacities at work in the relational processes of aesthetic reflection. The challenges facing my appropriation of Hegelian resources are suggested by the facts that Hegel rejects the Kantian notion of aesthetic ideas and deflates the significance of the sublime in aesthetic experience. To anyone familiar with Hegel's philosophy of art, it will seem reckless to turn to it for further elaboration of a nonconceptual form of aesthetic reflection. The promising content orientation of Hegel's aesthetics is vitiated by his subordination of aesthetic experience to determinate cognition. For Hegel the content of an art work is a single fixed theme wholly available to conceptual analysis, and so its meaning can be determined by concepts in a manner alien to the open-ended interpretive play of a Kantian sublime understanding. On that score, Hegel's devaluation of the sublime to an inferior artistic phenomenon stands opposed to my core theoretical aims.

Even so, a certain interpretive approach to the Hegelian system will provide just the material needed to flesh out the process of sublime understanding that Kant did not fully develop. Hegel approaches any subject matter by working his way up through one-sided or restricted material to an integrating peak of coherence, whether the peak be the Ideal of Beauty or the "completion" of philosophy. By focusing on a *mid-level* stratum of Hegel's system, one can identify the work of an aesthetic imagination that falls short of determinate cognition. Through this strategy I locate the interstices of Hegel's aesthetic theory where these powers of imagination come to the fore and do their work. One can also identify explicit and implicit encounters with the sublime that will show that it plays a more critical role in Hegel's aesthetic theory than he indicates. I reveal the production of Kantian aesthetic unity, in quite different ways in the two cases, in Hegel's accounts of the symbolic and romantic forms of art. The argument discloses an aesthetics of the sublime at work in these forms, and it finds a wealth of detail in these "imperfect" levels of Hegel's thought for elaborating the kind of indeterminate interpretive reflection that part I finds in Kant's aesthetic theory. In other words, my approach will locate a "Kantian-aesthetic moment" in the midst of Hegel's system. At this level of development, whatever his own final aims might be, Hegel effectively pushes Kantian conceptions of imagination and aesthetic reflection toward the model of a sublime understanding which I wrestle from them both. This use of

Hegel's system is explained further in the Interlude between parts I and II.

The overriding concern of my take on Kant and Hegel is this. Contemporary thinking about the power of the aesthetic, and the notion of sublimity, emphasize the indeterminacy, alterity, and heterogeneity of experiences that offer a felt counterpoint to the claims of cognitive validity. I want to draw these themes, and their attendant aesthetics of the sublime, out of the Kantian and Hegelian texts in which modernity's partition of cognitive and aesthetic experience was so decisively forged. This "partition," the *Teil* in the German *Urteil* or judgment, continues to stand in need of reflective reassessment. But the most valuable lesson to be learned from Kant's aesthetic theory, and Hegel's when it is cast in a certain light, is that for all its rich indeterminacy aesthetic experience still holds its own fund of validity. Sublime understanding in particular, as I will present it, has a normative dimension through which we build shared fields of intelligibility, albeit quite differently than determinate conceptual cognition does. By bringing out the implications of aesthetic indeterminacy in Kant and Hegel's theories while also preserving a notion of aesthetic validity, we can position the aesthetic as a feature of sense-making understanding at least as essential to us as thinking conceptually. Doing so allows us to realize—and to take responsibility for—the artistically creative dimension of our interpretive responses to each other and our worlds.

It is worth emphasizing just how unique Kant's embrace of aesthetic indeterminacy is. Not only is Hegel's grand philosophy of art committed to the conceptual determinacy of aesthetic experience (this is at least its Ideal). Even the British and Scottish empiricist aestheticians who precede Kant expect art to fulfill "Hegelian" (really, neoclassical) standards of strict unity and thematic determination, as I will show in the Interlude between parts II and III. Although both Hegel and the empiricists subordinate the imaginative "wit" of aesthetic play to the sound judgment of rational rules and determinate conceptual unity, only Kantian aesthetics embraces the "sound wit" of an aesthetic reflection that generates on its own an intersubjectively valid felt sense for orienting wholes of experience. It is above all this commitment to the playful indeterminacy of the aesthetic that recommends Kant's third *Critique* today, when artistic practice rarely accommodates an easy and conventional understanding. And it is above all a Kant-inspired aesthetics of sublimity that best captures the spirit and serves the needs of our sense-making pursuits today, both in and outside the sphere of art.

The key question for Kant's aesthetic theory—and really for the aesthetic at large if it is to have the import of being an autonomous source of intersubjective validity—is how aesthetic reflection can establish shared norms without appeal to conceptual rules or rational laws. My approach emphasizes the role of preconceptual *feeling* in Kant's view of aesthetic judgment, but I also thematize the special role the notion of *affinity* plays in the construction of aesthetic unity, as well as the contribution of a *transcendental affinity* to securing the validity of aesthetic reflection. We will see that in sublime reflection imagination freely responds to a rational demand for systematic unity, though it inevitably fails to present it. Imagination presents instead an aesthetic unity—in the form of a meaning-giving network of relations—that I will elaborate in contrast to the form of systematic unity as Kant presents it in the first *Critique*. This will bring out the transcendental bases of aesthetic validity, but it will also reveal an ineluctable *empirical* component to sublime reflection's discernment of sense-making affinities. The empirical dimension of aesthetic response will ultimately have decisive implications for the extent of universality sublime understanding can claim for its products.

The key conclusion of Part III is that salvaging a validity claim for this distinctively aesthetic form of sublime understanding requires "localizing universality." Reflective imagination can reveal and revise meaning-giving relational webs within specific historically bound communicative contexts. Yet it cannot demand of all humanity that it recognize the perspicacity of its play, for the intelligibility of its products relies in part on contexts of sedimented meaning-making shared by historically situated subjects. The validity of sublime understanding's inventions extends just as far as the circle of interpreters who adopt its specific revelations and make them parts of their worlds. Aesthetic autonomy, and the distinctive mode of validity it claims, loses the "strong" universality Kant hoped to establish for it, and it is here that my appropriation of Kant parts ways most significantly with his aims. But sublime understanding retains the "weak" universality of a norm-building practice pursued variously, with varying outcomes, in all our many and overlapping and cross-fertilizing linguistic communities.

A qualification or two might help to discourage misunderstanding. The Kantian sublime plays an important role for him as a bridge between aesthetic and moral experience, to the extent that imagination's "humiliation" in this judgment inspires respect for reason's powers. By casting the judgment of sublimity in the role of structuring a certain manner of *interpretive* activity, however, I have emphasized its relation to reason as an *intellectual* rather than moral power. This orientation will become most evident in chapter 3, where I focus on Kant's notion of the mathematical sublime while neglecting the moral freight of the dynamical sublime. I further defend this decision there. In general I have distanced my interpretation, for the sake of economy, from the implications of Kant's aesthetic theory for his moral and political philosophy. Given the conclusions I reach about the role sublime understanding plays in revealing and reworking shared webs of meaning, it should be clear that the ethical and political implications of aesthetic experience are ultimately unavoidable, as one would expect regardless of Kant. Suffice it to say that though they surpass the scope of this study, further exploration of the political dimensions of aesthetic reflection would need to elaborate these connections.

This qualification can be extended to my interpretive methodology as a whole. The aim of this study is to develop Kant's notion of aesthetic reflective judgment in directions that bring to light my version of a sublime understanding, and that prove relevant to contemporary concerns about interpretation, metaphor, and the relation of the aesthetic to conceptual cognition. To a large extent the argument maintains an allegiance to a Kantian philosophical orientation, in the sense that most of the major concepts with which the interpretation works get their substance and their interrelations from the critical philosophy. However, this study cannot be said to represent an explication of the text in any conventional sense. Combining the dual aims of extrapolation and conscientious regard for Kant's texts, I undertake laborious efforts to remain "true" to the spirit of the *Critique of Judgment* and many of its major claims, but I have sought to take Kant's aesthetic theory in a particular direction by emphasizing certain notions while neglecting others, and by weaving them together in unorthodox ways. Kant's third *Critique* provides essential equipment for articulating an aesthetics of sublimity, and a manner of interpretive sublime understanding that may not ultimately fit the cut of Kant's entire philosophy. For my purposes it need not, for my aim is to prod Kant into contemporary aesthetic territory rather than to heed his every intention.

The revisionist spirit of my approach takes on special significance when it comes to my interpretation of Hegel's thought. The "Kant-inspired" orientation of the project toward a non- or preconceptual aesthetic reflection means that most of Hegel's systematic concerns are thoroughly suspended or deferred here. This neglect of Hegel's own aims becomes most apparent in chapter 7, where my indifference to the classical Ideal of art that Hegel takes to be the pinnacle of artistic perfection is matched only by my theoretical reliance on the forms of art that Hegel finds less accomplished, or even destructive. My aim is to show that certain strata of the Hegelian system develop ideas that effectively expand notions central to a Kantian aesthetic of the sublime; Hegel develops these ideas in directions essential to the full articulation of my concerns. My exclusive focus on those "imperfect" levels of Hegel's system entails my occlusion of those "satisfactions" of the Concept by means of which Hegel thinks his system surpasses and puts to rest the decrepit phenomena on which I linger. His response to my interpretation might be, "Yes, but why remain at the level of mere reflective understanding?" Hence my approach cannot claim to be "true" to Hegel's thought, but only to put his system to a certain conscientious use, to demonstrate its power to illuminate a conception of sublime understanding ultimately inimical to his own purposes. This is, to be sure, an unusual treatment of Hegel, whom most writers either passionately attempt to refute or defend. I do neither, but rather wrestle from his system the makings of an aesthetics of sublimity he would likely disdain. Suffice it to say, then, that the challenge Hegel's own philosophy of art, and his systematic philosophy as a whole, pose to the orientation of this study remains to be met.

The *Oxford English Dictionary* defines *conceit* in a number of ways. A conceit can be "that which is conceived in the mind, a conception, a notion, an idea," or it can refer to "the faculty of mental conception; apprehension, *understanding*," though these meanings are largely obsolete today. Conceit can be a matter of "personal *judgment*, estimation." A conceit can be "a fanciful, *ingenious*, or *witty* expression; esp. a far-fetched *comparison* or elaborate and intricate figure of speech, image, etc." A conceit is "a fanciful notion, a *fancy*," which designates "the faculty of *imagination*" as its source. In all these senses, then, the "conceit" of this study is that it exemplifies the very practice of aesthetically reflective sublime understanding that it articulates.

I

Kantian Aesthetic Reflection

1

Kant's Theory of Reflective Judgment

Robert Musil's young Törless, yearning for blinding revelations of cosmic insight, makes the mistake of picking up one of Kant's critical works. His romantic, teenage fervor has not quite readied him to receive the master of Königsberg's system, and running his eyes over the dense pages leaves him feeling "as if some aged, bony hand were twisting and screwing his brain out of his head." Most students of Kant are familiar with this feeling from reading the *Critique of Pure Reason*, but the *Critique of Judgment* has its own share of brain-twisters, not to mention glaring inconsistencies, organizational confusions, and abrupt shifts of intention. Some of this has no doubt to do with the history of the work's composition, especially Kant's late "discovery" of reflective judgment, but it has as much to do with the profound magnitude of the task Kant set himself in this work. Given that he undertakes to resolve the question of whether there is any disputing about taste, as part of a strategy to justify a teleology of natural organisms and to bolster our hopes that the mechanism of nature can make a welcome home for our highest moral ideals, one can forgive Kant his not infrequent turbidity. For buried in the third *Critique* are not only remarkable insights into aesthetic experience and our relation to nature as moral beings. It also offers a view of an interpretive human understanding that builds normativity from aesthetically inflected materials, and that bears on a host of our contemporary theoretical concerns. The aim of part I is to unfold what I will come to call the sublime understanding imbedded in Kant's *Critique of Judgment*.

I begin by presenting Kant's founding distinction between determinate and reflective forms of judgment. This distinction brings out the schematizing function that imagination performs in the former, in contrast to the imaginative free play of aesthetic reflection. There are anticipations of Kant's third *Critique* view of reflective judgment in the *Critique of Pure Reason*; I look to the earlier notion of "transcendental reflection" to flesh out reflective judgment further. Because aesthetic reflection in particular does not result in thinking objects under concepts, I argue against the tendency to conceive reflective judgment as a power of empirical concept formation. For judgment to make any a priori claims, independent of the understanding's determination of concepts or reason's moral legislation, it must follow principles of its own. Hence reflection is the domain in which judgment comes into its independent own, and I explore Kant's account of "purposiveness" as the indigenous and operant principle of reflective judgment.

I argue that the upshot of this principle is that reflective judgment seeks out purposive unity—the appearance of intentional organization—among the diversity of presentations, or features of objects or situations, on which it reflects. Most clearly in aesthetic contexts, the reflective striving for unity assumes a regulative function: aesthetic experience for Kant will not fix on any specific purpose an object fulfills, will not think it just as a token of some conceptual type. Instead, an aesthetically reflective imagination will seek out an *indeterminate* purposive unity in its object. It will sense and explore suggestions of purposiveness free of any determinate cognition of purposes or concepts. The aim in the coming chapters will be to show that Kant's judgments of taste and sublimity enact this reflective search for purposive but indeterminate unity, each in their unique ways. This chapter concludes that whatever the character of the peculiar *aesthetic unity* imagination produces in its reflective play, it will assume a form quite other than the "technical" unity of a purpose or the "systematic" unity of a rational schema.

Two Kinds of Judgment

Kant conceives the faculty of judgment in general to consist simply in the ability to think the particular as contained under the universal.

Judgment enables one to subsume particular cases under general concepts, to recognize the given as an instance of a definite type.[1] Because Kant conceives of concepts as rules of subsumption, he locates the act of judgment in our decision that an individual case satisfies the conditions of a rule. Kant emphasizes this point in the *Critique of Pure Reason* when contrasting judgment with understanding: "If understanding as such is explicated as our power of rules, then the power of judgment is the ability to *subsume* under rules, i.e., to distinguish whether something does or does not fall under a given rule. . . ."[2] For Kant, the understanding provides rules of subsumption in the form of concepts, whether pure or empirical. Once given conceptual rules, the task of judgment is to recognize which of these rules each particular thing satisfies. Judgment organizes particulars under their determining concepts, but it does not itself produce the concepts under which it subsumes particulars: "judgment refers solely to the subject, and does not on its own produce any concepts of objects" (FI 208). Kant does not, then, consider judgment to be a "legislative" faculty, providing its own rules in the way that the understanding supplies categories to legislate over the cognition of objects, or in the way that reason legislates the moral law for itself. Judgment instead mediates between the particular and the universal without determining the character of either. It thus comprises a purely subjective activity of organizing and applying to various cases what is given it by other faculties. This will not mean that judgment produces nothing, however; judgment in the first instance produces those propositions in which it successfully relates particular and universal, subject and predicate. The absence of legislation in judgment will only mean that whatever other products it can claim will not assume the form of conceptual rules.

Kant distinguishes two main modes of judging in the third *Critique*, depending on the point of departure of the mediation carried out in the judgment. If a concept or universal—which Kant construes as a rule, principle, or law—is available to judgment, and judgment need only subsume a particular under it, a particular chair under the concept "chair," for example, then the mediation is a matter of *determinative* judgment. If, on the other hand, judgment has available only a particular for which it must find a universal—if, in a sense, it does not know what a thing is and so cannot state its concept, cannot find the rule that orders it—then the mediation is a *reflective* judgment (CJ 179). Kant had made, in his first *Critique*, a preliminary distinction between these two forms of judgment, which he called at that time "apodeictical" versus "problematical" uses of a judging reason.[3] The determinative judgment of his third *Critique* operates under the tutelage of the understanding and is thus productive of knowledge and bound up with the process of cognition. That is, the domain of determinative judgment as Kant presents it in the third *Critique* is just that of the manufacture of objective knowledge through the application of concepts that Kant explored in his first *Critique*.[4] Hence the application of the categories of understanding to the manifold of sensation in the constitution of experience provides a paradigmatic case of determinative judgment. Through the subsumption of particular objects under empirical concepts, again under the guidance of the understanding, determinative judgment provides knowledge of what those objects are.[5]

In the case of cognition of objects—determinative judgment as treated in Kant's first *Critique*—the mediation carried out in judgment consists in matching up the categories of the understanding with the raw material supplied by sensibility. Kant argues that this determination comes about by means of a "schematization" of the categories carried out by the imagination. The schema is a mediating representation that, according to Kant, is "homogeneous with the category, on the one hand, and with the appearance, on the other, and that thus makes possible the application of the category to the appearance" (CPR A138/B177). The schema serves judgment and cognition as a stepping-stone between the abstract content of a concept and the various objects that, despite their many differences, instantiate it. In the interest of clarity, Kant provides an example: "The concept *dog* signifies a rule whereby my imagination can trace the shape of such a four-footed animal in a general way, i.e., without being limited to any single and determinate shape offered to me by experience, or even to all possible images that I can exhibit *in concreto*" (CPR A141/B180).[6] This schematic representation of a dog, this template or, as Kant even calls it, "monogram" for doghood that links the concept to our sensible images of such creatures, is a creation of the *productive imagination*, by means, in the famous lines, of "a secret art residing in the depths of the human soul, an art whose true strategems we shall hardly ever divine from nature and lay bare before ourselves" (CPR A141/B180–181). The Kantian imagination plays an indispensable (if obscure) role in bringing together the concepts of the understanding and the material of sensation, for the particular images of objects in experience "must always be connected with the concept only by means of the schema that they designate" (ibid.). So, in the cognition of objects, imagination serves a mediating role central to the execution of determinative judgment; its schemata make possible the subsumption of particulars under concepts. In this process the understanding legislates the form of appearance, and the schematizing mediations of imagination subserve the aims of cognition.

But imagination plays a vital role in reflective judgment, as well, where the goal of producing knowledge of objects does not circumscribe its activity. Here, understanding does not delimit imagination, as it does in its role of cognitive legislator. Because reflective judgment, as we saw, is not provided with a concept under which to think its object, the schematizing activity of imagination does not apply. In *aesthetic* reflective judgment, imagination will instead contribute the nonschematizing element that distinguishes this reflection from the workaday activity of determinative judgment. This will be true of both of Kant's forms of aesthetic judgment. In the judgment of taste, the spontaneity of imagination accounts for the feeling of pleasure attending the beautiful, even as its free play must harmonize with the lawfulness of the understanding. In the case of the sublime, the failed effort of imagination to unite an overwhelming multiplicity in one comprehension accounts for the distinctive initial displeasure of this judgment. In sum, imagination plays an intimate role in all forms of judgment. But it comes most into its own in reflective judgment in particular, where it is freed from the task of schematization and the legislative prerogatives of the understanding in the domain of cognition. The degree of imagination's involvement in reflective judgment will become more definite as we proceed.[7]

The distinction between reflective and determinative forms of judgment can be amplified by considering Kant's appendix to the first *Critique*'s Transcendental Analytic, on "The Amphiboly of Concepts of

Reflection." Kant sought in the first *Critique* to secure the validity claims of knowledge by ascertaining the categorial grounds of cognition and constraining the application of experiential categories to their proper sensible domain. This task requires specifying the capacities and limits of our "various sources of cognition," namely sensibility and understanding. If we can determine what each of these powers can and cannot provide, and how those constraints govern how they interact, Kant thinks we will have a firm basis on which to justify our knowledge claims. He understands *reflection* to undertake this task: "*Reflection (reflexio)* does not deal with objects themselves in order to obtain concepts from them straightforwardly, but is our state of mind when we first set about to discover the subjective conditions under which [alone] we can arrive at concepts. It is our consciousness of the relation of given presentations to our various sources of cognition—the consciousness through which alone the relation of these presentations to one another can be determined correctly" (CPR A260/B316).[8] The passage reflects the third *Critique* position Kant takes, that reflective judgment does not itself produce concepts. Rather, reflection in the first *Critique* sense seeks to *locate* various presentations as products of sensibility or understanding, so as to avoid their being attributed to the wrong source or applied to the wrong domain. Explicitly locating the categories as concepts of pure understanding was such an act of reflection, and at this level the first *Critique* itself undertook the reflective work of properly locating a priori and a posteriori concepts under the sources of knowledge from which they arise.

But at a more fundamental level, Kant thinks this deliberate philosophical activity reflects a deeper *transcendental reflection* by means of which concepts spontaneously belong to their proper sources prior to the critical ascertaining of this fact. "I call *transcendental reflection* the act whereby I hold the comparison of presentations as such up to the cognitive power in which this comparison is made, and whereby I distinguish whether the presentations are being compared with one another as belonging to pure understanding or to sensible intuition" (CPR A261/B317).[9] Reflection as a transcendental acitivity provides an immediate and implicit "knowledge" of the cognitive faculties and their respective domains; it grounds the very facultative structure from which valid claims of knowledge will arise. As Dieter Henrich puts it, unlike the reflective work of the critical philosophy, "[transcendental] reflection always takes place. Without any effort on our part, we always spontaneously know (albeit, informally and without explicit articulation) about our cognitive activities and about the principles and rules they depend upon. Reflection in this sense is a precondition of rationality."[10] Transcendental reflection provides an immediate certainty of the proper configuration of the cognitive powers; it is the unconditioned *self-feeling* for the subject's well-functioning cognitive form. Jean-François Lyotard emphasizes the immediately *felt* self-coordination Kant takes transcendental reflection to provide: "Pure reflection is first and foremost the ability of thought to be immediately informed of its state by this state and without other means of measure than feeling itself."[11] At the basis of transcendental reflection, Kant thinks, lies an *immediately valid feeling* for the proper functioning of our cognitive powers. This certainty provided by transcendental reflection will become the primordial model of the universally valid feeling Kant ascribes to aesthetic reflective judgment.[12] The claim that something is beautiful will rely on an intersubjectively valid feeling *one legitimately has but for no reason.* Such a judgment will provide a visible instance of the prerational, precognitive felt certainty by means of which transcendental reflection grounds our rational and cognitive capacities.

As Kant indicated, reflection *compares* presentations in its effort to assign them to their proper sensible or categorial domains. He introduces "four headings of all comparison and differentiation" by means of which these presentations are located (CPR A269/B325). These headings—identity and difference, agreement and opposition, inner and outer, determined (or matter) and determination (or form)—first of all distinguish the character and domains of sensibility and understanding. Understanding will promote conceptual unity and determination, while sensibility will be determined by understanding despite the vast differentia and opposition of its matter. But furthermore, the headings prefigure the very categories understanding will employ in the manufacture of appearance. These "concepts of reflection" provide a preconceptual figuration of the determinative judgment the categories of understanding will complete. Concepts of reflection "differ from categories inasmuch as that they do not exhibit the object according to what makes up its concept (magnitude, reality), but exhibit in all its manifoldness only the comparison of presentations that precedes the concept of things" (ibid.). Reflection thus enjoys in the first *Critique* a certain priority over determinate conceptual cognition; it maintains the facutative distinctions by means of which sensibility and understanding will meet as complimentary sources of knowledge. As Lyotard puts it, in agreement with Henrich, "reflection is the (subjective) laboratory of all objectivities."[13]

Reflection in the first *Critique* compares and locates presentations prior to their categorial determination by the understanding. Similarly, in the third *Critique* reflective judgment works on presentations in the absence of determining concepts, whether pure or empirical. Given that aesthetic reflection operates without concepts of understanding, transcendental reflection would doubtless locate its presentations in the domain of sensibility, where we would expect imagination to play free of determining concepts. The headings of transcendental reflection attribute a preponderate degree of difference and opposition to the presentations belonging to the sensible domain in which aesthetic reflection will operate. This simply reflects the heterogeneity of the empirical realm in which reflective judgment seeks to make sense of uncanny particulars. While transcendental reflection places presentations in their proper transcendental "locations," aesthetic reflection faces the more empirically laborious task of comparing the presentations assigned to it in order to make sense of particular phenomena which the application of empirical and categorial concepts has left underdetermined.[14]

As indicated above, Kant conceives reflective judgment as the search for a universal—concept, rule, principle, or law—under which to subsume the particular. We judge reflectively in cases where we face an unfamiliar object or situation and wonder what to make of it; we seek general notions with which to make sense of something unknown or unusual. Reflective judgment may be broadly described as the effort to give structure and meaning to the uncanny, to whatever exceeds the grasp of our current categories and so resists cognition under determinative judgments. The discovery of an obscure artifact, for example, presents the challenge of puzzling out what its purpose and use must have been; we try out various concepts, and adjustments to them, in search of an explanation of the thing at hand. Or upon arriving in the middle of a complex conversation, we seek to reconstruct from the tone, manner, and statements of the participants the nature of the encounter in progress.[15]

The paradigm case for the purpose of exploring Kant's account of *aesthetic* reflective judgment will be the encounter with a work of art. The student of a work often faces the speculative challenge of gathering together the themes or images or other components of the work in order to reflect on what it might mean. That works of art require *reflection*, rather than determinate cognition, indicates that, for Kant, natural beauty and ingenious art provide us moments of uncanny wonder that no fixed concepts can explain or exhaust. How such reflection proceeds in its encounter with what lies "beyond" the current reach of concepts will become more definite later.

I indicated that reflective judgment searches for a universal with which to make sense of the particular, and the keyword in such an account must be the *search*. For especially in the case of aesthetic judgment, Kant does not think such reflection produces determinate knowledge or concepts. If we find a universal under which to think the particular, if we decide an artifact is a snow shovel, for example, then the judgment that enacts that subsumption, when we think the object under the concept "snow shovel," is a *determinative* one. The search for a concept, if successful, soon becomes subsumption under it. On this view reflective judgment—seeking, finding and applying universals to particulars—would seem only a handmaiden to judgment in its determinative mode. Hannah Ginsborg, for one, has argued that reflective judgment should be understood as a faculty of empirical conceptualization, as "a faculty which makes it possible to bring objects under empirical concepts in the first place."[16] This view is heavily influenced by the conception of reflection we saw in Kant's first *Critique*, where transcendental reflection grounds the very possibility of conceptualization. But as we have noted, Kant insists in the *Critique of Judgment* that judgment "does not on its own produce any concepts of objects" (FI 208). The interpretation of reflective judgment as a power of empirical concept formation violates this basic tenet of Kant's position. And if such a view exhausted the nature of reflective judgment, it would strip the *aesthetic* reflective judgment of the third *Critique* of its autonomy from the aims of conceptual cognition. As a form of reflection, aesthetic judgments remain free of determining concepts. If reflective judgment were a power of empirical conceptualization, its subspecies aesthetic reflection would presumably bring empirical particulars to concepts in some way or other. But such a claim would be altogether alien to Kantian aesthetic theory.[17]

There must be more to reflective judgment than initiating and completing a search for a concept. In the case of the aesthetic judgment of taste, for example, the reflection on beauty never results in disclosing a rule or concept by which to judge the object; the play of imagination makes this reflection precisely a matter of *not* judging by concepts, despite the understanding's role in the judgment. And in the judgment of the sublime, imagination bypasses the conceptual demands of the understanding in a very different interaction with the faculty of reason. Despite cases in which reflective judgment completes its work by, say, selecting the concept "snow shovel" and determining the nature of the thing, the concrete results of such reflection in the aesthetic domain assume a different form. If the snow shovel were a work of art, after all, recognizing it to be a token of the type "snow shovel" would hardly constitute an act of aesthetic appreciation and interpretation. Marcel Duchamp's *In Advance of the Broken Arm* may be "just" a snow shovel, but making sense of it as a work of art will require something different from knowing what the brute thing is. Thus, though Kant initially defines reflective judgment as the search for a universal under which to subsume a given particular, it is the character of the search, and the unusual results we will find it to have, rather than its completion in a concept, that is decisive for this form of judgment. The reflective aim of finding a universal to make sense of the particular should then be construed as a Kantian regulative ideal.[18] It motivates the efforts of reflective judgment to render the uncanny intelligible, but what this interpretive process produces will be very unlike a concept. The question becomes how to characterize the process of reflective judgment and its aesthetic varieties. Kant calls his account of this the principle of reflective judgment's operation (CJ 180; FI 218). Rather than serve as a handmaiden to the aims of conceptual determination, reflective judgment works from its own principle to produce results quite different from subsumption under concepts.[19]

Systematicity and Purposiveness in Reflective Judgment

We know that, for Kant, the constitutive role that a priori concepts have in forming our experience of sensible particulars exemplifies the cognitive success of determinative judgment. Every object of experience, to appear to us at all, must conform to the determining blueprint of the category of substantiality. Every instance of causal connection gets its basic character from the formative determination of such connections by an a priori concept of causality. Such transcendental concepts, in shaping any possible object of experience, cast a very wide net, and they represent a kind of least common denominator for how any object must look and behave. Because of their universal applicability, such concepts cannot accommodate, or specify, the gritty details of the many kinds of objects, or causal relations, that actually show up in the endless diversity of the empirical world. An a priori concept of causality may guarantee the validity of those determinative judgments in which we identify the pairing of cause and effect (assuming the judgment is correct). But its transcendental thinness offers us no guidance for distinguishing various kinds of more specific causal relations, such as those of interest to biology in contrast to those astronomers study. A priori laws of the understanding shape subjective experience as a *unified system* of appearances, at least at a most general level; but that generality extends no unity and systematicity to the heterogeneity of empirical particulars.

Kant states the problem, and begins to suggest the role reflective judgment plays in facing it, in the Introduction to the third *Critique*: "[S]ince the laws that pure understanding gives a priori concern only the possibility of a nature as such (as object of sense), there are such diverse forms of nature, so many modifications as it were of the universal transcendental concepts of nature, which are left undetermined by these laws, that surely there must be laws for these forms too. Since these principles are empirical, they may indeed be contingent as far as *our* understanding can see; still, if they are to be called laws (as the concept of a nature does require), then they must be regarded as necessary by virtue of some principle of the unity of what is diverse, even though we do not know this principle" (CJ 179–180). Kant supposes that the variety of empirical laws, or patterns of experience, must, as features of an experience of nature determined by transcendental rules, share in the systematic unity those rules provide at the categorial level. It will be the work of reflective judgment to seek unity in this vast manifold of experience, to expect a degree of order and coherence at the empirical level to complement the categorial structure of appearances. A priori laws of understanding cannot specify that structure, but Kant thinks a reflective judgment employing a *principle of systematicity* can legitimately expect the diversity of empirical experience to hang together as an ordered whole.

Kant introduces this principle thus: "[S]ince universal natural laws have their basis in our understanding . . . the particular empirical laws must, as regards what the universal laws have left undetermined in them, be viewed in terms of such unity as [they would have] if they too had been given by an understanding (even though not ours) so as to assist our cognitive powers by making possible a system of experience in terms of particular natural laws" (CJ 180). Because reflective judgment is "obliged to ascend from the particular to the universal," it must presuppose that all the particulars of experienced nature are amenable to organization under ever more comprehensive and encompassing universals. A principle of systematicity guides reflective judgment just because its search for the absent universal requires it to anticipate some ordered unity to be found in the contingent details of experience. Otherwise there would be no absent universal to seek out. For this reason, as he puts it in the First Introduction, Kant thinks it "subjectively necessary" for us to presuppose "that nature does not have this disturbing boundless heterogeneity of empirical laws and heterogeneity of natural forms, but that, rather, through the affinity of its particular laws under more general ones it takes on the quality of experience as an empirical system" (FI 209).

Two features of Kant's presentation of reflective judgment's principle of systematicity need to be emphasized. One is the role the notion of *affinity* plays in the reflective search for unity, for this will have major importance for the kind of unity and coherence a specifically *aesthetic* reflection will seek. I will come to this issue in a later chapter, and so will focus here on another feature of the reflective anticipation of systematicity: its attribution of *purposiveness* to the object of reflection. Reflective judgment, as Kant writes in the First Introduction, invites the subject to seek in its object "that special kind of systematic unity, the systematic unity in terms of the presentation of a purpose" (FI 219). Purposes are intimately related to concepts (as well as to rational ideas) in Kant's thought; both purposes and concepts provide what unity we find in objects, and in experience more broadly. As indicated above, Kant supposes that the principle of systematicity attributes to the diversity of empirical laws "such unity as [they would have] if they too had been given by an understanding (even though not ours)." We can begin to make sense of this by noting that Kant construes a unifying purpose as a special kind of concept which, as a concept, must be attributed to the constitutive activity of some understanding or other. For Kant, thinking of something as having a purpose requires thinking the thing as possible only on the basis of some prior concept of what that thing is meant to be. And locating the formative basis of a thing in a concept, furthermore, requires attributing that concept, that intention to form such a thing according to such a purpose, to an intending understanding.

Kant relates the notion of a purpose as a kind of conceptual cause to reflection's search for systematic unity in nature in a key passage from the third *Critique* Introduction: "Now insofar as the concept of an object also contains the basis for the object's actuality, the concept is called the thing's *purpose,* and a thing's harmony with that character of things which is possible only through purposes is called the *purposiveness* of its form. Accordingly, judgment's principle concerning the form that things of nature have in terms of empirical laws in general is the *purposiveness of nature* in its diversity. In other words, through this concept we present nature as if an understanding contained the basis of the unity of what is diverse in nature's empirical laws" (CJ 180–81). When reflective judgment anticipates unity within the apparent mere diversity of natural experience, it attributes to that experienced nature the purposiveness it would display were it the product of an intending understanding. The anticipation of such unity in reflective judgment implies the operation of a "*principle of purposiveness* for our cognitive power," because Kant regards unity among diversity as possible only by means of a purpose or intention informing that unity (CJ 184). Now Kant's close linkage of concepts and purposes implies that we make a determinative judgment when we fix the specific purpose of an object, especially a human artifact. Determining the purpose of a thing involves acquiring an adequate concept of it. When one realizes that the intended use of an object is to spread and smooth plastic building material, one verges on thinking it under the concept "trowel." But in reflective judgment, where we lack a concept of the object for which we seek a universal, we must also lack an understanding of its purpose. Kant does not think that the reflective anticipation of systematic unity could ever finally cognize nature as a determinate and purposive whole. The vast heterogeneity of natural experience denies any ascription of a perfected purpose to it. But he insists that we proceed, in our reflection on experienced nature, by treating what details of it we meet as belonging to a purposive whole, and by organizing that experience under the ever greater universals which would give the unity of a purpose to that whole, could we ever complete its ordering.

This anticipation of purposiveness motivates reflective judgment whether its object is the whole of experienced nature or specific objects. Reflective judgment seeks the universal to make sense of the particular not only in the diversity of nature, but in more local microcosms of organization. In aesthetic reflection we sense purposive order in what we find beautiful or sublime in nature or art. In teleological reflection we attribute purposiveness to individual living organisms. Especially in the case of aesthetic reflection, the expectation of purposiveness treats an object as if it were informed by a purpose even though the reflection does not grasp that purpose determinately. Treating an object as purposive does not fix its precise purpose, its conceptual cause, and so is compatible with the noncognitive operations of reflective judgment. Such reflection does not expose any objective or determinate property of its object, but through the attribution of purposiveness aims to make sense of the particular as implicated in an ordered whole, even though this making of sense cannot claim to produce anything cognitively determinate.[20]

How does Kant think that this expectation of purposiveness affects our reflection on an object's character? At one point in the "Analytic of

Teleological Judgment," Kant distinguishes the purposiveness found in products of art from that of natural purposes (the object of teleology) by presenting two requirements for the purposiveness of the latter, only one of which is fulfilled by products of art. He claims that, for something to be a natural purpose, "the possibility of its parts (as concerns both their existence and their form) must depend on their relation to the whole. For since the thing itself is a purpose, it is covered by a concept or idea that must determine a priori everything that the thing is to contain. But if we think of a thing as possible only in that way, then it is merely a work of art" (CJ 373). Kant goes on to indicate the second quality of a natural purpose, namely that its parts combine as a whole because they are "reciprocally cause and effect of their form"; but we require only the characterization of the purposiveness in works of art. Having a purpose, for Kant, requires the organization of parts into a whole that determines their relations to each other and to the whole. *Determining* in judgment the purpose of a thing requires grasping as a whole this organic unity of parts.[21] In the case of aesthetic reflection, however, the subject does not think the specific, determinate purpose of its object. The purposiveness we attribute to a work of art, for example, will arise from the subject's a priori expectation that all its parts come together as an organized whole. The absent universal that aesthetic reflection seeks would be the hidden conceptual cause, or intended purpose, forming the work into an expressive unity. In the case of reflection on nature as a possible system of experience, this principle requires judgment to seek unity among the variety of empirical laws, but at a more general level the principle of reflective judgment consists of *the expectation of and the search for purposive unity among a diversity of parts.*[22]

For reflective judgment, as we saw, the final comprehension of the purpose that informs a unity of the diverse must be construed as a regulative ideal. The "obligation" to construct that whole must be regarded as a subjective maxim of judgment that guides our reflection but does not determine its object.[23] To *determine* as a fixed quality the purpose of an object would be for judgment to determine its concept. Judgment might discover this concept and subsume its object under it in an act of determinative judgment, as when it determines that an artifact is a trowel. But a principle of reflective judgment cannot, for

Kant, produce this concept, this determination of purpose, itself. We must distinguish the use of a principle of purposiveness in reflective judgment, seeking unity in a diversity of parts, from any constitutive determination of purposes or their attendant concepts. Even in aesthetic judgment on a quite deliberately executed work of art, proper reflection on it neither begins nor ends with any determinate conception of its purpose (what it was meant to mean or express).[24] Kant does not think we could capture in a concept the "basis of actuality" of an object of beauty; thus we could not state its purpose in any decisive sense. Aesthetic reflective judgment, in order to be that, must refrain from attributions of purpose to objects of reflection.

Reflective judgment does nevertheless treat its object *as if* its various parts do cohere as a unity informed by a purpose or intention. That is, reflection presupposes purposiveness in its object, without cognizing its exact purpose. This subjective purposiveness—subjective because it does not determine the object's concept—is *the anticipation of an indeterminate unity* that lies at the heart of reflective judgment: "What is formal in the presentation of a thing, the harmony of its manifold to [form] a unity (where it is indeterminate what this unity is meant to be) does not by itself reveal any objective purposiveness whatsoever. For here we abstract from what this unity is *as a purpose* (what the thing is [meant] to be), so that nothing remains but the subjective purposiveness of the presentations in the mind of the beholder" (CJ 227). Kant also calls this subjective purposiveness in aesthetic reflection *purposiveness without purpose*. In reflective judgment, Kant claims that "we can at least observe a purposiveness as to form and take note of it in objects . . . without basing it on a purpose" (CJ 220). In the case of a work of art, then, reflective judgment approaches the work as something informed by a purpose or intention without cognizing that purpose in fact. Reflection addresses the work as the product of an intention that, in its manifestation in the work and its effect on the judging subject, cannot be encapsulated in a concept. It seeks to comprehend that purpose according to the principle of reflective judgment, that is, it seeks the unity of a purpose among the diversity of its constituent parts. Attributing purposiveness without purpose in reflective judgment thus amounts to regarding a work as an organic unity of interrelated parts without grasping that unity determinatively (in a concept).

The principle of purposiveness in reflective judgment motivates an expectation of unity, interconnectedness, and internal coherence among the components of an object of reflection. Aesthetic judgments on the beautiful and the sublime should, as varieties of reflective judgment, reveal this expectation in their workings and results. Because, as we saw, imagination provides the distinctive aspect of aesthetic reflection, we will do well to seek in its activity a manifestation of this expectation of and search for purposive unity.

Before proceeding to that in the next chapters, however, we may note that Paul Guyer has been critical of the role the ideas of systematicity and purposiveness (or "finality," as he translates it) play in Kant's aesthetic theory. It will be instructive to consider at this point some of his objections to these notions, because his critique of them raises the question whether aesthetic judgment ought to be seen at all as an instance of Kant's general theory of reflective judgment, as I wish to maintain. Guyer has argued that the general account of reflective judgment Kant provides in the two introductions to the third *Critique* bears little relation to his theory of aesthetic judgment and its mode of operation.[25] Guyer makes much of an important passage in the First Introduction, where Kant writes: "To reflect is to hold given presentations up to, and compare them with, either other presentations or one's cognitive power, in reference to a concept that this comparison makes possible" (FI 211). Kant gives the impression of distinguishing two forms of reflection, the first of which involves the comparing and relating of diverse presentations with each other, while the second involves relating presentations to their cognitive sources, as in the first *Critique* notion of transcendental reflection. Kant elaborates the *first* notion of reflection into the specific project of constructing a systematic unity out of the diverse empirical laws of nature. We have seen that this notion emphasizes an expectation of purposiveness in the search for a unity to make sense of the particular—and I maintain that this holds whether judgment reflects on the systematicity of nature or on a more local center of purposive unity, such as a work of art.

In regard to this *first* notion of reflection, Guyer argues that Kant's principle of systematicity, and the theory of reflective judgment it supports, must be irrelevant to Kant's account of aesthetic judgment. This is because, according to Guyer, when Kant embraces this principle of reflection he ascribes systematicity to nature as a property of its own, an objective property that reflective judgment can legitimately expect to find in nature.[26] If Kant in fact means to make such an ascription, then the reflective search for systematicity in nature must indeed bear little relation to his aesthetic theory, because aesthetic judgment makes no objective cognitive ascriptions. It rather concerns our subjective response to an indeterminate but purposive unity we sense in an object. Kant repeatedly insists, as we have seen, that reflective judgment in general offers no conceptual determinations constitutive of objects, but instead seeks to organize *our presentations* in relation to each other and their respective cognitive origins. But Guyer argues that Kant must be ascribing the property of systematicity to nature itself because he "presents it as the representation of a condition under which success in the fulfillment of our cognitive requirements can be rationally expected. . . ."[27] That is, nature must itself cohere as a systematic unity if it is reasonable to require reflective judgment to seek that unity out.

I would suggest that we can grant Kant a more consistent viewpoint by taking him to maintain that reflective judgment ascribes systematicity to "nature" as a *system of subjective experience*. As noted earlier, Kant thinks it "*subjectively necessary*" for us to presuppose that "through the affinity of its particular laws under more general ones it [nature] takes on the quality of experience as an empirical system" (FI 209).[28] Whatever order reflection finds in nature will be an order reflection introduces into *experience* beyond the broad order supplied by the categories of understanding. The rational expectation which the principle of systematicity fosters applies to *nature as we present it in appearance*; it requires that we organize that experience of nature according to principles that exceed our powers of conceptual understanding. Reflective judgment, in keeping both with Kant's accounts introductory to the third *Critique* and with his first *Critique* discussion of it, amounts to a kind of subjective housekeeping in which we compare and relate our presentations to give meaningful order to experience where empirical or other concepts are lacking. The search for systematicity in *experienced* nature, undertaken in reflective judgment, is not alien to Kant's account of aesthetic reflection, because in neither case does reflection make objective ascriptions about its objects.

In both cases, as we have seen, reflective judgment operates according to *regulative*, rather than *constitutive*, principles.[29]

The second form of reflective judgment suggested by the passage Guyer stresses refers to cases in which a presentation is compared not with other presentations, but with one's cognitive faculties. "To reflect is to hold given presentations up to, and compare them with, either other presentations or one's cognitive power, in reference to a concept that this comparison makes possible." This aspect of Kant's account follows his first *Critique* treatment of reflection as a process of "locating" presentations in terms of their proper cognitive sources. Guyer takes this second notion of reflection to be the exclusive source for Kant's theory of aesthetic judgment. "The latter possibility," he writes, "is Kant's ground for treating aesthetic judgment as a species of reflective judgment, for Kant will ultimately use the notion of a 'possible concept' to connote not merely possible concepts themselves but also the general condition for the application of concepts, the harmony between imagination and understanding."[30] Guyer takes this passage as Kant's justification for construing aesthetic judgment as a species of reflective judgment, but in fact he otherwise sees little reason to consider Kant's aesthetic theory in light of the general account of reflective judgment Kant provides.

In addition to his concerns about the principle of systematicity, objections to the notion of purposiveness also motivate Guyer to sever Kant's aesthetic theory from his broad views on reflective judgment. Guyer regards purposiveness or "finality" as an empty notion that "turns out to amount to *nothing but* an object's conformity to the requirements of the reflective judgment."[31] Reflection on experienced nature, according to the principle of systematicity, requires us to expect that its diversity will cohere as an ordered whole. When we treat nature as a system of experience, we attribute to it the purposiveness it would have were it the product of some intending understanding. That is, we treat it as a unity of parts ordered to some end. Guyer thinks the only relevant end here is whether nature conforms to the requirements of reflective judgment, so the notion of "finality" only repackages what the principle of systematicity already secures for reflective judgment. Because of the pervasiveness of this unhelpful notion in Kant's general account of reflective judgment, Guyer argues, we can learn nothing fundamental from it about the nature of aesthetic judgment. He concludes: "We may use the theory of reflective judgment to interpret Kant's model of aesthetic judgment, but not to identify the a priori principle of aesthetic judgment."[32]

Guyer thus seeks to distance Kant's account of the judgment of taste not only from Kant's general remarks on reflective judgment, but from the notion of purposiveness or finality as well. This idea is by any estimation central to every species of reflective judgment Kant treats in the third *Critique*, whether aesthetic or teleological. Guyer claims that finality adds nothing to Kant's theory of reflection and that it cannot offer a principle for aesthetic judgment. We have found that reflective judgment follows a principle of purposiveness that seeks in its object an interconnection of parts within a structured whole. The aim of the interpretation offered here will be to reveal the application of this principle in Kant's forms of aesthetic judgment, and to show the way this demand for unity is manifested differently in judgments of taste and of the sublime. Locating the operation of this principle in these judgments would firmly establish them as indeed species of reflective judgment, as Kant repeatedly claims them to be.

Hence my account will not accept the bifurcation Guyer detects in Kant's theory of reflection, between comparing presentations to each other versus relating them to our cognitive powers. Indeed, the construction of unity out of component presentations (from the first notion of reflection) lies at the heart of the reflective stance our cognitive powers assume toward their object (from the second). The aesthetic reflective "attitudes" imagination and our other powers assume in judgments of taste and of sublimity will enact the search for purposive unity among compared presentations. This approach preserves the key notion of Kant's view of reflective judgment, namely purposiveness, and it retains the central role of that notion in Kant's aesthetic theory. Though, as we will see, it produces unorthodox results of its own, my approach arguably does less violence to Kant's position than Guyer's rejection of purposiveness and his separation of aesthetic judgment from the rest of Kant's account of reflection. A primary aim of the next two chapters will be to justify this alternative by showing aesthetic judgment to be a true species of reflective judgment; that is, by locating the search for purposive unity in the judgments of taste and sublimity.

Varieties of Unity

Reflective judgment anticipates purposiveness in its object by sensing and seeking out the coherence of unified design. In the first *Critique* Kant had expressed this expectation of unity as a principle of systematization, a demand exercised by reason in organizing knowledge. Reason expects that all the content of experience will cohere as a systematic unity, and it propels us to discern the signs of that unity wherever they lie: "This unity of reason always presupposes an idea, viz., the idea of the form of a whole of cognition—a whole that precedes the determinate cognition of the parts and that contains the conditions for determining a priori for each part its position and its relation to the remaining parts" (CPR A645/B673). The integrity of reason as a unified faculty demands that its own ideas, as well as the wealth of knowledge supplied by the understanding and sanctioned by reason in critique, may precipitate an ordered whole.

Something of this drive for unity informs Kant's third *Critique* conception of reflective judgment, but we must be careful to recall that Kant conceives judgment as following *its own* principle (of purposiveness) in reflection; reflective judgment is not governed from without by a rational idea of systematicity. In fact, that idea of the form of a whole, as Kant presents it in the first *Critique*, makes use of *schemata* in ordering knowledge. Kant writes in the "Architectonic of Pure Reason": "For its execution the idea requires a *schema*, i.e., an essential manifoldness as well as order of the parts that is determined a priori from the principle of the purpose. A schema that is drawn up not in accordance with an idea—i.e., on the basis of reason's main purpose—but empirically, in accordance with aims that offer themselves contingently . . . yields *technical* unity. But a schema that arises only in conformity with an idea (where reason imposes the purposes a priori and does not await them empirically) is the basis for *architectonic* unity" (CPR A833/B861). The ultimate aim of reason, to organize its knowledge into a systematic unity, requires the guidance of an a priori schema to structure this architectonic.

But we noticed earlier that in aesthetic reflective judgment the schematizing activity of imagination is in abeyance; schemata are not applied in such judgments. Thus the coherence of diverse parts sought in aesthetic reflection cannot assume the form of technical unity as described above. Technical unities not only employ schemata but are also devised with reference to a determinate purpose. Neither can aesthetic unities be architectonic, for the ends of reason would then impose purposes on the object of aesthetic reflection. This would violate not only the indeterminacy of purpose maintained in such reflection, but would undermine the autonomy of reflective judgment. Not even a schema originating from an idea of reason should interfere with the nonschematic operations of aesthetic reflection.

Christel Fricke, for one, has distinguished two models of reflective judgment in Kant, the first of which parallels Ginsborg's account, noted earlier, of reflection as a power of empirical concept-formation. I argued that such a model cannot (at the very least) be the whole story because, most especially in the case of aesthetic reflection, judgment does not produce anything like a concept under which one could subsume particulars. Fricke suggests a second model, however, in which reflection undertakes something quite different from subsuming the particular under a new concept: "As an independent faculty the reflective faculty of judgement attempts to find a concept for the manifold by means of which this is not represented in the discursive unity of an objective concept, but by means of which it appears in the form of a systematic unity of a whole that is organized according to the representation of a purpose."[33] On the account developed in this chapter, reflective judgment does indeed *anticipate* the purposive unity of a system in its object. But because systematic unities require the application of schemata, and because schemata play no role in aesthetic reflection, it will turn out that the *aesthetic unity* discerned in such reflection does not achieve the form of systematic or architectonic unity at all. Aesthetic unities are not systematic unities, due to their lack of schematic organization, but also due to the fact, which will be considered in chapter 4, that for Kant systematic unities are essentially systems of classification. Thus though we know that reflective judgment's principle of purposiveness seeks a unity of diverse parts in an object viewed aesthetically, it is as yet unclear what sort of unity it comes to discern. The distinctive character of *aesthetic unity*—which will resemble neither the technical unity of an object cognized through a determined purpose, nor the architectonic unity of a system—remains to be seen.

Afforded this account of reflective judgment, we can now turn to Kant's more detailed treatments of aesthetic reflection, namely in the judgment of taste and the judgment of sublimity. The aim will be to determine where the principle of reflective judgment—seeking purposive (seemingly intended) unity among a diversity of parts—is most clearly at work in these judgments. We will find that this principle is active, as it should be, in the judgment of taste. On the unorthodox interpretation and appropriation of Kant that I will pursue, however, its operation will be best exemplified by the judgment of sublimity, as seen in the light of reflection on what Kant calls aesthetic ideas. We might already anticipate, in general accord with claims advanced by Rudolf Makkreel,[34] that a reflective practice of bringing coherence to diverse experience, yet without determining it through subsumption under a unified concept or purpose, will amount to a broadly enacted power of creative interpretation. This power will come to be what I call a sublime understanding.

2

The Taste of Aesthetic Reflection

What makes aesthetic experience so significant for Kant is its provision of a kind of validity based directly on a universal *feeling* rather than on discursive concepts. When you admire a beautiful flower, or a lovely representation of a flower—as in one of Robert Mapplethorpe's "innocent" floral compositions—your admiration is in some sense not specific to you. On Kant's view, aesthetic appreciation—of a kind to be clarified in this chapter—flows out of a universally shared structure of cognitive capacities. As such I can "demand" that others share the pleasure that something gives, because of the a priori sources of the feeling. I can legitimately judge that others ought to find the flower beautiful too; whether they will agree is another matter, but wherever intersubjective agreements about taste do bloom, aesthetic experience contributes to the building of shared values. When it comes, say, to one of Mapplethorpe's less innocent images, Kant might say that the feelings aroused will be more personally specific. Different people's interest in (or aversion to) what the work depicts, and what they think Mapplethorpe wants to do to them through his image, will complicate, to put it lightly, aesthetic response and its basis of validity. These contrasts—between nature and art, between innocent beauties and motivated acts of artistic expression—are decisive for Kant's conception of judgments of taste and their purview.

I introduce taste as a distinctive preconceptual relation between the cognitive powers of imagination and understanding. The "purposiveness without purpose" that aesthetic play discerns is found, I will claim, in an object's *formal* properties. That is, in the long-standing debate over the nature of Kant's aesthetic theory, I will adopt the position that his judgment of taste embodies a formalist aesthetic theory, one that would put aside all considerations of representational, symbolic, or expressive content when it comes to reflecting on works of art. This will precipitate an instructive dispute with Paul Guyer, who has made tremendous efforts to save Kant from a formalistic conception of aesthetic response. My view, carried through into chapter 3, will be that only Kant's judgment of taste is formalist, and that Kantian sublime reflection offers a more genial model for *interpretive* response to what a work might mean. In the case of taste, though, aesthetic imagination fulfills reflective judgment's search for purposive though indeterminate unity by exploring and playing with the pleasing designedness discerned in an object's form. Establishing the judgment of taste as a true instance of reflective judgment will be significant in itself: it will secure the relevance of aesthetic experience to reflective judgment's provision of an orienting felt sense for experiential wholes. This holistic sense will then take on its interpretive character in the judgment of sublimity, as a sense-making practice that delves into the meanings of art works, and that, more broadly, weaves networks of telling connections through metaphor and other creative means.

Because Kant took beauty in nature to be taste's modal object (as I will argue), this judgment offers little purchase on art's rich meanings. Further, taste's focus on formal features renders it averse to contemplation of the sort of contextual factors that enrich our responses to works of art as complexly historical products. In fact, Kant indicates at some points that the judgment of taste may not apply to human works of art at all, given the expressive purposes in them which might constrain imagination's play. Considering these issues will prompt an assessment of Kant's notorious distinction between free and dependent beauty, and will lead us to critical conclusions about the role of artist's intentions in aesthetic reflection. We will begin to see the contemporaneity of key features of Kant's theory in the view that a free imaginative response to art cannot be shackled to a recuperation of artistic intent.

Harmony of Form

In the judgment of taste one finds an object to be beautiful. Something about the object—broadly construed: it could be a thing, or a view, or a series of sounds, or the like—occasions a certain harmonious interaction between our powers of understanding and imagination. In this interaction, on Kant's view, a free play of the imaginative power spontaneously accords with the understanding so as to induce a feeling of pleasure. This feeling of pleasurable harmony is the content of a judgment in which we call something beautiful; it is beautiful because it inspires this distinctive relation of powers. The judgment of taste is reflective because in it we do not cognize the object according to any concept, even though imagination harmonizes in it with the power of concepts, the understanding. Imagination acts freely in the judgment of taste because its activity is not *determined* by its relation to the understanding; rather, its accord with the understanding arises spontaneously. The judgment is not based on conceiving an object, much less on cognition of any determinate purpose for the object; and yet the cognitive harmony the judgment expresses indicates that aesthetic reflection has discerned a kind of *purposiveness* in the object: "[If] a given presentation unintentionally brings the imagination (the power of a priori intuitions) into harmony with the understanding (the power of concepts), and this harmony arouses a feeling of pleasure, then the object must thereupon be regarded as purposive for the reflective power of judgment. A judgment of this sort is an aesthetic judgment about the object's purposiveness; it is not based on any concept we have of the object, nor does it provide such a concept" (CJ 190). The pleasurable harmony that serves as the basis for the judgment of taste indicates the "subjective purposiveness" of an object for reflective judgment. The harmony of faculties makes the judgment of taste a *feeling* for an object's purposiveness, and so the judgment does not think its purpose as a concept (CJ 221).

Kant of course claims that this judgment, though subjective, nevertheless enjoys a claim to universal validity. When we judge an object beautiful we do not merely express a subjective preference, Kant insists; we rather claim that everyone else ought to see its beauty. In lieu of a concept on which to base the validity claim of taste, Kant makes the basis for its universality the subjective condition of a harmony between cognitive powers. "[T]he way of presenting [which occurs] in a judgment of taste is to have subjective universal communicability without presupposing a determinate concept; hence this subjective universal communicability can be nothing but [that of] the mental state in which we are when imagination and understanding are in free play (insofar as they harmonize with each other as required for *cognition in general*)" (CJ 217–218). Kant bases the universal validity of this judgment on the commonality of this mental state to all judging subjects. Kant takes the spontaneous compatibility of imagination and understanding to be an essential component of the subject, a component without which the cognition of objects would, in fact, be impossible. Given that this harmony obtains necessarily for all cognizing subjects, the aesthetic pleasure that arises from it can be expected or "demanded" from every practitioner of taste. The judgment of taste may demand the assent of others because this *sensus communis* assures that the pleasure felt in the judgment is a truly universal feeling, rather than one specific to the chance predilections of a peculiar subject (CJ 237–240).

A second factor underlies the validity claim of the judgment of taste. When aesthetic reflection attributes purposiveness to its object, it discerns that designedness in the object's *form*. Kant regards the specific materials from which an object is made as potentially charming or agreeable to this subject or that, but the universality of the judgment must not be sullied by the "interest" in the object which such feelings of attraction imply. "A *pure judgment of taste*," as Kant writes, "is one that is not influenced by charm or emotion . . . and whose determining basis is therefore merely the purposiveness of the form" (CJ 223).[1] Taste attends to the form of an object because only the constancy of this aspect of it across all judges can warrant the judgment's claim to universality. What Kant regards as material in sensation, for example the vibrancy of a given color contrast, may in its empirical contingency appear variously to different viewers. Someone carried away merely by the sheer brightness of the gold paint surrounding Marilyn's head in Warhol's *Gold Marilyn Monroe* gives in to the "charm" of a sensation which carries no assurance of universal appeal. Only the formal aspect of an object of reflection can necessitate the a priori feeling of pleasure, and the claim to universality, which marks the exercise of taste: "If an object's form (rather than the material of sensation in its presentation) is judged in mere reflection on it . . . to be the basis of a pleasure in the presentation of such an object, then the presentation is also judged to be connected necessarily with this pleasure, and thus connected with it not merely for the subject who apprehends this form but in general for everyone's judgment of it" (CJ 190).[2] The judgment of taste, as an instance of aesthetic reflection, expects purposiveness in its object, in the way its parts unify as an articulated whole. This expectation of unity attends to the "form" of the object in question, and the universality of the judgment relies in part on the intersubjective availability and constancy of this form.

Given the primacy of form in the judgment of taste, we need to determine just what Kant means by "form" here. By this means we can clarify the operation of aesthetic reflection in taste, and discern the application of the principle of purposiveness in its search for unity among diverse parts. In the Third Moment of the Analytic of the Beautiful, Kant appeals to the *form of purposiveness*, or "purposiveness without purpose," as that to which the judgment of taste attends. The mere feeling reflection gets that an object is formed as if to fulfill some indeterminate purpose gives pleasure in the judgment: "the liking that, without a concept, we judge to be universally communicable and hence to be the basis that determines a judgment of taste, can be nothing but the subjective purposiveness in the presentation of an object, without any purpose . . . and hence the mere form of purposiveness, insofar as we are conscious of it, in the presentation by which an object is *given* us" (CJ 221). The form of purposiveness ultimately consists in an object's tendency to bring about the harmony of imagination and understanding—which harmony, as we have seen, produces the "liking" in beauty. If the form of an object, in some as yet unclear sense, provides the proper focus of taste, as Kant repeatedly insists, then it will be in this form that aesthetic reflection finds the "form of purposiveness" fulfilled.

Paul Guyer has questioned, however, whether this "form of finality" (as he translates it) is to be found exclusively in the purposiveness of *form*: "does formal finality necessarily pertain to the form of objects?"[3]

Guyer argues that in the appeal to the form of finality, that is, to sub-jective purposiveness, Kant does not show that any particular aspects of the object in question bring about the harmony of cognitive powers. "To attribute formal finality to an object is to claim that it is suitable for occasioning this state, but not to claim that it does so in virtue of any specific properties."[4] The subjective purposiveness attributed to an object of taste does not imply that the object pleases in virtue of any specific properties, Guyer argues, and so not in virtue of its formal character. Guyer finds Kant's entire account of purposiveness to be rather empty, and argues, as we have seen, that this finality "turns out to amount to *nothing but* an object's conformity to the requirements of the reflective judgment. . . . No further and more specific form, appearance, quality, or history of an object is invoked by calling it final. . . ."[5] Kant's loose use of "form of purposiveness" and "purpo-siveness of form" tend to suggest an aesthetic formalism that, accord-ing to Guyer, is neither required by the structure nor recommended for the well-being of Kant's theory of beauty. Subsequent formalist readings of Kant (exemplified by Clive Bell) have emphasized this dimension of his theory to its detriment, Guyer thinks.

If we are to understand what Kant means by clearly writing that aes-thetic judgment of the beautiful attends to the form of an object, we must determine what sense of "form" might account for the harmony of imagination and the understanding at the basis of taste. In the end, I will dispute Guyer's claim that the harmony of powers in taste need not be based on the object's form. Specifying this "form" will clarify where aesthetic reflection discerns the form of purposiveness, reflected in a unity of diverse parts, in the object of taste.

To what "form" of the object, then, does taste attend? Perhaps we may take the notion of "form" that Kant used in the first *Critique* to apply here as well. In that case the form of an object will simply con-sist in the structures given by the forms of intuition, namely space and time. This formal character of an object would, in keeping with the first *Critique*, be distinct from its material composition and those of its qualities the sensation of which varies with the subjective perspective of the observer.[6] Apprehending and reflecting on an object's form will involve exploring the temporal and spatial relationships among its various parts. In what way, then, would this focus on perceptual form account for the harmony of imagination and understanding in this judgment?

If the spatial and temporal form of a presented manifold of sensations, as apprehended by the imagination, "accords" with the faculty of concepts, that is, the understanding, then that form gives pleasure and the manifold is judged beautiful. This accord must be one between imagination and the forms of objecthood prescribed by the understanding. In the case of cognition, after all, experience arises for Kant from a determinate unification of the categories of objectivity supplied by the understanding with the spatially and temporally ordered presentations of imagination. In the judgment of taste the main difference is that this accord arises spontaneously rather than being legislated by the understanding to produce a determinative judgment. Despite this difference, it is still the spatio-temporal constructions of imagination that come into accord with the understanding. But why must imagination's activity satisfy the forms of objecthood? For the simple reason that if it is to accord with the understanding, no option except satisfying those forms exists. Because the understanding is the faculty of rules for the cognition of objects, there is nothing in the understanding (n.b.: with any a priori status) with which the imagination can accord except the forms of the appearance of objects.[7] Thus even in the judgment of taste an accord between these two faculties could only arise at that point where they are designed to meet, in the spatio-temporal form of appearance, even though the understanding's concepts are not applied determinatively.[8]

Yet so far this account of the harmony of imagination and the understanding suffers a serious failing, namely that *every* experienced object must satisfy the forms of intuition and the categories of the understanding.[9] Something in addition to the object's satisfaction of the lawfulness of the understanding must serve to distinguish it as beautiful. We must take into account the precise role of imagination, which, even as it conforms to the rules of the understanding, is not determined by those rules. Imagination, in reflecting on the form of an object, engages in what Kant calls a "free play of our presentational powers" (CJ 242). In this play imagination apprehends and reflects upon the spatial and temporal form of the object in such a way that it can harmonize with conceptual understanding without being governed by it.[10]

Imagination remains free in aesthetic reflection because no determinate conceptual rules are applied to the manifold of sensations. Yet even though concepts are not brought to bear *in the aesthetic judgment,* what is being judged must—as an object of experience—be a product of synthesis in accordance with the power of concepts. In aesthetic judgment the understanding, with the aid of the pure forms of sensibility, provides the only domain of lawfulness it has to provide, namely the form of appearance. It is within these formal constraints that imagination may freely entertain its powers of apprehension. The lawfulness of the understanding and the freedom of imagination thus achieve a mutual fit in which we feel the pleasure of beauty. We began by asking what sense of the "form" of the object provides for the possibility of this accord between faculties. It now appears that the spatial and temporal form of objecthood, as Kant has retained it from the first *Critique,* combined with a generous conception of the imagination's free play suffices to account for this possibility of harmony.[11] We need not appeal to any more elaborate notion of form in order to account for the harmony of faculties in the judgment of taste.

Guyer objects to this account of the purposiveness of form that taste finds in its object. He claims that "there is nothing in Kant's theory of the harmony of the faculties which can require that it be occasioned only by what the first Critique identified as the form of appearance."[12] But if the harmony is one between free imagination and the *lawfulness* of understanding, what else could occasion this harmony but the accordance of imagination's free activity with the form of appearance to which understanding gives the law? It would seem that "harmony" here can only mean a free exploration by imagination within the *formal* constraints placed by the understanding's rules of cognition. Guyer recognizes that the harmony of the faculties "can only be a state in which the imagination conforms to the understanding's demand for the unification of our manifolds of intuition, without the understanding performing its customary role of applying a concept to a manifold as the rule for its unification."[13] It should then be clear that the unity demanded by understanding is just that unity provided by the form of appearance. That demand specifies the constraints imagination must spontaneously "respect" in its free play in order to accord with the understanding.

Guyer argues that nonformal or (as we will see in the next chapter) conceptual aspects of an object can induce this harmony. He even suggests that precisely nonformal properties are especially potent for harmonizing imagination and the understanding: "the very fact that such features of objects are not pure a priori elements of their appearance and thus not susceptible to the schematism of the a priori concepts of the understanding makes it all the more likely that they could serve for the felt synthesis without concepts which founds aesthetic response."[14] We could grant that imagination might range over such elements in the course of its spontaneous play, but it would remain the case that the sort of unity demanded by the understanding places formal constraints on what features of an object can bear on an a priori harmony between these powers. In the judgment of taste the play of imagination harmonizes not with just any conceptual rules of the understanding, but with the a priori lawfulness of that faculty, and only as such can the judgment have an a priori claim to validity. Merely empirical and contingent elements provided to experience by sensation and by the understanding cannot serve as a basis for this harmony's claim to universal validity. So however much imagination might play with nonformal properties, or even conceptual or representational elements, only its presentation of *formal* unity can bear on its achieving the kind of harmony with the understanding which can demand universal assent. Hence Guyer's claim that nonformal properties can induce the harmony of powers distinctive of the judgment of taste potentially threatens the basis of validity of that judgment. To emphasize again: Kant's judgment of taste must be formalist because the specific accord at its basis is one between imagination and the understanding's rules for the form of appearance.

Closely related to the emphasis on aesthetic form in Kant's judgment of taste is his claim that the appearance of *design*, especially in works of art, gives form its power to harmonize our cognitive powers. The apparent order and well-formedness in an object of reflection inspires the play of imagination to an extent that the merely random or incongruous, Kant thinks, cannot. He links the notions of form and design in the Third Moment of the Analytic of the Beautiful: "[In] design the basis for any involvement of taste is not what gratifies us in sensation, but merely what we like because of its form. . . . All form of the objects of the senses . . . is either *shape* or *play*; if the latter, it is either play of shapes (in space, namely, mimetic art and dance), or mere play of sensations (in time). . . . [It] is the *design* in the first case and the *composition* in the second that constitute the proper object of a pure judgment of taste" (CJ 225). This notion of design links aesthetic form to the role of purposiveness in Kant's theory: imagination receives the suggestions of purposive activity that inspire its aesthetic reflection precisely through such well-formedness. Design is just the appearance of purposiveness in the form of an object, which spurs on imagination's play. Out of that play, if it freely conforms to the rules of understanding, arises the pleasurable harmony at the basis of the judgment of taste.

Guyer, however, has taken Kant to task for regarding the appearance of design as a criterion of beauty. He finds it empty as a means to distinguish what might be beautiful from what might not because, as he argues, we can all too easily imagine anything to be designed *in the sense of having a purpose*. "For *any* perceptual property an object might have, we may readily imagine a purpose which that object could satisfy. . . . And *within* any range of properties objects have, there are none that cannot be imagined to fulfill some conceivable purpose. . . . The appearance of design is a vacuous criterion for aesthetic judgment, for any appearance might satisfy some design."[15] For example, a mere puddle of water on the floor could be imagined to have been put there, designed by someone to wet people's feet. This installation, whatever its designedness, would hardly inspire aesthetic appreciation. But would the puddle suggest an *appearance* of design? Guyer is here confusing the question of whether something appears designed, that is, whether it carries the mark of design, and the question of whether it might have a purpose. One might attribute or assign a purpose to anything irrespective of its appearance; but many things with a purpose, such as the puddle of water, will not enjoy the appearance of design. Kant's design "criterion" of beauty obviously could not require that something satisfy a purpose, as Guyer seems to suggest, for such a criterion would turn aesthetic judgment into teleological judgment. Kant's point is rather that something that appears to be designed, that seems to show marks of intentional activity, that has the well-formedness of the purposive, is more likely to give rise to a judgment of beauty. Guyer exaggerates the connotation of purpose in design in a way that obscures Kant's emphasis on well-formedness as an indicator of purposive unity.

Even so, it would be a mistake to construe the presence of design as a sufficient criterion for judging something beautiful. It may be that many apparently designed things will betray too much uniformity or regularity in their design to inspire the play of imagination. "[W]here only a free play of our presentational powers is to be sustained . . . as in the case of pleasure gardens, room decoration, all sorts of tasteful utensils, and so on, any regularity that has an air of constraint is [to be] avoided as much as possible" (CJ 242).[16] Kant thinks that mathematical regularity, in particular, betrays the presence of human design without offering much opportunity for playful appreciation: "it does not allow us to be entertained for long by our contemplation of it; instead it bores us" (ibid.). Kant doubts that a series of uniformly distributed vertical lines, as in a bar code, say, will greatly entice imagination to experiment with its presentational powers. Some devotees of minimalist art might object to Kant's taste here, but his point is clear enough: too little appearance of design (as in the puddle of water) as well as too much uniformity inflict an "irksome constraint" on imagination's aesthetic play. The well-formedness of design might be a partial condition of aesthetic enjoyment, but it will not suffice to guarantee a judgment of beauty. Perhaps the fundamental tenet of Kant's theory is that no rule could be provided in advance that would allow us to pick out anything beautiful before putting it to the test of taste's imaginative response; misconstruing the presence of design as such a rule would violate Kant's entire approach.

Kant has been criticized for the excessive formalism of his judgment of taste, and Guyer's arguments in *Kant and the Claims of Taste* represent one of the most elaborate efforts to save Kant's aesthetic theory from its formalist tendencies. The motivations for making the effort are great: if Kant's theory limits the aesthetically relevant features of a work to its formal qualities of shape or sequence, he will have little to tell us about things we would like an aesthetic theory to illuminate, such as the representational and expressive powers of art, and our ways of ascribing meanings to it. We will see in the next chapter that making room in aesthetic judgment for appreciation of thematic content is precisely what

motivates Guyer's critique of Kant's perceptual formalism. And there is
no question that Kant provides many of the tools for formulating an
interpretive model of aesthetic appreciation, an aesthetic reflection
engaged in making sense of works as expressions of meaning. But that
model is to be found, on my view, not in Kant's judgment of taste,
which is indeed as formalist as Kant makes it out to be, but rather in
Kant's theory of sublime reflection. The desire to save Kant from a
barren formalism, though meritorious, does undue violence to the
judgment of taste by casting it in nonformalist terms. We should accept
the frequently evident formalist leanings of his theory of taste, and
leave it as formalist as any Greenbergian could like. After all, we can
and do on occasion appreciate natural beauty and works of art in
purely formalist terms, and Kant's judgment of taste provides an
account of how we are capable of this. The formalism of beauty does
not render Kant's entire aesthetic theory formalist, however, because we
can locate our means of appreciating the expressed content of art
works elsewhere in his theory. Specifically, in the next chapter I will
construe Kant's judgment of sublimity as an alternative model for how
we interpret the purposive unity of art works in terms of their expressed
content and meaning.

The Operation of Reflection in Taste

We have not yet determined, however, in what way the principle of
purposiveness actually operates in the harmony of cognitive powers
induced by purposive form. We have seen the indispensable role of
imagination in the judgment of taste, and presumably the aesthetic
reflective search for unity will appear in that power's play. Even as it
refrains from violating understanding's rules for the cognition of
objects, imagination's free exploration of its presentational powers
provides the distinctive element for sensing beauty. Here we will see
that in imagination's free activity it applies the principle of purposiveness to discern unity among the parts of an object's form. The perceptual form of a beautiful thing inspires the free activity of
imagination, but in this freedom imagination does not simply *reproduce* this form. A form that imposed itself too determinatively upon
the imagination would constrain the free harmony of powers distinc-

tive of the judgment of taste. This is why Kant insists that "where only a free play of our presentational powers is to be sustained . . . any regularity that has an air of constraint is [to be] avoided as much as possible" (CJ 242). Imagination does not here simply apprehend the form of a thing, but *produces* new ways to regard the object as a formal unity. It plays at inventing a variety of formal configurations within the limits placed by the perceptual form and the rules of the understanding. An object in which these limits do not unduly restrict imagination, in which there is room for imagination to play, may be judged beautiful.

In his first *Critique* Kant distinguishes the reproductive and productive powers of the imagination. Reproductive imagination is a power of memory that brings back to mind a previous empirical intuition. Because its activity is limited to recurrent experiences separated in time, reproductive imagination is, Kant writes, "subject solely to empirical laws, viz., to the laws of association" (CPR B152). Productive imagination, on the other hand, is a spontaneous power that *invents intuitions*. In the first *Critique* it is empowered to "determine sense [a priori] in terms of its form in accordance with the unity of apperception" and the requirements of the understanding (CPR B151).[17] In the *Critique of Judgment* Kant expands its powers and construes the free activity of the imagination in the judgment of taste as productive in the sense that it can be "the originator of arbitrary [*willkürlich*] forms of possible intuitions" (CJ 240).[18] Imagination freely takes in the form of the beautiful object by exploring various ways to construct a unity out of its elements. It acts creatively in that no rule in the form of a concept or determinate purpose guides its play or dictates its product.[19]

Consider an example of natural (though culturally tweaked) beauty, such as a complex arrangement of flowers.[20] Determinative judgment would cognize them as flowers and subsume them under that concept, or under the concepts of the specific species present. But if one considers the arrangement in its richness as a formal configuration, as a complex of shape, mass, density, line, and shadow, then the way in which imagination apprehends this wealth of perceptual material surpasses through appreciation the simple judgment of it as "flowers." Rather than settling on the concept, and dumbly claiming, "That's a bunch of flowers" (as one might say of Duchamp's ready-made,

"There's a snow shovel"), imagination plays with and varies its apprehension of its object. Imagination, so to speak, looks at the arrangement from this angle and that, it traces a tendril through to its source, it detects an apparent pattern within the spacing of leaves and buds, it contrasts the subtle structural and coloring differences between species, it lingers over specific details before relating them to some aspect of the rest. In short, we explore the possibilities within this complex for relating the whole and its parts. One's imagination is not limited to (not determined by) the concept "flower," yet its activity harmonizes with the understanding. That is, the formal configuration with which it plays is still the flower arrangement which the understanding, in its own right, cognizes in experience. As Rudolf Makkreel puts it, "The artistic imagination may not violate the categorial framework provided by the understanding, but it may explicate possibilities left open by that framework."[21]

Similarly in the case of art, formalist appreciation of a work occurs through a free imaginative exploration of features encompassed by the understanding's lawful governance over the form of appearance. To carry through the example, aesthetic appreciation of represented flowers, as in one of Mapplethorpe's floral compositions, can let imagination take in and play with the order and balance of the image in various ways. One might consider the curve of a stem in terms of its positioning within the frame, the gradations of texture and shade in the print's subject and background, how the manipulation of lighting and shadow bring out this or that feature of the subject, all in relation to the formal features of the flower itself as represented. Here, too, imagination plays without the constraint of concepts, in a specific sense: it might make use of a host of concepts in its formal exploration, just as it might in the case of natural beauty, but no concept determines its play nor dictates a show-stopping cognition of what the object is. This should be true for the concept "art" just as much as for "flower," though we will see shortly that the matter is more troubled than this, as there are elements of Kant's view that appear to raise questions about whether pure judgments of taste might be possible at all in relation to works of art.

For now it is clear that the productive activity of imagination provides the judgment of taste with the aspect distinctive of aesthetic reflection. Its free exploration defers determinative cognition of a manifold under a restrictive concept; but more importantly, productive imagination here employs the principle of purposiveness intrinsic to the operation of reflective judgment. This principle seeks well-formed unity among a constituency of parts. Productive imagination enacts this principle as it constructs alternative configurations out of the formal aspects of its object.[22] In the judgment of taste, the purposiveness of the beautiful object is confirmed by its possessing a richness of formal possibilities that can sustain imagination's experimental play. The harmony of cognitive powers is achieved when imagination, even as it spontaneously conforms to the understanding's rules for the cognition of objects, presents such an indeterminate purposive unity in a variety of ways. Thus we should not accept Guyer's segregation of aesthetic judgment from Kant's account of reflective judgment. For in sum, the judgment of taste enacts reflection's principle of purposiveness by playing constructively with the formal features of the beautiful thing.[23]

The Limits of Taste

Kant's aesthetic theory, I have maintained, adopts a perceptual formalism when it comes to the judgment of taste. But recall that aesthetic reflection anticipates unity in its object because it treats the object as something informed by a *purpose*, even if the reflection will not itself determine this purpose. The principle of purposiveness active in aesthetic reflection must, in order to accord with Kant's most basic claims, seek out a purpose that would unite the diverse parts of its object. It is by no means clear, especially in the case of human works of art, that a purely formal study such as that undertaken in the judgment of taste can alone suffice to shed light on this unity of purpose. There is more going on in a Mapplethorpe floral image than a play of light, texture, and geometry, and of course if one attempted an appreciation of beautiful form in the case of Duchamp's show shovel one would foolishly fall into just the trap he set for such a taste. One could play at presenting various formal configurations for Picasso's *Guernica* all day without getting any purchase on the aims informing the artist's work. Productive imagination, playing under the perceptual formalism of Kant's judgment of taste, would find a feast of formal unity to relish in this painting, but would remain all along oblivious to the probable meanings of the painting. Such a formally stunted judgment might have the poor taste to reproduce the image for use as wallpaper, given the feelings of harmony its forms induce in it. The expectation of purposiveness in reflection on a work of art must address itself not simply to formal considerations of the work's unity, but must seek as well to reflect on whatever unity its thematic content contributes to the work.

In this section I argue that Kant's account of the judgment of taste does not adequately address the expressive purposiveness of art for the reason that he takes beauty in nature to be the primary object of taste. Attention to Kant's distinction between free and dependent beauty will indicate that the pure formality of the judgment of taste tends to deny beauty to human artifacts because of the purposes that pervade them. Evaluating this distinction will help clarify the place of purposes and the role of artist's intentions in reflection on works of art. In the end, the need to include a work's thematic content among the objects of aesthetic reflection will encourage us to seek a form of judgment in which Kant finds a relation to ideas acceptable. That form will be the judgment of sublimity.

Conceiving reflective judgment as the search for purposive unity in an object would be of little use to an aesthetic theory if the search could not be undertaken in human works of art. In reflection on a work, searching for a principle to make sense of its parts as a coherent whole amounts to interpreting the thematic intention that gives the work meaning. The limitations on what the judgment of taste can illuminate about this arise from Kant's conviction that the unintended beauties of nature are the paradigmatic object of taste. In fact, on more than one occasion Kant appears to exclude human works of art altogether from the proper domain of the pure judgment of taste. For example, in the First Introduction he writes: "[W]e are dealing with the principle of merely reflective and not of determinative judgment (determinative judgment underlies all human works of art), and in the case of reflective judgment the purposiveness is to be considered *unintentional* and hence can belong only to nature" (FI 251). Kant's boldest claim in this version of his introduction, that all judgments of art are determinative, would imply that judging a work always involves thinking it under a definite concept supplied by a purpose or intention we know it to fulfill. If this were the case, the unity we attributed to the object would be the *technical* unity supplied by a determinate purpose, rather than the *aesthetic* unity productive imagination would discern in its object. Similarly, in the "Deduction of Pure Aesthetic Judgments" Kant seems to disqualify works of art as objects of *pure* aesthetic judgment. He writes: "[I]f the object is given as a product of art, and as such is to be declared beautiful, then we must first base it on a concept of what the thing is [meant] to be, since art always presupposes a purpose in the cause. . . . And since the harmony of a thing's manifold with an intrinsic determination of the thing, i.e., with its purpose, is the thing's perfection, it follows that when we judge artistic beauty we shall have to assess the thing's perfection as well, whereas perfection is not at all at issue when we judge natural beauty" (CJ 311). Kant seems to suppose that, when judging a depiction of the human form, for example, one must think a concept of human perfection in order to evaluate the success of the depiction of it. But if one takes concepts of perfection into account, then clearly judgment of the depiction is no longer purely aesthetic. If judging a work of art always involves presupposing a determinate purpose it fulfills, then the reflective construction of *aesthetic* unity from a work's features does not occur.

But these claims do not seem to be borne out in the third *Critique* as a whole. After all, Kant includes there an extensive—albeit unsatisfying—discussion of the fine arts as objects of aesthetic reflective judgment. Some commentators deny that Kant held nature in greater aesthetic regard than art; their motivation is typically to shore up the view that Kant's aesthetic theory does illuminate our responses to human art, and not just to natural beauty.[24] Theodore Gracyk, for one, argues that because Kant frequently means the term *Natur* to encompass "the sum of all objects of experience," the reflective expectation of purposiveness in *Natur* does not exclude art nor privilege the natural world. He concludes that "Nature's 'pride of place' is rather limited" in Kant's theory.[25] Yet Kant's preference for the *unintended* purposiveness of the purest beauties of nature lies largely in the fact that no matter how purposive such a beauty might be for a harmony of cognitive powers, we could never ascribe to it any determinate purpose, at least not without passing over into teleological judgment. Kant favors natural beauty because it bolsters the hope underlying the entire *Critique of Judgment*: that reflective judgment can reconcile, at least for regulative purposes, the mechanism of nature and the autonomy of the moral law, by finding beautiful signs that nature is purposive for the realization of the morally good. Only a *contingent* harmony between our cognitive powers and their objects can support this hope, so the intentional creation of beauty in art cannot serve the purpose, whether or not a work of art falls under the broad term *Natur*. The unintentional purposiveness of natural beauty plays a central role in Kant's architectonic project, so it seems misleading to underestimate its centrality to his aesthetic theory. The laudable aim of assuring the relevance of Kant's aesthetics to our responses to art does not require that we deny nature's pride of place in Kant's aesthetic lights. It requires instead, I suggest, that we acknowledge the formalist limits of the judgment of taste and look elsewhere in his theory for an account of our interpretive responses to meanings in the arts.

Kant clearly regards beauty in nature as the primary object of the pure judgment of taste, in large part because the purposiveness "found" there may be considered unintentional. Kant supposes that everyone enjoys the natural beauties of parrots, flowers, and crustaceans; our tasteful enjoyment of these beauties "is based on no perfection of any kind, no intrinsic purposiveness to which the combination of the manifold might refer" (CJ 229). There is surely more temptation to discover the satisfaction of a determinate purpose in a work of art, which is presumably the product of someone aiming to do one thing rather than another. Recall, however, that the purposiveness of beautiful form is not "found," strictly speaking, in either nature or art, but is rather ascribed to an object by the principle motivating reflective judgment. Aesthetic reflection does not ascribe objective properties to things as determinative judgment does, but rather cultivates a subjective relation between imagination and its object. We might well ascribe a definite purpose to a work of art, if we claimed to know the thematic intention of the artist, and characterized all the parts of the work as a whole brought to unity in the expression of that known intention. But in fact such a reading of the work would discern in it a *technical* rather than an *aesthetic* unity. Put another way, Kant's account of aesthetic reflection should commit him to the view that basing one's response to a work on a knowledge of the artist's intention destroys the indeterminate play essential to a properly *aesthetic* response. Kant should call critics who insist that interpretation of a work must be determined by artist's intent mere technicians of art. Kant, like all formalist aestheticians, should exclude considerations of intention from aesthetic judgment. If Kant were truly to maintain, as he seems to suggest in the First Introduction, that art works cannot but be thought under definite purposes, then reflection on them would never be aesthetic. Our *technical* assessment of a work would assign it a meaning based on the purposes or thematic intentions informing it, intentions we apparently know all about. Those putatively explicit intentions would come to determine an "aesthetic reflection" that had sought to root out of its object the mere form of purposiveness.

The problem is that Kant seems to believe that the *judgment* of a work of art, a work no doubt informed by artist's intentions, is automatically pervaded by those determinate purposes, and thus not sufficiently reflective. Kant seems to think that because a work of art is informed by the intentions of its creator, judgment of it must be determinative in accordance with one's cognizing those purposes in fact, and in concepts. It does not seem to occur to him that one could reflect on the purposive unity of a work's form *or* of its thematic content, *without knowing* the determinate intentions of the artist(s) who produced it, or without regard for those intentions, and thus without one's judgment being determined by them. Kant himself notes that even the botanist who does know "what sort of thing a flower is [meant] to be," namely the reproductive organ of the plant, simply "pays no attention to this natural purpose when he judges the flower by taste" (CJ 229). The teleological ascription of purpose is simply deferred in aesthetic appreciation. Perhaps even if the art critic did somehow know, like the botanist with her flower, "what sort of thing a [painting] is [meant] to be," by some privileged access to the artist's intentions, the critic could simply "pay no attention" to those purposes in order to preserve the free imaginative play of her *aesthetic* (rather than technical) response to the work. Then appreciation of, say, a Mapplethorpe floral composition could be as free of determination by a purpose, in this case the artist's intention, whatever that might be, as the botanist's admiration for a flower's beauty.[26]

The apparent incompatibility of a pure judgment of taste with judgment of an object informed by a purpose motivates Kant's distinction in the Third Moment of the Analytic of the Beautiful between free and dependent (or accessory) beauty. A look at the distinction will clarify the role of artist's intentions in our reflections on art. Kant draws the distinction in terms of whether response to an object presupposes a concept of its purpose: "Free beauty does not presuppose a concept of what the object is [meant] to be. Accessory beauty does presuppose such a concept, as well as the object's perfection in terms of that concept. The free kinds of beauty are called (self-subsistent) beauties of this or that thing. The other kind of beauty is accessory to a concept (i.e., it is conditioned beauty) and as such is attributed to objects that fall under the concept of a particular purpose" (ibid.). Kant has in mind as examples of free beauty "designs *à la grecque*, the foliage on borders or on wallpaper" that "represent nothing, no object under a determinate concept" (ibid.). Such designs inspire the play of imagination in part because they are sufficiently void of conceptual content, and so they do not threaten to tie down imagination's play. Kant takes such designs, and even more so their free-growing kin in nature, to be the model objects of the pure judgment of taste. This alone should indicate the limited purview of this judgment and the problems that arise in hoping for insight from it into the thematic complexities of art works. A taste that on formalist grounds could find similar enjoyments in wallpaper or *Guernica* requires tutelage from other dimensions of aesthetic evaluation.

In the case of accessory or dependent beauty, Kant has in mind organisms or artifacts animated by a purpose, or a concept of perfection, that must enter into judgment of them. "[T]he beauty of a human being...or the beauty of a horse or of a building . . . does presuppose the concept of the purpose that determines what the thing is [meant] to be, and hence a concept of its perfection, and so it is merely adherent beauty" (CJ 230). According to Kant, then, the beauty of a thoroughbred race horse is subordinate to the horse's assigned purpose as a race animal; a thoroughbred has the kind of beauty only an animal bred and trained for racing can have, and its beauty cannot be thought independently of its fulfillment of that purpose. Kant does not construe the beauty of all organisms as dependent on a purpose, however; he notes that "Many birds (the parrot, the humming-bird, the bird of paradise) and a lot of crustaceans in the sea are [free] beauties themselves [and] belong to no object determined by concepts as to its purpose, but we like them freely and on their own account" (CJ 229). It is worth noting that Kant's examples here tend toward the exotic, which suggests that their status as free beauties hangs on their having little assigned purpose in the culture from which Kant enjoys them. Perhaps a culture in which the bird of paradise played a central ritual function would assess its beauty through a dependent relation to a purpose. This sort of cultural variation suggests further that someone sufficiently distant from or oblivious or indifferent to the practices of thoroughbred racing could find a race-horse freely beautiful rather than dependently so. The distinction between kinds of beauties only grows more suspect the further one delves into it.

Kant makes two claims by drawing this distinction. He argues that attribution of a particular purpose to an object of reflection renders judgment of it impure; this point repeats the basic tenet that aesthetic reflection appreciates purposive unity *indeterminately*. But he also claims that certain kinds of entities cannot but be thought of in terms of their purposes or perfections, and whether they fulfill them, and thus cannot serve as the proper object of the pure judgment of taste. Included in this class, as Kant indicates, would be all apparent instances of human beauty. Presumably most works of art would fall into this class, as well; if Kant claims their beauty can only be appreciated as accessory to a purpose, namely what the artist intended it to be or to express, then judgments of dependent rather than free beauty will apply to art.[27] The obvious difficulty with Kant's distinction is that the concept-subordinate status of dependent beauty appears to violate the very nature of aesthetic reflection. If beauty is a felt harmony sensed by judgment without determination by concepts, how can dependent beauty, which presupposes a concept of a thing's purpose *in the aesthetic judgment of it*, be beauty at all?

This quandary has led commentators to either dismiss Kant's distinction entirely as an unfortunate confusion, or to attempt various charitable reinterpretations of it.[28] One can, for example, deny that dependent beauty is a separate *kind* of beauty alongside free beauty by arguing that the distinction is merely one between two judgmental attitudes one can take towards an object.[29] This approach still leaves one with the problem of how a judgmental attitude that takes an object's purpose into account can qualify as an aesthetic judgment. Alternatively, one can argue that dependent beauty is but a species of free beauty that adds some additional consideration without altering the nature of the judgment.[30] But the additional consideration taken into account in dependent beauty is a concept of the object's purpose, and again this judgment's status as authentically aesthetic remains in question.

Eva Schaper's treatment of this problem provides an instructive diagnosis of the formalist limitations of the judgment of taste.[31] She takes Kant to impose several conditions for something to qualify as a case of free beauty; the most important is found in Kant's statement that free beauty "does not presuppose a concept of what the object is [meant] to be" (CJ 229). She then argues that the most plausible reading of this condition would take it to apply differently to free beauty in nature and in art. In the case of free beauty in nature, Schaper writes, "judging something to be freely beautiful . . . is to disregard what the object could or should be, and this takes the form of disregarding its natural end or function. . . ."[32] But in the case of art, as we saw above, Kant emphasizes that "the foliage on borders or on wallpaper" which he offers as free beauties "represent nothing, no object under a determinate concept" (CJ 229). Schaper draws from this the conclusion that appreciating free beauty in art requires that we "disregard what the object could or should be, and this takes the form of disregarding what it could or might be in its representational aspect."[33] That is, Schaper thinks Kant commits himself to a nonrepresentational theory of art in which properly and purely judging a work aesthetically would require disregarding, say in the case of a painting, whatever the shapes on the canvas represent. One could appreciate the "rhythmic" spacing of columns and figures in David's *Oath of the Horatii*, so long as one ignored that columns and figures were what David spaced out. Such a position would be in keeping with an austerely formalist conception of aesthetic response, as it would be of a piece with Kant's preference for beauty in nature, where problems of representation do not arise. But the commitments Kant's distinction between free and dependent beauty might lead him to only heighten concern about the restricted usefulness of the pure judgment of taste, especially in the realm of art. For Schaper salvages a place for free beauty in art only by excising from aesthetic reflection any consideration of what a work of art is about or might mean. This relegates reflection on the expressive, representational, or symbolic content of a work to judgments of dependent beauty. Whether reflection on these concept-dependent features of a work of art can be regarded as properly aesthetic is, once again, by association with dependent beauty, left quite tenuous. "Reflection" on these dimensions of artistic content would be left no longer reflective at all, in fact, because they would purportedly be cognized under the rule of a known purpose or intention.

Before accepting this conclusion, however, we should examine the dichotomy that Kant has here posed. On the one hand, in the case of free beauty, the formal features of an object devoid of any determinate purpose is judged purposive for a harmony of cognitive powers. We find dependent beauty, on the other hand, where a concept of the object's perfection—its satisfaction of its purpose—somehow plays a role in judging it beautiful. But this dichotomy neglects the possibility that a work of art might be informed by the intentions of its producer without those purposes determining the reflection of the person judging it. In such a case judgment of the work would not be determined in advance by the artistic intentions which nevertheless animate it. The work would not count as a free beauty, void of all purposes, for it would indeed be informed by the intentions of its creator. But nor would the work count as a dependent beauty, since reflection on it would not "*presuppose* the concept of the purpose that determines what the thing is [meant] to be" (CJ 230).[34] That is, even though artists presumably fulfill specific aims and intentions in their works, those purposes need not determine our independent responses. Properly aesthetic reflection attributes aesthetic unity to an object, rather than the technical unity that would be ascribed in a judgment guided firmly by a known intention or purpose. Kant's dependent beauties are, in fact, ascribed a technical unity in accordance with a known purpose. But in *aesthetic* reflection one must be unaware of the intentions behind a work, unaware of them in any determinate conceptual form; or alternatively, one must ignore them for the sake of preserving the imaginative freedom of one's own inventive reflection on what the work might mean. If the botanist can manage a tasteful response to her flowers by "paying no attention" to her knowledge of what purpose they are meant to fulfill, the critic can appreciate a work of art independently of whatever intention the artist had in making it.

It turns out that Kant does admit the possibility of an abstraction from purposes that would allow aesthetic reflection to judge the beauty of something with a purpose by ignoring that determining concept of it: "A judgment of taste about an object that has a determinate intrinsic purpose would be pure only if the judging person either had no concept of this purpose, or if he abstracted from it in making his judgment" (CJ 231). Kant allows that one can simply segregate one's knowledge of something's purpose from the content of one's aesthetic judgment of it. Considering the strength of our common tendency to understand things in terms of purposes, and considering as well the variety of concepts that can determine our reflection on a thing, this capacity for abstraction must be quite powerful.[35] Kant, of course, makes this admission within the confines of the dichotomy he has posed. This power of abstraction from purposes is supposed to allow judgments of free formal beauty when it comes to objects that are pervaded by concepts of perfection and so would otherwise count as dependent beauties. Kant allows that even if one has a concept of an object's purpose, and no matter how laced with that purpose the object might be, aesthetic reflection on it can remain free of determination by that purpose. This allowance makes room not only for Kant's judgment of free beauty but also for the alternative I have suggested. The fact that a work of art is pervaded by the thematic intentions of its artist need not keep judgment of the work from being properly reflective, that is, not determined in advance by the intentions behind or in the work.

Kant grants the possibility of this either innocent or contrived "ignorance" of the purposes informing an object in order to reassert the priority of the pure judgment of taste. For my purposes this power of abstraction assures that one can reflect on the aesthetic form of a work of art by means of a pure judgment of taste, even though that work may be pervaded by artist's intentions. One "simply" ignores them when reflecting on the formal unity of the work, or more likely one has little purchase on them in any case. Kant's judgment of taste remains free of interest in the nonformal components of a work. But this gap between the responses of a judging subject and whatever actual intention is embodied in a work also allows aesthetic reflection to seek thematic unity in a work's *content* free of determination by those intentions. In this case one "simply" approaches a work of art expecting to find in it the purposive unity of a theme or themes without knowing or concerning oneself with the intentions of the artist. Kant's aesthetic theory can provide a model for this sort of free interpretive reflection, though not in the judgment of taste, due to its perceptual formalism. He can provide such a model because his overall conception of aesthetic reflection—above and beyond the anti-intentionalist leanings of taste's formalism—requires that imagination's play not be governed by any cognized purposes. The sometimes popular notion that the meaning of a work of art is decided once and for all by the intentions of the one(s) who made it does not find a friend in Kant.[36]

On the other hand, I do not think that we want a model of aesthetic reflection that requires that interpretation refuse any and every reference to the causal history of a work, its origins in the prerogatives of a certain artist of a certain class or race or gender or sexuality in a certain culture, motivated by certain concerns of importance at a certain time, responding to other developments in her field, and so on. Kant's formalist judgment of taste does require an oblivion to all such contextual factors, and thus itself unduly constrains the aesthetic play of an imagination eager to find meanings in things. The strange fruits of such constraint are evident, for example, in Patrick Hutchings's distress that Mapplethorpe's photographs of flowers might have an erotic edge to them: we cannot be appreciating the flowers as free beauties if we "advert to their *function* as sexual apparatus" and then "heap perversity upon logical and epistemological impropriety" by transferring our "concupiscence about sex" onto the poor things.[37] And apparently Duchamp "already trumped" Mapplethorpe by committing the more brilliant "perversity," in *The Bride Stripped Bare of Her Bachelors, Even,* of ascribing "carnality to the metallic and purely mechanical."[38]

Chapter 2

It would seem that we may only properly appreciate art by taking it to be about or mean nothing whatsoever, and these examples do reinforce a certain wisdom in being "against interpretation." As we will see, however, the interpretive model of aesthetic response I will elaborate from Kant's theory of the sublime does in principle allow inclusion of any number of contextual or other nonformal considerations that may contribute to elaborating meanings for works. The overriding condition will continue to be that one's attempt to discern the purposive unity of a meaningful whole in an object of reflection remain the play of a freely productive imagination (however "perverse"), rather than a determinate cognition circumscribed by a fixed concept or purpose.

We must seek a better model for reflection on a work of art than the judgment of taste provides. We need a form of aesthetic judgment more amenable to the interplay of ideas that give works their themes. The appreciation of form of which Kantian taste is capable does contribute considerably to our responses to art, as is evident to any admirer of Mondrian's sense of balance or Kurosawa's genius in composing camera shots. Even so, this formalism is inadequate on its own for plumbing the meanings of works; and doubtless, the most compelling analyses of formal structure in art benefit from a deep sensitivity to what the work might mean. We have not yet considered, however, Kant's other primary form of aesthetic judgment, namely the judgment of sublimity. The relation there between imagination and reason affords the sublime an involvement in ideas missing in the judgment of taste, and that relationship to ideas is auspicious for finding in the judgment of sublimity a properly *interpretive* conception of aesthetic reflection. The nature of the specifically aesthetic unity that such reflection produces remains to be seen, though we know that it will be neither a systematic unity prescribed by reason nor a technical unity prescribed by some specified purpose. Turning to the sublime will illuminate the imaginative production of indeterminate unity we pursue in the act of aesthetic interpretation.

3

Sublime Reflection

Reading a fiction like Vladimir Nabokov's *Pale Fire* can be "frustrating." Its poem by John Shade and its commentary by Charles Kinbote, neither of whom are what they seem, interact at multiple levels of deception and irony. Shade cannot speak for his poem himself, having seemingly been killed by one lunatic or another, and his self-appointed literary executor (as it were), cannot be trusted on anything but his own self-worth. Kinbote discerns his fantastical autobiography in Shade's lines only by appeal to "draft variants" of questionable provenance, but even this may only be semblance if Kinbote might be Shade's own ironic reimagining of himself. The reader struggles to make sense of all this and much more as an expressive whole, and if the novel truly affects her, she finds an unfolding wealth of material to play with and think through. She finds: the subtle semantic order and relating of characters behind the cryptic "Resemblances are the shadows of differences"; the systematic ambiguity in the title, given its reference to *Timon of Athens* and Kinbote's misunderstanding of it (his "Zemblan" translation is off); the references to *Lolita* and the equivocal relevance of Kinbote's own sexual appetites; the extraordinary hint-trove of the "index"; the meaning of *kinbote*, its reversal of "botkin"; and on and on. By bringing all these aspects together, relating them into an "idea" the novel might plausibly convey, the reader interprets the work. It provides such a rich site of interconnected meanings and suggestive avenues of response, however, that it defies any total comprehension. Nabokov's readers admire it for that very reason, and would object to any quick and easy, reductive assessment of its meaning. I would argue in fact that its admirers *feel the sublime* when they seek failingly to encompass all that it induces them to think. A rich work of art defies our efforts to determine the whole of its possible meaning. Our open-ended interpretive response to the challenge it poses is well modeled, I want to claim, by a Kantian sublime reflection.

The last chapter sought a model of aesthetic reflection in Kant's judgment of taste. Though we found in it the use of reflective judgment's principle of purposiveness, the perceptual formalism of that judgment constrains the search for unity which taste undertakes. Specifically, the judgment of taste appears to afford little reflection on whatever complex of meaning and thematic content informs a work of art. We must seek a model for a properly interpretive reflection in a form of aesthetic judgment more amenable to a relation to the ideas that, for Kant, give art its content. Imagination's interaction with reason in sublime reflection will afford it that relation to ideas. First I introduce the Kantian sublime, focusing on the mathematical variety, and I resolve questions that arise about the applicability of this judgment to human products of art. I advance an unorthodox reading of Kant's doctrine of *aesthetic ideas,* and I claim that reflection on them assumes the form of a judgment of sublimity. This linkage will provide a resolution for uncertainties about the roles of form and expression in Kant's theory. By this means I expose a sublime reflection that interprets a work's thematic content as an expressive but indeterminate whole. This will place Kant's judgment of sublimity at the center of a broadly construed, interpretive aesthetic understanding, and I begin to explore some of the implications of this result. Especially in relation to Kant's theory of expression and his "latent" theory of metaphor, the contours of a sublime understanding will begin to emerge.

Aesthetic Reflection on the Sublime

Kant customarily distinguishes the beautiful from the sublime in terms of the relation of cognitive powers that pertains to each of them. In the case of the beautiful, a harmonious interaction between imagination and the understanding arises from reflection on the form of an object. In the case of the sublime, to contrast, neither this relation of powers nor this concentration on form obtains: "The beautiful in nature concerns the form of the object, which consists in [the object's] being bounded. But the sublime can also be found in a formless object [*das Erhabene ist dagegen auch an einem formlosen Gegenstande zu finden*], insofar as we present *unboundedness*, either [as] in the object or because the object prompts us to present it, while yet we add to this unboundedness the thought of its totality. So it seems that we regard the beautiful as the exhibition of an indeterminate concept of the understanding, and the sublime as an exhibition of an indeterminate concept of reason" (CJ 244). Though Kant refers here to the beautiful and the sublime in nature, the same bound/unbound distinction applies to the work of art as well. The form of an object or work sets its spatial and/or temporal boundaries, so the question will be what aspect of the thing can open the *un*boundedness of sublimity. It will be important to keep in mind what many of Kant's readers have failed to notice, but which Rudolf Makkreel has observed, namely that "Kant does not write that the sublime can be found *only* in a formless object, but that it can *also* be found there. . . . Thus what is judged to be sublime is not necessarily formless."[1] The experience of the sublime must arise from a presentation of unboundedness, but nothing in Kant's account implies that an object with formal limits cannot give rise to this experience by means of some qualities it possesses other than its formal structure.[2] Among those who have missed this point is Jacques Derrida, who has argued that "the sublime is to be found, for its part, in an 'object without form' and the 'without-limit' is 'represented' in it or on the occasion of it, and yet gives the totality of the without-limit to be thought."[3] His reference to an "object without form" obscures the passage from Kant quoted above, where Kant states that the sublime can *also* be found in formless objects, not that it must be found in them alone.[4] The intricate formal structure of *Pale Fire* hardly precludes the encounter with sublimity one undergoes in the effort to make sense of it.

Not only the primacy of form but also the relevant relation of cognitive powers is altered dramatically in judgments of sublimity. As did understanding in the judgment of taste, the faculty of reason plays a primary role in sublime reflection. It does so by supplying the thought of "totality" to reflection on an object not readily grasped in such a way due to some "unboundedness" that accrues to it. This gap between reason's attribution of totality and an experience of unboundedness that appears to fall short of reason's expectations is filled by imagination. As in the judgment of taste, a relation between imagination and another power accounts for the distinctive character of the judgment. Yet unlike the judgment of beauty, where imagination and the understanding *harmonize* in reflection on the form of an object, in the case of the sublime imagination and reason are in *conflict*.[5] For in this judgment reason demands that its object be comprehended as a totality, and yet imagination proves itself incapable of doing so. The sublime object defies imagination's effort, required of it by a relation to reason, to present it as a whole (about which more later).

Recall that it was productive imagination which sought out purposiveness in the judgment of taste, in which it variously took in the formal unity of an object. The purposiveness of sublime reflection, however, lies instead in imagination's *failure* to encompass such unity: "[O]ur imagination, even in its greatest effort to do what is demanded of it and comprehend a given object in a whole of intuition (and hence to exhibit the idea of reason), proves its own limits and inadequacy, and yet at the same time proves its vocation to [obey] a law, namely, to make itself adequate to that idea. Hence the feeling of the sublime in nature is respect for our own vocation [*Bestimmung*]" (CJ 257).[6] Imagination's inability to present a whole instills a respect for reason's power to think of totality in ways that cannot be sensibly grasped. Judgment of the sublime thus ultimately serves to exalt reason at the expense of imagination. For our purposes, however, in seeking a satisfactory model for aesthetic reflection on an art work's thematic content, we will want to concentrate primarily on the very process of judging sublimity, rather than the respect for reason that issues from the judgment.[7] We will find that, for Kant, the meaningful content of a work is presented in *aesthetic ideas*. Treating interpretive reflection on these ideas as an act of judging the sublime will illuminate the sort of reflective operation we seek.

Earlier I suggested that the judgment of sublimity will prove exemplary of reflection on thematic material because of the amenability of the sublime to ideas. It is precisely the altered relation of cognitive powers in this judgment that makes a place in it for ideational content. Kant claims that "in order for the mind to be attuned to the feeling of the sublime, it must be receptive to ideas," for only by this receptivity can the limitations of the sensible be shown by comparison with reason's idea of totality (CJ 265). The relation between imagination and reason in this judgment orients imagination toward ideas in a way that radically alters the content of its judgment. "[I]n judging a thing sublime," Kant writes, the aesthetic power of judgment "refers the imagination to *reason* so that it will harmonize subjectively with reason's *ideas* ([though] which ideas they are is indeterminate)" (CJ 256). Because imagination proves itself in this judgment *inadequate to exhibit reason's ideas,* the harmony to which Kant refers will ultimately prove unattainable, though this failure serves the purpose of awakening our respect for reason's powers. Furthermore, the fact that imagination cannot exhibit reason's ideas guarantees the aesthetic nature of the judgment. Though the imagination may play with ideas in judging the sublime, its reflection on them will not be determined by reason. The form this play takes will become clear as we proceed.

Because reason is a dual power, both cognitive and practical in its activity, the agitation brought on by imagination's inadequacy produces two distinctive judgments of sublimity, depending on to which aspect of reason the imagination "refers" its distress. Reason has both intellectual and moral prerogatives, and Kant's distinction between the mathematical and the dynamical varieties of the sublime arises from this division. In the judgment, then, "the imagination will refer this agitation either to the *cognitive power* or to the *power of desire,* but in both cases the purposiveness of the given presentation will be judged only with regard to these *powers* (without any purpose or interest). The first kind of agitation is a *mathematical,* the second a *dynamical,* attunement of the mind" (CJ 247). In the case of the mathematical sublime, imagination seeks a relation to intellectual ideas of reason. Such ideas include the classics of God, freedom, immortality, eternity, etc; but sublime reflection will extend as well to political and personal themes "exemplified in experience," as Kant writes, "such as death, envy, and all the other vices, as well as love, fame, and so on" (CJ 314). In these cases we will see imagination responding to reason's generic demand for totality by seeking to present such ideas with a completeness that, by going "beyond the limits of experience," hopes to *express* rational ideas.[8] A judgment of the mathematical sublime, in response to the thematic content of a work of art, will seek (and fail) to unify the work's meaning as a whole "by means of an imagination that emulates the example of reason in reaching [for] a maximum" (ibid.). These passages belong, in fact, to Kant's discussion of *aesthetic ideas,* and the aim of my appropriation of Kant will be to substantiate the claim that interpretive reflection on these ideas assumes the form of a judgment of mathematical sublimity.

In the case of the dynamical sublime, one is overwhelmed by the threatening might of nature, yet one feels the superiority of practical reason over any mere natural force. As they did to Tallulah Bankhead in *Lifeboat,* "thunderclouds piling up in the sky" and "the boundless ocean heaved up" "raise the soul's fortitude above its usual middle range and allow us to discover in ourselves an ability to resist which . . . gives us the courage [to believe] that we could be a match for nature's seeming omnipotence" (CJ 261). Aside from the obscurity in Kant's account regarding the role imagination actually plays in this response to nature's might,[9] there are two reasons why my interpretation of Kantian sublimity will largely ignore the dynamical kind. First, dynamical sublimity seems generally less applicable to art, and Kant's discussion of it is indeed suffused (exclusively, at that) with natural imagery. There are surely works of art that seek to convey an experience of dynamically sublime *subject matters,* as in the Gothic and horror genres of literature and film, or even in an IMAX production that tries to make nature's power to engulf us as vivid as possible (while safely seated). But my concern is with the sublimity of an interpretive mode of response to art generally, rather than with the supposed sublimity of certain topics. The act of judging the mathematical sublime will in fact offer a better model of aesthetic interpretation, as it will capture our manner of responding to the aesthetic ideas which for Kant give art content, whatever the subject matter might be.

And second, Kant's account of dynamical sublimity invariably makes it a relation to practical (moral) ideas of reason. Nature's might threatens our physical frailty but reminds us of a supersensible vocation in rational autonomy, while nothing merely natural, however powerful, could ever be held in such esteem. It is truly through the dynamic sublime, rather than the mathematical, that Kant links his aesthetic theory to his moral philosophy, as he also does with his claim that beauty can be a *symbol* of morality (about which more follows). It would be unduly restrictive, not to mention threatening to the autonomy of the aesthetic, to link all responses to art to moral ideas. Much great (and poor) art doubtless addresses moral and ethical concerns, though it is surely counterintuitive to think that *all* art has such a dimension or makes such a reference, however much Kant (or Tolstoy) might be tempted by the thought. Hence the respect for reason's moral vocation in the experience of the sublime, which saturates Kant's account of the practical implications of the dynamical variety, will not serve as a primary focus of this treatment.[10] Instead, imagination's relation to intellectual ideas generally in the mathematical sublime will afford this judgment a more inclusive and varied purchase on the range of thematic material which is expressible in art, for Kant, through aesthetic ideas.

There are, however, some difficulties that arise in applying the judgment of sublimity to works of art. Kant begins his account of the mathematical sublime with the following observations. In our judgment of the vast, unbounded objects that typically inspire feelings of sublimity, we estimate the greatness of their magnitude, according to Kant, by reference to the absolute measure provided by reason: infinity as a whole (CJ 254). In seeking this measure, imagination begins an additive regress which overwhelms its powers of comprehension.[11] That is, the aesthetic estimation of magnitude by imagination suffers a maximum that, when exceeded by some object or experience, induces the conflict between imagination and reason indicative of the sublime. Imagination is unable to present the measure in terms of the intuition of totality which reason expects of it. Yet the displeasure of this inadequacy gives way to a pleasure in the realization that reason evinces a power that transcends the limitations of our phenomenal being (CJ 259). The fact that in this account imagination seeks to meet *the measure of infinity* explains why Kant typically appeals to examples of the most vast manifestations of crude nature to illustrate the effect. Human artifacts of limited size, much less works of art, most of which can fit (or be performed) inside a room, would seem to fail for Kant to suggest the infinite sufficiently. They cannot be sublime, so it seems, because their measure is so small.

Apart from this regress to infinity in the mathematical sublime, however, we can distinguish another line of argument in Kant's account. The power of imagination is limited by a maximum of comprehension which it cannot exceed. Now, Kant's use in the mathematical sublime of the terms "apprehension" and "comprehension" closely parallels his account of the power of imagination in the first *Critique*. "Apprehension" corresponds to the earlier work's "synthesis of apprehension," in which a manifold of sensible intuition is "gone through and gathered together" as a single moment (CPR A99). "Comprehension" corresponds to the "synthesis of reproduction in imagination," in which the mind grasps whole series of presentations by holding past ones in memory alongside current ones and relating them (CPR A100).[12] The limit of comprehension ascribed to imagination in the *Critique of Judgment* amounts to its inability to indefinitely retain a growing volume of apprehension. But this limitation beyond which imagination cannot go—and which prevents the imaginative comprehension of infinity— also applies to imagination's effort simply to comprehend all the parts of a sufficiently great object as a whole. Imagination runs into difficulty in trying to comprehend an object as a unity—the more parts, the more *complex*, the more difficult the task—whenever it faces something vast, elaborate, or *complex* enough to overwhelm its powers.[13]

In other words, some threshold exists beyond which the immensity or complexity of an object of reflection overwhelms imagination, which cannot take it all in. Kant's own examples of the great pyramids and St. Peter's basilica play into this simplified reading of what overwhelms imagination. The comprehension of such edifices "is never complete," for the subject "has the feeling that his imagination is inadequate for exhibiting the idea of a whole, [a feeling] in which imagination reaches its maximum, and as it strives to expand that maximum, it sinks back into itself," swooning before the grandeur of its object (CJ 252). Reason's superiority over imagination appears in these examples in the failure of imagination to comprehend the whole, but without recourse to the rather "baroque" regress to infinity that forms the main line of Kant's argument.[14] That account may capture the rational extreme of sublimity in the idea of infinity, but Kant's worldly examples attest to the potential sublimity of finite objects of reflection. In the case of St. Peter's, for example, not just the size but the ornate complexity of the interior overwhelms imagination's effort to comprehend all its details as a whole. Judging it sublime requires a regress only to the limit of imagination's comprehension, rather than to infinity. Hence it is conceivable, and compatible with Kant's account, that the judgment of sublimity can apply to even a small work of art, when reflection on the *complex* of its parts overwhelms imagination's effort to comprehend the purposive unity of the whole.[15] It is just such a complex of textual, narrative, symbolic, and allusive elements that the reader of *Pale Fire* undergoes the frustrated pleasure of interpreting.

There remains a second difficulty that we must revisit and again set aside. Treating reflection on the content presented in a work of art as a judgment of the sublime entails allowing such judgments to apply to human artifacts. Yet on some readings Kant dismisses this possibility, for reasons other than their magnitude. As was the case with the judgment of taste, the determination of an artifact by its specific purposes threatens to exclude proper aesthetic judgment of it: "A pure judgment about the sublime . . . must have no purpose whatsoever of the object as the basis determining it, if it is to be aesthetic and not mingled with some judgment of understanding or of reason" (CJ 253). A human artifact, to be judged determinatively and teleologically in terms of its intended purpose, would not appear to admit of proper sublimity. Determination by a purpose would seem to too tightly bind such an object for it to possess the boundlessness that arouses feelings of the sublime. Kant concludes: "[W]e must point to the sublime not in products of art (e.g., buildings, columns, etc.), where both the form and the magnitude are determined by a human purpose, nor in natural things *whose very concept carries with it a determinate purpose* (e.g., animals with a known determination in nature), but rather in crude nature" (CJ 252). The infinite extent of the heavens above or the might of a stormy, raging sea serve for Kant as preeminent inducements to feelings of sublimity. As was the case with the judgment of taste, Kant prioritizes aesthetic experience of nature, and appears to leave little room for authentic judgment of the sublime in the case of human works of art. And yet Kant equivocates on this matter more than the above statements reveal. After all, Kant uses the pyramids at Giza and St. Peter's basilica as examples of how imagination is overwhelmed by the mathematical sublime. These are artifacts if there ever were such. So Kant allows that aesthetic reflection on an artifact can assume the form of a judgment of sublimity. Furthermore, Kant grants on other occasions that the sublime may be found in works of art: "[T]he exhibition of the sublime may, insofar as it belongs to fine art, be combined with beauty in a *tragedy in verse*, in a *didactic poem*, or in an *oratorio*; and in these combinations fine art is even more artistic" (CJ 325).[16] And he remarks in the *Anthropology* that "the *representation* of the sublime can and should be beautiful in itself. . . ."[17]

The problem would not seem to be whether the sublime may be presented in works of art, but whether the degree of purposiveness typical of human artifacts hinders true sublime reflection on them, because such reflection is not determined by specific purposes. Of course, we have already visited this problem in the case of judgments of taste, and the solution offered in the last chapter serves just as well here. Even though an artifact may be informed by purposes, aesthetic judgment of it, whether it be of its beauty or of its sublimity, need not be determined by those purposes. We do not invariably approach works of art in cognizance of their creator's intentions and aims; nor do we insist that aesthetic reflection must await our cognizance of them. Kinbote might go overboard in discarding Shade's poetic intent, but then that depends on who Kinbote really is; in any case, the reader of *Pale Fire* finds herself on her own in making sense of the novel, and would do herself an aesthetic disservice by wanting Nabokov to give it all away. We have seen that a judgment which did take the nod from a known intention would ascribe a determinate technical, rather than free aesthetic unity to its object. And we have also seen that Kant grants the possibility of our ignorance of the purposes informing a work; he even grants that we may abstract from what knowledge we have of them, in order to engage in proper aesthetic reflection.

Thus the intentionality of a work of art as an expressive artifact need not deter a sublime reflection on it, in which we would freely seek to discover what the work might mean. For this reflection to proceed it need only be the case that the work not be so dominated by ideas and intentions that their obvious determination of the work cuts short aesthetic reflection.[18] Works of art must be subtly purposive, they must be "free from all constraint of chosen rules" (CJ 306) if they are to sustain feelings of sublime incomprehension. No matter how "punctiliously" the artist executed her intentions in a work, such purposiveness need not hinder our reflection on its expressive unity unless her execution is done "painstakingly" (CJ 307). A work that wore its point plainly on its sleeve, say by emblazoning it across the work, as in some of Barbara Kruger's political art, might reveal authorial intent too baldly to inspire a properly sublime reflection (though this need not keep it from being beautiful). So many interpretive avenues intersect in *Pale Fire*, on the other hand, that no single synoptic intent could seem to encompass it. In any case, the role of purposes in works of art poses little problem for reflecting on them through judgments of sublimity.[19]

Sublimity and Aesthetic Ideas in Art

In the last chapter I took issue with aspects of Paul Guyer's interpretation of the harmony of faculties in a judgment of taste. I argued that reflection on the form of appearance of an object suffices to account for the relation between imagination and the understanding in that judgment. Even as it conforms to the lawfulness of the understanding, the free spontaneity of imagination in appreciating beauty arises from its productive exploration of an object's formal unity. We saw that Guyer resists this account of that harmony, and we are now in a better position to see why he does so. For his motives lead us directly to the issue of aesthetic ideas and their role in judgment of a work of art. Guyer claims that an account of harmony which rests upon the form of appearance cannot reserve the proper place for aesthetic ideas in our contemplation of a work: "[T]he theory of aesthetic ideas which Kant expounds later in the third Critique must derive from Kant's own exploitation of the gap between the general idea of the harmony of the faculties and the particular formalist opinions of the third moment."[20] If we explain the harmony of cognitive powers in judgments of taste solely in terms of imagination's sporting with the form of appearance, Guyer argues, then aesthetic ideas will be squeezed out of the judgment. For "it is clear that the constituents of an aesthetic idea are *not* limited to pure spatial and temporal forms."[21] Guyer appeals to Kant's example of Jupiter's eagle (CJ 315) to maintain that aesthetic ideas "work by presenting conceptual contents in addition to such forms. . . ."[22] We shall consider the "constituents" of aesthetic ideas later in this chapter.

But first we must recognize the assumption motivating Guyer's argument, namely that the content of aesthetic ideas is supposed to play a role in the judgment of *taste*. Now, Kant does state in the "Deduction of Pure Aesthetic Judgments" that "beauty in general (whether it be beauty of nature or of art) may be called the *expression* of aesthetic ideas" (CJ 320). Guyer takes this to mean that "the explanation of our pleasure in the contemplation of a work which presents aesthetic ideas is the same as that of our pleasure in beauty, namely, the harmony of the faculties."[23] Guyer seeks to explain the response to aesthetic ideas in terms of the reflection on beauty that occasions the harmony of taste. Because an aesthetic idea (as we will see in more detail) is an intuition presented to reflective judgment, its *presentation* possesses a formal unity which may come to the attention of taste. That is, the thematic material of aesthetic ideas may be presented by means of form. The element of pleasure in viewing the presentation of an aesthetic idea will derive from its beautiful form, and to that extent Guyer is correct. Yet the fact that a beautiful form may convey or express aesthetic ideas does not imply that this thematic content will be assessed by the same judgmental means as the form which expresses it. Contrary to Guyer's insertion of an aesthetic idea into a reflection on beauty, nothing in Kant's account suggests that the *thematic content* of aesthetic ideas comes to the attention of *taste*. I will argue instead that the feeling of pleasure in aesthetic judgment refers to the restful contemplation of the beautiful form that presents an aesthetic idea, but that the contemplation of its content may be more adequately characterized as an experience of sublime *agitation*. Instead of regarding judgment of a work of art as taste's appreciation of beautiful form-and-content, as Guyer does, I will argue that judgment of a work involves two stages or moments of judgment, one that reflects upon its beautiful form, and a distinct second stage which grapples with its sublime content. Separating these two moments of judgment renders the form of appearance perfectly adequate to explain the harmony of imagination and the understanding in the appreciation of beauty. For then reflection on the content of aesthetic ideas will not need to be rationalized into the judgment of taste. Instead, on my appropriation of a Kantian aesthetics of sublimity, making sense of aesthetic ideas will be the work of a sublime reflection.[24]

What initial temptation is there to link the content of aesthetic ideas to judging the sublime? Both the sublime and the presentation of aesthetic ideas in fine art introduce into aesthetic reflection a role for ideas as opposed to the formal intuitions of sense predominant in the judgment of taste. When faced with the sublime, as we have seen, imagination proves itself unable to achieve an exhibition of ideas of reason. The thought of totality that reason expects of imagination proves beyond imagination's capacity to present. But Kant's account of aesthetic ideas offers a precise parallel to this relationship: he understands an aesthetic idea as an imaginative intuition that strives to express a rational idea but cannot. Kant thinks of both aesthetic and rational ideas as *boundless*, inaccessible in one way or another to the form of cognition. This already suggests the element of sublimity in each of them. They defy determinate cognition each in their respective ways, and thus arouse in imagination a feeling of being overwhelmed (which engenders respect). Specifically in the case of aesthetic ideas, Kant claims that they are not so formless as to have no relation to concepts, but rather that their wealth of content is so great as to exceed the bounds of comprehension in any determinate concept: "In a word, an aesthetic idea is a presentation of the imagination which is conjoined with a given concept and is connected, when we use imagination in its freedom, with such a multiplicity of partial presentations that no expression that stands for a determinate concept can be found for it. Hence it is a presentation that makes us add to a concept the thoughts of much that is ineffable" (CJ 316).[25] The language of the ineffable, of that which overwhelms the imagination and defies comprehension as a determinate whole is redolent of the Kantian sublime. The task is then to show how well Kant's account of judging the mathematical sublime captures imagination's interpretive response to the excessive material of aesthetic ideas. Furthermore, sublime reflection's failed effort to comprehend as a whole the "multiplicity of partial presentations" involved in an aesthetic idea will provide an exemplary case of reflective judgment's principle of purposiveness in action, seeking to relate all the parts of a work into an expressive, meaningful whole.

So far we have seen that sublime reflection involves a relation between imaginative intuition and reason's demand for totality. Of a piece with this, aesthetic ideas, as products of imagination, try to give expression to ineffable ideas of reason. In the first *Critique* Kant had tentatively drawn the distinction between these two kinds of ideas, and he saw them as wholly alien to each other. Using the language of "ideals of sensibility" rather than of "aesthetic ideas," he wrote that these are "creatures of the imagination concerning which no one can offer an explication and give an understandable concept. . . . [They] amount less to a determinate image than to a design that hovers, as it were, at the mean of various experiences; they are characteristics such as painters and physiognomists claim to have in their minds and are supposed to be an incommunicable shadowy image of these people's products. . . . [They] may, although only improperly, be called ideals of sensibility; for they are meant to be the unattainable models of possible empirical intuitions, yet provide no rule capable of explication and examination" (CPR A570–571/B598–599). Here the imagination's "ideals of sensibility" appear to bear little relation to rational ideas. In the *Critique of Judgment*, however, Kant treats the two as more intimate counterparts. He contrasts the aesthetic ideas presented by imagination in fine art with rational ideas in the form of an inverse reflection: "An *aesthetic idea* cannot become cognition because it is an *intuition* (of the imagination) for which an adequate concept can never be found. A *rational idea* can never become cognition because it contains a *concept* (of the supersensible) for which no adequate intuition can ever be given" (CJ 342). Kant understands aesthetic and rational ideas as symmetrical opposites, both of which defy, from starting points the other can never reach, acts of schematization that would bring together intuition and concept in determinate cognition. In fact, Kant sees more in their relation than mere structural opposition; for the aesthetic ideas that comprise the thematic content of art serve in some sense to express indeterminately ideas of reason.

Some commentators have suggested that aesthetic ideas function for Kant as *symbols* of rational ideas.[26] Rudolf Makkreel, most notably, has argued that beauty can be a symbol for the rational idea of the moral good, as Kant famously claims, because beauty expresses aesthetic ideas.[27] Makkreel's position aims to unite Kant's §59 claim that beauty is the symbol of morality with his (just visited) §51 claim that beauty "may be called the *expression* of aesthetic ideas" (CJ 320). He does so by arguing that the beautiful expression of an aesthetic idea "can supply a symbolic analogue" for a directly unpresentable rational idea.[28] It will be important for later developments to focus for a moment on why I think that construing aesthetic ideas as symbols of rational ideas is mistaken. The problem lies in the role of analogy in Kant's theory of symbolism.

In "On Beauty as the Symbol of Morality" (§59), Kant distinguishes schematic and symbolic exhibition of a concept. Exhibition or *hypotyposis*—the vivid sketching or illustration of an idea—involves providing an intuition that matches up with a concept and confirms its objective reference (CJ 351). In the case of an empirical concept, such as "dog," an intuited or experienced *example* confirms the concept's reality. When it comes to an a priori concept or category of the understanding, its sketching intuition or schema is given along with it a priori. But although schematic exhibition provides "direct" and "demonstrative" illustration of concepts, symbolic exhibition fleshes out ideas via the indirect route of *analogy*:

All *hypotyposis* (exhibition, *subiectio ad adspectum*) consists in making [a concept] sensible, and is either *schematic* or *symbolic*. In schematic hypotyposis there is a concept that the understanding has formed, and the intuition corresponding to it is given a priori. In symbolic hypotyposis there is a concept which only reason can think and to which no sensible intuition can be adequate, and this concept is supplied with an intuition that judgment treats in a way merely analogous to the procedure it follows in schematizing; i.e., the treatment agrees with the procedure merely in the rule followed rather than in terms of the intuition itself, and hence merely in terms of the form of the reflection rather than its content. (CJ 351)[29]

Instead of providing an intuition that literally embodies the content of the concept, which is impossible in the case of rational ideas, symbolic exhibition appeals to an incongruent entity whose concept shares analogical features with the original. Symbolic exhibition, according to Kant, "performs a double function: it applies the concept to the object of a sensible intuition; and then it applies the mere rule by which it reflects on that intuition to an entirely different object, of which the former object is only the symbol" (CJ 352).

Kant illustrates this obscure formula with his famous analogy between a despotic state and a hand mill. Even though the *intuition* of a hand mill (imagine a food mill or ricer) bears no direct relation to despotism or any concept of government, the *action* of the mill in grinding down resisting objects can symbolize the overlording power of the despotic state. The isomorphism lies not in their respective appearances, which share no similarity; it lies instead in a similarity between "the rules by which we reflect on the two and on their causality" (ibid.).[30] The analogy at work could be specified as: the material fed through a hand mill is to its operator, as the subjects under an absolute monarchy are to the despot. The analogy does not license the inference that a despotic state is (literally) a machine, like the hand mill, so the intuition deployed in the analogy is not informing us about despotism directly. Instead, the analogy only suggests a rule covering the relationship of cause and effect present in each set of relations.[31] We imagine an agent feeding material into the mill as he turns its handle, and we *conceive a rule* for the actions and consequences or effects involved which we transfer to the domain of government and its leaders. The analogy gives flesh to our understanding of the abstract notion "despotism," not to mention that it dramatizes our assessment of the institution.

Kant in fact distinguishes two kinds of analogy. Quantitative analogies in mathematics allow one to infer a fourth term D from the ratio A:B::C:D when A, B, the relation between them, and C are known (CPR A179/ B222). Such an analogy or proportion is constitutive of the value of D; that is, it allows one to determine D's exact magnitude. If I know that the relation between 2 and 4 in the ratio $2:4::3:x$ is multiplicative, then I know that x is precisely 6. A qualitative analogy, to contrast, does not provide determinate knowledge of the fourth term. The rule it does provide expresses "only the relation to a fourth, but not *this* fourth *member* itself" (ibid.), so the only determinate content of the analogy is the isomorphic, relational rule it captures (the problem lies in the fact that the rule-content *is* determinate; see below). This rule aids in "seeking the fourth member in experience" (CPR A180/B222). The hand mill analogy, for example, aids in the identi-

fication of despots: when you see a state apparatus mangling its subjects' freedoms the way a hand mill crushes through force, you know
you're dealing with a tyrant. The distinction between quantitative and
qualitative analogy must be noted because, as some commentators
have stressed, only the latter functions in symbolic exhibition.[32]

For §59 of the third *Critique*, it is the intuition of beauty, of course,
which offers a symbolic exhibition of the (directly unintuitable) rational idea of the morally good. In the appreciation of beauty we experience, Kant thinks, a direct and disinterested liking reflective of a
capacity for judging universally, free from the influence of merely sensuous charms. Moral reflection similarly involves the production of
universal rules free from the influence of inclination, and so aesthetic
experience offers an intuitive embodiment of the self-legislative vocation of practical reason (CJ 353–354). Through this analogy, "Taste
enables us, as it were, to make the transition from sensible charm to a
habitual moral interest without making too violent a leap" (CJ 354).
We saw above that the determinate rule-content of a qualitative analogy is typically a causal relationship between ground and consequent
which is present on both sides of the analogy. In the case of aesthetic
and moral experience, the common causative ground is a free productivity of universal norms, of taste in the former case and of the
moral law in the latter. The analogy expresses an isomorphism
between the effect, an experience of beauty, brought about by the
free causality of taste, and the effect, the moral good, brought about
by the free causality of practical reason.

Now the problem with construing aesthetic ideas as symbols is that
the analogical rule-content of a Kantian symbol is too determinately
specifiable. The analogy involved can be reduced, in fact, to a complex
simile. Beauty can symbolize morality because aesthetic experience is
like moral reflection due to the disinterested and free universality common to both. Kant enumerates four ways in which they are alike (at CJ
353–354), and as Guyer has noted, Kant's fleshing out of the analogy
"should exhaust the content of the assertion that beauty is the symbol
of morality."[33] The meaning of a Kantian symbol can be determined by
specifying the rule governing the analogy, and this determination of
meaning is entirely at odds with the *inexhaustibility* of meaning Kant
attributes to aesthetic ideas. The meaning of an aesthetic idea cannot

be determined by *any* rule, certainly not by an analogical one, and so aesthetic ideas cannot have a *symbolic* function in Kant's sense of the term.[34] Aesthetic ideas are not structured as analogies, and hence they do not exhibit rational ideas (or anything else) symbolically.[35] They do not *exhibit* concepts or ideas at all, in fact; instead, they *express* an indeterminate and expansive range of meaning that no rule, concept, or rational idea can encompass. The relationship between aesthetic and rational ideas is one of indeterminate expression, rather than symbolic exhibition: the unbounded complex of "kindred presentations" brought to mind as an aesthetic idea, and which imagination seeks to make sense of, does not despite its richness symbolically exhibit the rational idea it expressively intimates, any more than reflection on aesthetic ideas, in all their sublime unboundedness, could be determined by the ideas of reason they express.

Makkreel maintains that "Beauty can serve as the symbolic presentation of a rational idea because it is also the expression of a mediating aesthetic idea."[36] I suggest rather that beauty is the symbol of morality only because aesthetic *judgment* has a structure analogous to the structure of moral judgments. When the Kantian subject senses beauty in nature, it senses that nature is amenable to the acts of autonomous judgment that make morality possible; in this sense, natural beauty symbolizes the moral good. Kant's claim that beauty is the expression of aesthetic ideas does not bear on beauty's symbolization of morality, because aesthetic ideas are not structured by the analogical rules that would make them symbols in Kant's sense. On my view, beauty "expresses" aesthetic ideas in that they may be *conveyed* through a beautiful form; aesthetic ideas in turn *express* rational ideas *indeterminately* by striving (and failing) to emulate reason's synoptic vision of a totality of meaning. Makkreel is correct, and strikingly original, in his claim that "aesthetic ideas are interpretive in approximating rational ideas;"[37] but they are so as expansive expressions of meaning, not as rule-bound analogical symbols.

In Kant's aesthetic theory, artistic genius gets credit for recognizing and handling the rich subject matter of aesthetic ideas. He regards genius as "a *talent* for producing something for which no determinate rule can be given" (CJ 307). Genius creates in the work of art a presentation "for which an adequate concept can never be found." No determinate rule or concept could be rich enough to capture all that this presentation evokes in reflection; hence the mistake in construing aesthetic ideas as analogies. The fertile content of the aesthetic idea, never to be reduced to a fixed determination, must be distinguished from the beautiful form by which the artist presents it. These two aspects differ in their source and in the talent required to produce them: "Genius can only provide rich *material* for products of fine art; processing this material and giving it *form* requires a talent that is academically trained, so that it may be used in a way that can stand the test of the power of judgment" (CJ 310). Ironically, on one interpretation of *Pale Fire*, the poet Shade has a largely uninspired grasp of form, while his usurping interpreter Kinbote has brilliance to spare but no taste. For Kant, the work of fine art presents the subject matter of aesthetic ideas within the frame of a determinate formal arrangement. This form of the work produces the harmony of cognitive powers in which imagination intuits formal unity in its object, and the judgment of taste fulfills the principled aim of aesthetic reflection to that extent. In contrast to that judgment of taste, the material of the aesthetic idea remains indeterminate, alluded to by the beautiful form, but in no strong sense determined by it. In fact, as we will see in more detail, much of an aesthetic idea's content will arise from *outside the work*, and so cannot be encompassed by the work's mere formal properties, nor can it be judged by taste.

A work and its ingenious creator present aesthetic ideas through the work's form. No doubt that beautiful form may be to the liking of taste, but the ideas are not judged by that standard. Beauty does not bear on the flurry of reflection aesthetic ideas inspire. To characterize properly reflection on their unbounded content, we must understand what occurs in productive imagination's response to them. "By an aesthetic idea . . . I understand that presentation of imagination which prompts much thought, but to which absolutely no determinate thought, i.e., no concept, can be adequate; consequently, no language can entirely grasp it and render it intelligible." The aesthetic idea seeks to go "beyond the limits of experience" by evoking whole complexes of allusive thought, more than any single experience can provide. Because it does not serve to exhibit any fixed concept, the potential for articulation of its content remains quite open. One might think of aesthetic ideas as the spur to an open-ended exploration of meaning or significance. The idea "prompts much thought"; it possesses content in which a variety of concepts may play roles, though this does not imply that one could complete the articulation of what can be thought in it. The aesthetic idea is an imaginative intuition "to which no concept can be completely adequate," and its allusive connotations cannot be *bounded* by any final determination.[38] The hallmark of the aesthetic idea is the *inexhaustibility of its content*, and this feature of it confirms its affinity with the sublime. On my view, in fact, we interpret aesthetic ideas via a sublime reflection.

Sublime Reflection

Kant presents the aesthetic idea, in its expressive relation to reason, as connected to a particular concept, even though the reflection it inspires soon *exceeds the bounds* of any single concept: "If a presentation of the imagination is imputed to a concept, as belonging to the exhibition of it, and yet it by itself prompts so much thought as could never be comprehended in a determinate concept, and by which the concept itself aesthetically expands [*ästhetisch erweitert*] in an unlimited [*unbegrenzte*] way; in this way, then, the imagination is creative and thus sets in motion the power of intellectual ideas (i.e., reason), specifically by making reason think more, at the prompting of [such a] presentation . . . than can be grasped and made distinct in the presentation" (CJ 315).[39] The unlimited or boundless (*unbegrenzte*) content of the aesthetic idea *defies comprehension* by any one concept. In this sense, its sublimity is patent: all that the idea suggests surpasses the maximum of comprehension imagination faces in the experience of vastness. In fact, sublime reflection's role in our response to aesthetic ideas appears precisely in the *aesthetic expansion* emphasized above, which I interpret as a version of the *aesthetic apprehension and comprehension* undertaken by imagination in judging the mathematical sublime.[40] The flood of allusion and implication set loose by the aesthetic idea provides imagination "a multitude of kindred presentations" (CJ 315) that it apprehends as an expanding series. Imagination seeks to *comprehend* this multiplicity as a unified whole, but the boundless wealth of the aesthetic idea soon overwhelms it. The very same enactment of imaginative powers that gives rise to a judgment of sublimity, in response to the very same rational demand for totality, propels the expansion of meanings in aesthetic ideas.

Kant's account of the mathematical sublime perfectly captures the overwhelming nature of this expansion: "when apprehension has reached the point where the partial presentations of sensible intuition that were first apprehended are already beginning to be extinguished in the imagination, as it proceeds to apprehend further ones, the imagination then loses as much on the one side as it gains on the other; and so there is a maximum in comprehension that it cannot exceed" (CJ 252). The expansion of material prompted by the aesthetic idea overwhelms imagination's capacity of comprehension. Sublime feeling lies precisely in imagination finding itself "inadequate . . . for exhibiting the idea of a whole" (ibid.), and in seeking but failing to produce a unified meaning for the aesthetic idea, imagination performs an aesthetic reflective judgment of sublimity. Indeed, just as in sublime reflection imagination, in its free response to reason's desire for totality, reaches the maximal limit of its comprehension, aesthetic ideas are produced, as Kant writes in the midst of his primary discussion of them, "by means of an imagination that emulates the example of reason in reaching [for] a maximum" (CJ 314). Though the form of an aesthetic presentation may be judged by taste, reflection on its content, that is, on its aesthetic ideas, instead requires the interpretive powers of a sublime reflection.

Three other commentators (to my knowledge) have approached this interpretation. First, Paul Crowther has linked aesthetic ideas to the sublime in art, though his account emphasizes the sublime *effects* of the scale of a work or the profundity of the message its aesthetic ideas convey.[41] My account differs considerably by discerning the work of sublime reflection in the very process of interpreting aesthetic ideas.[42] Second, Sarah Gibbons sees a structural similarity in the imaginative capacities involved in both judgment of the sublime and the presentation of aesthetic ideas, but she does not hold that sublime reflection itself responds interpretively to aesthetic ideas. She takes the two activities to be quite different, in fact, because she claims that "judgements of fine art," in contrast to judgments of the sublime, "are more closely bound up with the schematizing function of imagination." Unlike the vague sense for the whole which the experience of sublimity offers, "[fine] art continuously offers new conceptual tools with which to grasp the particular."[43] My interpretation of Kant's theory has shown that reflective judgment can only be taken to produce unique aesthetic unities of its own if its activity suspends the schematizing function of imagination. If aesthetic reflection produces new conceptual tools for grasping particulars, it ultimately serves the aims of determinative judgment. My interpretation frees aesthetic reflection from this subservience by modeling the response to aesthetic ideas on a judgment of sublimity. This judgment cannot schematize its object as a conceptual whole, but rather finds in the aesthetic idea precisely what Kant would have it find, an overwhelming, indeterminate multitude of connotation.[44] Third and finally, Robert Wicks has argued a position very similar to my own, though he does not elaborate sublime reflection as a model of interpretation.[45]

My claim that the formal appearance and the thematic content of an aesthetic object are assessed by two different kinds of judgment, namely of beauty and of sublimity, respectively, serves in fact as an alternative solution to a long-standing debate in the literature concerning the respective roles of "form" and "expression" in Kant's aesthetics.[46] There is an unmistakable tension in the third *Critique* between the apparent formalism of the judgment of taste and Kant's treatment, later in the text, of the expressive content of the various fine arts. For how indeed can a pure aesthetic judgment that appears to have no truck with concepts or representations of affairs contribute to our reflection on the thematic material imparted by a work of art? The standard solution to this difficulty has been to loosen up, to the point of all-inclusiveness, the array of elements that contribute to the harmony of cognitive powers in the judgment of taste.[47] Kant's repeated insistence that taste attends solely to form is either reformed out of existence, or the notion of "form" is rendered flexible enough to include thematic content within it, thus bringing the expressive power of aesthetic ideas back into the fold of judgments of beauty. In short, proponents of this solution assume that the judgment of taste is the only game in town, and then invent elaborate means to make room for aesthetic ideas in that judgment. Once one recognizes the facility of judgments of sublimity for characterizing reflection on aesthetic ideas, one need no longer do violence to the perceptual formalism of taste. My solution has the advantage that it retains Kant's formal judgment of taste as it stands. It avoids the temptation to force aesthetic ideas into taste's limited compass, by locating interpretation of them in a separate sublime reflection.

How, then, should this reflection on aesthetic ideas be further characterized? Imagination's effort to construe an aesthetic idea as a purposive whole will amount to *interpreting* the idea. Interpretation has typically been construed as a process of making sense with an eye for the whole, and the imaginative response to aesthetic ideas in sublime reflection embodies just such an interpretive process. Interpretations seek to make holistic sense of all the parts of a work; Kant indicates that the "aesthetic attributes" of an expressive work ignite the expansion which overwhelms imagination's limits of comprehension. It is through these attributes that aesthetic ideas indirectly and symbolically convey ideas of reason. He sums up much in the following passage:

> Those forms which do not constitute the exhibition of a given concept itself, but rather only, as supplementary presentations of the imagination, express the concept's implications and its kinship with other concepts, are called (aesthetic) *attributes* of an object, an object whose concept is a rational idea which as such cannot be exhibited adequately. Thus Jupiter's eagle with lightning in its claws is an attribute of the mighty king of heaven, as the peacock is of the magnificent queen of heaven. These attributes, unlike *logical attributes*, do not present the content of our concepts of the sublimity and majesty of creation, but rather something different, something that prompts the imagination to spread itself over a multitude of kindred presentations that arouse more thought than can be expressed in a concept determined by words. These aesthetic attributes yield an *aesthetic idea*, which serves that rational idea in lieu of a logical exhibition of it, but it properly serves to enliven the mind by opening up for it a view into a vast realm of kindred presentations. (CJ 315)[48]

The complex of beautiful form in a work presents aesthetic attributes which do not determine the content of the idea but instead serve to arouse the mind to a quickening in which reflection upon the indeterminate meaning of the idea occurs. In this expansion a "view" is opened up for imagination into "an immense realm of kindred presentations" all in some way related to the thematic unity of the work. By "presentations" (*Vorstellungen*) Kant does not mean merely mental images, but rather anything that can come before consciousness, mental content generally. The constituent parts of aesthetic ideas may be images, feelings, or memories, concepts or ideas which serve to flesh out the content of the idea, so long as no particular presentation, conceptual or otherwise, determines the reflection on the entire complex. Kant grants that "even an intellectual concept may serve . . . as an attribute of a presentation of sense" (CJ 316), so a sublime reflection on aesthetic attributes can attend to all the sorts of nonformal elements left out of the judgment of taste, including contextual factors. The "multitude of kindred presentations" imagination seeks to unify in its response to a work will clearly include elements that "reside" *not in the work itself,* but in the subject reflecting on the work or in her cultural milieu. Aesthetic ideas open up for imagination a "view" into "an immense realm," and some of what sublime reflection draws from that realm to include in its sense-making response is drawn from outside the work. Indeed, one cannot hope to make sense of *Pale Fire,* for example, without locating the *Timon of Athens* passage from which its title comes, and which Kinbote hopelessly misreads.

In fact, Kant's account suggests that we could think of the aesthetic idea as a *product* of imaginative reflection, rather than as a given something waiting to be discovered in a work.[49] We have seen that *productive imagination* plays a primary role in reflective judgment generally. Here, too, though the aesthetic attributes of a work initiate the expansion of imaginative comprehension by supplying suggestive material, imagination acts creatively in seeking a means to make of this material a whole. Kant writes that "the imagination ([in its role] as a productive cognitive power) is very mighty when it creates, as it were, another nature out of the material that actual nature gives it" (CJ 314). Of course, the same applies to the material given to imagination by a work of art, especially inasmuch as fine art is for Kant the domain for presenting aesthetic ideas. In this constructive process imagination seeks to present as a whole all that the work suggests to it, and Kant writes that "such presentations of the imagination we may call *ideas*" (ibid.). There is thus a strong sense in which the aesthetic idea is produced by the sublime reflection imagination visits on the thematic content of a work. So though in one sense aesthetic ideas are exhibited in works of art, in another sense we may regard an aesthetic idea as the *outcome* of a process. The end result of sublime reflection's interpretive response to a work just is an aesthetic idea. On this view, imaginatively produced aesthetic ideas constitute interpretations of a work's meaning (for better or worse, as Kinbote's follies make clear). This conclusion suggests that the *genius* Kant sees at work in an artist's presentation of aesthetic ideas "gives the rule to art" just as much in the response that re-produces aesthetic ideas in sublime reflection. To the extent that interpreting a work well involves reinventing it, aesthetic response to artistic genius will require an ingenuity of its own, as is evident to any reader of *Pale Fire*; its author did, after all, famously expect his readers to be "little Nabokovs." To the extent that sublime reflection as much "invents" as "discovers" the themes it discerns in a work, the partial comprehension of aesthetic ideas will be the outcome of a "genial" process in which artistic invention invites as inventive an interpretive response.[50]

The implication that the very object of sublime reflection extends beyond the bounds of the work, into the specificity of the reflecting subject, and her surrounding context, will be explored further in the next chapter, because it will have considerable implications for the validity claim of sublime reflection. Suffice it for now to say that imaginative reflection on an aesthetic idea seeks to comprehend as a meaningful whole the multitude of thoughts, references, and implications the idea arouses for it. The judgment undertaken here is reflective, for even as imagination seeks to comprehend this diversity of material as a whole, its constructive activity is not controlled by any fixed determination of the work's meaning or the artist's intention. The independence of aesthetic reflection from what would be the technical project of ascribing a meaning to a work based on a knowledge of the artist's aim only strengthens the claim that imagination produces aesthetic ideas in its interpretation of a work, rather than receiving them prepackaged from the work. But furthermore, the status of aesthetic ideas as products of a reflective form of response to art implies that the meanings that sublime reflection ascribes to works remain *indeterminate* and *open-ended*. Sublime reflection fails to comprehend a work's expressive purpose as a determinately unified whole. Instead, it produces in aesthetic ideas partial and incomplete insights into a work's plausible meaning(s). Sublime reflection never completes its response to a work: it is precisely the inexhaustibility of aesthetic ideas that makes interpretation of them sublime. We might stop responding to the powerful reflective inducement a work provides, and return to the workaday world of conceptual determinacy. But the appreciation of indeterminate purposive unity at the core of Kant's aesthetic theory implies that we could not (in principle) finish interpreting an object of aesthetic reflection. An "interpretation" that declared, "*Pale Fire* means *X*, end of story," would feign possession of a knowledge it cannot have through aesthetic means. Worse yet, such misplaced confidence would defeat the point of sublime reflection's agitating encounter with indeterminacy—in other words, would relieve the pressure it puts on determinately established habits of understanding.

I will pursue these themes further in the next chapter, in the context of exploring in greater detail the notions of aesthetic unity and validity that issue from Kant's account of sublime reflection. It should by now be evident that pushing Kant's aesthetic theory in the direction I do shows that the third *Critique* can offer a savory model of interpretation to those contemporary theorists taken with the possibilities of semantic indeterminacy and the deferral of conceptual unity. Sublime reflection as a form of interpretive response favors the inexhaustibility of artistic meaning, the disunity of inventive takes on it, and, as we will see, the multiplicity of plausible interpretations of a work.

Kant typically segregates considerations of beauty from the experience of the sublime, though we have seen him refer to their intermingling. To the extent that he recognizes any symbiotic relation between the two, it usually assumes the form of a beautiful product of art serving to present some archetypally sublime subject matter, such as a formally beautiful painting of a windswept mountainscape after the manner of Caspar David Friedrich. Kant thus only explicitly grants that beautiful works of art can present sublime *themes*, say of nature's might or of lofty moral sentiments. I have tried to show that, with some adjustment to Kant's theory, one can interpret judgments of taste and of sublimity as forming two distinct but intimately related moments or stages of reflection on art. In his account of the sublime in nature, then, Kant distinguishes beauty and sublimity in terms of the feelings they inspire: "The mind feels *agitated* in the presentation of the sublime in nature, while in an aesthetic judgment about the beautiful in nature it is in *rest-*

ful contemplation" (CJ 258). My account indicates that aesthetic reflection on a work of art can be understood to involve both a restful contemplation of its beautiful form and an agitated exploration of what its sublime content, its aesthetic ideas, mean.

An advantage of this rendering of Kant's theory is that it makes Kantian aesthetic judgment more welcoming to reflection on products of art. We have seen that the formal strictures of the judgment of taste appear to discourage response to the representational or thematic components of a work. Kant certainly grants reflection on aesthetic ideas, but it is unclear how the judgment of taste can accommodate it. These difficulties can be resolved by regarding interpretation of the thematic content of art as a sublime reflection. Both judgments can then fulfill their respective functions in aesthetic response, with a standard Kantian distinction between form and content serving to specify the focus of each moment of judgment. The relation between imagination and the understanding in taste is fulfilled in reflection on a work's formal unity, while the relation between imagination and reason in the sublime is fulfilled in reflection on a work's meaning. Locating both forms of judgment in reflection on works of art thus shows art to be a locus for the variety of aesthetic relations between cognitive powers. If both beauty and the sublime reside in the work of art, in its form and its unbounded meaning, then reflection upon that work provides a thorough exercise of our cognitive powers, something which beauty or the sublime in isolation cannot. Throughout his third *Critique*, as we have seen, Kant prioritizes beauty and sublimity in nature over what human works of art can accomplish. But the symbiosis of formal beauty and semantic sublimity in art shows it to bring together what the contrastive phenomena of restful beauty and dynamic sublimity in nature rend asunder.

One issue remains. Recall one of Kant's few remarks on the co-presence of beauty and sublimity in art: "[T]he exhibition of the sublime may, insofar as it belongs to fine art, be combined with beauty in a *tragedy in verse*, in a *didactic poem*, or in an *oratorio*; and in these combinations fine art is even more artistic" (CJ 325). As noted earlier, the "insofar as" would seem to suggest that Kant thinks there could be art that affords no sublime reflection. Indeed, he observes in the *Anthropology* that "it is only because music serves as an instrument for poetry that it is *fine* (not merely pleasant) *art.*[51] Apparently poetic language lends the content of aesthetic ideas to music which otherwise falls short of being *fine art* because it offers only a formal, temporal play of sound to taste.[52] Because I have argued that sublime reflection on a work attends to the content of the aesthetic ideas that it presents, it will indeed be true that the combination of beauty and sublimity will exist solely in those works that present aesthetic ideas. Kant's example of foliage on wallpaper (CJ 229) may be beautiful without eliciting a judgment of the sublime, since this regular pattern is not likely to present aesthetic ideas. But because it is of the essence of the *fine art* of genius to express such ideas, both judgments will typically obtain in reflection on such works. In other words, my argument implies that the greater artistry Kant grants to fine art which combines beauty and sublimity is achieved in the presentation of aesthetic ideas as a rule.[53] If aesthetic ideas are in fact *produced* by imaginative reflection on art, as suggested earlier, rather than being merely *given* to us by the work, then there is ample room to think of all fine art as offering, at least in principle, an occasion for an open-ended interpretive response.[54] There will then be as much (or as little) richness of expression and meaning in a work, including all music, as one comes prepared to "find" in it (which is not to say that some art will not be judged bad). Even so, I will suggest in chapter 9 that in fact some art—especially much modernist and postmodern art (hence the appeal to Nabokov)—compels a more sublimely indeterminate reflection than art does as a rule.

Aesthetic Ideas and Metaphor

The analogical form of reflection involved in Kantian symbols has led some commentators to discern in Kant's account of them a theory of *metaphor,* though Kant does not discuss metaphor as such.[55] Metaphors have been construed as implicit analogies since the time of Aristotle, who characterizes metaphor as "the application [to something] of a name belonging to something else," most importantly (though not exclusively) through the use of analogy.[56] Kant's own language mirrors this formulation. A symbol works "a transfer of our reflection on an object of intuition to an entirely different concept" (CJ 352–353); this transference *(metaphora)* is the etymological core of the meaning of "metaphor." The hand mill Kant calls a symbol might as easily be called a metaphor for despotism, as in "the despotic state is a machine." On such a view, a metaphor would be just an analogy with the "ratio" it expresses left implicit for its audience to unpack. Beauty would be a metaphor for morality whose meaning can be unpacked by specifying the rule-content at the core of the analogy relating the two, just as Kant unpacks it in section 59.

But in addition to sensing a theory of metaphor in Kant's account of symbolization, commentators have also found a second and competing, latent conception of metaphor in the doctrine of aesthetic ideas.[57] Francis Coleman treats aesthetic ideas as metaphorical expressions whose richness and ambiguity suggest more meaning than can be related in literal uses of language. "According to Kant," Coleman writes, "'aesthetic ideas' . . . are quasi-sensuous or aesthetic examples of analogical reasoning. The metaphor, for Kant, is not mere ornament; it enjoys cognitive value."[58] We have seen that aesthetic ideas are not in fact structured as analogies; nor are they metaphorical by virtue of an analogical structure. Like most recent theorists of metaphor, Coleman takes Kantian aesthetic ideas, as instances of metaphor, to enjoy an "intrinsically indeterminate" wealth of possible meaning, which Coleman does not see that they would not have were they truly analogies.[59] As in the experience of sublimity that comes with seeking to unify the "multitude of kindred presentations" in an aesthetic idea, the ambiguities of metaphorical meaning defy determination by simple concepts, or replacement by a literal paraphrase (much less an analogical rule). In the more elaborate treatment of metaphor in chapter 8, we will see that the account of metaphor embodied in Kant's aesthetic idea prefigures the contemporary "interactionist" school of thought on metaphor, which itself contrasts with the analogy tradition reflected in Kant's theory of the symbol.

Metaphors produce an indeterminate unity between disparate realms of experience by allowing us to understand one thing in terms of another, to combine ideas and images in a revelatory way.[60] Metaphors typically transfer some set of features we associate with one thing or domain onto another, and by this juxtaposition shed new light on the "target" domain. A metaphor like "time is money" links our temporality to a series of monetary and economic connotations that habituate us to thinking of time as something that can be spent, saved, budgeted, invested, used profitably or wasted, and so on. The meaning of a metaphor is indeterminate and open-ended because the range of connotations and linkages it allows varies across hearers and is always open to addition. Metaphors illuminate patterns of *affinity* that organize experience, often in powerful ways, by relating the diverse into an indeterminately expressive unity. Indeed, in the next chapter the role the notion of affinity plays in Kant's theory of judgment will come to assume paramount importance for understanding the structure of aesthetic unity and the sort of claim to validity products of aesthetic reflection can make.

As we have seen, aesthetic ideas do not directly present a concept, but rather, as Kant writes, "express the concept's implications and its kinship with other concepts" in an expansion of connections that "arouse more thought than can be expressed in a concept determined by words" (CJ 315). In this overwhelming flood of connotation aesthetic ideas convey a wealth of meaning beyond our means to state literally, beyond imagination's means to present schematically, just as the metaphor invokes an open series of relationships by means of which we gain insight into some other thing. Aesthetic ideas "try to approach the exhibition of rational concepts" (CJ 314); in the course of sublimely failing at this they offer in their metaphorical character an allusive expression of ideas which we cannot present determinately. And aesthetic ideas function thus not only in relation to the highest flung ideas of reason, but wherever their transfer of presentations brings more to the illumination of a new domain than can be encapsulated in a determinate concept. The aesthetic ideas found in art elaborate experiential themes such as death, envy, love, and fame; but in their metaphorical richness they "give these [ideas] sensible expression in a way that goes beyond the limits of experience, namely, with a completeness for which no example can be found in nature" (ibid.). Kantian aesthetic ideas thus function metaphorically in their marshaling of kindred material for an expressive elaboration that oversteps the bounds of particular concepts to convey a meaning no literal paraphrase could replace. Indeed, if the aesthetic unity produced by sublime reflection has a metaphorical character, then as Robert Yanal has claimed, "the search for metaphorical meaning is a kind of reflective judgment," more specifically a key instance of sublime reflection.[61] This suggestion will take on more importance as I proceed, and as the special role of sublime understanding in disclosing and extending the networks of sense-making relation that run through our habits of mind becomes clear. In Hegel's aesthetic theory we will once again discern the coalescence of sublimity and metaphor seen here in Kant, not to mention the role this complex plays in exposing and reworking habitual patterns of thought. Only in chapter 8 will the significance of metaphor for sublime understanding be fully articulated.

In chapter 1 we found that a principle of purposiveness guides reflective judgment toward a search for organic unity among the constituent parts of its object. In aesthetic reflection, in its separate modes, this principle motivates productive imagination to construct purposive unities out of the material with which it plays. In the case of taste, we saw that the lawfulness of the understanding demands the unity of the form of appearance. Imagination spontaneously conforms to this demand by intuiting formal unity, or a variety of such configurations, in its object. In this chapter I have argued that Kant's judgment of sublimity applies the same principle of purposiveness.[62] In this case, imagination freely attends to reason's demand for totality by seeking to comprehend as a coherent whole the thematic material presented in a work. Where the outcome of tasteful judgment was an intuition of formal unity, sublime reflection results in the imaginative production of aesthetic ideas. Those ideas constitute indeterminate and open-ended interpretations of a work's meaning. Now, because imagination freely accords with the understanding in judgments of taste, but fails to meet reason's demand for totality in judgments of sublimity, the products of sublime reflection possess an indeterminacy and plasticity unusual for the product of a legitimate form of *judgment*. In sublime reflection on aesthetic ideas, the subsumptive and systematic prerogatives of Kant's general theory of judgment meet their greatest challenge from an interpretive reflection that, without being subsumptive or systematic, nevertheless makes a claim to validity. The implications of this for a model of aesthetic reflection, and the sort of demand for agreement that its products can make, will be explored in the next chapter.

4

Aesthetic Unity and Validity

In its interpretive responses to works of art, sublime reflection produces something very unlike a concept. Imagination's task in its fashioning of aesthetic ideas is to construct from the attributes of a work a "unifying" set of relations. But I have argued throughout that the unity sought in aesthetic reflection cannot assume the form of the technical or architectonic unities Kant describes. We attribute technical unity to objects in accordance with a definite purpose we know them or want them to fulfill. The design specifications for an automobile present technical unity. In the case of a work of art, ascribing technical unity to it would amount to treating it as a machine—designed according to the specifications of a known artistic intention—"built" to crank out a fixed meaning. Interpretive "reflection" on the work would be determined in advance by that purpose if technical unity were what it sought. But nothing predetermines the free play of imagination in aesthetic response, so for it works of art do not have invariably prescribed meanings; the unity it seeks in them is not technical.

Systematic unities, on the other hand, are regulated, as we have seen, by an a priori rational "schema which originates from an idea" (CPR A833/B861). The indeterminately expressive function of aesthetic ideas militates against their sort of unity being construed systematically. In sublime reflection imagination faces an expanding array of attributes that it seeks to comprehend as an organic whole. No schema, whether derived by imagination from a concept of the understanding or an idea of reason, directs its interpretations. If that were the case, imagination would not be freely at play with its material; it would instead follow the principles of another cognitive power, and we would not have a case of aesthetic reflection.

The bottom line is: given that imagination tries but *fails* to exhibit a rational whole in sublime reflection, what it does produce cannot enjoy a determinate technical or systematic unity for the simple reason that it is not wholly unified at all. But neither is an aesthetic idea just a disunified mess, as we will come to see more clearly. If not technical or systematic, then, what does a properly aesthetic "unity" look like? What sort of ordering issues from imagination's effort to present aesthetic attributes as a whole? Insofar as aesthetic ideas constitute interpretations, as I have suggested, what manner and degree of unity do they enjoy? And *as* interpretations of a work's plausible meaning, how do these imaginative unities justify their claim to offer valid insights?

To address these questions, I begin by considering some implications of Kant's theory of expression. If aesthetic ideas stand in an expressive relation to rational ideas, this relationship will help clarify the kind of unity, and the kind of validity, these products of sublime reflection will have. This discussion occasions a comparison of the sort of intersubjective validity claims Kant's judgments of taste and sublimity make. I argue that we can better understand the validity of sublime reflection's interpretations by contrasting Kant's detailed notion of systematic, rational unity with the sort of aesthetic unity a productive imagination invents. Doing so exposes the role a notion of "affinity" plays in aesthetic reflection, and this clue motivates a visit to the first *Critique*'s "A" edition Transcendental Deduction, where Kant presents affinity as an a priori condition of all conceptual knowledge. I will make a case that the notion of affinity in fact establishes both transcendental and empirical dimensions for the production of aesthetic unity. In part III this result will have a decisive influence on the extent of universality sublime understanding can claim for its insights.

The Questions of Unity and Validity

As a start, the fact that an aesthetic idea expresses some indeterminate rational idea may have bearing on the sort of unity imagination will construct as it reflects on a work of art. The expressed rational idea does not impose a schema on reflection, and yet it plays a shaping role by delineating the range of aesthetic attributes suitable for expressing it. With this point in mind, we must revisit a previously cited passage and more carefully untangle its import. Kant characterizes the aesthetic idea thus:

> If a presentation of the imagination is imputed to a concept, as belonging to the exhibition of it, and yet it by itself prompts so much thought as could never be comprehended in a determinate concept, and by which the concept itself aesthetically expands in an unlimited way; in this way, then, the imagination is creative and thus sets in motion the power of intellectual ideas (i.e., reason), specifically by making reason think more, at the prompting of [such a] presentation . . . than can be grasped and made distinct in the presentation (though the thought does pertain to the concept of the object presented). (CJ 314–315)[1]

Now, Kant uses the term "concept" inconsistently in this passage. He normally attributes concepts to the understanding, and he means as much when he describes a presented aesthetic idea as something that prompts more thought than can be grasped in a "determinate concept." But his other uses of "concept" in this passage refer instead to rational or intellectual ideas.[2] An aesthetic idea is a presentation of imagination which belongs to the partial expression of a rational idea, not a concept of the understanding. Thus when Kant concludes this statement with the proviso that "the thought does pertain to the concept of the object presented," he means that the array of attributes brought to mind in an aesthetic idea (the object) all bear on or relate to the intellectual idea (the "concept") expressed. All the aesthetic attributes with which imagination plays are supposed to contribute to intimating that rational idea (or ideas).

The idea in question thus serves a behind-the-scenes *normative* role: it regulates just what "multitude of kindred presentations" the aesthetic idea ought to bring to mind. That is, for the aesthetic idea to fulfill its expressive function, its specific attributes, and the specific way they are related in sublime reflection, must be subject to some standard of rightness. Not just any attempt to comprehend a group of aesthetic attributes as a meaningful whole will orient reflection toward the expressive aim of the group. Kant gives the impression that ingenious works of art inspire an overwhelming rush of allusion and memory, but this flood of material can only constitute an aesthetic idea if two conditions are fulfilled. First, the material must be suitable for expressing (albeit incompletely) the idea(s) in question. And second, the organization of this material into an expressive whole, as attempted in sublime reflection, must succeed in pointing in the right direction by provoking thought on the idea(s) the material was "meant" to express.

The problem with this normative role, which ideas of reason seem to play in sublime reflection, is that the person judging the work does not have at her disposal those very guiding ideas. Sublime reflection *freely* seeks out a thematic unity to make sense of a work's attributes; that unity is not imposed on reflection by a dictate of reason. Imagination *produces* aesthetic unity on its own, and no other cognitive power determines the outcome of its free play. If ideas of reason imposed a structure on aesthetic ideas, if imagination merely received through aesthetic ideas a gift of rational unity, judgment of them would not be reflective. Aesthetic unity would really be systematic, specified by a rational schema, rather than the spontaneous product of imagination's reflective power.

But Kant does not allow this prospect: aesthetic ideas cannot be systematically unified, for that would make them sensible instances of rational ideas, and Kantian rational ideas as such cannot be instantiated. And on my account, aesthetic ideas are constructed by a process of imaginative comprehension structurally destined, as a sublime reflection, to lack any sort of determinate unity. Thus rational ideas play a paradoxical role in this reflection: they seem to provide a norm for judging whether aesthetic ideas truly manage to (partially) express them. And yet the aesthetic reflection itself, in order to be that, cannot be guided by any rule imposed from without. The fact that an array of aesthetic attributes expresses a rational idea would seem to require that imagination organize them in some certain way in order to make proper sense of them. And yet imagination's production of a network of relations among aesthetic attributes cannot be subject to the rule of reason.[3]

This apparent normative dimension to free reflection on aesthetic ideas, this paradoxical normativity without the imposition of a rule, raises questions about the validity claim that judgments based on this model of reflection can make.[4] Typically for Kant, judgments receive their warrant from the integrity of the universals that are applied in them. The objective reference of cognitive judgments derives from the transcendental pedigree of the categories which the understanding applies to experience. The binding force of moral judgments relies on their underlying universal principles of autonomy as supplied by reason. In the case of aesthetic judgments the basis of their claim to validity, to a demand for agreement from others, is quite different, precisely because no conceptual rule can serve as a standard here. Without cognition of any concept or purpose or artistic intention underlying its object, aesthetic reflection is in a sense on its own, and the legitimacy of its judgments must have another basis. How, then, does the evident normative role of ideas of reason affect the validity of a reflection that is meant to occur free of determining rules? What demand for agreement can imagination make for the web of relations it constructs in sublime reflection without appealing to a conceptual rule or systematic idea that would justify its construction?

We are left with a pair of intimately related issues: we need to clarify further the specific manner in which imagination seeks purposive unity among aesthetic attributes in sublime reflection (the question of aesthetic unity). And second, we need to explore what claim to validity its product can make, in the absence of any justificatory rule, but under the obscure influence of the ideas of reason intimated by that product (the question of aesthetic validity). We can begin to address these issues by revisiting Kant's own account of aesthetic validity in the third *Critique*. The relationship between imagination and reason involved in sublime reflection's claim to validity will then motivate us to shift back to the question of aesthetic unity, and consider what the *Critique of Pure Reason* can show about the contrast between it and systematic unity. We will learn from the first *Critique* that "affinity" plays a key role in the "look" of aesthetic unity. This progress will return us once again to the question of validity, which we will then be better positioned to answer.

A brief recitation of Kant's account of aesthetic validity can begin by focusing on the judgment of taste and by stressing the centrality of *feeling* to Kant's grounding of the demand for agreement made by aesthetic judgments. The harmony of cognitive powers attending a judgment of beauty manifests itself as a feeling: "there must be one attunement in which this inner relation [of imagination and the understanding] is most conducive to the (mutual) quickening of the two mental powers with a view to cognition (of given objects) in general; and the only way this attunement can be determined is by feeling (rather than by concepts)" (CJ 238–239). In a determinative judgment the shared basis that grounds a public demand for agreement is the intersubjectively available concept under which something is subsumed. When I claim that a Braeburn is a kind of apple, or that this apple is a Braeburn, the validity of my claim relies on the communal integrity of my concepts (as well as my proper application of them). But in aesthetic judgment concepts play no validating role. Kant instead locates the basis of taste in a fundamental relation between cognitive powers. This relation obtains in all knowing subjects, and it is accessible to us only at the level of feeling. The felt harmony of imagination and the understanding must be a universally valid feeling, for that harmony is required for the possibility of cognition as such: "this subjective relation suitable for cognition in general must hold just as much for everyone, and hence be just as universally communicable, as any determinate cognition, since cognition always rests on that relation as its subjective condition" (CJ 217).

The judgment of taste can demand the assent of others, according to Kant, because the feeling of pleasure in the harmony of cognitive powers rests not on any contingent attraction to the agreeable but on a cognitive relation common to all. This harmony produces what Kant calls a *common sense*, a feeling of pleasure shared by all subjects: "[T]his attunement itself, and hence also the feeling of it (when a presentation is given), must be universally communicable, while the universal communicability of a feeling presupposes a common sense" (CJ 239). The relationship between imagination and understanding which is constitutive of cognition is felt in the judgment of taste in their free, preconceptual accord. The *sensus communis* that enjoys this harmony grounds the universal communicability of the claim "This is beautiful." So when I praise the beauty of a sunset, Kant thinks I do not express a mere personal liking akin to a preference for fudge ice cream. Instead, I am reporting that the imaginative play which the sunset inspires in me has awakened a pleasurable feeling from the deepest and most universal structures of my cognitive self, of *any* cognitive self. If others let their imaginations range over this sunset, they too ought to feel the same universal pleasure awaken in them.[5]

In the case of sublime reflection, which I will focus on from here forward, the situation is more complicated. We have seen that this judgment begins with imagination's attempt to emulate the example of reason and that power's demand for totality: "in judging a thing sublime [the aesthetic power of judgment] refers the imagination to *reason* so that it will harmonize subjectively with reason's *ideas* (which ideas they are is indeterminate)" (CJ 256). We saw earlier that imagination seeks to satisfy reason by construing its object as an exhibition of rational ideas. But the limits of imaginative comprehension, its inability to sustain an intuition of unity as complete as that found in ideas of reason, frustrates the effort. This conflict between cognitive powers produces a feeling of displeasurable inadequacy: facing the sublime one "has the feeling that his imagination is inadequate for exhibiting the idea of a whole, [a feeling] in which imagination reaches its maximum, and as it strives to expand that maximum, it sinks back into itself, but consequently comes to feel a liking" (CJ 252). On my view, imagination's sublime failure to exhibit rational ideas results in its indeterminate expression of them in aesthetic ideas.

The liking imagination inspires through this effort is the *respect* we feel for the superior powers of reason. Kant notes that at an everyday level, when we judge something large through an aesthetic estimation of magnitude, "we then always connect with the presentation a kind of respect, as we connect a [kind of] contempt with what we simply call small" (CJ 249). But in the case of sublime reflection, where Kant takes imagination to judge something large absolutely in response to reason's demand for totality, the respect we feel is not for any object but for reason itself. Kant thus places the primary value of judgments of sublimity in their kindling of respect for our rational vocation as intellectual and moral beings: "our imagination, even in its greatest effort to do what is demanded of it and comprehend a given object in a whole of intuition (and hence to exhibit the idea of reason), proves its limits and inadequacy, and yet at the same time proves its vocation to [obey] a law, namely, to make itself adequate to that idea. Hence the feeling of the sublime in nature is respect for our own vocation" (CJ 257). It should be noted that the *sublime* feeling of inadequacy which imagination undergoes, in which it feels violently stretched to the limit of its powers, is quite distinct from the *moral* feeling of respect for reason in which the sublime feeling finally issues. Distinguishing these feelings is critical, for Kant argues that the feeling of respect—the felt regard for reason's idea of freedom and its demand for totality in thought—is really the precondition for the arousal of sublime feeling. In order for the sublime feeling to arise, imagination must first freely respect a rational demand that we present totality.

For this reason, Kant claims that no *sensus communis* can ground sublime reflection. The universality of the pleasure at the basis of taste relies on a harmony of cognitive powers which can be expected in everyone because it conditions the possibility of cognition as such. But our capacity to feel the sublime is more tenuous because it is mediated by the feeling of respect: "taste we demand unhesitatingly from everyone, because here judgment refers the imagination merely to the understanding, our power of concepts; in the case of feeling, on the other hand, judgment refers the imagination to reason, our power of ideas, and so we demand feeling only under a subjective presupposition (though we believe we are justified and permitted to require this presupposition in everyone): we presuppose moral feeling in man" (CJ 266). Kant thinks we can *require* the feeling of respect from everyone, but we cannot *expect* that this feeling will motivate one and all, because respect for our rational vocation is a *cultivated* feeling that may or may not find support in a given cultural milieu. "It is a fact," Kant writes, "that what is called sublime by us, having been prepared through culture, comes across as merely repellent to a person who is uncultured and lacking in the development of moral ideas" (CJ 265). Because our capacity for sublime feeling hangs on our preparedness to feel respect for reason, the claim to validity in sublime reflection will not be communicated to whomever lacks this moral feeling. As Lyotard puts it, "the demand in sublime feeling does not properly belong to sublime feeling. The demand comes to sublime feeling from the demand to be communicated inscribed in the form of the moral law. . . . If one does not have the Idea of freedom and of its law, one cannot experience sublime feeling."[6] Hence the validity claim of sublime reflection rests on an a priori feeling of respect for reason's ideas, but this judgment's intersubjective reception is somewhat less secure than Kant's judgment of taste, because the expressive import of the sublime work of art will only be suggested to those who have regard for the rational ideas which aesthetic reflection seeks to present.[7]

Lyotard overemphasizes, however, imagination's relation to *reason as moral legislator.* I argued earlier that Kant's mathematical sublime, rather than the morally weighted dynamical sublime, would better model a broadly construed account of imagination's production of aesthetic unity. The mathematical sublime arose from imagination's response to reason as a *cognitive power* productive of intellectual ideas, while the dynamical sublime arose from its response to reason as a morally legislative *power of desire* (CJ 247). So in fact imagination's reflective response to reason's intellectual demand for totality can be understood apart from reason's role in providing moral ideas. Even the feeling of respect can be understood apart from its distinctive moral function. Kant defines respect most generically as "[the] feeling that it is beyond our ability to attain an idea *that is a law for us. . . .*" Kant goes on to write that "the idea of comprehending every appearance that may be given us in the intuition of a whole is an idea enjoined on us by a law of reason" (CJ 257). This comprehension is just what imagination seeks in sublime reflection. That is, *aesthetic reflection shows its respect for reason's demand for totality when it attempts to unify the attributes of aesthetic ideas.* In this sense, respect for reason's law is built into the very process of reflective judgment; its search for intelligible unity in uncanny phenomena is motivated by the demand for unity which reason makes. In other words, the respect for reason evident in sublime reflection's interpretive striving can be articulated in broad intellectual, rather than specifically moral terms (which, as we have seen, has the advantage of widening the range of meanings expressed through aesthetic ideas).

Even without reference to the moral dimension of the Kantian subject's vocation, however, the validity claim of sublime reflection still depends on a cultivated feeling of respect for rational unity. Reflective imagination only seeks to comprehend aesthetic ideas as purposive wholes in response to a demand from reason. Hence the validity claim of the aesthetic unity imagination produces can only be communicated to whomever shares the regard for unity to which the judgment responds. Recall that the claim to validity made by a judgment of sublimity is not that everyone will in fact accede the sublimity of something, but that they ought to find it sublime. Sublime reflection expects approval of its interpretive response to a work because it feels that its take at least partially expresses a unified meaning which imagination cannot entirely comprehend. Whether others will agree depends on their sensitivity to the ideas conveyed through the work; even more so, it depends on their cultivated willingness to seek unity in the manner reflective judgment and reason would have them. The fact that the validity claim of sublime reflection depends on conditions of acculturation will gain import as we proceed.

Reflective Affinity

We cannot further refine this account of aesthetic validity without clarifying the manner in which imagination's constructive activity proceeds to the limit that induces sublime feeling. As an interpretive activity, sublime reflection expects others to appreciate its insights into a work; we need to understand just what those insights look like, as specifically aesthetic unities, in order to see why they could make a claim on our agreement. Unfortunately, Kant provides little direct guidance for specifying the imaginative comprehension undertaken in this reflection. I want to argue, however, that it is possible to develop an account of imagination's construction of *aesthetic* unity in contrast to Kant's detailed discussions of the structure of *systematic* unity. Recall that in sublime reflection, on my account, imagination, freely emulating reason's demand for totality, attempts to exhibit a rational idea. For Kant, ideas of reason are themselves the source of systematic unity; a rational idea organizes thought into systematic form.[8] Thus when imagination emulates reason in sublime reflection, it attempts to construct a systematic unity from the aesthetic attributes at its disposal; only thus could its effort count as an attempt to exhibit a rational idea. But the limitations of imagination dictate that what it produces from this effort—namely (on my account) a partial *expression* for the idea in the form of an aesthetic idea—falls short of reason's systematic products. Kant explores the character of systematic unity, and the principles of its construction, in the *Critique of Pure Reason*, specifically in the section "On the Regulative Use of the Ideas of Pure Reason," as well as in the First Introduction to the *Critique of Judgment*. By studying these passages, I suggest, we can determine what principles imagination *attempts* to employ in its reflection on aesthetic attributes. We can then clarify the manner of its constructive activity and the structure of the product, an aesthetic idea, which issues from imagination's "impaired" application of these principles.[9]

The first thing that becomes apparent in the first *Critique* is that Kant construes systematic or architectonic unity as a structure of *classification*. Reason organizes our welter of concepts and experiences by grouping together like phenomena into categories that can be placed in a hierachical system of kinds. Kant introduces this notion by means of an example, that of the diverse appearances of "power" in the human mind. We encounter in ourselves such various mental powers as "sensation, consciousness, imagination, memory, ingenuity, discrimination, pleasure, desire, etc." (CPR A649/B677). Faced with this unseemly disunity, reason employs "a logical maxim [which] commands us at the outset to diminish as much as possible the seeming diversity by comparing [these powers] and thereby discovering their hidden identity" (ibid.). Reason gathers together disparate appearances of power and dispels their apparent heterogeneity by postulating their unity in a "basic power" *under which they can be subsumed* as cases of it: "[A]lthough logic does not at all ascertain whether there is such a power, the idea of such a power is at least the problem posed for a systematic presentation of the manifoldness of powers. The logical principle of reason demands that we bring about this systematic unity as far as possible; and the more the appearances of one power and another are found to be identical to each other, the more probable does it become that these appearances are nothing but different manifestations of one and the same power" (ibid.). The construction of systematic unity proceeds by taming the diversity of phenomena to fit a structure of classification. The subsumption of particulars under systematic ideas is not determinative in the way cognitive judgments are. The organizing ideas posited by reason cannot be exhibited in appearance; that is, we cannot demonstrate that a basic power underlies all functions of the mind, we instead use this notion as a heuristic device in our investigations of mentality. Thus the identification of diverse appearances as manifestations of systematic ideas must be construed as a merely regulative ordering of experience. In any case, the classificatory impetus of systematic unity is apparent in Kant's treatment of rational ideas as ways of grouping likenesses under unifying themes.

The *hierarchical* nature of systematic classification is especially apparent in Kant's First Introduction to the *Critique of Judgment*, where the project of introducing unity into the diverse phenomena of nature requires reflective judgment to employ "a principle by which we present nature as a system for our judgment, a system in which dividing the diverse into genera and species enables us, by making comparisons, to bring all the forms we find in nature to (more or less general) concepts" (FI 212, n.21). Systematic unity in the First Introduction assumes the form of a pyramidal structure of genera and species into which the diversity of nature can be fit. The hallmark of reflective judgment in this mode is its expectation that such a structure of classification suits nature: "reflective judgment, by its nature, cannot undertake to *classify* all of nature in terms of its empirical variety unless it presupposes that nature itself *makes* its transcendental laws *specific* in terms of some principle. Now this principle can only be that of [nature's] appropriateness for the power of judgment itself" (FI 215). The organization postulated by reason in the systematic unity of its ideas is one in which everything can be located in a hierarchy of lower and higher forms. Kant takes the completion of such a system of classification to be beyond the means of human endeavor. But the unity of reason demands that we expect to find hierarchical structure organizing natural diversity, and that we design our investigations around looking for it.

Returning to the first *Critique,* Kant delineates three principles of systematization reason employs in its construction of systematic hierarchy. The first two principles of *homogeneity* and *specificity* most clearly reflect the project of classification central to reason's aim: "The logical principle of genera, which postulates identity, is opposed by another one, viz., the principle of *species*. The principle requires of things— regardless of their agreement under the same genus—manifoldness and diversity, and makes it a precept for the understanding to be no less attentive to these than to identity. . . . Thus reason shows here a twofold interest—two interests that conflict with each other: on the one hand the interest of *range* (generality) as concerns genera, on the other hand the interest of *content* (determinateness) in regard to the manifoldness of species" (CPR A654/B682). The principle of specificity guides the separation of kinds in terms of their dissimilarity and is thus a force for multiplication and differentiation. Its work, however, serves the purposes of the principle of homogeneity, which orders the multiplicity of species into a hierarchy of kinds. Because the goal of systematic unity is a structure of classification, the principle of homogeneity has priority over specification; that is, the end of creating a system serves as a check on the multiplicative prerogative of the other principle.

Kant calls his third rule the principle of *affinity* or *continuity*. This condition demands that a system of classification enjoy smooth transitions between all its levels of hierarchy and its adjacent forms: "Hence reason prepares the understanding's realm by these means: (1) by a principle of the *homogeneity* of the manifold under higher genera; (2) by a principle of the *variety* of the homogeneous under lower species;—and, in order to complete the systematic unity, reason adds (3) also a law of the *affinity* of all concepts, a law that commands a continuous transition from every species to every other species through a step-wise increase of difference. We may call these three rules the principles of the *homogeneity*, of the *specification*, and of the *continuity* of forms" (CPR A657–658/B685–686). Kant excludes from systematic order any abrupt shifts between one organizing concept and the next. The hierarchy of genera prescribes that each step to higher genera be fully explicable, with a minimum of novelty added at each stage. The principle of affinity promotes the construction of a unified pyramid of classification, because it requires that all phenomena be seen to belong to one continuous field of relations. Kant takes the unity of this field to mean that system reaches its greatest unity at its peak: "there are not different original and first genera that are, as it were, isolated and separated from one another (by an empty intervening space); rather, all the manifold genera are only divisions of a single highest and universal genus" (CPR A659/B687). In sum, systematic unity assumes for Kant the form of a pyramidal hierarchy of classification structured by principles of homogeneity, specification, and affinity.

Now the question is: how do these principles bear on the character of *aesthetic* unity? We saw that imagination seeks in sublime reflection to exhibit a rational idea; this requires that it attempt to construct the systematic unity typical of reason's ideas. My account would have it that when imagination proves incapable of in fact satisfying this demand, it instead expresses the ideas indeterminately through construction of an aesthetic idea. The "unity" of this product will thus assume a form that arises from imagination's application of the systematizing principles. But its application of them is limited by its specific powers in aesthetic reflection and by the limits of its capacity for comprehension. We can, then, elaborate the nature of aesthetic unity by considering to what extent imagination is capable of utilizing each principle of systematicity in its play. This will allow us to assess what sort of unity would arise from imagination's truncated use of these principles. We will find that the principle of affinity plays a key role in sublime reflection's production of aesthetic unity.

It should be apparent that the principle of homogeneity will "suffer" the most at the hands of the imagination's specific mode of play in sublime reflection. Applying a principle of hierarchical subsumption would discount imagination's activity as aesthetic, for to apply it imagination would need to make use of schematizing powers which it reserves for more cognitive pursuits. Put more strongly, aesthetic imagination cannot employ a principle of homogeneity simply because it does not have at its disposal conceptual genera under which to group and subsume like phenomena. Imagination does not cognize the rational idea(s) that a set of aesthetic attributes seems to intimate. Imagination's alienation from the idea it seeks to intuit renders it incapable of homogenization, because that ordering of classifications must be guided by the very rational schema that imagination lacks.[10] Thus the most we can infer about the nature of aesthetic unity from imagination's inability to employ the principle of homogeneity is that *aesthetic unity will not include any hierachy of subsumption in its structure.* In the course of its reflection imagination may group together aesthetic attributes in terms of some similarity or other; but such grouping cannot be taken to the point of subsuming them under a concept or genus. Indeed, as in the case of metaphor, discerning striking but unlikely parallels between disparate phenomena is a key component of aesthetic reflection's power to make sense of or shed new light on a thing. But this does not entail, as metaphorical expression does not entail, subsuming the related items under an exhaustive concept. At most aesthetic imagination can intuit similarity between attributes for the purpose of relating those attributes nonhierarchically to other elements it seeks to comprehend.

It should also be apparent that the principle of specification is particularly *well* suited to imagination's reflection on aesthetic ideas. In sublime reflection imagination apprehends a multiplicity of attributes the distinctness of which it must recognize and maintain as it seeks to relate them in their diversity. Without a principle of subsumption provided by a rational schema, imagination cannot presume to rank the relative importance of the attributes it relates. It can only respect the differentia of the multiplicity at its disposal and construct a network of relations on an "egalitarian" basis. The importance of specification in aesthetic reflection is just the flip side of the deemphasis on homogeneity. In the absence of a classificatory hierarchy, imagination must relate attributes not in terms of the subsumption of one under another, but rather in terms of their illuminating similarities and differences. This feature of aesthetic unity also shows up in metaphor, which presents one domain as quite different than, but nevertheless remarkably isomorphic with another. Thus imagination's active employment of the principle of specification indicates that aesthetic unity will be marked by a *sustained differentiation of attributes* in which none is considered more determining of the overall unity than the next.

Finally, how will imagination's attempt to employ the principle of affinity affect the character of aesthetic unity? In its weakest formulation this principle just dictates that imagination expect the attributes upon which it reflects to indeed be amenable to supporting a network of relations. In this sense the principle of affinity merely reflects the anticipation of purposive unity sought for in aesthetic reflection. But as we saw above, in the case of constructing a *systematic* unity the principle of affinity makes a much stronger demand, that the elements related in a system form a *continuous* field of very tight-knit classifications. However, the shifting priority of the other principles in imagination's reflection (as opposed to reason's thinking) suggests that this strong demand for continuity cannot be made in the case of relating aesthetic attributes. The deemphasis on homogeneity in aesthetic reflection, and the priority of the principle of specification—in other words the priority of preserving a heterogeneity of attributes—suggests that imaginative comprehension will relate attributes as much in terms of their differences as in terms of their similarities. In this context the principle of affinity will not demand a network of immediate relations among subtle shifts of position in a system of genera. Rather, as in the case of metaphor once again, it will demand instead construction of a network of relations among quite dissimilar objects. In fact, because the hallmark of the aesthetic idea is to contain more than can be thought in any concept, the elements it links together must be sufficiently disparate and mutually uncanny to surpass conceptual determination. This, of course, is what makes aesthetic ideas sublime.

Metaphors embody precisely this structure, in that they disclose affinities between the most far-flung ideas, things, and experiences. The metaphor "time is money," for example, relates two grossly distinct phenomena in ways that have come to affect our idioms and ways of behaving in innumerable ways. The meanings and impact of the metaphorical connection surpass what the concepts of time or money can make sense of on their own. The production of aesthetic unity "goes beyond experience" precisely through this bold relating of disparate things. We might suspect, then, that the very possibility of metaphor arises from the imaginative "misuse" of rational principles of system-building.

In the case of aesthetic responses to art, imagination's search for affinity will motivate it to construct a network of far-flung relations among previously or putatively unrelated features of a work and all it brings to mind. So the inventive construal of a work's possible meanings involves a productive imagination that engages in a *connective activity of sublime reflection.* It demonstrates its interpretive ingenuity by sculpting diversity into a newly expressive, partial whole. Aesthetic unity generally will assume the form of indeterminately unified, relational networks which disclose unexpected affinities among disparate elements. The Kantian aesthetic ideas that constitute proffered interpretations of art will suggest through those relationships what a work might mean.[11]

Aesthetic Validity

This result returns us to the question of validity: how does imagination's production of affine networks satisfy Kant's account of the intersubjective agreement demanded by sublime reflection? Recall that the basis for agreement in a judgment of sublimity is the intuition of a unity that imagination, in its effort to comprehend a group of aesthetic attributes as a whole, reaches for but fails to grasp in the way reason would have it. The feeling of pleasurable displeasure that this effort gives rise to enjoys an element of universality because it reflects a feeling of respect for reason's idea of totality which, Kant thinks, we can require of everyone. It should be apparent that the production of reflective affinity fits the contours of sublime reflection's claim. The construction of unexpected affinites between disparate attributes reveals imagination's *feeling of respect* for reason by reaching for the systematic unity of rational ideas. Further, this effort pushes imagination to the limit of its comprehension and induces the *sublime feeling* of frustration, as it finds itself unable to sustain too complex a network of affinities. This account of sublime reflection includes both the respect for reason and the frustration in imagination indicative of the feeling that grounds its universality.

For Kant, the universal validity of aesthetic judgments is based on a priori conditions peculiar to the constitution of a feeling and knowing subject. Given the central role the disclosure of affine networks plays in aesthetic reflection, we can further clarify the nature of aesthetic validity by investigating the transcendental status of affinity. It happens that Kant discusses affinity as a transcendental condition of all experience in the "A" edition Deduction of the *Critique of Pure Reason.* Little work has been done to elaborate the forms of reflective validity which Kant treats in the *Critique of Judgment* in relation to the first *Critique*'s conditions for the possibility of experience, and hence for the possibility of determinative judgment. I want to do just a bit of that work, in order to demonstrate both the relevance and the limitations of affinity as a transcendental basis for aesthetic unity and validity. We will see that affinity provides both a transcendental *and an empirical* ground for the validity of aesthetic reflection.

One of Kant's primary aims in the first *Critique*, of course, is to establish a firm foundation for empirical knowledge by determining "what are the a priori conditions on which the possibility of experience depends;" these conditions will prove to give experience an immutable form that structures our knowledge of appearances.[12] Accounting for this structure explains how it is possible that "cognition is a whole consisting of compared and connected presentations," connected as a whole precisely by virtue of the applicability of that form to all appearances. In the "A" Deduction Kant finds an explanation for this experiential unity in his doctrine of a "threefold synthesis" consisting of "the *apprehension* of presentations that are modifications of the mind in intuition; the synthesis of the *reproduction* of these presentations in imagination; and the synthesis of their *recognition* in the concept" (CPR A96, 97).

The initial synthesis of apprehension "goes through and gathers together" the manifold as intuited spatially and temporally, while the final synthesis of recognition in concepts organizes presentations under categories that dictate the form of appearance. But Kant thinks that *prior* to the synthesis of recognition "we must assume a pure transcendental synthesis of imagination that itself underlies the possibility of all experience"; this synthesis of reproduction grounds the possibility of presentations being *associable and comparable as such*, that is, grounds their reproducibility in orderly ways (CPR A101). The imaginative maintenance of the temporal field of presentations allows temporally separate presentations to be gathered and compared. Only if presentations are a priori associable can the synthesis of recognition organize them under categories. Rules of understanding "[present], when appearances are given to us, the necessary reproduction of their manifold," but a *productive* imagination grounds their original belonging together: "the principle of the necessary unity of the imagination's pure (productive) synthesis prior to apperception is the basis for the possibility of all cognition, especially of experience" (CPR A106, 118). For Kant, at least in the "A" Deduction, productive imagination— which in another context responds to the indeterminate richness of aesthetic ideas—makes possible the very application of understanding's categories to the manifold. It accomplishes this by first constituting that manifold as a continuous field amenable to determinate conceptual structuration.

Kant asks how particular instances of empirical association are made possible by the preconceptual work of productive imagination. He answers that "the basis for the possibility of the manifold's association, insofar as this basis lies in the object, is called the manifold's *affinity*" (CPR A113). Affinity is the *indeterminate associability* of the manifold: it grounds the possibility of rule-governed connections between appearances, and it is produced *prior* to rule-determination under categories.[13] This affine manifold will get determined in the end by conceptual rules, and Kant concludes that "the affinity of all appearances (whether near or remote) is a necessary consequence of a synthesis in imagination that is based a priori on rules" (CPR A123).[14] Imagination's synthetic work will be determined conceptually by what the synthesis of recognition in concepts and the work of understanding contribute to the construction of objectively valid knowledge. *But in an aesthetic context,* imagination plays with its productive powers independent of conceptual determination. In lieu of cognizing its object through the understanding's rules, aesthetic imagination "reverts," as it were, to the product of its prior moment of synthesis, namely the associability of the whole. Put another way, imagination reflects aesthetically on what the extent of its connective powers, when free of rule determination, allow it to. That is, imagination explores the indeterminate affinity of the manifold.

In the case of conceptual knowledge, the synthesis of recognition under the unity of apperception produces a *necessary* unity of presentations according to categorial laws. In the absence of rule determination, what necessity can aesthetic judgments claim? As a transcendental condition of any possible experience, everyone must be able, according to Kantian principles, to recognize the affinity of the manifold. When productive imagination plays aesthetically, it celebrates the differential affinity it "finds" in its presentations despite the absence of ordering rules. Imagination can insist on the validity of its connective play precisely because its play *reveals a transcendental condition,* namely the affinity of all presentations, for which it is ultimately responsible. Imagination enjoys its relation-building powers, and this pleasure demands a universal communication: its basis in a transcendental condition indicates that everyone may enjoy it. At this formal, transcendental level whatever pleasure imagination receives from *any* associative play rests on a transcendental condition, and imagination is thereby warranted in expecting others to also find pleasure in such reflection.

This a priori pleasure in connectivity would render every relation aesthetically valid, were it not for the fact that the principle of purposiveness in reflective judgment constrains the play of imagination to the presentation of relational networks that feel *designed* despite their lack of conceptual determination. Imagination's relationship with the understanding in judgments of taste, and with reason in judgments of sublimity, constrain it to seek coherent order among parts. In the case of beauty, imagination intuits the formal affinity of a manifold and plays with the variety of ways in which its object can be regarded as purposively organized. Sculpting order in the absence of conceptual rules, imagination feels pleasure in and articulates the transcendental affinity upon which all conceptual ordering is based. The validity of the judgment rests on the way in which this imaginative intuition and expression of preconceptual order appeals to a transcendental condition. When enjoying beauty, imagination shows that the affinity of the manifold is the aesthetic condition of all cognition.

In the case of sublime reflection, I have focused on the role it plays in assessing the meaning of a work of art. We saw imagination answer reason's demand for systematic unity by producing the loose relational network of aesthetic unity in its response to aesthetic ideas. Reason demands that imagination comprehend and exhibit a rational idea; unable to do so, imagination achieves instead the expressive intimation of rational unity in the differential, affine network of aesthetic unity. In producing a network of attributions, in relating the thematic material of a work as a whole, imagination interprets the work. It does not decide artistic meaning, but it suggests plausible routes of interpretation, ways in which a work conveys purposive design at the level of its significance. As is the case for the formal affinity of beauty, sublime reflection is transcendentally valid when it produces interpretive affinity from among the aesthetic attributes of a work. The interpretation it produces is thought valid when it reveals the aesthetic unity of design and relational coherence in the work. Without ever completing a work's meaning, imagination explores what it could mean by straining to relate features of the work, *and response to the work*, as an affine whole.

This last emphasis helps to distinguish the status of the validity claimed for judgments of taste from the claims of sublime reflection. In the first, the form of the work bounds the set of features imagination plays with in its reflection. Formalist aesthetic theory embodies just this orientation, that only perceptual features present in the work bear on aesthetic response to it. The boundlessness of the sublime, however, implies that there can be no already established limits on what features of a response may contribute to sublime reflection's development of an illuminating interpretation.[15] As we have seen, Kant indicates that aesthetic ideas prompt a "multitude of kindred presentations," "more thought" than is contained in any single concept or even in the work itself. This rush of material, while relevant to appreciating the work, is tied to the contingent specificity of the particular interpreter. The collection of attributes from which sublime reflection constructs an affine manifold is not constant; it varies with the experience of the respondent, with what the work "brings to mind" in each case. The boundlessness of what may become a relevant element of an interpretive network introduces into sublime reflection the possibility of multiple valid outcomes, and this variation itself reflects the search for indeterminate unity which reflective judgment aspires to. A work of art may sustain a variety of plausible interpretations; far from undermining the validity of each, this variation instead celebrates the rich power of a work to embody free affinity of the manifold in manifold ways. I noted earlier that advocates of the view that the meaning of a work of art is determined by artist's intentions do not find a friend in Kant; champions of the alternative view that works allow room for a variety of plausible "readings" do.

On my interpretation of Kant, then, one who constructs organizing affinities among putatively unrelated phenomena has a basis for expecting others to recognize that affinity as well. Reason demands unity among our vast welter of presentations, and reflective judgment seeks that purposive coherence throughout our experience. When aesthetic reflection encounters a work of art and senses in it the expression of an intended meaning, it seeks to make sense of the work's features as a communicative whole. Imagination interprets the work reflectively, which means that it does not merely subsume it under a concept: the declaration, "that is a painting," does not constitute an interpretation. Nor does imagination cognize the work as having a determinate purpose: it plays with making sense of the whole without having a meaning forced on it from without, in particular not from a putative knowledge of artistic intent. In the absence of any rule of unification, imagination produces a partial understanding of how a work's attributes cohere with a certain expressive trajectory. As a sublime reflection, interpretation of a work must always fall short of the completed, unified understanding reason demands. Sublime reflection offers partial new insight into what defies our total comprehension, and it delivers those insights in the form of interpretive networks of affinity, piecing diverse materials together into indeterminately expressive "un-wholes." When imagination construes the attributes of a work as an expressive complex of relationships, it makes a claim that its striving for unity has produced a view, which Kant calls an aesthetic idea, into a possible meaning of the work. The basis of validity for making such a claim lies in the cultivated regard for rational unity which sublime reflection freely emulates, and in affinity's transcendental pedigree.

Now, of course, as cases of paranoia make plain, it is altogether too easy to sense hidden affinities among widespread phenomena.[16] Just because sublime reflection induces someone to discern uncanny affinities and advocate their perspicacity does not mean that others will acknowledge any insight in that person's imaginative fancy. There must be more to warrant the demand that others accept the affinity of an imaginative construction than merely this intuition of connectedness. The expressive relation of aesthetic attributes to rational ideas indicates that the network of affinity that imagination constructs must fulfill a *disclosive* function: aesthetic unity must illuminate the ideas brought into play by this network. The value of an aesthetic idea will largely lie in the extent to which it enhances our understanding of the thematic attributes it relates. The affinity it discloses between apparently unrelated things must fulfill some explanatory or interpretive aim that makes it useful to others. Only the cumulative acclamation of others who find the connections made by an aesthetic idea instructive can strengthen its claim to validity. So for example, a metaphor like "time is money," which does structure our beliefs and actions, will have meaning for people, whereas "time is cheddar" will not. The disclosive power of aesthetic ideas shows that, though logically prior to full-fledged cognitive judgments, they fulfill a truth-telling function by which the value of particular products of sublime reflection can be assessed. The paranoid's disclosure of a conspiratorial system of affinities will fail this test of aesthetic validity when it proves unilluminating to others.

The disclosive function of aesthetic ideas indicates that the affinities they produce must be distinguished from a merely arbitrary play of association. It is *productive* imagination that pursues this connective activity, whereas Kant locates the laws of empirical association in the merely reproductive imagination. Again praising the productive imagination in its creation of aesthetic ideas, Kant writes that "In this process we feel our freedom from the law of association (which attaches to the empirical use of the imagination); for although it is under that law that nature lends us material, yet we can process that material into something quite different, namely, into something that surpasses nature" (CJ 314).[17] What happens in construction of an aesthetic idea is a process of "association" that does not randomly toss together just anything; instead, this connective reflection creates a compelling precedent for relating things whose connection had before been concealed (or nonexistent). Empirical imagination merely associates phenomena under the guidance of memory and repetitive experience; it cannot demand that others follow or adhere to its personal, idiosyncratic associations. Productive imagination, on the other hand, surpasses experience by connecting things that had been taken to be unrelated. And in doing so this reflection makes a demand for agreement that others recognize the perspicacity of the affinities it has disclosed. In part II we will learn from Hegel's philosophy of mind and his aesthetic theory that the relationship of sublime reflection to empirical (or contingent) association is more complex than we can presently formulate. In the Interlude between parts II and III, I will contrast the relational play of sublime reflection with the role of the association of ideas in British and Scottish empiricist aesthetic theory.

So far we have considered the transcendental basis of the validity claims made by aesthetic reflection. The intuition of indeterminate unity in a beautiful form, and the expression of relational coherence in aesthetic ideas both appeal to transcendental affinity as the pre-conceptual ground of purposive design. Now, Kant's categories of the understanding, as a *transcendental* basis for cognition, can account for how I can experience objects at all, but they cannot account for the empirical details of why I am experiencing one object, this keyboard, rather than some other. Similarly, the role of a priori affinity in founding the possibility of aesthetic reflection provides no account of why some associative play, some imaginative networks of relation "work," and some do not. For example, using the case of metaphor again, affinity as a transcendental basis for aesthetic validity can account for the very possibility of metaphor, but it cannot explain why "time is money" works and "time is cheddar" does not. Transcendental affinity ultimately provides only a *formal* measure of the preconceptual basis to which aesthetic reflection appeals. Put another way, transcendental affinity justifies the practice of inventing sense-making patterns of relation, but it can provide no guidelines for which products of this practice will achieve an intersubjectively shared validation.

This fact is most evident in sublime reflection's production of the relational, aesthetic unity of interpreted meanings. The case of paranoid delusion reminds us that associative play can all too easily discern networks of relation and concealed symbolic orders in anything. These felt affinities can assume all the rich articulation of formally plausible interpretations (to the extent that they are internally consistent), but whether they or any other interpretive construction of affinity will meet with intersubjective agreement is an *empirical* and *ideological* question. What it seems appropriate to relate, and how it seems appropriate to relate it, will depend on the culturally variable assumptions of interpreters. In the case of art specifically, the range of attributes thought relevant to aesthetic reflection is the product of cultural traditions and social practices, histories of aesthetic theory and art criticism, struggles over limiting or expanding artistic categories, conflicts of taste within and across social groups, and so forth. The possible diversity of response built into the boundlessness of sublime reflection reveals the empirical dimension of affinity in the variable attributes different subjects will take as relevant to construing the significance of a work. What affine networks of interpretive reflection will find a sympathetic ear at any given time will depend on what given interpreters are prepared to see, and on how those interpreters have been prepared to make their takes. Just as Kant would have it, there can be no rules for predicting taste, much less for what we will find sublime. Insofar as the sublimity of an interpretation lies in its power to pave avenues of revelation unthought by previously given categories, its productivity always exceeds the reach of established rules.

Part III will further explore the inevitable empirical component of the intersubjectively meaningful patterns of affinity sublime reflection claims to disclose. We will see that although it does not entirely undermine the validity claim of sublime reflection, this empirically "local" dimension does limit what universality, what extent of agreement, sublime understanding can hope for its interpretive products.[18]

I have extrapolated from Kant's aesthetic theory a sublime reflection that produces disunified structures of affinity. Instead of ordering like particulars in a hierarchy of subsumption, these webs disclose telling connections among an array of diverse particulars. This kind of reflective act is the play of a productive imagination that casts a net of sensemaking relations over that which exceeds our conceptual grasp. Imagination's perpetual failure of determinate comprehension, and its frustrated yet exhilarated expression of aesthetic ideas, reflects the aesthetics of sublimity in which I have construed Kant to have positioned our interpretive responses to art. When imagination responds to the uncanny sublimity of art, it manages at best a partial and disunified take on what a work means. But it will turn out that the vague sense for the whole that it does accomplish offers a kind of understanding unavailable to determinate cognition. To develop this aesthetics of sublimity further, and to reveal the sublime understanding it engenders, we need to explore the rich incarnation of imaginative reflection to be found in Hegel's system. Often despite himself, Hegel will help us to better understand the meaning-giving play of sublime reflection and its responses to both art and our shared worlds.

Interlude: Turning to Hegel

The philosophical revolution launched by Hegel in response to Kant is, of course, complicated. The complexity derives, in part, from the variety of intervening figures—Fichte and Schelling, Hamann and Schiller—who helped precipitate Hegel's transformation of the critical philosophy. It also derives from the fact that Hegel's "dialogue" with Kant lasted decades and affected most every feature of his work. I can hardly offer here a thorough evolutionary history of German "idealism," nor can I treat in detail the many facets of Hegel's adoption, rejection, and profound transformation (to mimic a familiar Hegelian structure) of Kant's perspective. We can begin to discern those elemental differences in Hegel's views most relevant to this study—his reworkings of imagination, reason, and aesthetic experience—by considering the brief critique of Kant that Hegel gives in his introduction to the *Lectures on Aesthetics*. Hegel praises Kant for recognizing "the absoluteness of reason in itself" because Kant conceived reason as a power to think the totality.[1] Kantian reason can *think* of totality as a regulative idea for organizing experience, but it cannot accomplish the totality of an exhibited system of experience. So, according to Hegel, Kant failed to think this idea through because he "fell back again into the fixed opposition between subjective thinking and objective things" (ibid.).

Hegel aims to radicalize reason by showing its power, in his construction of an encyclopedic system, to unify everything of significance that leads up to and gives shape to his time. Hegelian reason will achieve what Kant's could only dream of once he had granted reason only an inner dominion and trapped it within a competition of subjective faculties. This left him, according to Hegel, "with no alternative but to express the unity purely in the form of subjective Ideas of Reason, for which no adequate reality could be demonstrated . . . [and] whose essential inner character remained unknowable by thinking" (LFA 57; 13:84). Hegel thinks a primary obstacle to fulfilling reason's thought of totality is Kant's tendency to separate the subjective and objective into irreconcilable domains, each of which must retreat onto separate transcendental ground, namely the noumenal subject and the thing-in-itself. Kant only postulated their unity "in what he called the *intuitive understanding*," which would dissolve the opposition of thought and reality; but Kant "makes this dissolution and reconciliation itself into a purely *subjective* one again, not one absolutely true and actual," because Kant denies that such an understanding could belong to us (LFA 57; 13:84–85). Hegel intends to overcome this opposition by advancing his systematic Concept as a locus of absolute unity *achieved* by reason, a unity in which subject and object, thought and reality, can commingle and recall their matrimony.

Kant certainly did posit the notion of an intuitive understanding as a heuristic *contrast* to the kind of understanding a discursive human intellect can have. As he characterized it in the *Critique of Pure Reason*, intuitive understanding would be "original," indeed "divine," an understanding "through whose presentation the objects of this presentation would at the same time exist" (CPR B72, 145, 139). Human understanding synthesizes material it receives through a sensible intuition distinct from its conceptualizing powers, while the intuition of this divine understanding is itself intellectual: it would produce objects in their sensible existence in the very act of thinking them. The concepts of a discursive understanding, whether empirical or categorial, must apply to the cognition of intuited material; they do not originate an intuition of their own. As Kant argues in the *Critique of Judgment*, the very fact that we can conceive an intuitive understanding as a mere possibility hangs on the discursive nature of the human intellect, because the very notions of possibility and actuality are artifacts of our limited understanding. For an intuitive understanding, which intuits the actuality of whatever it thinks, there can be no distinction between possibility and actuality, as is reflected in the ancient tradition of conceiving God as pure actuality (CJ 401–403). And further, Kant's entire conception of reflective judgment indicates the challenges facing a discursive understanding, which must strive to make unified conceptual sense of the diversity of the particular. It is an empirical question whether we humans will make any (limited) progress toward that goal, while an intellectual intuition *immediately* thinks the totality as an existing system: "Such an understanding as well as its presentation of the whole has no *contingency* in the combination of the parts in order to make a determinate form of the whole possible" (CJ 407). So for Kant the intellectual intuition of a postulated intuitive understanding "lies absolutely outside our cognitive power," and this conclusion reflects the whole tenor of the critical philosophy, in that it guarantees that "the use of the categories can likewise in no way extend beyond the boundary of objects of experience" (CPR B308).

Hegel was hardly so averse to the notion of an intuitive intellect. From his earliest published writings, particularly in the essay *Glauben und Wissen* that appeared in Hegel and Schelling's *Critical Journal* in 1803, Hegel forged a link between an absolute power of reason and imaginative intuition. He in fact claims, as he will claim again in the *Encyclopedia*, that "the imagination is nothing but Reason itself . . . , [though] it is only Reason as it appears in the sphere of empirical consciousness."[2] Hegel goes even further when he claims that Kantian productive imagination leads to the kind of intuition of rational unity which Kant attributes to intellectual intuition: "The Idea of this archetypal intuitive intellect is at bottom nothing else but that same Idea of the transcendental imagination that we considered above. For it is intuitive activity, and yet its inner unity is no other than the unity of the intellect itself, the category immersed in extension, and becoming intellect and category only as it separates itself out of extension. Thus transcendental imagination is itself intuitive intellect."[3] Like Kant, who granted imagination's intuitions a constitutive role in empirical experience, Hegel will also emphasize imagination's allegiance to cognition. But Hegel goes much further by attributing powers to imagination that cooperate with reason in overcoming the very distinctions between the empirical and the rational which Kant reified. Both imagination and reason, traditionally opposed as intuitive and intellectual powers, will contribute to the presentation of an intuitive intellect's systematic unity, at least once history's narrative has brought their full powers to fruition. We will see that the role Hegel grants to imagination in *presenting the unified idea* has crucial implications for his aesthetic theory and the place of the sublime in it, as well as for my approach to his work. His radicalization of reason's power to unify the particular in a necessary system will be matched by his racheting up the productivity of artistic imagination into a power to present determinate unities in sensuous form.[4]

In addition to his valorization of imagination as an ally of reason, as early as *Faith and Knowledge* Hegel also singles out Kant's notion of reflective judgment for special praise. Hegel describes it as "the most interesting point in the Kantian system, the point at which a region is recognized that is a middle between the empirical manifold and the absolute abstract unity. But once again, it is not a region accessible to cognition. Only the aspect in which it is appearance is called forth, and not its ground which is Reason."[5] For Kant, reflective imagination can only sense a totality beyond its reach, a totality it cannot cognize and exhibit. As we saw in part I, Kantian imagination presents, in its failure to exhibit a rational unity, an expressive aesthetic unity of a less determinative sort. But Hegel's appropriation of Kantian reflective judgment, in keeping with his radicalization of absolute reason and his alliance of imagination with it, renders the products of this judgment *unified determinations of the particular.* John McCumber has argued that the constructive method of Hegel's systematic philosophy, and the constant generation of new general truths in Hegelian narrative, indicates a *"massive appropriation from Kant"* of the doctrine of reflective judgment.[6] On such a view, one can regard the development of Hegel's encyclopedic system as a great exercise in reflective judgment in which the particularity of human experiences and conceptual distinctions are brought into unified, organic relation.[7]

Hegel remains true to these ideas much later in his career. In the early sections of the *Encyclopedia of the Philosophical Sciences* (1830) he again links reflective judgment and the idea of an intuitive intellect, though in a way that reflects his own appropriation of them. In his *Encyclopedia Logic* discussion of the Critical Philosophy, he writes: "The principle of an *intuitive understanding* is ascribed to the *reflecting faculty of judgment*, i.e., an understanding in which the *particular*, which is *contingent* for the *universal* (the abstract identity) and cannot be deduced from it, would be determined through this universal itself; and this is experienced in the products of *art* and of *organic* nature."[8] Kant, of course, did not attribute a power of intellectual intuition to any part of human subjectivity. When Hegel links reflective judgment with a power to intuit totality he reveals his intention to hold that the imaginative products of such reflection present the Idea in sensuous form. We must be careful to recognize that in Hegel's appropriation of reflective judgment, the demonstrative activity of imagination and reason determinately presents the content of the systematic Idea. Unlike Kantian reflective judgment, which only anticipates rational totality without getting it, Hegelian "reflective judgment" unites intuition and thought in the organic whole of the Idea expressed in Hegel's encyclopedic system. Hegel thinks that the play of reflection in Kant's third *Critique* offers an intimation of what his own system brings to fulfillment. Even though Kant maintains that rational ideas cannot be exhibited in intuition, Kant points the way (against the grain of his own thought) to Hegel's Idea of a rational totality in the products of aesthetic and teleological reflection.[9] Hegel claims that even if Kant refuses the actualized Ideal of reason, "the *presence* of living organisations and of artistic beauty shows the *actuality* of the *Ideal* even for the senses and for intuition. That is why Kant's reflections about these objects were particularly well adapted to introduce consciousness to the grasping and thinking of the *concrete* Idea."[10] Beauty will be, for Hegel, one concrete form the Idea takes, and his system another. Chapter 6 will provide a detailed look at Hegel's account of beauty as the sensuous appearance of the Idea.

For the moment we need only take the indications of Hegel's opportunistic response to Kant that he gives in the introduction to his *Lectures on Aesthetics*.[11] We saw that in Kant's case aesthetic imagination judges without the aid of a concept, and that this lack of determination frees imagination to construct the network of relations found in aesthetic unity. Hegel, however, interprets Kantian aesthetic judgment in a way that *attributes a determinate concept to beauty*: "The beautiful [for Kant] . . . is to invoke a universal pleasure directly without any such relation [of correspondence to universal concepts]. This only means that, in considering the beautiful, we are unaware of the concept and subsumption under it, and that the separation between the individual object and the universal concept, which elsewhere is present in judgment, is impermissible here" (LFA 58–59; 13:86–87). Where Kant took subsumption under concepts to be the feature critically *absent* from aesthetic judgment, Hegel finds the interpenetration of a work and its determinate concept or animating theme. A work of art is for Hegel so unified with its theme that we cannot distinguish the presentation from what it presents; nevertheless, it presents an organically unified content with a determinateness wholly alien to Kant's view. Hegel's gloss on Kant here says much more about Hegel's view than about Kant's. And again, in his discussion of the role of purposiveness in Kant's aesthetic theory, Hegel blends aesthetic and teleological judgment in a way that attributes determinate purposes to beauty: "Any natural product, a plant, for example, or an animal, is purposefully organized, and in this purposiveness it is so directly there for us that we have no idea of its purpose explicitly separate and distinct from its present reality. In this way the beautiful too is to appear to us as purposiveness" (LFA 59; 13:87). We saw in chapter 1 that Kant thought that aesthetic objects fulfill only some features of the purposiveness of natural purposes, and that this indeterminate purposiveness of the beautiful is what allows it to support the free play of productive imagination. For Kant, an object of aesthetic reflection, however purposive in its stimulation of reflective judgment, cannot be taken to embody a determinate purpose because it cannot be determined by a concept. But for Hegel, who takes reflective judgment to construct rational unities, aesthetic objects express the determinate content of their concept or theme, and find their purpose fulfilled in determinately expressing that concept.

In short, Hegel's summation of Kant's aesthetic theory in the *Lectures on Aesthetics* provides instead a vision of Hegel's own theory: "Thus Kant sees the beauty of *art* after all as a correspondence in which the particular itself accords with the concept" (LFA 60; 13:88). But Kant saw the beautiful to accord only with the *power* of concepts, not with a particular concept; this indeterminacy remains the case even for my interpretation of Kant, in which the content of a work of art is best approached through sublime reflection. The accordance of particular and determinate universal that Hegel discerns in Kant's aesthetics exists, in fact, exclusively in Hegel's. He does finally concede that Kant falls short of Hegel's interpretation of him: "But this apparently perfect reconciliation is still supposed [by Kant] at the last to be only subjective in respect of the judgment and the production [of art], and not itself to be absolutely true and actual" (LFA 60; 13:88–89). The "subjectivity" of aesthetic judgment, its reference to felt rather than objective conditions, accounts for why Kant separates beauty from the cognition of determinate concepts and purposes. With Hegel all of this changes, and the beauty of art becomes a means for sensuously exhibiting determinate thematic unities.

It will be helpful to illustrate this radical change by looking at Hegel's response to the Kantian doctrine of aesthetic ideas. To a large extent, Kant's aesthetic idea is an artifact of his contention that ideas of reason cannot be exhibited in intuition. The aesthetic idea serves as an intuitional counterpart to rational ideas in that they expressively intimate rational ideas without attaining their systematic unity. Because Hegel expects art to achieve a sensuous expression of the Idea as a rational whole, one can imagine that the aesthetic idea does not fare well in his account. As early as *Faith and Knowledge*, Hegel opposed Kant's unbridgeable gap between aesthetic and rational ideas. Referring to Kant's contrastive definition of the two, for which no concept can be adequate to the intuition of an aesthetic idea, and no intuition can be adequate to demonstrate an Idea of reason, Hegel pithily responds: "As if the esthetic Idea did not have its exposition in the Idea of Reason, and the Idea of Reason did not have its demonstration in beauty." By maintaining a gap between aesthetic and rational ideas, Hegel argues, Kant fails to seek "an intuition of the absolute identity of the sensuous and the supersensuous. . . ."[12] Hegel takes this intuition, and its elevation to thought, to be the final end of reason, once reason has been unchained, that is, from the shackles of Kant's faculty-oriented subjectivism.

For Hegel, there can be no gap between aesthetic and rational ideas. His conception of beauty as intuition of the Idea cannot allow intuitions to express rational ideas in Kant's merely indeterminate fashion: "Since beauty is the Idea as experienced or more correctly, as intuited, the form of opposition between intuition and concept falls away."[13] In that their opposition falls away, the thematic Idea expressed in art is for Hegel both aesthetic and rational, intuitive and intellectual, sensuous and supersensuous, at once. Hence the Idea presented in the beauty of a coherent theme will *not* assume for Hegel the form of a Kantian aesthetic idea.[14] The content of an Hegelian artistic Idea will possess the determinacy and organic unity of a product of reason for which the place of every part is determined in the whole, whereas Kant's aesthetic idea falls short of such unity and achieves only a loose network of relations between its parts.

Thus Kant's aesthetic idea has no place in Hegel's theory. In the process of collapsing the opposition of aesthetic and rational ideas, Hegel rejects the loose connections forged by the former in favor of the latter's expression of achieved organic unity. This position accords with Hegel's radicalization of reflective judgment, and by the time of the *Encyclopedia* he will briefly refer to Kant's doctrine of the aesthetic idea as an example of his predecessor's underestimation of reason and imagination's powers of reflection.[15] John McCumber notes Hegel's rejection of the aesthetic idea and relates this to the way Hegel reorients reflective judgment toward the production of systematically ordered ideas: "The key to the nature of reflective judgment thus does not reside for Hegel in its lack of concepts but in what Kant would call its purposiveness: the attribution to experience of a guiding center (in a work of art, of its guiding conception) which organizes that object over time and does not apply to any other."[16] As we saw above, Hegel's artwork has a guiding conception, its Idea, which organizes its content as an organic whole. By emphasizing the guided purposiveness of art Hegel attributes a teleology to products of reflective judgment, products that come to have a definite purpose and determinate conceptual content alien to Kant's aesthetic idea. Hegel replaces Kantian aesthetic reflection's production of an affine network resistant to conceptual determination with a reflection that produces identity between a concept and its sensuous appearance.[17]

We have seen that in Kantian sublime reflection, imagination produces a network of relations in the partial interpretive unity of an aesthetic idea. This affiliation between aesthetic ideas and sublimity suggests that Hegel's rejection of the former does not bode well for his view of the latter. In a Kantian experience of the sublime, imagination is unable to comprehend as a unity the multiplicity of parts on which it reflects. This overwhelming of an imagination without unity in its comprehension conflicts with the dominant notion of Hegel's aesthetic theory, that beauty is the sensuous presentation of thematic unity in the Idea. The organic wholeness of Hegel's beauty leaves little room for the decentered confusion of the sublime. And in fact, in the introduction to his *Lectures on Aesthetics* Hegel summarizes what he takes to be the "chief results" of Kant's third *Critique* without mentioning the sublime at all (LFA 83–89; 13:56–61).[18]

One might suggest that none of these developments bodes well for finding in Hegel the sort of indeterminate, sublime reflection we discerned in Kant's third *Critique*. The flower of that reflection, on my view, is a Kantian aesthetic idea, and Hegel rejects that doctrine. Hegel's conviction that "reflective judgment" can produce systematic conceptual unity opposes the search for a nonsystematizing imaginative reflection whose products defy conceptualization. Nevertheless, part II will contend that by adopting a certain interpretive strategy toward Hegel's system, one can locate features of Hegel's accounts of imagination and aesthetic response that amplify a Kantian aesthetics of sublimity. Against the grain of Hegel's systematic thought, this approach will illuminate a reflective locus of nonconceptual and nonsystematic aesthetic unity and validity at a certain mid-level stratum of his system. Chapter 5 will pursue this aim in Hegel's *Encyclopedia* theory of imagination, while chapters 6 and 7 will take up the rich articulation of art in his *Lectures on Aesthetics*.

Throughout his *Encyclopedia* system, Hegel aims to consummate reason's grasp of totality by constructing an organic unity to house and interrelate the fruits of Western thought. Hegel's system seeks to demonstrate the achievement of such a reason as the finest outcome of that culture and its history. For the purposes of this study, whether Hegel succeeds in this project is irrelevant. The systematic end of Hegel's philosophy will not bear on my appropriation of it, though constant vigilance will be required to steer clear of his orientation toward achieved totality. Hegel's system culminates in what he takes to be the highest forms of reason's unification of thought and world, namely art, religion, and philosophy. But he also seeks to narrate spirit's arrival at these perfections, starting from its most humble origins. For example, the third part of the *Encyclopedia of the Philosophical Sciences,* the *Philosophy of Mind,* recounts the growth of rational cognition from its first stirrings in the contingency and unfreedom of what Hegel calls the natural soul. Human spirit for Hegel does not realize its powers easily, much less eternally, but must struggle to gather itself out of its murky natural origins. Thus the *Encyclopedia* "Anthropology," the first part of the *Philosophy of Mind,* recounts soul's effort to save itself from natural contingency and such irrational phenomena as clairvoyance and madness.

That is, not every moment of Hegel's system depicts reason's triumph, even though reason's thought of totality will, in the end, prevail. So in the *Lectures on Aesthetics,* Hegel sees the perfected expression of beauty in a classical Ideal, but this achievement is preceded and followed by forms of art that fall short of expressing the Idea. And Hegelian reason does not simply leave behind the less sophisticated or even decrepit moments of its early development. As an organic unity, all the phenomena Hegel treats remain indispensable parts of the whole. As we will see in chapter 5, early features of mind's development continue to shape it well beyond their inception. By the end of his *Philosophy of Mind,* Hegel's conception of imagination has become so implicated in the systematizing destination of rational cognition that one might forget its lowly origins. But the habits Hegel's mind learns early do not cease to inform it as it grows to maturity. They just prove unhelpful for mind's mature effort to consummate its rational powers. By recalling features of Hegelian imagination that precede its integration into reason's systematic aims, and by focusing on moments in Hegel's aesthetic theory where artistic production fails to intuit the Idea, we can construct an account of imaginative reflection distinct from the systematizing cognition at which Hegel ultimately arrives. Hegel takes aesthetic imagination to achieve determinate expression of concepts. But not all the time: when it does not, we may discern another level of reflection at work, perhaps not as grand as thinking the totality, but for the purposes of this inquiry into the aesthetics of sublimity, a more interesting one.

I will study Hegel's *Encyclopedia* account of imagination in order to detail the aesthetically reflective powers it employs in the *Lectures on Aesthetics,* where he says less about imagination. In Kant's case, we had to distinguish carefully the schematic, cognitive functions of imagination from its nonconceptual aesthetic activity. Similarly with Hegel, the ultimately cognitive mission of imagination in the *Encyclopedia*, which for Hegel means its allegiance to reason's aims, will require us to distinguish carefully imagination's powers from their systematic employment. In Hegel's case, we can steer imagination clear of a systematic goal by recalling early features of its development, which Hegel deemphasizes in the end, but which remain among its powers and will contribute to a reflection not allied to reason's achievement of system. With this account of imagination in hand, we can study those artistic products that also fall short of a rational Ideal. By seeing these lesser art forms as the works of an imagination marked by early features of Hegel's conception of it, we can unearth an account of connective sublime reflection that will extend what we first discerned in Kant's work.

Note that nothing about this strategy denies the systematic aim of Hegel's work, nor does it question whether Hegel accomplishes that aim. The strategy betrays only an interest in a lesser stratum of Hegel's system, where he discusses phenomena that pose obstacles to the development of reason's systematizing powers. My interpretation of Hegel's system follows a path away from his systematic philosophy by concentrating on features of it that contribute little to reason's ultimate aim. But my interpretation attempts neither to "refute" Hegel's system nor even to concern itself with issues of refutation. As was indicated in the introduction, this study aims to develop a certain "Kant-inspired" aesthetic perspective. It turns out that features of Hegel's mature *Encyclopedia* system elaborate on ideas relevant to a Kantian aesthetics of sublimity at levels of that system's development prior to the reconciling satisfactions of Hegel's Absolute Idea. Given the orientation of this study, Hegel can profoundly contribute to articulation of a sublime reflection, and the aim of part II is to recover from the midst of Hegel's system his "inadvertent" supplementation of Kantian aesthetic indeterminacy. Because I take this approach, Hegel's own systematic concerns are thoroughly suspended or deferred here. My interpretation seeks to make a "conscientious" use of Hegel in that it takes pains to engage his system in the fine grain of its detail; but my purposes are alien to Hegel's, and this study no more pretends to debunk Hegelian systematicity than it pretends to do justice to Hegel's ownmost intentions. Instead, my interpretation "mines" Hegel's aesthetics in two senses: it mines the veins of Hegel's thought that can be put to building a Kant-inspired conception of a sublime understanding, and it thereby makes his aesthetic theory "mine" by steering it toward my ends.[19]

What my approach does betray is a commitment to the indeterminacy that is central to Kant's conception of the aesthetic, but is only marginal to Hegel's. I will argue in chapter 6 that the cognitive unity and determinacy of Hegel's "classical" Ideal of Beauty rests on the unity of an Ideal social world. If the art of the last century has had any consistent theme, it has been rather the disunity and fragmentation of social life and the multiplication of contrary perspectives. The diversity of our contemporary narrative self-understandings, our critical suspicions about the political dimension of knowledge, our feeling of hurtling into a very uncertain future—our "form of life" calls for an aesthetics of sublime indeterminacy, rather than an Hegelian cognitivist appropriation of the aesthetic, and it is really no wonder that the sublime has become so fashionable. My elaboration of sublime understanding in part III will indicate that embracing, along with Kant, the indeterminacy of aesthetic experience allows us to preserve a notion of aesthetic validity Other than the cognitive. It allows us to conceive the aesthetic as a source of lived interpretive understanding as fundamental to our sense-making practices as more determinate cognitions.

We will see that Hegel does discuss the sublime in his *Lectures,* and that it occupies precisely one of those "moments of failure" that will have central importance for my interpretation. But in addition to his explicit discussion of sublimity, we will find, even in the *Encyclopedia Philosophy of Mind,* that moments of sublimity surface repeatedly at the interstices of Hegel's theory where imagination acquires and exercises its various powers. In both the *Encyclopedia* and the *Lectures* we must pay close attention to indications of struggle with the sublime, for where imagination fails to present determinate unity lies the promise of locating in Hegel the conceptually transgressive products of a sublime understanding.[20]

II

Mining Hegel's Aesthetics

5

Constructing Hegel's Imagination

We find it natural to associate, at least in daily parlance, madness and the inspired productivity of artistic genius. When we do, "imagination" plays a vital role in securing the connection, for we think of that power ambivalently as a source of creative invention that can also, unleashed, lure us into a den of phantasms. We fancy imagination to be the wellspring of the communicative power of art, but that same power threatens in madness to sever those under its sway from the human community. A Van Gogh or a Nietzsche exemplifies for European culture the sometimes thin line between genius and madness. The membrane between them is porous because we construe both as products of a kind of organic excess, and because both madness and ingenuity violate our accepted norms. In terms of the violence they do to received patterns of thought and habits of acting, the most salient difference between madness and ingenuity may be that the inspired artist (or philosopher) manages to build new intersubjective norms, new visions of intelligibility to revise the old. The mad person, like the paranoiac, lacks a shareable vision. The fascination of Nietzsche or Van Gogh is that imagination made them both communicatively ingenious and solipsistically mad.

Madness and imagination are linked to artistry in the "Psychology" Hegel advances in the third division of his *Encyclopedia of the Philosophical Sciences* (1830), though it takes some work to see this. My aim here is to do that work and to show, more specifically, the central role the notion of "habituation" plays in Hegel's close relating of madness, imagination, and art. It will turn out that Hegel's interweaving of these four notions must be understood against the background of his critique and transformative appropriation of the doctrine of the association of ideas, which he begrudgingly inherited from the eighteenth-century empiricists. To map this conceptual structure I will consider in this chapter (1) Hegel's account of the origins of madness in the "soul" of his *Encyclopedia* "Anthropology"; (2) his characterization of madness and his notion of habit formation as its cure; (3) the origin of key imaginative powers in habit formation; and (4) Hegel's full account of imagination in the *Encyclopedia* "Psychology."

We will see that Hegelian imagination begins to appear in the *Encyclopedia* first as a purely arbitrary and potentially maddening play of association, then as an empiricist-inspired, associative power of habit formation. Hegel's "full-grown" version of imagination as a determinately cognitive power will build normative habits of thinking in the form of abstract concepts or categories. This concept-formative imagination will exemplify Hegel's radicalization of the Kantian doctrine of reflective judgment; unlike Kant's aesthetically reflective imagination, Hegel's reflective imagination will project conceptual *determinacy*. But we will see in chapter 6 that Hegelian imagination, as a power of ingenious artistry has, in the end, a "de-habituating function" by virtue of the way it draws on its primordial resources of mad inspiration to surpass habitual patterns of thinking. Hegel's imagination will be both a source of "sober" and customary cognitive categories and a playful transgressor of those habits. By the close of part II I will have identified those moments in Hegel's aesthetic theory where imagination dehabituates not only our sense of what is "natural" or "given" in our ways of thinking, but also our very confidence in conceptual determinacy. In those moments will I locate the alternative productivity of a sublime understanding.

Madness Originates in the Feeling Soul

A proper understanding of Hegelian imagination, artistic and otherwise, requires tracing its origins from the earliest formation of mind in the *Encyclopedia*. Hegel treats those beginnings as the birth of human soul. Consideration of that category will not only allow us entrée to Hegel's treatment of madness; it will also clarify the formation of those imaginative capacities that Hegel deemphasizes in his later account. Hegel locates the soul at the beginnings of his *Encyclopedia* "Anthropology" in a narrative of cognitive development that treats traditional categories of mental capacity as stages in the natural fruition of our most advanced powers of reason. He begins his account with the notion of "soul" as that in which the first "*awaking* [n.b.] of *Consciousness*" out of the sleep of mere material nature occurs.[1] Soul comes into being as the simple starting-point of an emergent consciousness when nature surpasses its particularized corporeality by realizing a universal interiority as its other. The birth of soul "means that Nature itself sublates its own inadequacy to truth: it means that Mind presupposes itself no longer as the universality which in corporeal individuality is always self-externalized, but as a universality which in its concretion and totality is one and simple. At such a stage it is not yet mind, but *soul*" (PM §388, 29/43).[2] Nature takes on soul when nature opposes itself to its material existence, when it separates its universality from the ubiquity of its matter and so makes possible the creation of a universe of subjectivity and thought. Hegel construes soul as a sort of Aristotelian "prime matter," the original stuff from which all the features of mind will be crafted (PM §389, 29/43). As such soul is at first practically devoid of qualities, and is only an extremely plastic capacity for transformation. Out of soul will unfold every ability of mind: feeling, perception, imagination, and reason. But in the beginning soul proffers only a site for the development of immaterial universality, a counterpoint to nature. Indeed, the soul begins with so little differentiation that it requires eight paragraphs of development into the "Anthropology" for it to reach, in paragraph 395, the determinacy of individual souls. Only at that point can we begin to speak of the souls of individual subjects (though they are far from yet having a subjectivity).

Though soul begins as a breeding ground for universality, Hegel sees in its breakup into individuals a loss of universality that makes them subject to the vicissitudes of nature: "The soul is further de-universalized into the individualized subject. But this subjectivity is here only considered as a differentiation and singling out of the modes which nature gives," that is, it has not yet the free subjectivity of consciousness where the universal will be recovered (PM §395, 51/70).

This *natural subjectivity* of the individual soul means that its entire content derives from what just happens to affect it from without. The difference between individual souls comes only from what contingencies of immediate nature have happened to pass through them and left some mark. The content of the soul of natural subjectivity is arbitrary and circumstantial, because the soul does not yet give any law of its own to its character: "This *natural* subjectivity is not as yet a self-determining one following its own laws and acting according to necessity, but a subjectivity determined from outside, tied to *this* space and *this* time and dependent on contingent circumstances" (PM §400 Zu, 75/100). Only by ordering itself into a structured whole common, at least in its fundamentals, to all subjects will the soul achieve a degree of necessity with which to oppose natural contingency and with which to recuperate its status as universal.

As noted earlier, Hegel uses the metaphor of waking to characterize the birth of soul from material nature. He further expands this metaphor when the individual soul achieves its next stage of determination by distinguishing itself from its natural circumstantial content. By paragraph 398 the soul has awakened, or been born, again, and from its new perspective it seems, in its former state of submission to natural contingency, to have been asleep: "The distinction of individuality, as a *being for itself*, from its *mere* being, this immediate judgment is the *waking* of the soul, which confronts its self-absorbed natural life, in the first instance, as one natural quality and state confronts another state, viz. *sleep*" (PM §398, 65/87).[3] Soul has awakened to its power to differentiate itself into moments, into components, as it will later divide itself into powers and capacities. Thus Hegel construes the waking of soul as the acquisition of judgment: the waking "is itself the *judgment* [*Urteil*: primary partition] of the individual soul—which is self-existing only as it relates its self-existence to its mere existence, distinguishing itself from its still undifferentiated universality" (ibid.). The capacity for judgment originates the long struggle of soul to overcome its contingency and natural subjectivity. The differentiating activity of judgment will produce a multiplicity of moments in the soul. Unlike the welter of "contingent modifications" that trouble the sleep of natural subjectivity, however, judgment produces differences that make a difference: judgment distinguishes parts that will come to comprise the key features of a whole subjectivity.

Hegel distinguishes these sleeping and waking states of soul in terms of the ordering of content prevalent in each. In the waking state we find a concrete interconnection of phenomena that makes of experience and personality a unity. Waking consciousness appears as "a concrete totality of features in which each member, each point, takes up its place as at the same time determined through and with all the rest" (PM §398 An, 66/88). Not only will all the moments of the waking soul fit together as a faceted whole, but each of its particulars will depend on the whole for its content and function. The soul of Hegel's "Anthropology" strives for, but has not accomplished such a full awareness and integration of itself. As we will see, only by forming habits will it wake up completely. For now, it seems that the awakening soul seeks from its earliest moments to make of itself the sort of organic unity prescribed by Kantian reflective judgment. Considering Hegel's emphasis on unification in the waking of consciousness, it should not surprise us that, later in the *Philosophy of Mind*, Hegel concedes that "in the notion of a power of *reflective* judgment [Kant] touches upon the *Idea* of Mind" (PM §415 An, 156/202). Kant only touches upon it, because reflective judgment's search for purposive unity never produces a systematized whole. Only with Hegel is reason's idea of totality in fact consummated. In any case, the waking of the soul will come more and more to be implicated for Hegel in a process of reflection which creates a systematically integrated unity of its parts.

For the soul asleep a quite different picture emerges. While the waking soul aims to become a holistically integrated organism, its poor cousin the sleeping soul wields a capricious power over its "picture[s] of mere ideas and images. . . ." It engages in a subjective picture-thinking in which the manifold "contingent modifications" of its content "are in the main only externally conjoined, in an unintelligent way, by the so-called laws of the so-called *Association of Ideas*; though here and there of course logical principles may also be operative" (PM §398 An, 66/88).[4] Given over to its natural content, the sleeping soul links together its ideas and images in a manner ranging from the insipid to the fantastic, with little regard for the sort of "concrete interconnection in which each part stands with all parts" sought by the waking soul. The sleeping soul *merely* associates its parts; and Hegel has little regard for the "so-called" laws of association, as he will emphasize again in the *Encyclopedia* "Psychology." Of course, for his eighteenth-century empiricist predecessors, from Locke to Hume and beyond, association had the status of a fundamental basis of mental life on which all our ideas are built. For Hume in particular, association is *the* means by which imagination builds up the complex ideas and cause-effect relationships on which custom or *habit* is based.[5] By positioning association as a primitive kind of subjectivity, something to be supplanted by more accomplished mental powers, Hegel expresses his disdain for this empiricist psychology. As we will see in more detail, however, the power of association remains active in the full development of Hegel's conception of imagination. I will argue that the sleeping and waking souls come to form the flip sides, the dual nature of that power. Imagination as agent of associative caprice, imagination as creator of a unified normative order: this dichotomy will become most pressing as we seek out a Hegelian imaginative power that produces the normativity of affine networks of relation which are neither capricious nor systematic in form.[6]

Hegel takes the soul that is both sleeping and awake, the soul that has made this first partition, to be a soul sufficiently cognizant to feel its content as its own. In awakening to the difference between itself and its sleeping substance, the soul looks upon its contingent modifications from a distance that cannot refute its attachment to those determinations. The soul feels the unity of its sleeping and waking states even as it separates them out; and it becomes in recognizing this unity a *feeling soul* (PM §404, 94/124). Just as in the birth of soul nature took on subjective inwardness, so in the waking of soul its sleeping substance becomes the content of its inner sensorium. This soul is not yet cognizant of a subject-object distinction, its sensations are not to its knowledge received from without. But soul is acquiring an interior that will become sophisticated enough to cognize objects external to it. The feeling soul needs "to raise its substantiality, its merely virtual filling-up, to the character of subjectivity, to take possession of it, to realize its mastery over its own" (PM §403, 92/122). As it wakes up further, it will construct from its inner substance the unity of a conscious subject.

But at present the soul is stuck in an intermediate stage. It has begun to make judgments of its own, but it cannot yet organize what it differentiates. The partitioning power of the judgment signals the emergence of an intelligence that will devise rules of order for its "given" substance, but this power is born into the soul's continued acquiescence in its contingent natural circumstance: "on the one hand, soul is still fettered by its substantiality, conditioned by its naturalness, while, on the other hand, it is beginning to separate itself from its substance, from its naturalness, and is thus raising itself to the intermediate stage between its immediate, natural life and objective, free consciousness" (PM §402 Zu, 89/118). This double nature of the feeling soul leads Hegel to construe it as the unity of sleeping and waking. Not only has soul awakened to judgment by dividing itself in two, but its two sides coalesce in that the waking soul discovers its own power to order its material from within the very sleeping substance on which it works. The soul that awakes was and still is the soul asleep, and what it wakes to formed first in the dreams of the latter. Thus Hegel writes that "the soul's abstract being-for-self in the waking state obtains its first fulfillment through the determinations which are ideally contained in the soul's sleeping nature, in the soul's substantial being" (PM §399 Zu, 72/96). It will become clear that no matter how far mind progresses, this early partition of the soul will continue to leave its mark: soul will become so wide awake as to achieve self-awareness, but the primordial soup of contingent association in its sleeping substance will not cease to nourish it. When making art especially, imagination will rely on that natural store of inspiration.

Hegel's treatment of the feeling soul as a unity of waking and sleeping states valorizes the contribution of the latter to the sustenance of the whole, and yet he regards this intermediate condition with some ambivalence. This waking sleep of the soul that feels gives rise to some of the most bizarre passages of the "Anthropology," and that in a work that rarely shies away from the bizarre. Due to its intermediacy, Hegel writes, "this stage of mind is the stage of its darkness" (PM §404 An, 94/124). The feeling soul lives under a shadow; it is "not yet as *its self*, not a true subject reflected into itself;" its loose grasp of itself means that "the individuality of its true self is a different subject from it—a subject which may even exist as another individual" (PM §405, 94/124). Hegel depicts a unity of the waking and sleeping souls, yet just as often the soul awake looms over its sleeping half as a vague apparition, an abstract construction alienated from its origins. The feeling soul in the person of its sleeping self can be made to sense its waking mind as an alien presence possessing it from without—rendering the soul subject to such phenomena as magical possession, clairvoyance, "magnetic somnambulism," and "animal magnetism" or hypnotism, all of which Hegel discusses at length.[7] Despite his initial analysis of the feeling soul as a unity of waking and sleeping parts, the soul that feels appears in the "Anthropology" primarily and most vividly as a soul at odds with itself, a soul in which the slumber of natural contingency vies with the waking order of things for control of a fragile mind.

Out of this volatile mixture of sleep and waking arises, in Hegel's narrative, the insanity of "dreaming while awake" in which soul must struggle to generate for itself an ordering of its content out of the dank nest of its natural subjectivity. In Hegel's account of insanity we will witness the waking soul's struggle to rein in the associative play of its sleep, and to regiment rogue elements of its substance that refuse to take part in the whole subjectivity it constructs. In the cure of insanity we will see a constructive process that fashions from a "hostile" multiplicity of parts a unifying network of determinate, stable relations.

Hegel's feeling soul is an *aesthetic* soul in the broad sense. And to survive insanity it depends on an *aesthetic reflection* to generate and stabilize the ties that will bind it together. But in keeping with Hegel's radicalized reflective judgment and his alliance of art with the comprehension of rational unity, this aesthetic soul will evolve into a subject committed to the waking destination of the determinate whole. As this chapter proceeds, we will discover that this reflective process to cure the soul's insanity provides the basis for Hegel's conception of imagination, in both its cognitive and aesthetic modes. In Hegel's genesis of mind, I will argue, the imaginative power is born out of saving the soul from madness.

Habituation Cures Madness

Hegel's soul has, by paragraph 407, begun to take on the contours of a proper subject, though it does not yet count as a consciousness employing a fixed subject-object distinction. Rather, soul has reached a state of subjective "self-feeling," an *aesthetic subjectivity* that exists as a process of self-differentiating judgment. The particularity of the soul arises from the unique array of things it feels within it: "The sensitive totality is, in its capacity as individual, essentially the tendency to distinguish itself in itself, and to wake up to the *judgment in itself*, in virtue of which it has *particular* feelings and stands as a *subject* in respect to these aspects of itself" (PM §407, 122/160). This soul senses its potential for self-possession, and out of its manifold feelings it will construct the unity of a conscious subject. But at this stage its content is still the welter of contingent modification given it by nature. As such the self-feeling soul is one "susceptible of disease" because its particular feelings are bound up in "the element of corporeality which is still undetached from the mental life" (PM §408, 122/161). Each moment of the soul's natural subjectivity may, in its arbitrary "willfulness," threaten the project of self-fashioning on which mind has embarked.

The power that particular moments of feeling now have in the soul makes possible its madness. Hegel takes the self-feeling soul to lose itself to insanity when it becomes possessed by or engrossed in a single fixed feeling or idea that defies integration into a unified subject:

The fully furnished self of intelligent consciousness is a conscious subject, which is consistent in itself according to an order and behavior which follows from its individual position and its connection with the external world, which is no less a world of law. But when it is engrossed with a single phase of feeling, it fails to assign that phase its proper place and due subordination in the individual system of the world which a conscious subject is. In this way the subject finds itself in contradiction between the totality systematized in its consciousness, and the single phase or fixed determination which is not reduced to its proper place and rank. This is Insanity. (PM §408, 123/161)

Hegel's formulation of the conflict that makes for madness—a conflict between a fixed phase of feeling and the "individual system" of a conscious subject—presents a problem which must be resolved for my interpretation to proceed. In blunt terms, the latter figure in this conflict, the "fully furnished self," does not at this stage of the soul's career exist; it has not yet been reached in the logical development of the text. Hegel's mind only attains the form of a systematized totality of experience, at the very earliest, late in the "Phenomenology of Mind" (PM §§413–439), that is, in the second subsection of the "Subjective Mind" section of the *Encyclopedia* "Philosophy of Mind." The soul that succumbs to madness, however, resides in the final moments of the "Anthropology," Subjective Mind's first subsection, and we will see that the full-fledged subject of the "Phenomenology" is in fact a *product* of the soul's recovery from madness. By casting the conflict of insanity as he does in §408, Hegel anticipates a formation of mind that will only arise to play such a part some twenty paragraphs later in the logical progression of his system.

Hegel admits as much in the *Anmerkung* to §408, where he states that "in considering insanity we must . . . anticipate the full-grown and intelligent conscious subject, which is at the same time the *natural* self of *self-feeling*" (PM §408 An, 123/161). The full-grown subject will still be for Hegel the self-feeling soul because, in Hegel's system, mind's progress to higher grades of development does not imply that it leaves behind its former selves. Mind's history accumulates, and it can on occasion be affected in its higher forms by what came before. This will be apparent, for example, in the way the associative thinking of the sleeping soul will recur as a feature of imagination's activity when that capacity finally arises in §455, fifty-seven paragraphs after the original partitioning of the soul into its waking and sleeping parts. Hegel *illustrates* the experience of insanity in the "Anthropology" by using features of mind that have not yet been treated at the point of those paragraphs. He does so because, of course, in experiential terms madness is a malady that undermines full-fledged subjects. But for Hegel's systematic unfolding of mental capacities, madness, as a compromised form of consciousness, will appear prior to the introduction of true consciousness. For this reason, the fixed idea of the mad soul of §408 must be seen to oppose not the "fully furnished self," which has not yet been introduced into the system, but rather the waking soul that is trying to become the organic whole that Hegel anticipates in these passages. At this point in Hegel's systematic development of "mind," the waking soul provides an abstract opportunity for the contingent disarray of the soul to achieve a structural unity.

It is this potential, and the soul's attempt to realize it, that the fixed idea of insanity opposes when it violently resists integration into the subjective whole. In the context of the "Anthropology," prior to the emergence of true consciousness, it only makes sense to understand the fixed idea of the madman as opposing the production of a fully awake and unified subject, rather than as opposing an already unified subject. The latter, it will turn out, is in fact the outcome of the cure for insanity that the formation of habits will provide. Only by understanding madness as a malady of the soul, the cure of which produces the organically whole subject, will we be able to recognize in the cure of habit-formation the seeds of Hegel's conception of imagination and its own dual nature. In what follows, this aim will require that I qualify Hegel's claims about madness in order to emphasize that, at this point in soul's systematic construction, only by resolving the obsessions of madness will the unified rational subject come into being.[8]

The struggle of madness as a conflict between the sleeping and waking parts of the soul helps to explain Hegel's characterization of insanity as a kind of waking dream in which the two sides vie for control. Madmen "are *dreaming while awake* and are *dominated* by a *fixed idea* which they cannot harmonize with their objective consciousness [n.b.]" (PM §408 Zu, 126/165). Hegel divides his account of this somnolent madness into three stages.[9] This division not only isolates distinct kinds of madness; it also organizes these kinds into a narrative progression in which the soul reaches its most violent realization of the conflict within its content. At first the waking soul loses whatever hold it has over its ideas, and then secondly a particular idea among its sleeping substance comes to dominate its attention. The conflict between the organic unity sought by the waking soul and a rogue idea that defies inclusion in the whole is fully apparent in Hegel's third stage, where "the lunatic *compares* his merely subjective idea with his objective consciousness [n.b.], [and] discovers the sharp difference existing between the two. . . ." Soul's recognition of its pathology results in a "more or less despairing effort to overcome the *discord*" of the two (PM §408 Zu, 131/172).

We distinguished earlier the activity of the sleeping and waking parts of the soul in terms of the former's merely associative play in contrast with the work of the latter to make an integrated whole of its mental content. Hegel's account of the early stages of madness indicates that the malady arises from a weakening of the waking soul that brings to the fore the associative disorder of the soul asleep. The core condition of Hegel's first stage of insanity is something he calls "rambling mind," in which soul is overwhelmed by a kind of indiscriminate free association. The rambling mind's interest in everything "springs from an inability to *fix* one's attention on anything definite, and consists in the malady of stumbling from one object to another." The waking soul's drive for unity is undermined by a play of contingency as it "stumbles" from one arbitrary association to the next. Illustrating this in the language of the mind's later organization, Hegel writes, "The rambling mind always stems from a weakening of the power of the rational consciousness to hold together the totality of its mental representations." The play of sleeping soul blurs the view for the whole of its waking half.

Once this play which threatens the unity of the soul takes hold, "madness proper" can arise, where "the natural mind which is shut up within itself . . . acquires a *definite* content and this content becomes a *fixed idea*" (133/174). That is, the soul becomes fixated on a particular idea among the rambling heterogeneity of its associations. Some part of the soul identifies itself with this content, and opposes itself to the rest. The soul becomes decentered as its fixed idea opposes itself to the effort of the waking soul to give order to the play of association. At this second stage the conflict between the fixed idea and the aims of the waking soul is not yet explicit to the madman; the "*simple* lunatic" is so lost in his fixation that he "has no *definite awareness* of the *contradiction* which exists between his fixed idea and the objective world" (135/176). The lunatic who thinks he is Napoleon, or who believes there is a horse and carriage in his stomach, is controlled by an arbitrary notion that obscures the soul's waking powers.

But even in its opposition to itself the soul is still a composition of parts, and in the final stage of insanity, which Hegel calls "mania" or "frenzy," the soul's waking half resurfaces sufficiently for the maniac to realize his duality. In this conflict "the maniac himself has a vivid feeling of the contradiction between his merely subjective idea and the objective world, and yet cannot rid himself of this idea but is fully intent on making it an actuality or on destroying what is actual" (ibid.). The double personality of the lunatic is complete, for he identifies himself with a moment of associative play on which he fixates, and yet he knows that his self lies elsewhere. "[I]n mania, where one particular idea usurps the authority of the rational mind, the particularity of the subject manifests itself unchecked, and the natural impulses and those developed by reflection belonging to this particularity consequently throw off the yoke of the moral laws rooted in the truly universal will, with the result that the dark, infernal powers of the heart are set free" (PM §408 Zu, 135-136/177).[10] Hegel again in this passage anticipates later formations of mind; but the dilemma of the madman is clear. The maniac is trapped in a nightmare of contradictory desires: he wants both to become a rational subject and to obsess over the sharp particularity of the contingent modifications in his sleeping soul, modifications that must be brought under control, rather than set loose, for his rational potential to be fulfilled.

Before turning to Hegel's cure for this malady of the soul, and to the subject produced by this cure, we would do well to cast another interpretive light on the struggle between waking and sleeping in madness. The waking soul, faced with the associative disorder of contingencies in its sleeping substance, seeks to fashion its arbitrary parts into an organic unity. Soul follows in this process the same prerogative that Kant's imagination did in fashioning the sense-making unity of an aesthetic idea in sublime reflection. Of course, imagination also sought unity in Kant's judgment of taste, but only a *formal* unity, while sublime reflection, and Hegel's waking soul, seek to unify a *content*, in this case soul's. Kantian imagination proved unable to comprehend an array of aesthetic attributes as a systematic unity, though its effort produced an aesthetic unity of relations. Here, too, in Hegel's account of madness, rogue elements of the sleeping soul's associative play defy comprehension by the waking soul's projection of organic unity. The Kantian sublime resists presentation as a whole, and Hegel's mad soul attempts to prove itself sublime when it defies the unifying aims of its awakening.

The profound difference, of course, is that Hegel's aesthetic soul will overcome the sublimity of madness. It will succeed in producing the organic unity of a subject out of that which defies it, its sleeping substance. The waking soul wins where Kantian imagination loses—which reflects Hegel's downgrading of the sublime and his radicalization of reflective judgment. But we will see that the imagination, which will issue from the waking soul's success, will retain as its own dual nature both the power to construct unity and the capacity for associative play which the soul must here disavow to save itself. Hegel's imagination will become both a master of unity and the agent of its destruction. We will see in chapter 7 that, where the Kantian sublime surreptitiously surfaces in Hegel's aesthetic theory, imagination will be at work—undermining, in a play of association, its own production of unity. Hegel's aesthetic imagination will turn on itself, as the sleeping soul turns on the waking, injecting a sublime disorder into its own constructions. Hegel's *merely* associative imagination will achieve less than Kantian imagination does in constructing an aesthetic idea, while Hegel's unifying imagination will, in overcoming the sublime, achieve more than Kant's. In the struggle between these powers of imagination in Hegel's theory, we will find an imaginative power of aesthetic reflection that generates and validates relations of affinity neither merely contingent nor unified by a concept.

Keeping this trajectory in mind, how does the soul recover from its fixation on a moment of its feeling? The possibility of recovery lies in the fact that, even though the obsession of the sleeping soul dominates the madman, he is still dreaming *while awake*: his waking soul still struggles to survive and can come to reassert its formative power over the play of the soul's mad dream. In the sick soul, "along with an insanity connected with a *particular* idea, there also exists a consciousness which in its other ideas is rational, and from this a skillful psychiatrist is able to develop sufficient power to overcome the particular fixed idea" (136–137/179). The intense hold that the maniac's obsession has on her must be loosened so that this rogue element can be integrated into the system of subjectivity the waking soul seeks to construct.[11] The maniac's fixed idea must be stripped of its hubris to assert independence from the rest of the soul. It must be stripped of its claim to sublimity, its claim to exceed comprehension in the whole of a conscious subject, its claim to present something alien to a systematic unity. The soul that casts off its submission to this false god comes to master its content: "the soul which is no longer confined to a merely subjective particular idea by which it is displaced from the center of its concrete actuality, has so completely received into its ideality the immediate and particularized content presented to it, has come to feel so at home in it, that it moves about in it in freedom" (PM §410 Zu, 144/188). When soul feels at home *(eingewohnt)* in its content, no particular moment of its substance is uncanny to it; it possesses the whole and can begin to form from it a functional unity. Hegel claims in the same passage that "This being-at-home-with-oneself we call habit [*Gewohnheit*]." In habit-formation the productive activity of the waking soul will realize the self-control to overcome the rebellious power of its obsessive dreams. The exercise of habits will produce the "fully furnished self" of rational consciousness and, as we will see shortly, will contribute to the emergence of Hegelian imagination.

Hegel introduces habit-formation as a power of the soul in §410 of the *Encyclopedia*.[12] In habituation the soul takes control of its content through a process of abstraction: "The soul's making itself an abstract universal being, and reducing the particulars of feelings (and of consciousness) to a mere determination of its being is Habit" (PM §410, 140/183). Habit liberates soul from its obsession with a fixed idea because it assumes the view for the whole the waking soul demands: "[I]n habit . . . man relates himself not to a contingent single sensation, idea, appetite, etc., but to himself, to a universal mode of action which constitutes his individuality, which is posited by himself and has become his own and for that very reason appears as free" (PM §410 Zu, 144/188). Soul recovering from madness finds itself again the controlling force under which all its modifications fall. By organizing its content into a structure of habits, by imposing a regiment of habitual *repetition* on its associative play, soul invents patterns of behavior by means of which it asserts its autonomy through submitting itself to rules: "But since the repeated activities of man acquire by repeated exercise the character of habit, the form of something received into recollection, into the universality of mental inwardness, the soul brings into its bodily activities a universal mode of action, a *rule*, to be transmitted to other activities" (PM §410 Zu, 146/191). By means of this repetition, soul organizes the multiple occurrences of particular feelings under abstract categories: "This process of building up [*Sicheinbilden*] the particular and corporeal expressions of feeling into the being of the soul appears as a *repetition* of them, and the generation of habit as *practice*" (PM §410, 141/184).[13] Soul diminishes the monadic isolation of each of its contingent modifications by establishing patterns of likeness among them and organizing them accordingly. By this means soul cements relations between the feelings it repeatedly experiences, and in cementing patterns it gives the stamp of necessity to their recurrence. Necessity arises in the soul from "the universal that is related to mutually external singulars," that is, when the establishment of a universal category, however abstract, projects into the soul's future the expectation of continued instances of the feelings organized (PM §410 Zu, 144/189). Far from the capricious play of the sleeping soul, soul that finds itself in the formation of habits can expect one thing to follow on another with reliable repetition.[14]

To reveal the origins of Hegelian imagination, it is crucial to emphasize the organization of *like* feelings in habit formation. By overcoming the soul's obsession with particular feelings, habituation tames the associative disarray of the sleeping soul by subsuming feelings under categories of sameness. The power of the lunatic's fixed idea dissolves when habit formation makes it just another in a series of similar feelings, over all of which soul asserts its control by unifying them under an *abstract universal*: "The universal to which the soul relates itself in habit, in distinction from the self-determining, concrete universal which exists only for pure thinking is, however, only the abstract universality produced by reflection from the repetition of many single instances" (PM §410 Zu, 144/188). Habits, for Hegel, assume the form of abstractions which treat repeated instances of feeling or behavior as all the same, ignoring their differences, for the sake of the mental stability that the habitual expectation of sameness affords.

We will see in the next section that this abstractive power of judgment which emerges in habit formation becomes a central capacity of imagination. Hegel anticipates later developments when he writes in the *Anmerkung* to §410 that "Habit on an ampler scale, and carried out in the strictly intellectual range, is recollection and memory" (143/187). Recollection and memory are the first and third moments of representational thinking in the "Psychology" subsection of the *Philosophy of Mind*; imagination serves as the middle term between them. Imagination will retain the power to organize categories of likeness: that is to say, the aspect of mature Hegelian imagination that will engage in empirical concept-formation, in the production of abstract universals, originally acquires that talent, in Hegel's systematic development of "mind," from the soul's habit-formative recovery from madness. What role imagination plays in the production of *concrete universals*, and what features of its early development contribute to that part, remains to be seen.

It will become critical, however, to determine what other constructive powers Hegelian imagination has. For at present, in habit-formation's cure for insanity, the waking soul has overcome the formlessness of its sleeping self by imposing a principle of homogeneity upon its associative play. In madness soul experiences its own substance as sublime, defiant of subsumption under universals. But in habit-formation soul diminishes the threat of incommensurable difference by focusing on the similarity of repeated experiences. That is, habit-formation emphasizes precisely the search for homogeneity that Kantian aesthetic reflection sidestepped in producing an affine network of relations between *disparate* phenomena. Habit-formation's production of "categories" reflects Hegel's intended radicalization of reflective judgment toward the determination of rational unities. We will soon see habituation elevated into a properly imaginative power of empirical concept formation, perpetuating cognitive imagination's ordering of similitudes. In habit-formation Hegel's imagination generates normative order by relating like things; the question will be whether his imagination can also, as an aesthetic power, produce normatively binding affinities across spaces of heterogeneity.[15]

Kant praised productive imagination for creating, in aesthetic ideas, "another nature out the material that actual nature gives it." In doing so, Kant thought, imagination demonstrates its "freedom from the law of association . . . ; for although it is under that law that nature lends us material, yet we can process that material into something quite different, namely, into something that surpasses nature" (CJ 314). By the close of Hegel's "Anthropology" we see a power that will become imagination overcoming the associative play of the soul asleep to produce the "second nature" of habit (PM §410 An, 141/184). Recall that the second nature Kant's imagination produces is an aesthetic idea. Hegel in fact one ups Kant here, for the second nature that issues from the origins of Hegel's imagination in habit formation will be the Kantian subject itself. Habit formation produces the "actual soul" (PM §§411–412) which becomes the Kantian object-related subjective consciousness Hegel treats in the subsequent subsection of the *Philosophy of Mind*, his "Phenomenology of Mind."[16]

Hegel construes the generation of the conscious subject by means of habit formation as "the Soul's work of art" (PM §411, 147/192). If Kant's imagination produces aesthetic ideas, Hegel's budding imagination cuts its first teeth on creating the Kantian subject *as a work of art*, a free creation that establishes its own normative order.[17] Hegel thus constructs the Kantian subject as the product of an aesthetic reflection, a universalization of feeling through the repetition and normative ordering of habit. Though again, this retooled Hegelian reflective judgment produces universals to a degree alien to the Kantian aesthetic. Hence the aesthetic subjectivity that soul realized in self-feeling has now been launched on a trajectory toward determinate unity. Less and less will it retain the indeterminate play so distinctive for Kant's conception of aesthetic unity. It is indeed notable that Hegel's "Anthropology" account of *genius* makes it the mark of the "self-possessed and healthy subject [who] has an active and present consciousness of the ordered *whole* of his individual world, into the *system* of which he *subsumes* each special content of sensation, idea, desire, inclination, etc., as it arises, so as to insert them in their proper place" (PM §408 An, 123/162).[18] We will see this process of making a whole subject repeated in Hegel's *Lectures on Aesthetics*, where the (by then more sophisticated) artistic genius molds her subjectivity into a unified and presentable theme. Imagination will be in full flower at that point, and only then will we be able to ascertain whether Hegel's imagination has occasion to produce less determinate, aesthetic unities of relation similar to those that come from the Kantian imagination's encounter with sublimity.

The "artistry" of habituation molds from soul's associative material a unified subject, and at present the unpresentable sublime of soul's sleeping substance has been conquered by the waking subject and its habits.[19] We should expect that a subjectivity built on a foundation of abstract universality (habit) will not last long in Hegel's systematic development of "mind." The concrete universality of the Concept, which mind realizes in art, religion, and philosophy, surpasses such abstractive attention to sameness and repetition. The "work of art" which soul achieves through habituation will no longer count as art by the time imagination has become able to create beauty, for Hegel conceives Beauty as at odds with abstract universality—as a sensuous reconciliation of unity and diversity in which *disparate* elements freely cohere as a thematic whole. To become capable of this feat imagination, as I will show, must recuperate and redeem the associative play of the now dormant sleeping soul. Full-grown Hegelian imagination, in possession of its mature artistic powers, will recover that play of difference and defy the habits born of its own birth from madness.

Hegel's Many Imaginations

To a large extent one can understand Hegel's "Anthropology" as the dramatization of a struggle between opposed psychical powers: a contingent play of "natural" association, which gets entirely out of hand in madness, is tamed by the awakening of a "spiritual" power of rule-bound habituation. It should be apparent that this drama mimics the interplay of association and habit in empiricist psychology, which had to appeal to rules of association to give a structure of custom (in our ideas and moral sentiments) to the otherwise potentially capricious play of imagination. Hume remarks in the *Treatise*: "As all simple ideas may be separated by the imagination, and may be united again in what form it pleases, nothing wou'd be more unaccountable than the operations of that faculty, were it not guided by some universal principles, which render it, in some measure, uniform in all times and places."[20] Of course, the tenuous lawlike status of Hume's principles of association led him to the skepticism about knowledge of causal relationships that inspired Kant to seek a transcendental ground for the categorial constitution of fundamental structures of experience.

Hume's claim that a reproductive imagination simply associates perceptions based, for one, on their resemblance or similarity assumes that similarity is simply given in perception. That is, he cannot explain how imagination forms ideas by recognizing "given" similarities, when the subject must already possess some ideas or concepts before it can discern similarity between objects.

Kant maintains, to the contrary, that imaginative schemata determined by categorial rules of the understanding *produce* patterns of similarity in experience. Now to the extent that Hegelian imagination, by the end of its "anthropological" development, shares with empiricist imagination the production of arbitrary habits based on repetitive similitudes "given" through feeling, it also shares with empiricism a poor understanding of the epistemic conditions for the possibility of recognizing similarity. Hegelian mind will achieve the insight that nothing is "given" immediately only near the completion of its development. By then it will be apparent that the goal of thinking the systematic totality of the Concept was the mediating precondition undergirding all of mind's lesser talents, including habit formation. For Hegel, as I have intimated, that consummation of thought begins in abandoning abstract universality and its fascination with repetitive sameness for the "unity in diversity" of the concrete universal. Given Hegel's hostility for the empiricist laws of association, we must keep in mind that, however critical a step forward habituation represents in his narrative, Hegel will ultimately repudiate the "artistry" of its repetitive rules in favor of more adept arts of unity building.

We can now turn to Hegel's account of full-fledged imagination, in the *Encyclopedia* "Psychology," and determine what of its powers surpass the habitual repetition of sameness. We will find that imagination embodies key features of the anthropological subjectivity discussed in the previous sections, both in its capacities and in the material on which it works. It will prove essential to carefully relate Hegel's formal treatment of imagination in §§455–459 to both the associative play of the sleeping soul and the rule-generating activity of habit-formation, for in these opposed phenomena lie the dual nature of imaginative "cognition." Hegel does treat imagination, as Kant does, as an agent of cognition, mediating between intuition and concepts. As with Kant, however, we will need to ascertain imagination's reflective powers outside a purely cognitive context. This will prove especially difficult in Hegel's case, because every road on the map of his system leads to thought of the Idea as a realized whole. Ultimately, the strategy of retaining the marks of Hegelian imagination's anthropological prehistory will help us develop an account of an aesthetic reflection that falls nicely short of producing the systematic unity which Hegel seeks.

I indicated that Hegel includes imagination among the representational powers of the "fully furnished self." That self, replete with a solid subject-object distinction, takes shape in the *Encyclopedia* "Phenomenology" (PM §§413–439), which follows the "Anthropology."[21] Only in the later "Psychology" (§§440–482) do all the powers of mind unfold. For my purposes, the key feature of this "phenomenological" development up into the "Psychology" lies in the fact that, throughout, the "content" of soul, subject, and mind remains the same. That is, the natural array of contingent modifications which individualize the feeling soul, and whose play drove the waking soul mad, becomes the "intuitions" on which Hegel puts mind to work at the outset of the "Psychology." Intuition as Hegel presents it "confines itself . . . to seizing the *unexplicated* substance still wrapped up in the inessentials of the external and contingent" (PM §449 Zu, 200/255). That is, intuition provides an externalized, spatio-temporal form for the felt modifications soul has had from its beginnings. Representational thinking, then, in the powers of recollection, imagination, and memory, will organize and conceptualize that same content as a reinternalized array of mental images.

Recollection (§§452–454), the first step toward forming representations, builds up a great manifold of imagistically rendered moments of *contingent and unrelated intuition*: it produces a "night-like mine or pit in which is stored a world of infinitely many images and representations, yet without being in consciousness" (PM §453 An, 204/260).[22] In other words, recollection generates an imagistic reconstitution of the "natural" content of the *sleeping soul*. As was noted earlier, mind's progress in Hegel's *Encyclopedia* does not imply that it leaves behind its previous incarnations. The development of mind requires for Hegel the structured unity of all its moments, high and low. Here the disarray of the soul asleep reappears as the "subconscious mine" of images which recollection makes from the content of the feeling soul. When dealing with its pit of feelings, soul fell into the abyss of madness; it recovered by forming habits that normalized its feelings, grouping like ones together. In madness soul fancied itself sublime, beyond comprehension as a whole; but the successes of habit formation gave the lie to its "sublimity." Now again, in the recollection of the sleeping soul's disordered content, mind faces a "multitude of kindred presentations" potentially defiant of unification. Once again, mind faces the prospect of a sublimity within itself beyond its means to grasp as a whole. Imagination, born of habituating madness, will have the task once again of bringing a rule-bound order to this dark mine. The question will be whether representation deals with its "mine pit" of images any differently than waking soul handled its array of feelings.

Imagination meets this need by not only mechanically grasping the intuitive content of the soul in the form of images, but by also processing that content; imagination, Hegel writes, "becomes a recollection which affects the *content*, *generalizes* it, thus creating *general* representations or ideas" (PM §451 Zu, 202/258). Faced with the disarray of the sleeping soul, reconstituted by recollection from its "dark mine" of images, imagination gives structure to this mass much in the way habit-formation responded to the particularities of the soul in recovering from madness. We will see, in fact, that just as recollection revives the contingent content of the sleeping soul, imagination recapitulates habituation's appeal to homogeneity as a means to bring that morass under control. Imagination, which in this guise Hegel terms *Einbildungskraft*, "fashions for itself a content peculiar to it by *thinking* the object, by bringing out what is universal in it, and giving it determinations which belong to the ego" (ibid.). What is universal in an array of images, for the purpose of producing abstract representations or concepts, will be whatever makes them similar, and so amenable to a habitual recognition and subsumption. But we will find as well in Hegel's account imaginative powers that promise two things: the disturbance of a habituation to abstract categories, and the production of networks of indeterminate unity in a properly Kantian aesthetic reflection.

Hegel treats imagination in paragraphs 455 to 459 of the *Encyclopedia* "Psychology."[23] The first issue a reading of Hegel's account must face is the distinctively artifactual condition of his text at this point. Throughout the 1830 third edition of the *Encyclopedia* one must balance a focus on Hegel's main paragraphs and *Anmerkungen* with an often considerable reliance on the *Zusätze* added by Boumann in 1845. These multiple sedimentary layers do not entirely coincide in these paragraphs. Paragraph 455 treats what Hegel calls "reproductive imagination" *(reproduktive Einbildungskraft)* and its *Anmerkung* provides a critique of the empiricist tradition concerning the association of ideas. The *Zusatz* to the paragraph outlines Hegel's account of imagination and distinguishes at least three forms, namely "reproductive," "associative," and "creative" imagination. Hegel terms the first two *reproduktive* and *assoziierende Einbildungskraft*, whereas he calls creative imagination *Phantasie*; the terminological distinction will prove most important as we proceed. But it is not clear how Hegel's critique of the association of ideas in the *Anmerkung* relates to his *Zusatz* account of associative imagination. To compound the difficulties, §456 then seems to treat creative imagination *(Phantasie)* as the second form, and explicitly enumerates it as such, while associative imagination seems to form only a transition from the first. Creative imagination will divide into symbolic and sign-making forms, while §456 appears to consider only the former. The *Zusatz* to this paragraph refers to a "productive imagination" *(produktive Einbildungskraft)*, but it is unclear whether Hegel means this to be synonymous with symbolic imagination *(symbolisierende Phantasie)* or with creative imagination *(Phantasie)* as a whole.[24]

One can adopt various strategies for allaying some of the confusion of the text. Willem de Vries, for one, chooses to dismiss as an unhelpful interpolation by Boumann the division of imagination given in the *Zusatz* to §455. Disregarding that addition's distinction between reproductive and associative imagination, deVries claims that "if attention is paid to the architectonic mentioned in the main paragraphs, it is clear that Reproductive Imagination and Associative Imagination are one and the same, and that the three divisions of Imagination are (a) Associative or Reproductive Imagination, (b) Symbolic Imagination, and (c) Sign-making Imagination."[25] Although this solution does respect Hegel's enumeration, I suggest a slightly different division of the subject. Paragraph 455 and its *Zusatz* treat reproduction and association as processes by which imagination produces general representations. Creative imagination's instantiation of symbols is covered in §456, while §457 treats mainly *Phantasie*'s instantiation of its products in signs (its *Zusatz* draws out the distinction between symbols and signs). Paragraph 458 completes the discussion of signs and sign-making imagination. One can see, then, two main forms of imaginative activity, a first that constructs general representations or concepts *(Einbildungskraft)*, and a second *(Phantasie)* that creates symbols and signs; the great difference in the products of these two modes of imagination will become clear as we proceed. Reproductive and associative imagination fall under the moment of generalization, but they are not simply one and the same, as de Vries claims; I will carefully distinguish them below. Both symbol and sign-making imagination fall, of course, under creative *Phantasie.*[26]

We must first, then, consider the generalizing imagination, or *Einbildungskraft*, introduced in §455, which mines the pit of images in the subject to produce "universal" representations. We will see, more precisely, that *Einbildungskraft* produces *abstract* universals. It begins as reproductive imagination, "where," Hegel writes, "the images issue from the inward world belonging to the ego, which is now the power over them" (PM §455, 206/262). Reproduction calls forth images from its inner store, and freely selects particular moments from the contingent modification of intuition. Hegel thus takes *Einbildungskraft* to possess the entire content of the pit of images, and he understands this imagination as a power that works this still contingent content up into more general representations. *Reproduktive Einbildungskraft* begins this process by isolating particular aspects of an image, such as the color of a rose; it produces further images of such aspects of its content, though what it focuses on is arbitrary. It might isolate the color or the thorns of the rose, or the box that it came in, or the height of the person who delivered it. But in any case it is by mining deeper into the soul's images for particular features that reproductive imagination initiates the process of working this content into concepts.

For this reproductive "output from its universal mine" associative imagination will provide "a *general* representation for the *associative relation* of the images which according to circumstances are more abstract or more concrete ideas" (ibid.). *Assoziierende Einbildungskraft* goes farther than reproductive imagination: it connects images of particulars to subsume them under general representations, and it undertakes this process of abstraction by comparing images for their similarity. "That which connects the single images to one another," Hegel writes, "consists precisely in what is common to them" (PM §456 Zu, 209/266). This imagination connects the red in the rose and the red of a fire truck under a general representation of "redness." Or, in another kind of abstraction, associative imagination ignores the redness of a toy wagon and a fire truck, instead connecting them under the general idea "vehicle." Its abstractions are arbitrary, because *Einbildungskraft* is free to select out whatever features it pleases from whatever images it pleases, but it produces general concepts nevertheless. It produces, in fact, that sort of concept Hegel designates an *abstract universal*, in which an array of particulars is construed as all the same, and subsumed under some likeness they share, to the occlusion of their specific differences. As a power of abstract universal formation, then, associative *Einbildungskraft* relates particulars strictly according to their likeness.[27] As such, it must be emphasized that the *merely* associative, maddening play of the sleeping soul, which we found habit-formation to overcome, has no place in Hegel's account of "associative imagination," for the very reason that this generalizing aspect of Hegel's full-fledged imagination is his "psychological" reformulation of habituation as it appeared in the "Anthropology." That is, the use associative *Einbildungskraft* makes of abstract sameness in order to structure mind's pit of images *repeats* the waking soul's habituation of madness. That aspect of imagination which organizes similitudes, and which began to coalesce in soul's recovery from madness, reaches its completion in associative *Einbildungskraft*. As a projector of sameness, Hegel's generalizing associative imagination does not make connections with respect to *difference* in the manner that was central to the production of affinity in Kant's account of sublime reflection.

As noted above, Hegel presents a biting critique of the empiricist association of ideas in the *Anmerkung* to §455. Echoing his "Anthropology" attack on the empiricists, he treats such merely associative "thinking" as a purely arbitrary play with no claim to universality. "The so-called *laws of the association of ideas* . . . are not *laws*, just for the reason that there are so many laws about the same thing, as to suggest a caprice and contingency opposed to the very nature of law" (PM §455 An, 206/262–263). As we saw at the beginning of this section, empiricist psychology sought to rein in the play of imagination by attributing lawfulness to the operations of association. From the post-Kantian perspective of transcendental philosophy, those "laws" must appear as arbitrary as the very trains of association they purportedly shape. "The train of images and representations suggested by association," Hegel writes, "is the sport of vacant-minded ideation" (207/263), precisely because he thinks it lacks the validity of the abstract universals his own associative *Einbildungskraft* fashions. We must carefully distinguish Hegel's critique of empiricist association from his account of *Einbildungskraft,* for he clearly wishes to locate the latter within a process of cognition in which he thinks the former has no part. By recasting reproductive and associative imagination as generalizing movements of thought, Hegel seeks to salvage them from their involvement in mere capricious association. In fact, the ultimate justification of imagination's production of abstract universals will lie in its contribution to the higher cognitive mission of speculative reason, and in its position within the systematic totality of the rational Idea. So if associative *Einbildungskraft* is the full realization of habit in the realm of thought, it is not so greatly different from empiricist association; Hegel acknowledges as much when he remarks in §456 that "even the association of ideas is to be treated as a subsumption of the individual under the universal, which forms their connecting link" (209/265). In the end, the real difference between empiricist association and Hegel's generalizing imagination will come from the justification of the latter as an integrated component of mind's organic unity.

Empiricist imagination could engage in the most arbitrary and contingent associations, linking images any way it pleased, or it could follow lawlike principles, however tenuous their status as law. *This duality remains in Hegel's conception of associative Einbildungskraft.* I have emphasized its contribution to concept formation and hence to cognition, but Hegel grants that imagination may also forgo its cognitive duties and revert to mere associative play. "I have, for example," Hegel writes, "the image of an object before me; to this image is linked quite externally the image of persons with whom I have talked about this object, or who own it, etc. Often the images are linked together only by space and time" (PM §455 Zu, 208/265). In such instances *Einbildungskraft* connects images in a subjective fashion indifferent to the production of abstract universals. So we can in fact distinguish two associative activities of *Einbildungskraft*: the first, given in Hegel's main account of a generalizing imagination, constructs abstract representations, or empirical concepts, on the basis of homogeneity between images. Hegelian imagination's generalizing power is its most determinately cognitive one. As such, it maps onto Kant's occasional treatment of reflective judgment as an imaginative power of concept formation, which we saw to be just the sort of activity that Kantian *aesthetic* reflection, playing at the production of purposive unity in the absence of determining rules, does not pursue.

But second, associative *Einbildungskraft* engages in the contingent play of connecting disparate images guided only by subjective caprice. Note that this duality in Hegel's conception of mature imagination repeats the original partition of the soul, whose waking part sought a universality it first realized in habituation, while its sleeping part played with mere associations to the point of driving soul mad. This continuity indicates that the associative play of the sleeping soul survives as a power of full-fledged imagination. It is this merely associative aspect of imagination that must bear the critique Hegel gives of the empiricist association of ideas; he thinks this play has nothing to offer to the cognition of universality in representational thinking. Even so, Hegel does grant a positive connotation to this play of ideas in the *Zusatz* to §455. Referring to the play of *wit*, Hegel remarks that it "connects ideas which, although remote from one another, none the less have in fact an inner connection" (209/265). These clever connections between disparate ideas, of course, depend on the constructive activity of mind as much as its resemblance-based general representations do; that is, the "inner connection" of ideas is hardly given in them. Hegel seems to see in wit the sort of creative tension between disparity and affinity on which we saw the connective activity of sublime reflection capitalize. As in the exemplary case that metaphor has provided, the connections made here are not merely contingent, for they come to express something compelling. But neither do they fit the mold of the abstract concepts *Einbildungskraft* constructs in its allegiance to cognition. We will find in Hegel's aesthetic theory a repeated linkage between this *positive wit* and an imaginative activity that constructs relations of affinity across disparity. Though we are not yet prepared to discern just what admixture of imaginative powers Hegel takes to be responsible for this creative process, the capricious play of association will likely have a part. In chapter 6 I will argue that this inventive capacity for bringing expressive unity to the diverse and remote lies at the heart of Hegelian imaginative artistry. And in those instances where imagination falls short of expressing *determinate* unity I will locate the operation of a properly sublime reflection.

Following the generalizing activity of *Einbildungskraft*, Hegel locates a second phase of imaginative power in the special products of what he calls *Phantasie*. This creative imagination produces symbols and signs that, each in quite different ways, represent the content imagination works up from intuition. Hegel introduces *Phantasie* in §456, though without yet mentioning its sign-making component: "Intelligence is the power that wields the store of images and ideas belonging to it, and which thus freely combines and subsumes these stores in obedience to its peculiar tenor. Such is creative imagination [*Phantasie*]—symbolic, allegoric, or poetical imagination—where the intelligence gets a definite embodiment in this store of ideas and informs them with its general tone" (PM §456, 209/265–266). *Phantasie* is a power still productive, as Hegel takes all representational thinking to be, of "syntheses," in the sense that the imagistic material, "in which the subjective principles and ideas get a mentally pictorial existence, is derived from the data of intuition" (209/266). *Phantasie* still works with the particular content of the feeling soul, passed on through intuition and recollection, and so must mine and transform the same pit of images available to *Einbildungskraft*. It is, however, unclear from Hegel's *Encyclopedia* treatment of *Phantasie* whether its products are distinctively its own, or whether it only gives objective form, in a perceptible symbol or sign, to those representations supplied it by the generalizing *Einbildungskraft* that precedes it.

But Hegel indicates that *Phantasie* produces symbols shaped by some higher order of *purpose* or *principle.* He writes that "[I]ntelligence is more than merely a general form: its inwardness is an internally definite, concrete subjectivity with a substance and value of its own, derived from some interest, some latent concept or Ideal principle, so far as we may by anticipation speak of such" (PM §456, 209/264). By referring to an imaginative product shaped by a determinate interest Hegel anticipates the contours of his aesthetic theory, where the symbolizing activity of *Phantasie* will play a central role. The presentation of a complex theme in a work of art should seem to require a more sophisticated synthesis of material than that supplied by the abstract generalizations of *Einbildungskraft.* We will see that, in keeping with the contours of Hegel's system, artistic *Phantasie* will surpass the abstract universals of associative *Einbildungskraft* to present, in sensuous form, the reconciling satisfactions of concrete universality.

Hegel divides *Phantasie* into symbol- and sign-making types. The first produces an image or object that itself expresses the content of imagination. The other produces signs that arbitrarily denote some content without directly expressing it in the manner of Hegelian artistic symbols. As a crude example, an upward-pointing arrow symbolizes the message "this way up" by expressing that meaning through its very form (and contextual cues), while a sign with the letters and spaces "this way up" on it expresses the meaning through arbitrary shapes. Symbolic imagination "selects for the expression of its general ideas only that sensuous material whose independent signification corresponds to the specific content of the universal to be symbolized" (PM §457 Zu, 212/269). Because symbolic imagination manifests itself in the image, its products enjoy an identity of content between the symbol and what it symbolizes. Hegel makes it clear that he locates the productive activity of art in the powers of this symbolizing *Phantasie.* The "ideating activity" of what he here calls "productive imagination . . . forms the formal aspect of art; for art represents the true universal, or the Idea in the form of sensuous existence, of the image" (PM §456 Zu, 210/267). The focus will be on symbolizing *Phantasie* as we turn to the *Lectures on Aesthetics.* For Hegel the identity of content between symbol and symbolized will mean that imagination produces works of art which wholly and determinately express a thematic Idea. We will focus on this orthodox work of symbolizing *Phantasie* in chapter 6. But as we will see in chapter 7, imaginative encounters with sublimity crop up in Hegel's *Lectures on Aesthetics* whenever the expressive function of art breaks down or has yet to develop. In those instances *Phantasie* will draw on its inheritance of mad associative play to dehabituate the homogenizing abstract concepts of Hegel's generalizing imagination.

I have traced the ever more sophisticated work of a mind that organizes the contingent modifications from which it began. The awakening mind first confronted the associative disarray of the sleeping soul in its response to madness. We have there and elsewhere seen mind assert itself over the wild heterogeneity of its particularity by inventing patterns of homogeneity to organize the soul's parts. The production of rules by habit-formation and the working up of concepts both appeal to resemblance to categorize soul's content under higher genera. We saw that in overcoming madness, mind dispelled the soul's claim to sublimity; mind made of the soul an ordered whole of rule-bound habits, and so gave the lie to the sleeping soul's presumption of sublimity, its pretense that it could not be presented as a whole. But we have also seen that the contingent variegation of the soul remains in mind's higher forms, and becomes in fact the nocturnal mine of images from which imagination constructs its generalized products. By reviving the content of the soul in images, recollection revived this associative morass.

The question then arises: does the revival of the soul's contingent feeling in images *also* resuscitate a potential for sublime unpresentability? John Sallis has posed this question after a fashion, as part of an effort to resist the systematizing destination of imagination in its cognitive submission to reason. He asks whether the pit of images retains a sublimity (though he does not use this term) that defies comprehension by the generalizations of cognizing imagination: "The question is whether the nocturnal pit can be so thoroughly illuminated by the light of presence or whether there do not remain withdrawn in its dark depths slumbering images that are not simply at the call of spirit. And does the nocturnal pit perhaps cast its shadow over the entire course of imagination? Do even those images brought forth from the pit by reproductive imagination not bring along something of its darkness, mixing it then into that play of images from which spirit would draw up universality? Is there in that play of images a dark residue, something not recoverable in universality, something resistant to that subjugating of images that would make them in the end only the mirror for spirit?"[28] Sallis argues that Hegel exaggerates the power of imagination to subjugate the pit of images. Hegel casts imagination as a power capable of overcoming the sublime by valorizing its homogenizing capacities in the "Psychology" while relegating its transgressive manifestations to the "Anthropology." "The strategy is one of systematic displacement and consequent repression," writes Sallis. "Certain forms of imagination are displaced from psychology to anthropology, to a phase where . . . the subject is [still] susceptible to disease." Sallis sees madness itself as a primordial instance of imaginative activity; to be mad is to be at play in the pit of images, the sublime potential of which Sallis hopes will continue to threaten the cognitive mission of imagination in the "Psychology."[29]

For my purposes, hoping to undermine Hegelian imagination's allegiance to speculative reason must give way to discerning what alternative destination it might have in the aesthetic realm. We have twice seen the felt content of Hegel's aesthetic soul offer up an experience of sublimity, when the disarray of the soul asleep and the nocturnal pit of images threaten to defy comprehension as a whole. In the latter case, we saw the contingent play of mere association counteracted by the unifying power of generalizing imagination, and the potential sublimity of the mine of images was denied by the homogenizing production of abstract concepts. Yet in Kant's case we saw an *aesthetically* productive imagination respond to the sublime neither by sinking into merely contingent, associative play, nor by constructing a conceptual unity from what it faced (because it was incapable of this). Rather, Kantian sublime reflection constructed an interpretive aesthetic unity in order to express indeterminately an idea beyond its means to determine. We have seen Hegelian imagination engage in the associative play it learned from the sleeping soul's madness, and we have seen it engage in the unifying acts of categorization it first practiced as habit-formation. But can Hegel's imagination construct the sort of indeterminate unity central to an aesthetics of sublimity?

I will turn to Hegel's *Lectures on Aesthetics* to pursue this question. There, a symbolizing imagination will produce sensuous expressions for *determinate* themes, and Hegel will thereby reject Kant's claim that beauty cannot be cognized in a concept. But as in the *Encyclopedia* separation of the anthropological from the psychological, not all aesthetic experiences will realize the highest truth-telling powers of art. Not all aesthetic experience will manage to comprehend and present a unified whole, and in those interstices of Hegel's theory we will see the symbolizing efforts of imagination face the unpresentable sublime. Not only will Hegel's aesthetic theory clarify the sort of symbols produced by *Phantasie*, which is a matter left unresolved by the *Encyclopedia* "Psychology." His theory of art will also show us what *Phantasie* comes up with when faced with something beyond its comprehension. In the process Hegel will help flesh out the sort of sublime reflection we found in Kant's aesthetic theory.

6

Phantasying Art

Hegel's elaborate study of art works and their significance in his *Lectures on Aesthetics* promises to advance our elaboration of an interpretive aesthetic reflection. In part I we learned that Kant's judgment of taste, with its concentration on aesthetic form, proves an inadequate model for reflection on expressions of meaning. Kant's privileging of beauty in nature in his judgment of taste led us to sublime reflection as a potential model of interpretation. We saw that what sense imagination makes of a work's meaning assumes the form of an aesthetic idea, an affine network of attributes that partially expresses a rational unity beyond imagination's means to comprehend. The need to orient this account of aesthetic sublimity toward judgment of meaningful works of art would seem to find a champion in Hegel. His *Lectures* provide an intensive exploration of art animated by an aesthetic sensitivity Kant lacked. Hegel's determination, early in the *Lectures*, that the Ideal of Beauty will not be found in nature, but rather in the "spiritual" products of human art, is a promising improvement over Kant.[1] Hegel offers a philosophy of artistic expression that may provide theoretical tools for articulating imagination's interpretive production of aesthetic unity.

As we saw in the Interlude, however, Hegel's aesthetic theory is at the same time doubly inimical to the aims of this study. Hegel takes art to participate in reason's systematic goal of articulating the Idea. To that end he understands works of art to provide, in a sensuous form, the expression of a *determinate* content. We will see more clearly in this chapter the extent to which Hegel takes a work of art to have "one true theme" that organizes all its parts into a unified and conceptually determinable whole. This cognitive determination of art's content entails, as we know, his rejection of the Kantian doctrine of aesthetic ideas. We know, too, that the intimate relation between aesthetic ideas and sublime reflection entails Hegel's demotion of the latter to a decrepit aesthetic phenomenon, and we will see this more clearly in chapter 7. Hegel's commitment to art as a means to articulate the Idea will motivate his disfavor for a sublime aesthetic experience that claims to exceed comprehension by concepts.

In this chapter I consider the orthodox center of Hegel's aesthetic theory, in which *Phantasie* does achieve determinate expressions of meaning. I confirm the role of this imaginative power in artistic production and aesthetic reception as Hegel conceives them in the *Lectures*. His *Encyclopedia* account of the symbols *Phantasie* produces leaves unclear their difference from the abstract concepts of a generalizing imagination. I elaborate the character of Hegelian determinate aesthetic symbols and emphasize their status as "concrete" rather than abstract universals. This difference brings out the sense in which Hegel's aesthetic imagination overcomes our reliance on established patterns of conceptual thinking by presenting more organic unifications of diverse material. I argue that Hegelian imagination, as a power of ingenious artistry has, in the end, a "de-habituating function" by virtue of the way it draws on the relational play of the sleeping soul to surpass received habits of thought. But this transgressive power will still *determine* unities of artistic meaning, and the question for chapter 7 will be where, on the margins of Hegel's theory, imagination instead produces the indeterminate relational networks of sublime reflection.

Imagination and Reflection in Hegel's *Lectures*

We saw in chapter 5 that Hegel locates artistic production in a symbolizing imaginative power. This *Phantasie* produces symbols that Hegel takes to express wholly the content of what they symbolize (in contrast to Kantian aesthetic ideas). Hegel retains this view in his *Lectures*, where he argues that "the artist must act creatively and, in his own imagination [*Phantasie*] . . . with profound sense and serious feeling, give form and shape throughout and from a single cast to the meaning which animates him" (LFA 174; 13:229). Whereas Kant tied productive imagination to genius and the exhibition of indeterminate aesthetic ideas, Hegel attributes the production of aesthetic truth to symbolizing *Phantasie.* "[This] productive activity of imagination [*Phantasie*] whereby the artist takes what is absolutely rational in itself and works it out, as his very own creation, by giving it an external form, is what is called genius, talent, etc." (LFA 283; 13:366). Imagination, specifically symbolic *Phantasie,* will be the power through which rational unity is expressed in sensuous form.

The various productive and reflective powers of imagination play key roles in Kant's aesthetic theory because he sought to provide an account of subjective forms of judgment and of the interplay of cognitive powers involved in aesthetic appreciation. The unavoidable fact that Hegel does not share this subject-orientation raises a set of related problems we must consider before proceeding. Hegel recognizes the need to specify some psychological origin for artistic production; he does so when he remarks in the *Lectures* that "since the work of art springs from the spirit, it needs a subjective productive activity as its cause. . . . This activity is the imagination [*Phantasie*] of the artist" (LFA 280; 13:362). But beyond this Hegel does not have a lot to say about imagination in the *Lectures.* Instead, his aesthetic theory focuses on the content of works of art and their manner of expressing a rational ideal. Hegel is much more interested in works and their contribution to cognition of the Idea than in the productive imagination that creates them *or* the reflective imagination which judges them. Stephen Bungay has noted that "it is not part of Hegel's aim to discuss the artist or artistic production, as there is nothing philosophical to be said about either."[2] But Hegel has as little interest in providing a theory of aesthetic judgment, Bungay also notes, because Hegel views such concern as a symptom of the mental faculty subjectivism at the core of Kant's work. Hegel's focus is the nature of aesthetic symbols, and neither their origins in the artist nor their reception in judging subjects occupies his attention for long.[3]

The minimal detail on imagination and aesthetic response in the *Lectures* poses two problems for my approach, but I think they can be readily resolved. First, recall that chapter 5 discerned a gap in Hegel's

Encyclopedia account of imagination: a gap between the abstract universals produced by generalizing *Einbildungskraft* and the concrete symbols produced by *Phantasie*. Imagination in its symbolizing function would seem to unify material at a more sophisticated level than the mere subsumption of like phenomena enacted in imagination's formation of empirical concepts. The fact that Hegel devotes little space in the *Lectures* to discussing the productive work of symbolic *Phantasie* might threaten to leave our account of what it produces incomplete. Hegel's *Lectures* would then not clarify what the *Encyclopedia* left uncertain. But however much the *Lectures* as a whole focuses on symbols themselves, rather than the imagination that produces them, those symbols will be the product of *Phantasie*. We will see in the next section that, in their ideal form, Hegel takes aesthetic symbols to unify an array of disparate parts under the strict organization of a determinate theme. *Phantasie's* products thus differ greatly from the general representations of associative *Einbildungskraft,* which subsume only similar images under an abstract category. Even without much discussion of the artist's imagination, then, we will be able to differentiate Hegelian aesthetic symbols from the subsumptive concepts of generalizing imagination. That is, Hegel's theory of symbolism will itself specify for us the fruit of *Phantasie's* artistic powers. In the end, it will also illuminate the sort of aesthetic unity that falls short of the determinacy of such symbols.

Hegel's indifference to the workings of the artist's mind poses no problem, but we cannot follow his reticence concerning aesthetic judgment. This second problem may seem more intractable. An account of reflective imagination seeks to articulate how we respond aesthetically to objects in the absence of guiding concepts. To the extent that Hegel provides us a philosophy of artworks and their content, rather than an aesthetic of appreciation and judgment, we are faced with a gap between what we need and what Hegel has to offer. But, in fact, Hegel's account of artistic content in its ideal form establishes its own standard for what counts as an appropriate response to a work. Because Hegel takes art at its best to express a determinate content in a unified way, the aim of grasping that content in its unity guides the interpretive work of the respondent. That aim also provides a standard for assessing the quality of competing interpretations of a work.

We will see more clearly in the next section that the concrete universals of Hegel's aesthetic symbolism organize an array of material under the guiding unity of a specific theme. John McCumber has characterized the universal in a work of art thus: "The properly 'aesthetic' universal must be . . . fully defined by, and indeed identical with, its function of organizing just the particular set of individual details it does organize, and no others. . . . As presented by the work of art to the spectator, the guiding conception of the work is not something the spectator can freely invent: it is a limit to his experience."[4] For Hegel a work presents one definite theme, and it becomes the constraining task of the spectator to reconstruct that theme from the features of the presentation. Aesthetic reflection begins from these isolated details of the work, which in their particularity "[afford] the spectator an independent enjoyment." But these details only have their place in the work as means to the expression of its guiding theme. The particular in an aesthetic presentation, McCumber writes, "is subordinated to the work as a whole and can be viewed in terms of the contribution it makes to that work."[5] The student of a work must discover the determinate conception that gives meaning to all its details. She must articulate this unifying theme so that she can return to the work's parts and understand their place in and contribution to the whole. The particulars of the work's content are reconciled with its determining theme, and the whole is reconciled to her effort of comprehension, when "the spectator, having penetrated to a clear understanding of the work's guiding conception, returns to the work itself to see how its specific details express that message. . . ."[6]

This process of reconstructing the thematic unity of a work generates its own standard for evaluating differing interpretations. Clearly an account of a work that fails to make sense of or ignores major parts of it will be inferior to one that clarifies the role of those parts in the whole. Even for a Kantian sublime reflection, a reading of *Ulysses* sensitive to the symbolic order linking the work to the *Odyssey* will be preferable to an interpretation that misses the symbolism. But in great contrast to Kant, for whom interpretation constitutes an open-ended imaginative play, interpretation on Hegel's terms *ends* when it comprehends the fixed meaning ordering a work's parts.[7] Because a work of art is for Hegel an organic unity in which nothing belongs that does not contribute to expressing its one true theme, interpretations of a work can be judged by the extent to which they grasp a theme that can be shown to account for *every* detail in it. In Kant's case the nature of sublime reflection, and the indeterminacy of artistic meanings, allowed the possibility of multiple plausible interpretations of a work. For Hegel, *the correct* interpretation of a work would be that *one* that comprehends the guiding theme and the part every feature of a work plays in expressing it. For Hegel, the one true theme of a work specifies the one correct interpretation of it; there might be many differing responses to a work, but only the one that grasps the expressive unity of its parts will count as the interpretation of its meaning. For Hegel, quite the contrary to Kant, a work will embody a determinate unity of unambiguous expression, and aesthetic response will be bound to the task of taking in that expressive whole as a unity of definitive relations.

Thus, though Hegel has little to say in his *Lectures* about the nature of aesthetic reflection and the imagination at work in it, his theory of artistic content allows us to extrapolate an account of what reflection on a work must undertake. And though Hegel does not explicitly provide a theory of aesthetic judgment, he shows what form he thinks aesthetic response should take by himself pursuing the aim of discerning the organic unity of a work in all the interpretations of art he advances in the monumental purview of the *Lectures.*

Hegel's theory of artistic content requires our reflective response to art to assume a form quite different from the aesthetic unity we have seen a Kantian sublime reflection produce. The positive potential of Hegel's system to illuminate a Kantian sort of aesthetic unity will only be disclosed by sidestepping the center of Hegel's theory and the Ideal of Beauty he presents there. Hegel's aesthetic of determinate beauty, in which reflection finds a guiding conception to order its relating of disparate parts, must be passed over in our search for those moments in Hegel's theory when imagination faces an indeterminate unity of parts without conceptual guidance. The unified products of symbolizing *Phantasie,* in which the meaning of every part is determined by its contribution to expressing the symbolized whole, cannot accommodate the imaginative play of a reflection which relates affine particulars *qua* particulars, without subsuming them under or subordinating them to a determinate idea or theme.

Phantasie predominates in the Hegelian ideal of complete expression, to which he thinks the lesser powers of imagination which we have seen can contribute little. We will see most clearly in chapter 7 his hostility to the merely associative play of imagination, which in the context of the *Lectures* he often refers to just as *Einbildungskraft*. According to Hegel, this everyday, essentially reproductive form of "imagination [*Einbildungskraft*] rests on the recollection of situations lived through, of experiences enjoyed, instead of being creative itself. . . . But the productive fancy [*Phantasie*] of an artist is the fancy of a great spirit and heart, the apprehension and creation of ideas and shapes, and indeed the exhibition of the profoundest and most universal interests in pictorial and completely determinate sensuous form" (LFA 40; 13:63).[8] It will be critical to keep in mind that in the *Lectures on Aesthetics* Hegel distills much of the elaborate treatment of imagination in the *Encyclopedia Philosophy of Mind* into a stark contrast between symbolizing *Phantasie* and the capricious play of associative *Einbildungskraft*. In fact, Hegel's entire account of *generalizing* imagination plays little role in his aesthetic theory. This further confirms the broad gap between its homogenizing abstract universals and the reconciling unities of artistic symbolization. We will see that where the mere association of elements does come into play in the *Lectures,* it invariably assumes the form of linking *dissimilar* particulars in opposition to the subsumptive work of generalizing imagination's categories of likeness. In the next section we will see again that *Phantasie* relates disparate parts as well, but it organizes them under the rule of a determinate concept or theme. *Phantasie*'s Ideal standard of organic unity can only serve to discredit the more "humble" relational work of mere association. But recall from chapter 5 that Hegel granted, though he did not develop, a positive connotation for the play of wit involved in the association of disparate images and ideas. Hegel's *Lectures* will develop the productive potential of associative imagination, but only on the margins of his theory.

To locate in Hegel's philosophy of art theoretical tools to enrich our account of sublime reflection and its production of aesthetic unity, we must focus on moments in his account of art's development that can support a certain balance of imaginative activity. In both the symbolic and romantic forms of art, where the unifying power of Hegelian symbols is not achieved, we will find the associative caprice of imagination seeking to unify disparate parts in keeping with the goal of *Phantasie*, only to produce aesthetic unities of a Kantian sort. This capricious imagination, which surfaced first in the sleeping soul and was retained as mere association in Hegel's theory of imagination, will resurface in the *Lectures* in those cases where aesthetic reflection lacks a determinate conception to guide its projection of unity. This mixture of associative and symbolizing imaginations will coincide with a Kantian productive imagination that constructs an affine network among attributes to (partially) express a rational idea. This combination of Hegelian imaginative powers will result in the production of aesthetic unities that neither succumb to a merely contingent, associative play, nor assume the organic, systematic unity of Hegel's Ideal.

And to anticipate once again, the activity of reflective imagination in symbolic and romantic art will be intimately tied to experiences of sublimity. Those encounters with the "threat" of sublimity, which propelled the construction of the unified subject out of the contingent mass of the sleeping soul, will appear again in Hegel's aesthetic theory. But with the aid of what we now know about Hegelian imagination, we will be able to discern in a properly aesthetic context the work of a reflective imagination that, in the face of a sublimity beyond its comprehension, produces loose relational networks with a claim to validity, a claim to extend understanding, despite the absence of any conceptual rule.

Phantasie's Idea of Beauty

Before we can address what Hegelian imagination produces when it falls short of determinate presentation, we must visit the orthodox center of his philosophy of art. At its peak artistic production achieves, at a sensuous level, that reconciliation of thought and externality which motivates Hegel's construction of the systematic Idea as a whole. The achieved presentation of beauty consists, for Hegel, in the external appearance of the Idea in its truth. He writes, "when truth in . . . its external existence is present to consciousness immediately, and when the Concept remains immediately in unity with its external appearance, the Idea is not only true but beautiful. Therefore the beautiful is characterized as the pure appearance of the Idea to sense" (LFA 111; 13:151). In the *Lectures* art elevates natural contingency toward the necessary unity of thought by having the Concept take possession of and express itself through the sensuous. Beauty mediates these two sides in order to produce the dialectical tension of a *sensuous thought*: "[T]he sensuous aspect of a work of art, in comparison with the immediate existence of things in nature, is elevated to a pure appearance, and the work stands in the *middle* between immediate sensuousness and ideal thought" (LFA 38; 13:60). Beauty is the Concept made flesh, and Hegel makes clear its priority in determining the unity of beauty: "[In] this unity the Concept is predominant. For, in accordance with its own nature, it *is* this identity implicitly already, and therefore generates reality out of itself as its own; therefore, since this reality is its own self-development, it sacrifices nothing of itself in it, but therein simply realizes itself, the Concept, and therefore remains one with itself in its objectivity" (LFA 106; 13:145). Even prior to the feat of beauty, sensuous nature was but the Concept's own vague shadow; art recalls their unity in sensuous form while maintaining the predominance of thought. Although the Concept may come into its sensuous own in this reunion, we will see that much of the contingency and particularity specific to the sensuous must be banished from the artist's subjective conception and its outer presentation in order for the Idea to exist as beauty.

The fact that beauty consists in the sensuous expression of the Concept indicates the intense cognitive orientation of Hegel's aesthetic theory. Works of art for Hegel embody themes that have the imprimatur of the Concept's truth: "[B]eauty is only a specific way of expressing and representing the true, and therefore stands open throughout in every respect to conceptual thinking, so long as that thinking is actually equipped with the power of the Concept" (LFA 91-92; 13:127). What appears in beauty is the artist's concept or specific thematic intention, fashioned and executed by *Phantasie*. This determinateness of beauty indicates the radical difference between Kant's and Hegel's aesthetics. For Kant, the judgment of beauty arises from a reflection in which no determinate concept limits the play of imagination. But for Hegel, beauty plays a role in the realization of the true Idea; what beauty expresses must, then, be circumscribed and definite so that the sensuous material can vividly embody its specific intent. Where Kant thought the meaning of a work should expand indefinitely in the aesthetic idea's "multitude of kindred presentations," Hegel expects a work to present its one true theme so completely that only the slow-witted (or those not equipped with the power of the Concept) could sense any ambiguity in its meaning. Where Kantian aesthetic reflection is not determined by artist's intentions, Hegel takes a work of art to express fixedly the intention we must discern in the rational unity of its product. Where Kant took fine art to present what is inexpressible in concepts, Hegel demands full expression of a determinate theme, and evinces a strong hostility to excuses appealing to inexpressibility.[9]

No matter how determinate Hegel takes the thematic content of art to be, however, artistic production requires that the theme be expressed in the form of *sensuous truth*. Thus though the truths of beauty take their inspiration from the Concept, art does not present that final unity of the Idea which only the medium of philosophical discourse can accommodate. The idea expressed by a work must take priority over the means of expression, but the sensuous nature of those means constrains what art can express: "[It] is art which sets truth before our minds in the mode of sensuous configuration, a sensuous configuration which in this its appearance has itself a loftier, deeper sense and meaning, yet without having the aim of making the Concept as such in its universality comprehensible by way of the sensuous medium; for it is precisely the *unity* of the Concept with the individual appearance which is the essence of the beautiful and its production by art" (LFA 101; 13:140). Art's sensuous mode of expression guarantees for Hegel its separation from philosophy.[10]

Furthermore, works of art must be understood to express *particular*, restricted themes suited to the concrete particularity of the sensuous medium they appear in. When Hegel's systematic Concept appears in beauty, what appears is really a limited and specific theme, rather than the content of the Concept itself in all its complexity: "What we called the content, the meaning [of a work of art], is something in itself simple (the thing itself reduced to its simplest yet most comprehensive determinations) in distinction from execution" (LFA 95; 13:132).[11] In Hegel's famous example, Achilles's wrath is the simple "content" or theme of the *Iliad*, while all the vast and complex features of the epic provide the "form" for expressing that theme.[12] A work of art addresses a theme such as the wages of anger, or fidelity in love, and every part of the work exists only to express it; such a theme might merely appear as a microscopic moment in the grand structure of the Concept itself.

The restricted themes of art bear the Concept's stamp of approval because they deal with matters of profound depth and human concern. The perfection with which great works exhibit the restraint of courage, or evoke the pangs of love, gives expression to truths as necessary as the Concept's own self-organization. Beauty achieves a microcosm of the Idea's rational unity: "It is only by virtue of a genuine and inherently substantial content that restricted and mutable existence acquires independence and substantiality, so that then both determinacy and inherent solidity, content that is both substantial and restrictedly exclusive, are actual in one and the same thing; and hereby existence gains the possibility of being manifested in the restrictedness of its own content as at the same time universality and as the soul which is alone with itself" (LFA 155; 13:205). The sensuous medium of beauty's expression requires that its themes be particular, but this does not detract from its universal import. A work of art not only expresses its restricted theme, but also "expresses" the prerogatives of the Concept in that it has a structure in which every part gets its meaning from the determinate unity of the whole. Using a distinction made by Nelson Goodman, we might say that a work of art *expresses* its particular, limited theme, while at the same time it *exemplifies* the universality of the Concept by sharing a similar form.[13] We need to clarify this form in order to understand the nature of the symbols *Phantasie* exhibits in art.

At the level of the Concept, Hegel takes the unity it provides to consist not in the mere subsumption of like particulars under an abstract generalization, but rather in the organization of disparate parts into a meaningful whole. The Concept provides a locus of unity to make sense of a manifold of parts, such that when it makes a sensuous appearance, "the externally separated parts, into which it unfolds, it can so combine and retain in unity that now every part of its unfolding makes this soul, this totality, appear in each part" (LFA 153;

13:203). What had been a contingent collection of natural and sensuous material gets ordered, under the influence of the Concept, into an expressive whole. In the case of works of art, this whole gets its unity from the one central theme that every part of a work can join the chorus of expressing, and find its own voice by intoning that theme. So to present a theme adequately, the artist must sculpt her available material into a whole in which nothing irrelevant to the expression of that theme remains. "The work of art," Hegel writes, "evinces its genuine originality only by appearing as the *one* personal creation of *one* spirit which gathers and compiles nothing from without, but produces the whole topic from its own resources in a single cast, in one tone, with strict interconnection of its parts, just as the thing has united them in itself" (LFA 296; 13:383). *Phantasie* presents to aesthetic experience a determinate theme expressed through a relational unity of subordinate parts which appear to find themselves at home in expressing this theme.

Hegel maintains that this *form* of the work places constraints on what topics can be presented in it; the organic and determinate unity of beauty limits the thematic content that can appear beautiful. Subjects lacking a compelling internal coherence cannot be presented beautifully. Dieter Henrich has even suggested that the strict *formalism* of Hegel's theory comes to overpower its apparent emphasis on a content-based analysis of art works. Hegel's aesthetics, Henrich writes, "offers a theory of the meaning of the work, an aesthetic of content more rigorous than anything comparable before or since, while on the other hand the content which appears is defined purely as form."[14] Even so, a theory of aesthetic merit that demands thematic unity from works cannot by that means alone specify what topics will be amenable to such presentation. Much of Hegel's *Lectures* explores the sorts of subject matter in which artistic production can achieve this beautiful unity of meaning. In the process, Hegel also delimits where *Phantasie* fails to meet this demand, where a measure of formlessness or deformity marks its productions. There, as in Kant, we will find an encounter with the sublime propel imaginative reflection to produce a less determinate kind of aesthetic unity.

But where *Phantasie* does create unified works, Hegel considers this product a *symbol* because of the identity of content between the work and what it expresses. The whole theme appears wholly in the work, without remainder or ambiguity, and so the correlation between symbol and symbolized, between a work and its theme, is complete. Symbols typically share only some particular feature(s) with what they symbolize (as in the analogical function of Kantian symbols), and we will see in chapter 7 that despite the symbolizing function of *Phantasie* in his aesthetic theory as a whole, Hegel delineates an entire zone of "symbolic art" whose symbols fail to express the ideas toward which they reach. For now, it should be clear that at the height of its powers *Phantasie* produces a microsystem of disparate parts that as a whole expresses one determinate theme. Products of *Phantasie* thus differ greatly from the abstract universals of Hegel's generalizing imagination; those concepts only subsume like instances under general representations without drawing connections between dissimilar particulars. They differ as well from the aesthetic unity produced in Kantian aesthetic ideas, where no determinate theme or concept governs the relation among parts constructed by an imagination overwhelmed by the wealth of material with which it plays.

Some readers of Hegel have underestimated the extent to which he views aesthetic content as "open throughout in every respect to conceptual thinking," as he says. William Desmond, in particular, interprets Hegel's views in a way that leaves much openness and indeterminacy in a work's content.[15] He even suggests that Hegel adopted Kant's doctrine of aesthetic ideas. While defending Hegel from the charge of "totalitarian closure," which purportedly comes with the presentation in art of fixed and determinate themes, Desmond notes that "In advance of Hegel, Kant . . . speaks of aesthetical ideas as straining after a maximum of completeness, like the ideas of reason. Kant, of course, does not fall foul of the accusation of 'totalitarian closure.' Might we not see Hegel as developing the Kantian insight concerning aesthetical ideas, instead of, as the charge implies, reversing it."[16] But this suggestion does not recommend Desmond's broader view of Hegelian "openness" in aesthetic content, because it should be clear from the Interlude above that Hegel explicitly rejects the aesthetic idea. His rejection of it heralds his turn to a cognitive theory of aesthetic content, in the sense that he takes the "one true theme" of a work to be fully expressible in concepts, and succinctly so.

The extent to which a work assumes for Hegel the form of a strict unity of parts, each subordinate to the expression of a single, determinate theme, militates against Desmond's claim to find rich indeterminacies of meaning in Hegel's vision of ideal art.[17]

We should not conclude, however, that Hegel takes the theme of a work to so lord over its parts that they disappear into it. As noted earlier, no matter how subordinate the means of expression must be to the theme a work seeks to express, Hegel insists that the unified presentation of this theme must not artificially force together its disparate parts. This determinate thematic unity must rather be grounded in the organic coherence of parts which integrate freely. The unity of the work of art must not be merely necessary, but must have the strength to handle the independence of its diverse contents. "In the beautiful object," Hegel writes, "there must be both (i) *necessity*, established by the concept, in the coherence of its particular aspects, and (ii) the appearance of their *freedom*, freedom for themselves and not *merely* for the unity of the parts on view. . . . The necessity must not emerge in the form of necessity itself; on the contrary it must be hidden behind an appearance of undesigned contingency. For otherwise the particular real parts lose their standing as existing on the strength of their own reality too, and they appear only in the service of their ideal unity, to which they remain abstractly subordinate" (LFA 115; 13:157).[18] The presence of contingency within the unity of the work softens the potential brutality of an overdone insistence on necessity. This "appearance of undesigned contingency" is no mere gloss of accident meant to conceal the strict necessity of a work's theme; this element of contingency, rather, plays an essential role in the properly sensuous exemplification of the Concept. The aesthetic presentation of sensuous thought requires that the necessity of the idea or theme expressed accommodate the ineluctable contingency of the sensuous material in which it appears. Paradoxically enough, contingency is thus essential to the presentation of aesthetic necessity.[19] In fact, this balance maintained between necessity and contingency applies to Hegel's conception of systematic philosophy as a whole. Just as the artist must do justice both to the necessity of her theme and to the independent contingency of its parts, so philosophy as well "consists generally in coming to know the necessity that is hidden under the semblance of contingency; but this must not be understood to mean that contingency pertains only to our subjective views and that it must therefore be set aside totally if we wish to attain the truth."[20] In both cases, the will to unifying conceptions must be tempered by an affirmation of the open-ended influence of the contingent.[21]

Nevertheless, the sensuous presentation of a strictly unified theme requires that much in the way of natural contingency must be cleared away so that the form of the Concept can inhabit the means of expression. Sensuous beauty requires the element of contingency to authenticate it, but beyond this ambiguous point incidental material must be eradicated from the presentation, for "the task of the work of art [is] to grasp the object in its universality and to let go, in its external appearance, everything that would remain purely external and indifferent for the expression of the content" (LFA 164; 13:217). In particular, Hegel indicates that when executing a worthy theme from her intentions, the artist must banish a good measure of subjective contingency in order to present the theme of the work in its essence. The subjectivity of the artist must serve as a pure medium for the germination of a coherent concept. It must become at one with whatever theme it seeks to realize. The artist must be able "to forget his own personality and its accidental particular characteristics and immerse himself, for his part, entirely in his material, so that, as subject, he is only as it were the form for the formation of the theme which has taken hold of him" (LFA 288; 13:373). The artist must be possessed by the depth and power of a theme to which her idiosyncratic accidents of personality contribute little.[22]

Recall from chapter 5 that Hegel construes the generation of a conscious subject in habit formation as "the Soul's work of art" (PM §411, 147/192). Suppressing the contingent, associative play of the sleeping soul (which will reappear in *Einbildungskraft*'s mere association of ideas), the waking soul organizes itself under unifying categories in the subsumptive activity that will become generalizing imagination. Here again, in the more sophisticated activity of symbolizing *Phantasie*, subjective contingency in the artist must be constrained so that a determinate unity of parts may be fashioned to express the theme of a work. The idiosyncrasy of the artist as a natural subject must give way to the unifying work of beauty: "[The] originality of art does indeed consume the accidental idiosyncrasy of the artist, but it absorbs it only so that the artist can wholly follow the pull and impetus of his inspired genius, filled as it is with his subject alone, and can display his own self, instead of fantasy [*Beliebigkeit*] and empty caprice, in the work he has completed in accordance with its truth" (LFA 298; 13:384). Once again subjective play must be tamed to make room for expressions of unity, though now that unity no longer assumes the form of repetitive habits or abstract concepts. Instead, in artistry *Phantasie* accomplishes the production of organic unities of *disparate* parts in the form of artistic symbols. Mere association, linking images and ideas without unifying them as a determinate rational whole, can on its own offer little to the production of fine art (in Hegel's sense). This is because it *lacks a theme or idea* to guide its play. In mere association, as we have seen, imagination engages in a "sport of vacant-minded ideation"; the relations it pursues "suggest a caprice and a contingency opposed to the very nature of law" (PM §455 An, 207/263). The presentation of beauty, at the peak of imagination's unifying powers, overcomes this subjective contingency in which a capricious imagination is implicated. But I want to suggest in the next section that *Phantasie* acquires its power to unify the diverse from the only of Hegel's imaginative functions which admits a taste for alterity. It gets it from the play of contingent association, though *Phantasie* will guide that play toward the expression of unity.

Phantasying Art: Dehabituation and Re-Determination

Hegel emphasizes that, in its production of aesthetic symbols, *Phantasie* relies for inspiration on "natural gifts" of its subjectivity. It turns out that imagination has enjoyed those gifts since the early development of the soul. *Phantasie* has, Hegel writes, "a sort of instinct-like productiveness, in that the essential figurativeness and sensuousness of the work of art must be present in the artist as a natural gift and natural impulse, and, as an unconscious operation, must belong to the natural side of man too" (LFA 40; 13:63). This alone suggests the ties of artistic creativity to the natural play of feeling in the soul. But, of course, the continuity of felt content we have seen throughout mind's development indicates that even *Einbildungskraft* works that same material when it constructs homogenizing concepts. What makes *Phantasie*'s fashioning of this material artistic, and in some sense a more "natural" impulse?

Both the abstract universals of *Einbildungskraft*, and the artistic symbols of *Phantasie* serve to unify an array of particulars. As we have seen, in the case of *Einbildungskraft* an array of *similar* phenomena gets subsumed under a concept that captures the commonality of the particulars while ignoring their difference. We saw that this abstractive power of Hegelian imagination arose first in habituation's cure for madness. In the context of artistic production, though, imagination as *Phantasie* has the task of uniting an array of disparate parts brought together for some expressive end. Where *Phantasie* does create such unified works, the whole theme appears wholly in the work, without remainder or ambiguity, and so the correlation between symbol and symbolized, between shape and meaning, is complete. This identity is what we saw Hegel attribute to *Phantasie*'s productions in the *Encyclopedia*, and we can now see the extent to which its products surpass the abstract concepts of *Einbildungskraft*. Aesthetic symbols are structured to express some universal theme, are ordered by this principle or purpose, and undertake a unifying reconciliation of diverse natural materials to this end. *Einbildungskraft*, by contrast, only recognizes and sustains, with its concepts, patterns of repetitive likeness.

Phantasie, in order to produce the expressive unity of artistic symbols, must bring diversity into relation with itself. The key to understanding *Phantasie* is to recognize from where it acquires this capacity. It is not evidenced by *Einbildungskraft*, which only relates what is similar, but rather in the mere associative play imagination inherited from the sleeping soul. Both functions of full-fledged imagination rely on that felt associative content, which remains continuous throughout mind's development. *Einbildungskraft* "summarizes" that material by grouping like phenomena, but artistic *Phantasie*, as a natural gift and impulse, responds to it in a manner that preserves its profusion of diverse feeling. The images from which *Einbildungskraft* produces concepts are subordinated to the formation of that abstract universal: only what is similar in them is relevant to the concept, and the remainder can be ignored as *Einbildungskraft* abstracts that shared quality. But Hegel makes it clear, as we saw before, that an artistic symbol cannot force parts into an arbitrary unity, but must respect the individuality of all its parts. Otherwise, Hegel writes, "the particular real parts lose their standing as existing on the strength of their own reality too, and they appear only in the service of their ideal unity, to which they remain abstractly subordinate" (LFA 115; 13:157). It was the independent reality of all the felt moments of the soul which threatened it with madness. That array has since become the mine of images *Phantasie* works on to produce symbols, and Hegel attributes to *Phantasie* a regard for preserving the real diversity of this array it inherited from the soul.

But even as imagination respects that diverse particularity, the thematic purpose or principle *Phantasie* fulfills in producing an artistic symbol gives an expressive coherence to the array of particulars it relates. *Phantasie* does not merely reproduce the associative disarray of the sleeping soul any more than *Einbildungskraft* does. *Phantasie* preserves the felt diversity of particulars even as it brings expressive unity to them. Most importantly, Hegel claims that it can do so because the unity *Phantasie* expresses through its symbols reveals the related parts' *own* unity. Hegel's Concept not only relates a manifold of parts into a self-contained unity with some expressive aim; the Concept unifies parts that express their true nature for the first time in their involvement in that community of parts. Only when given a context by the thematic purposiveness of the Concept do the contingent particulars of sense take on meaning: "[T]he Concept is so much the absolute unity of its determinations that these do not remain independent and they cannot be realized by separating themselves from one another so as to become independent individuals, or otherwise they would abandon their unity" (LFA 108; 13:147–148).[23] The relational structure of the Concept mimics the form of Hegel's systematic Idea as a whole. That Idea is embodied in the *Encyclopedia*, where particular phenomena—such as insanity, the morphology of sea shells, the notion of "measure," the institution of marriage, and the powers of imagination—are given meaning by their participation in a faceted whole.

Hegel tailors this notion of the Concept to the case of beauty, where *Phantasie* restores unity to the associated particulars it handles: "[Although] the difference of the particulars is *real*, their *ideal* conceptually adequate unity must all the same be restored within them; they are particularized in *reality* but their unity, mediated into *ideality*, must also exist in them" (LFA 110; 13:150). In a sense, then, *Phantasie* redeems the associative play of feeling in the sleeping soul by disclosing in art a unity and coherence in that play. Soul was by itself incapable of discerning the order underlying the play of its associations, and the apparent disorder got out of hand in madness. Habituation resolved the problem to an extent by subordinating the moments of the soul to the homogenizing repetitions of habit, and this ordering function became the concept-forming talents of *Einbildungskraft*. But artistic *Phantasie* capitalizes on these structural developments to recover the free relational coherence of soul's play, drawing on that rich deposit of "natural" unity to produce symbols whose reconciling holism surpasses the abstract concepts of habitual *Einbildungskraft*.

Recall Hegel's comment, noted earlier, that imaginative wit "connects ideas which, although remote from one another, none the less have in fact an inner connection." We can now better see that this alludes to his conviction that the unifying products of imagination *restore* to objects of experience a coherence *of their own,* which they possess *through* their inextricable intertwining with mind's powers of cognition. The habituated abstractions of *Einbildungskraft* fall short of realizing that "speculative" unity, and Hegel's elaboration of a more accomplished imaginative power in *Phantasie* represents his ultimate rejection of the habit-driven imagination of the empiricists. We noted that they took patterns of similarity to be simply given in perception, and failed to justify (provide a ground for) imagination's power to form abstract ideas on the basis of similarity. In the context of Hegel's brand of transcendental philosophy, imagination can be said to restore to the particular *its own* unity precisely because whatever coherence experience has, whether in homogenizing patterns of abstract universality or in the organic "unity over diversity" that Hegel embraces, mind's progressive determination of experience provides the only available, the only necessary justification. The natural play of association in the soul turns out to have a reconciling coherence, obscured by habituation and by *Einbildungskraft* but brought to expression by artistic *Phantasie,* for the very reason that it was never a "natural" given at all: for Hegel, it awaited the realization of its altogether mediated nature in the Idea formed from spirit's highest powers.

We can see now that Hegel's way of contrasting *Phantasie* and *Einbildungskraft* reflects his larger commitment to valorizing the unifying powers of reason over the (merely) conceptual, representational thinking of "the understanding." *Einbildungskraft* is the imaginative power most strongly allied with abstract cognition, as is evident in the homogenizing effects of the concepts it forms. This everyday way of thinking, pursued within the rubric of a firm subject-object distinction, gained its everydayness from the formation of those repetitive habits that, in Hegel's *Encyclopedia* account, gave birth in the first place to the conscious subject aware of its objects. Throughout his systematic philosophy Hegel aims to supplant the abstractions of this habituated understanding with the overarching unity he attributes to speculative reason (the very unity exemplified by the Idea the *Encyclopedia* represents). *Phantasie*, in its artistic efforts to unify the diverse, steps beyond the abstract universals of understanding and its imaginative proxy, *Einbildungskraft*. Hegel grants to its symbolic products a truth-telling function; this aligns it with religion and philosophy as the "media" in which reason pursues the realization of *concrete* universality. Among the various functions of imagination Hegel recounts in the *Encyclopedia*, he accords only *Phantasie* the status of a "nominal reason," the further development of which produces our highest rational powers (PM §457 An, 211/268). By casting imaginative artistry as a stepping-stone to reason, Hegel distances the highest accomplishments of imagination from the origins of that power in habit formation. By this means Hegel "saves" imagination from being merely the agent of arbitrary habit it was for his empiricist predecessors.

By producing aesthetic symbols with a unity beyond the means of *Einbildungskraft* to conceive, *Phantasie* undermines the habitual ease of abstract conceptual thinking. By demonstrating a respect for the particular diversity of what it unifies, *Phantasie* denies the "natural" validity of concepts which ignore difference in order to force a crude unity. Those concepts, produced by *Einbildungskraft* under the aegis of understanding, reflect the partial origins of imagination in habit-formation. Artistic imagination, though, *dehabituates* such patterns of thinking by disclosing a more organic unity of the diverse, a unity homogenizing concepts miss. And *Phantasie* "denatures" those habits precisely by drawing on the other half of imagination's origins, in the associative play of the sleeping soul. The madness habituation cured was the frenzy of untamed diversity in thought, and at these higher levels of mental development Hegelian imagination recovers that associative diversity, and puts it to the purpose of expressing unity. The sleeping and waking souls of Hegel's *Encyclopedia* "Anthropology" became the merely associative and the generalizing halves of imagination, respectively. The former sacrificed unity to diversity in the horror of madness, while the latter sacrificed diversity to unity in the straitjacket of habit. Only in *Phantasie,* among the powers of imagination, do unity and diversity coalesce, through its production of concrete universality in artistic symbols. That is, when the artistry of *Phantasie* resists conceptual habits and recovers the diversity of association in the sleeping soul, it makes the initial stabs at the speculative unity which Hegel's systematic reason will ultimately accomplish. Hence the soul's mad play not only inspires the labors of artistic imagination, which recollects its origins in recovering that play; it also prefigures the very strivings of Hegelian reason, in which the tempering purpose of holistic truth-seeking will bring order to that associative play.

Hegel's philosophy of art is frequently chided for its conservative devotion to classical ideals of beauty and its adherence to the requirement that art express "national" character and cohesion. These criticisms may be just, but my account of madness, habit, imagination and its artistry in Hegel's *Encyclopedia* and his *Lectures on Aesthetics* suggests an alternative way of viewing art in Hegel's thought. In its "maddening" opposition to habitual thinking, artistic imagination challenges what seems "natural" to its audience, just as philosophical reason challenges our most closely held and taken for granted conceptual dichotomies. A classically conservative theory of art would hold that a beauty *given* in nature sets the standard for human imitations. Hegel's expressed indifference to natural beauty, indicated by its cursory treatment in the *Lectures,* exemplifies his conviction that art plays a role in the constant challenging of any allegiance to natural essences or abstract representations of a "given." Against such uncritical habits of thought, imaginative artistry dehabituates customary patterns of thinking by offering alternative visions of "unity over diversity" to test the homogenizing status quo. Surprisingly enough, the dehabituating work of *Phantasie* suggests surprising allegiances between Hegel's philosophy of art and the grand tradition of aesthetic dehabituation that followed him, from Nietzsche to Heidegger, Adorno, Derrida, and Lyotard, and throughout the avant-garde prerogatives of twentieth-century art.[24] Hegel stands as one of the optimistic founders of that tradition; this would make artistic *Phantasie,* in its revisionary projections of human possibility, a force for conceptual revolution.

But there is a difference that makes all the difference between Hegel and these critical inheritors of his tradition, between Hegel and the Kantian aesthetic indeterminacy which these thinkers also draw on. The difference is that, for Hegel, art remains a cognitive locus of truth. Art dehabituates abstract determinations of taken-for-granted conceptual thinking only to replace them with concrete determinations of rational unity. Hegel's Ideal art *re-determines* the habitual "given," transforms it into a concretion of reason's systematic Idea. By comprehending the particular as a determinate expression of organic unity, art fulfills, to the extent it can, Hegel's radicalization of reflective judgment not only as a power of empirical concept formation (in *Einbildungskraft*), but also as a power capable of exhibiting a totality of meaning (in *Phantasie*). But contrary to Hegel, the point of aesthetic dehabituation in its twentieth-century legacy has been to question the limits of determinacy, and test the implications of admitting ineluctable indeterminacy into thought, meaning, and our self-understanding. Lyotard has suggested that our century is particularly burdened (or blessed) with an aesthetics of sublimity for which "the stake of art" has become "to be witness to the fact that there is indeterminacy."[25] This would be not only an indeterminacy of what has not yet been rendered determinate in our systems of thought, but also an irreducible indeterminacy that marks the limit of our cognitive powers.

Now, Kantian sublime reflection does admit indeterminacy into aesthetic experience, it does embrace the unique status of the aesthetic as a foray into the Other of unified understanding. At the same time, as an interpretive engagement with uncertain meanings, it offers a *partial* sense for experiential wholes which exceed our total comprehension. Sublime reflection legitimately claims to convey a felt sense for the whole, some features of which it expresses through the networks of affinity it discloses, but it also acknowledges the limits of its presentational powers. Hegel, too, lauds the dehabituating benefits of art's defiance of conceptual categories. But by replacing abstract concepts with the determinacy of rational Ideals, he occludes the element of aesthetic sublimity we would need to make any sense of the prerogatives of much modernist and especially postmodern art.

Philippe Lacoue-Labarthe sees the cognitive determinacy of Hegel's Ideal as "a gigantic 'war-machine' directed against aesthetics in general . . . and intended, under the pretext of correcting its mistakes (its inability to grasp the beautiful in its *concept*) to contain the danger which its 'establishment' represented. . . ."[26] The danger aesthetics represents to Hegel is its establishment of a noncognitive locus of truth, of a felt validity irreducible to concepts. Hence the importance of Hegel's encyclopedic progression from "anthropology" to "psychology": it leads an initially *felt* aesthetic sense for unity (in the waking soul) into the conceptual fold of first abstract and then concrete universality. Hence the privileged position of sublimity as a threat: it claims to exceed conceptual comprehension as such, to establish, as Lacoue-Labarthe writes, "the paradoxical [aesthetic] locus where truth could be *revealed* as undiscoverable, unrepresentable. . . ."[27] The maximal import of aesthetic indeterminacy lies not in a mere resistance to determination, but in its provision of a non- or precognitive sphere of validity. The affine networks of relation that sublime reflection produces reveal webs of shared meaning that cannot be encapsulated in discursive concepts or schematized as a rational system. And the felt dimension of these "subliminal" meanings implicate each person's interior habits of thought in the patterns of affinity that sublime reflection exposes and reworks.

Recall that in the aesthetic expansion attending production of a Kantian aesthetic idea, the "multitude of kindred presentations" the Kantian subject ranges over in its free play allows a variety of plausible interpretations of some object. But in Hegel's case the determinacy of artistic meaning does not allow room for interpretation to include those subjective elements. The range of elements allowed into Hegelian interpretation is established in and by the work, with perhaps the allowance of some contextual features drawn from the work's historical setting (of which the work's meaning is really a reflection, the artist's time grasped in sensuous form). That is, Hegelian artistic symbols are bounded, and so not sublime: bounded by the work's fixed meaning and the determinate intention of its creator. Kant's analytic of the sublime is of such importance precisely because the validated indeterminacy of meaning that sublime reflection embraces is the centerpiece that makes the aesthetic a "competitor" of cognitive understanding. Those aesthetic unities of relation, as we will see in part III, comprise a widespread background of sublime understanding that complements the more determinate products of unified conceptual cognition. Hegel's cognitive theory of determinate artistic meanings instead returns the aesthetic to the status of handmaiden to cognition.

Lyotard contrasts Kant's acceptance of the ineliminable conflict between imagination and reason in the experience of sublimity, with Hegel's rendering the two powers "homogeneous" by regarding imagination "as reason arrested in one of its formations, in one of its acts, . . . as a reason temporarily limited, . . . [that] will not fail [in the end] to pass these limits."[28] While Hegel's reason no doubt goes on to surpass its encounters with the sublime, my concern lies in what aesthetic reflection accomplishes in Hegel's theory at those points when the conflict does come to a head. We may assess what Hegel contributes to an understanding of the aesthetic unity produced in those cases without regard for what he takes speculative reason to go on to produce in his system. We do know that the sublime reflection in question will not be found at the level of Hegel's artistic Ideal. The powers of imagination which we suspect will contribute to the construction of aesthetic unity are suppressed in *Phantasie*'s Ideal productions.

Hegel locates this peak of perfection in his classical form of art, the mid-point of his narrative, following the symbolic form but preceding the romantic. In the "classical art" of Hellenic culture, as Hegel casts it, we will not find the loose aesthetic unity produced by sublime reflection. This can come as no surprise when one sees that "for the classical artist," according to Hegel, "the content must already be there cut and dried, given, so that *in its essential nature it is already determined for imagination* [*Phantasie*] as settled, as belief personal or national, or as a past event perpetuated by tales and tradition" (LFA 438–439;

14:28).[29] In the classical art of *Phantasie*'s ideal, Hegel repeats for us, "the content is determinate and the free shape is determined by the content itself and it belongs to it absolutely, so that the artist seems only to execute what is already cut and dried on its own account in essence" (LFA 439; 14:29).[30] In the face of such determinacy of content and appropriate form, the spectator charged with drawing this content from the work's sensuous existence will seek to make sense of the work's parts all as parts of a whole determined by that theme.[31] But the aesthetic reflection I have sought to articulate has no (and finds no) theme or concept to determine and adjudicate its relating of parts.

In a strong sense the determinate unity of Hegel's classical Ideal reflects the coherence of the social world from which it arises. More accurately, it reflects Hegel's nostalgic construal of Greek culture as an Arcadian past when thought and sensuality coalesced perfectly. The artist of Hegel's Ideal work of art has a genius for presenting necessary totalities of meaning because he supposedly has been nurtured by such a balanced and "rational" form of life. It may well be that Hegel's Ideal of Beauty can bloom only as the delicate flower of a certain Mediterranean soil. If his Ideal of determinate expression needs the sustenance of a rationally balanced and unified social world, it may be a rare occurrence indeed, and it would likely aver to put in an appearance in our thoroughly disunified and fragmented historical present. Arthur Danto has suggested that the stunning variety of contemporary art reflects our own uncertain identities: we cannot need one kind of art in particular when we do not even know who we each are, much less who "we" are.[32] Given the disruptive (sometimes destructive), critical (sometimes cynical) prerogatives of much modernist and especially postmodern art and popular culture, we have more to learn about ourselves from an aesthetics of indeterminacy, of the kind to be drawn from Kant's reflections on the sublime, than from Hegel's determinate Ideal. We have been dehabituated, by the end of this millenium, of a confidence in rational unity and our capacity to achieve it. I will insist in part III, however, that this "humility" does not keep a sublime understanding from forwarding our sense-making efforts to the extent that it can.

Hegel makes the preceding remarks about the essential determination of the classical artist's material when he is moving to the classical form of art from the symbolic form he had just treated. In these same passages Hegel characterizes symbolic art as that "troubled quest" in which "an imagination [*Einbildungskraft*] that runs riot without proportion and definition," produces "expositions of the content [which] remain themselves only enigmas and problems, and they testify only to a wrestling for clarity and to the struggle of the spirit which continually invents without finding repose and peace" (LFA 438–439; 14:29). Perhaps this struggle of the spirit in symbolic art reveals the efforts of an imagination that falls short of Ideal productions. This imagination might produce something like a Kantian aesthetic unity, with the help of those other imaginative powers that resist the determinacy of Hegel's Ideal. If so, the contours of an indeterminately sublime reflection might be recovered from the un-Ideal margins of his theory. We could then leave Ideal Beauty to the ancients, and embrace the sublime disunity, and the unscripted creative potential, of our own disordered present.

We turn now to Hegel's accounts of the symbolic and romantic forms of artistic expression. We will see imagination seek and fail to produce a determinate unity of parts, and produce aesthetic unity instead. In keeping with the Kantian standpoint from which I began, that imaginative production will bear the mark of an engagement with sublimity.

7

Aesthetic Unity in the Hegelian Context

What do riddles and metaphors, poems and the "prose of life," have in common? According to Hegel, they push us to reach for interpretive meanings we cannot quite capture. In a riddle, this unsatisfied striving lasts only as long as the answer is withheld. But aesthetic experience as Hegel conceives it encounters moments—when unfolding a complex metaphor, or unpacking a dense poetic text, or even when reflecting on the complexities of our lived worlds—when determinate comprehension runs out of steam. Hegel values these moments less than those Ideal instances, however rare, when art prefigures the achieved unity of form and content, of subject and world which Hegel thinks only philosophy can ultimately guarantee. But by dwelling on those moments, where they crop up in Hegel's *Lectures,* we can elaborate the sort of indeterminate sublime reflection I have thematized.

We know that the Ideal unity that Hegel's systematic reason and his symbolic artistry achieve takes time. On the way to these perfected determinations of content, less consummate phenomena get positioned as flawed steps in a progression that ends in reason's triumph. In the case of the *Encyclopedia Philosophy of Mind,* even bizarre features of the psyche were located in an account of imagination's formation as a subordinate of rational thought. Hegel later ignores those features imagination acquired through its "history" that do not contribute to the production of rational unity, such as the play of mere association. But they remain among its powers, and they will play critical roles in the aesthetic reflection developed in this chapter. Hegel's *Lectures on*

Aesthetics offers no exception to this pattern. In his narrative of art's development, as we know, the realization of Ideal Beauty is preceded by the symbolic art form. While symbolizing *Phantasie* produces works thoroughly organized by a single theme, the "symbolic" form fails to produce such ideally expressive symbols. In this prior moment, aesthetic content can only point toward a unity it cannot fully express. This should sound much like a Kantian aesthetic idea. In the "romantic" art that Hegel takes to succeed the classical form, aesthetic imagination again finds itself unable to unify a determinate content, though for different reasons than obtained in symbolic art. We will find that in Hegel's "imperfect" forms of art imagination produces, with the aid of powers Hegel devalued in his encyclopedic account of it, the indeterminate aesthetic unity of a sublime reflection.[1] And as we have come to expect from moments of indeterminacy, both the symbolic and the romantic forms will bear the mark of an aesthetics of sublimity.

Symbolic Art and the Hegelian Sublime

If Hegel's Ideal of Beauty is met in the classical form of art, then the "symbolic form" that precedes it hardly qualifies as art under Hegel's schema. Symbolic art does not achieve the reconciliation of concept and sensuous externality that makes art, at its peak for Hegel, a harbinger of the conciliatory potential of philosophy. In fact, at this premature stage of art's development, not only a fit between concept and the means of expression is lacking; Hegel also thinks the very content of this art lacks determinacy, and so the efforts to express it cannot reach "true" artistry. "The first form of art," he writes, "is . . . rather a *mere search* for portrayal than a capacity for true presentation; the Idea has not found the form even in itself and therefore remains struggling and striving after it" (LFA 76; 13:107). This lack of determinate content in the symbolic form and the struggle undertaken to comprehend its absent unity already suggest the importance of this part of Hegel's aesthetic theory to our purposes. The symbolic form of art evinces precisely that unfulfilled search for unity that premised Kantian imagination's production of "mere" aesthetic unity. Kant's imagination, seeking to meet reason's demand for totality, sought in sublime reflection to comprehend a content beyond its means to present, and produced instead the indeterminate unity of an aesthetic idea. So will Hegel's, as we will see.

We must first be sure to distinguish the role of symbolizing *Phantasie* in Hegel's aesthetic theory as a whole from the imaginative products of the symbolic form of art.[2] As we have seen, a true Hegelian aesthetic symbol gives complete expression to its definite meaning (the symbolized). But "from the very start we must at once distinguish the symbol in its own independent characteristic form, in which it serves as the decisive type for artistic vision and representation, from that sort of symbolism which is just reduced to a mere external form, explicitly not independent" (LFA 303; 13:393). The form the symbol takes in the symbolic form of art is not "independent" precisely because it does not enjoy the full expression of content that would stamp it as Ideal. Instead, symbols under the symbolic form will approximate to aesthetic ideas, which can only point toward a content beyond their means to express fully. The "definite meaning" of a Kantian aesthetic idea is unavailable; here, too, in Hegel's symbolic form of art, the absence of a determinate meaning or theme leaves imagination to its own devices in seeking to decipher its object.[3] Hegel writes of the "merely symbolic" symbol that it "by its very nature remains essentially ambiguous. . . . [For] the look of a symbol as such raises at once the doubt *whether a shape is to be taken as a symbol or not,* even if we set aside the further ambiguity in respect of the *determinate* meaning which a shape is supposed to signify amongst the *several* meanings for which it can often be used as a symbol through associations of a more remote kind" (LFA 306; 13:397). Unlike the products of symbolizing *Phantasie,* what an aesthetic symbol of the symbolic form symbolizes is unclear.[4] Its meaning cannot be definitively determined, and its meaning can vary across the interpretations of different "readers" of the symbol. This ambiguity implies that, unlike the univocity of interpretation required by the "one true theme" of Hegel's Ideal works of art, works of the symbolic form will allow the sort of variety in interpretation embraced by a Kantian aesthetic. To this extent, Hegel's symbolic form in effect constitutes the Kantian moment of his aesthetic theory.[5]

Recall from chapter 6 that Hegel's aesthetic of content orients his analysis toward the character of art works themselves; for the most part, he is not concerned with aesthetic *reception*. Thus in his account of symbolic art he analyzes ambiguous symbols that point toward a "determinate" content that is in fact not yet definite and that they cannot present definitively; but he has little to say about how an aesthetically judging subject would respond to these symbols. As we saw before, one can reasonably project an account of aesthetic productivity and response from Hegel's characterization of the artistic products in question. But if works of the symbolic form do not symbolize a definite content in the manner of symbolizing *Phantasie*'s Ideal products, it is unclear at this point to what imaginative activity Hegel would attribute their production. Something less sophisticated than full-fledged *Phantasie* must be at work in their creation, for they do not meet its standards of determinacy. For my purposes, sharing Hegel's indifference to the opaque operations of artistic creativity, the focus will again be on what imaginative activity plays a part in responding to ambiguous symbols. We will find that only by reinstating the "merely" associative powers of *Phantasie* can reflective engagement with the symbolic form of art be clarified.

Hegel divides the symbolic into three moments, the overarching theme of which is "a continuing struggle for compatibility of meaning and shape" (LFA 317; 13:411). The harmonious meeting of a determinate meaning fully expressed in a definite shape will arise only in the transition to the classical form of art, while symbolic art knows only disharmony, the unsatisfied reach toward the universal.[6] It struggles with its ignorance of the Idea in three stages: it begins, first of all, as an "unconscious symbolism" that does not yet sufficiently understand the difference between the universal and the particular and so vaguely identifies the two (LFA 323–361; 13:389–466). Here the particular is taken as an immediate manifestation of an obscure universal presence or power; the *distinction* between meaning and shape, which motivates artistry to render them perfectly compatible, is not yet grasped. Hegel discusses here such phenomena as animal worship, fire in Zoroastrianism, and the Egyptian pyramids.

The second stage of symbolic art, which Hegel calls the "Symbolism of the Sublime," understands the distinction between meaning and its presentation, but the difference between them appears insurmountable. As in Kant's sublime, no presentation can fully express a meaning which defies comprehension. The obscure content of the symbol, despite its lack of definition, remains superior to its only poor means of expression. This absent meaning of the symbolized makes the presented symbol itself "known as its negative, external to it, and its servant. In order to express *itself* therein, the meaning cannot allow this existent to subsist independently, but must posit it as the inherently deficient, something to be superseded—although it has for its expression nothing other than precisely this existent which is external to it and null" (LFA 318; 13:413).

Finally, Hegel calls the third stage of symbolic art the "Conscious Symbolism of the Comparative Art-Form" (LFA 378–421; 13:486–539). In this art, Hegel argues, the meaning to be presented attains some definition, but the link between this meaning and its sensuous presentation has become so tenuous that, far from identifying a harmonious unity between them, one is just seen as an illustration of the other, "for comparison's sake." Here Hegel writes that symbolization itself "becomes a conscious severance of the explicitly clear meaning from its sensuous associated picture; yet in this separation there remains at the same time an express *relation*, but one which instead of appearing as an *immediate* identity, asserts itself only as a mere *comparison* of the two, in which the difference . . . comes to the fore just as clearly. This is the sphere of the symbol known as a symbol: the meaning known and envisaged on its own account in its universality, the concrete appearance of which is expressly reduced to a mere *picture* and is compared with the meaning for the purpose of its illustration by art" (LFA 318; 13:412). The status and import of the comparative art form—under which Hegel treats examples as diverse as fables, proverbs, riddles, allegories, similes, and *metaphors*—will require considerable clarification later.

It will be best, in fact, to anticipate in brief the interpretive strategy of the coming pages. Recall the Kantian structure of sublime reflection presented in chapter 3. Faced with a diversity of elements, imagination sought to comprehend them as a whole, and underwent an experience of sublimity when it failed to. In lieu of a conceptually determined rational unity, imagination produced instead an aesthetic idea. This aesthetic unity assumed the form of a loose network of connections between disparate images, objects, and ideas. Metaphors were seen to be an emblematic product of this form of aesthetic reflection. In Kant's case aesthetic unity had no systematic structure and could not be captured by or subsumed under any definite concept. Despite the absence of any such conceptual rule, this reflection claimed some validity, some disclosive value for its products. The remainder of this section and the next will argue that Hegel's account of the sublime and its passage into comparative art repeats the structure of sublime reflection we saw in Kant's aesthetic theory. In Hegel's sublime, *Phantasie* faces a particular whose universal meaning it cannot grasp. But the symbolizing function of the particular leads imagination to seek some unified comprehension of its object. In the absence of any definite meaning, imagination compares elements of its object to construct relationships that emphasize, as Hegel indicated above, the parts' differences as much as their similarities. The comparative art of Hegel's symbolic form will be the product of an imagination that has passed through an experience of sublime incomprehension to construct a properly aesthetic unity, neither amenable to conceptual determination nor merely contingent in its outcome.

In the symbolic form of art, as we have seen, the Idea has not yet been sufficiently worked out for a satisfactory external formation of it to be found. At this early stage "the relation of the Idea to the objective world [is] a *negative* one"; the Idea "is itself unsatisfied by such externality, and, as the inner universal substance thereof, it persists *sublime* above all this multiplicity of shapes which do not correspond with it" (LFA 77; 13:108). Hegel thus demotes the sublime to a rudimentary form that falls short of the reconciliation of thought and world at which art aims. The experience of sublimity expresses the schism between the thought of the universal and the finite world of sense. It emphasizes this crucial distinction, yet without resolving it in the sort of sensuous manifestation of the universal which art will later accomplish: "Sublimity lifts the Absolute above every immediate existent and therefore brings about the liberation which, though abstract at first, is at least the foundation of the spirit. For although the meaning thus elevated is not yet apprehended as concrete spirit, it is nevertheless regarded as the inner life, self-existent and reposing on itself, which by its very nature is incapable of finding its true expression in finite phenomena" (LFA 362; 13:466–467). Hegel regards the sublime as that which exceeds the bounds of sense and defies presentation in finite form. The sublime is the unpresentable beyond, and Hegel associates it primarily with our relation to the sacred and with attempts to symbolize it in religious iconography. The presentation of the sublime serves to point toward the sacred while at the same time expressing the futility of seeking to present the sacred in the merely finite. "This outward shaping which is itself annihilated by what it reveals, so that the revelation of the content is at the same time a supersession of the revelation, is the sublime" (LFA 363; 13:468).

In keeping with Hegel's location of the sublime primarily in spiritual art, Paul de Man has interpreted Hegel's symbolic sublime as "the moment of radical and definitive separation between the order of discourse and the order of the sacred."[7] The discursive symbol can only point toward the sacred order which it cannot articulate and from which it is forever alienated. The sublime universal that, in this early stage of art's development, refuses to appear in any concrete form, signals an unacceptable schism in the unity of the Idea. The stage of classical art to follow will make the reconciliation of thought and externality possible, at least until romantic art again sullies this unity. Of particular interest in de Man's reading is his claim that for Hegel the sublime poses a challenge to the concept of mind, which de Man takes to be "the monotheistic principle of philosophy as the single field of unified knowledge."[8] Because the sublime of symbolic art separates the universal from sensuous immediacy, it forfeits the project of constructing a systematic unity of knowledge. Its premature acceptance of this schism must be overcome if a unity of the universal with concrete particulars is to be achieved. Hegel must resist the experience of sublimity and must relegate it to a rudimentary stage of art's development, because it contradicts what he takes to be the very point of art—to affect a sensuous manifestation of the Idea—while the sublime expresses only the Idea's absence. Hegel resists the "threat of sublimity" in his *Lectures* as assiduously as he did in the *Encyclopedia* construction of a unified subject. But in his aesthetic theory we will discern somewhat different results for imagination's encounter with the sublime.

Aesthetic Unity in the Comparative Art-Form

The sublime's deferral of the determinate universal sets just the stage we need for an aesthetic reflection that seeks some coherence in its object without the aid of definite concepts or fully realized themes. As in the Kantian sublime, Hegel's *Phantasie* has found itself incapable of presenting a determinate unity of meaning. But *Phantasie* still seeks a manifestation of the universal in its particular, as did Kantian imagination when it treated the particular as an expression of some rational idea. Aesthetic reflection's presupposition of purposive unity led Kant's imagination to construct what coherence it could for its object: the aesthetic ideas produced by sublime reflection were its product. Here too, Hegelian imagination will respond to sublime incomprehensibility by seeking out what relational coherence it can muster. Hegel considers this process and its products under the "comparative art-forms" that immediately follow his analysis of the sublime.

In the absence of the truly symbolic, perfectly symbiotic relationship between form and content required by the Ideal of beauty, Hegel takes comparative art to effect a *purely subjective linkage* between some topic and a depiction of it. "[If], within this actual cleavage [between meaning and shape]," Hegel writes, "shape and meaning are to be brought into a relation of inner affinity, as symbolic art requires, then this relation lies directly neither in the meaning nor in the shape, but in a *subjective* third thing which, in its subjective vision, finds aspects of similarity in both, and in reliance thereon illustrates and explains the independently clear meaning through the cognate individual picture" (LFA 321; 13:416–417). Hegel has in mind here things such as parables, where a simple narrative is used to illustrate a moral lesson. The linkage of story and moral is merely subjective because many features of the story will bear only a contingent relation to expression of the moral, or they will only serve to convey the moral rather than being the embodiment of an Ideal content.

Three key aspects of Hegel's account of comparative art need emphasis: (1) Hegel's sudden introduction of explicitly known meanings; (2) his location of the needed subjective element in the artist; and (3) his emphasis on the subjective relating of depiction and meaning. In the previous moment of art's development, *Phantasie* lacked any definite meaning under which to think its object. Suddenly in comparative art, *Phantasie* invents a link between an expressive shape and an "explicitly known" topic. Hegel writes that in the comparative art form "the meaning is not only explicitly known but is *expressly* posited as different from the external way in which it is represented. In that case, as in sublimity, *the meaning, thus explicitly expressed, does not essentially appear in and as the meaning of the shape given to it in such a way.* But the relation of the two to one another no longer remains, as it did in the preceding stage, a relation grounded purely in the meaning itself; on the contrary, it becomes a more or less accidental concatenation produced by the subjective activity of the poet, by the immersion of his spirit in an external existent, by *his wit and his invention* in general" (LFA 378; 13:486–487).[9] If Hegel grants to comparative art a relation to a definite meaning, it is only because the "true" unity of concept and means of expression has been so sundered in this art that the link between them relies entirely on the subjective wit of the artist. The relationship here between shape and meaning, then, falls far short of that in Ideal Beauty.[10] But furthermore, this meaning does not even appear as the meaning of the shape, Hegel claims; thus the explicit link between them is evident *only* in the conscious intention of the artist. The producer of comparative art, Hegel writes, "kens both the inner essence of the meanings he has adopted as the content of his work and also the nature of the external phenomena which he uses in a comparative way for their better illustration, and he puts the two together *consciously* and intentionally on account of their discovered similarity" (LFA 379; 13:487). Only for the artist is the connection between meaning and shape immediately evident, for it exists only in her forging of it.

We have prepared in advance for the need to reorient Hegel's aesthetic theory toward an account of aesthetically reflective *reception* and judgment of works. Here the need is paramount. For from the perspective of the audience of comparative art, the meaning attached to an object in the artist's intentions is not evident. As was the case in treating Kant's distinction between pure and dependent beauty, aesthetic reflection on the purposive unity of a work is carried out with indifference to the known or unknown intentions of the artist. Thus aesthetic reflection on the comparative art form must seek out the meaning which the particular is supposed to illustrate. Despite Hegel's claim that comparative art involves the linking of shape and a definite meaning, that link is not apparent to aesthetic reflection. From *its* perspective, the linking inspired by comparative art cannot be an immediate attachment of a meaning to the shape. Instead, the reflection encouraged by comparative art will involve relating features of the given particular in the attempt to find a definite meaning. In other words, the reflection on comparative art will construct *aesthetic ideas*, loose networks of meaningful connection forged in the absence of conceptual determination. This may seem for the moment like a radical extrapolation from Hegel's position, but his examples will show that the work of interpreting comparative art lies in making links among confusedly disparate material.

Hegel distinguishes two species of comparative art. In one the artist begins with a particular presentation and produces a universal meaning with which it can be compared. In the other she has a meaning in mind for which she procures an illustration (LFA 380; 13:489). This distinction may seem to map on to Kant's division of reflective and determinative judgments. After all, reflective judgment seeks a universal under which to think the particular, and determinative judgment shows the particular to instantiate a given universal. This may suggest that we should seek cases of aesthetic unity in the first form, Hegel's "Comparisons Originating from the External Object." He treats under this category such aesthetic forms as fables, parables, and proverbs. For example, Hegel discusses Aesop's fables, where natural relations between animals are deployed to illuminate some ethical maxim (LFA 384–388; 13:492–498). In such cases, from the perspective of an aesthetic audience, the meaning of the fable must be worked out in our judgment, and so a measure of aesthetic reflection comes into play. But the relation of comparison between the particular and the meaning it illustrates is too determinate in these cases for them to help us. In judgment of such a work, the meaning soon discerned in it becomes the organizing principle under which we explain the whole. The sustained indeterminacy of the aesthetic idea is not at home here.

Oddly enough, then, we find the Hegelian construction of aesthetic unity, rather, in the second species of comparative art, "Comparisons

Which Start from the Meaning." This seems odd because the determinate meaning of an object must be lacking in a reflection which produces aesthetic unity. But again, only the *artist* begins with a meaning and seeks a depiction with which to compare it. From the perspective of its audience, the configuration always comes first, and its meaning must be sought out. Hegel writes: "[The] separateness of the two sides [meaning and shape] is the presupposition and therefore their association is (a) a purely subjective enlivenment of the meaning through a shape external to it and (b) an interpretation of a real existent equally subjective through its bearing on the other ideas, feelings, and thoughts of the spirit" (LFA 396; 13:508). Aesthetic reflection will *interpret* the particular in an effort to formulate a meaning that makes sense of it. Because we are far from the Ideal of Beauty, this reflection will not discern a determinate theme which animates every part of the work. Meaning and presentation remain separate, as Hegel says, for all symbolic art. But reflection on comparative art will construct what coherence it can, by relating the disparate parts of the work with the aid of the associative powers of imagination. This will involve relating the particular to other "ideas, feelings, and thoughts" it brings to mind, to the "wealth of kindred presentations" it brings on. In short, the search for meaning in Hegel's comparative art forms results in the imaginative production of aesthetic unity. We can develop this interpretation in a series of examples.

Hegel's forms of comparative art include riddles, metaphor, and simile.[11] The riddle begins as a series of clues for which we anticipate a solution, but if it is effective we are stumped, unable to grasp the answer that would make sense of them. The strange juxtaposition of clues seems to defy their bearing on a single answer. The suspense we feel, while scrambling through our ideas for a solution, may be seen as a rudimentary form of the sublime suspension caused by whatever resists conceptual understanding. Hegel writes of the riddle that its component clues "are associated together in a disparate and therefore striking way. Therefore they lack a subject embracing them together into a unity and their deliberate concatenation and connection one with another has as such absolutely no sense, although, on the other hand, they do all the same point to a unity in relation to which even the apparently most heterogeneous traits nevertheless acquire sense and meaning again" (LFA 398; 13:510). In the solution to the riddle lies the missing unity that holds together the scattered clues. The clues are related in a "disparate" and "striking" way, and in seeking a solution we must tease out their connections and discern their point of convergence. Making sense of the clues requires puzzling out which of their similarities matter, what the contrasts between them show, and at what level of abstraction to think them. Our response to a riddle is thus akin to the process of "detective work" with which we characterized reflective judgment at the outset of part I.

The riddle challenges our skills to piece together the clues into a revealing whole: "The riddle in this respect is the conscious wit of symbolism which puts to the test the wit of ingenuity and the flexibility in combining things, and its mode of presentation is self-destructive because it leads to the guessing of the riddle" (ibid.). Riddles provide only a brief and unrepeatable exercise of reflective judgment, for once the solution is guessed or given the game is over. Riddles are not cases that induce a sustained aesthetic reflection, but for the duration of the solution's absence imagination must seek connections among the clues without the aid of any guiding conception (the missing solution). That is, *Phantasie* must employ its associative powers without the determining control of a fixed idea. We will develop the import of this shortly, but it should be recalled that the "wit of ingenuity" which Hegel discerns in this exercise of an associative *Phantasie* confirms his *Encyclopedia* reference to a positive revelatory potential for wit in "mere" association.[12]

Metaphor and simile will provide us with the most significant cases of the construction of aesthetic unity in Hegel's account of the comparative art form. Hegel understands both metaphor and simile as devices by which we gain insight into one thing in terms of its likeness and contrast with another. In metaphorical uses of language "the purely bacchanalian delight of fancy [*Phantasie*]" discloses or creates relations among disparate experiences: "[Metaphor] may arise from the wit of a subjective caprice which, to escape from the habitual [*um dem Gewöhnlichen zu entfliehen*], surrenders to a piquant impulse, not satisfied until it has succeeded in finding related traits in the apparently most heterogeneous material and so, to our astonishment, combining things that are poles apart from one another" (LFA 407;

13:522).[13] In the construction of or reflection on metaphors, Hegelian imagination seeks that balance of affinity and heterogeneity which marks the network of relations in a Kantian aesthetic idea. Metaphors forge relationships between disparate domains of experience, and through these connections they supply a wealth of content and connotation to our language that cannot be encapsulated in any single determination.[14] By discerning patterns among our ideas and experiences, metaphorical reflection produces a web of interrelation that can supply new meanings for things. But these are meanings expressed in aesthetic ideas, that is, in forms that defy complete articulation.

Hegelian imagination can produce such meaning only with the aid of its associative powers. Recall that from as early in the *Encyclopedia* as the "Anthropology," Hegel identified the association of ideas with "subjective caprice," the contingent relating of content in the sleeping soul. In metaphor we see this associative caprice display a *positive wit* by producing relations among images, ideas, and experiences, relations that open up new perspectives. Metaphorical connection in Hegel's comparative art not only relates and contrasts the subject and predicate of simple metaphors. Rather, as in a Kantian aesthetic idea, imaginative invention also generates whole complexes of association, complexes of diverse material that overstep the bounds of any given conceptual form or thematic limitation. Hegel writes of both metaphor and simile that this combinatorial caprice "expresses the boldness of the imagination [*Phantasie*] which, having something confronting it—whether a single perceptible object, a specific situation, or a universal meaning—works on it and evinces its power to bind together things lying poles apart and connected externally, and so to drag into our interest in one topic the most varied material, and, by the labour of the spirit, to chain to the given topic a world of heterogeneous phenomena. This power of imagination [*Phantasie*] in inventing shapes and, by ingenious relations and connections, binding together the most diverse material is what in general lies at the root of simile" (LFA 411; 13:527).

In short, my interpretation of Hegel's symbolic art form shows metaphorical and similative connections across disparate objects of reflection to be a paradigmatic product of aesthetic reflection. In one manifestation, reflective judgment produces metaphors. We have found in the comparative art of Hegel's symbolic form a strengthening of the theoretical structure surrounding Kant's conception of aesthetic ideas. In both cases, the striving to express an unpresentable unity evinces an experience of sublimity. The outcome of the encounter is the production of the relational network, redolent with metaphorical meaning, of an aesthetic idea.[15] The coalescence of indeterminate expression, sublimity, and metaphor which we discerned in Kant's aesthetic theory has surfaced again in Hegel's *Lectures*, in one of those "deficient" zones of expression which fall short of presenting a conceptually or systematically determined unity.

But with Hegel, ironically enough considering his antisubjectivist commitments, we are even better positioned to specify the confluence of imaginative powers involved in producing aesthetic unity. In chapter 5 we saw that what would ultimately become an *assoziierende Einbildungskraft* first arose in the contingent play of the sleeping soul. The play of this nascent imagination was soon occluded by the drive for subsumption under definite categories, which is a power the soul acquired in its habit-formative recovery from madness. Hegel's final conception of generalizing imagination is dominated by this subsumptive activity of concept-formation, while the contingent association of unlike ideas is relegated to the anthropological backwater of cognitive prehistory. Finally, the *symbolisierende Phantasie* of artistic production and reflection became one of the highest fruits of imagination's development. But that symbolizing *Phantasie* cannot be at work in the comparative art form, because these products manage only the indeterminate expression of Kantian aesthetic ideas, rather than the transparent symbolic expression of Hegel's Ideal *Phantasie*. In comparative art, the associative powers of imagination participate in the generation of metaphorical meaning by forging disclosive links between putatively unrelated phenomena. In this imaginative reflection the contingent association of ideas and the wholly expressive products of symbolizing *Phantasie* meet in the work of an *assoziierende Phantasie*, an imagination which discerns or produces meaningful connections neither wholly contingent nor systematically unified.

This admixture of powers is seen in a passage where Hegel refers to what associative imagination *(Einbildungskraft)* can achieve when guided by *Phantasie*'s (unfulfilled) symbolizing prerogative. Hegel refers to the "pleasure of comparing" that comes with "the orgy of imagination's [*Einbildungskraft*] power"; left to this play, *Einbildungskraft* would produce only the capricious association of the soul asleep. But this caprice can at times "[betray] a wit of combination which is more *spirituel* than a mere witticism"; with *Phantasie* to bend mere association toward the presentation of a whole, imagination can surpass a wholly contingent play to produce something more compelling. In such a case, in an elaborate metaphor or simile, for example, an associative *Phantasie* can produce a "dwelling on one and the same topic which thereby is made the substantial center of a series of other ideas remote from it" (LFA 411–412; 13:527–528). In such cases, *Phantasie,* short of presenting the determinate symbol of its highest powers, produces the indeterminate unity, the allusive expression of a Kantian aesthetic idea. Under the influence of *Phantasie*'s (truncated) aim of symbolic expression, productive imagination achieves in comparative art a reflective *wit*, one to which Hegel attributed a power to disclose meaningful connections among disparate ideas.

The connectivity first evidenced in the dark origins of the sleeping soul comes to fruition in Hegel's symbolic form of art. Indeed, for commentators who interpret the moments of artistic development as stages in the production of a self-conscious subject, the symbolic form reflects the standpoint of a nascent consciousness struggling with the natural subjectivity of Hegel's anthropological soul. Christoph Helferich links symbolic art to the *Encyclopedia* "Anthropology" explicitly: "The symbolic art-form is the *inception* of art, and its corresponding consciousness rises to the level of 'wonder,' i.e., the subject lives 'no longer' as an unconscious accessory of nature, but has 'not yet' attained a clear consciousness of itself. . . ."[16] Imagination faces the uncanny sublime in symbolic art just as the soul striving for unity faced the hostile multiplicity of its potentially mad fixed ideas. The difference is that in the comparative art of the *Lectures,* the associative play of imagination produces something of value. In the *Encyclopedia* the soul's play was suppressed in favor of the subsumption under categories deemed necessary, in habit-formation, for the construction of a stable subject. But the "threat of sublimity" faced down by habit-formation, and again later in the conceptual regimentation of the representational subject's mine of imagery, has a different outcome in

Hegel's symbolic art. As in the aesthetic idea, associative *Phantasie* responds to the symbolic sublime by generating what aesthetic unity it can, short of "Ideal" determinacy, in relational networks of metaphorical meaning.

We can now turn to the romantic form of art, which follows the demise of Hegel's classical Ideal. Again imagination will be faced with a sublime absence of unity. Associative wit will surface again as a locale of reflective invention. And we will see imagination respond to the romantic sublime in a way that will boost the import of the aesthetics of indeterminacy nestled in Hegel's system.

Romantic Art, Subjective Humor, and the Sublime

In the progression of art forms presented in Hegel's *Lectures*, the unity of Idea and the sensuous is achieved in the classical Ideal. Where symbolic art lacked a content sufficiently articulate to receive thorough presentation, classical art represents for Hegel the completed union of sensuous expression and determinate theme. But in the "romantic" form of art that follows, this unity of thought and actuality collapses once again. Art and its participants realize that no corporeal form can do full justice to the inward depth of subjectivity. In romantic art, "the spirit knows that its truth does not consist in its immersion in corporeality," and so "spirit is pushed back into itself out of its reconciliation in the corporeal into a reconciliation of itself within itself." The identity of subjective theme and objective presentation in the classical Ideal is sacrificed in romantic art so that spirit may develop its content in ways inexpressible in sensuous form. Hegel writes: "The simple solid totality of the Ideal is dissolved and it falls apart into the double totality of (a) subjective being in itself and (b) the external appearance, in order to enable the spirit to reach through this cleavage a deeper reconciliation in its own element of inwardness." Hence romantic art begins as a meditation on the universal content of subjectivity; it presents the divine simplicity of "absolute inwardness, and its corresponding form is spiritual subjectivity with its grasp of its independence and freedom" (LFA 518–519; 14:128–129).

This initial characterization of the romantic form already indicates its importance for my interpretation. We have sought the moments in

Hegel's aesthetic theory where symbolizing *Phantasie* fails to present a determinate unity of theme and expression. At those points Hegel's account can illuminate the reflective production of aesthetic unity. Like symbolic art, romantic art also fails to present a determinate content, but for different reasons than obtained in the earlier form. Artistic endeavor has developed subjectivity to a point that it requires other means to express itself than sensuous art can provide. Hegel thinks it finds these means in religion and philosophy, but for now the task of romantic art must be, as Albert Hofstadter writes, "to show sensuously the ultimate inability of the sensuous to satisfy the spirit's true need."[17] That is, romantic art once again faces the sublime transcendence of a content inimical to sensuous presentation. Romantic art, constrained by the sensuous, can only point toward a content it cannot wholly express, and Hofstadter, for one, has seen the link to Kantian aesthetic ideas that this suggests. Romantic art, he writes, "cannot literally show infinite spiritual freedom sensibly, because sensible form is incapable of receiving that content. Like the Kantian expression of an aesthetic idea, the sensible form can at most adumbrate an infinite meaning that it cannot formulate."[18] This sublimity may suggest that all romantic art as a whole will provide material for a theorization of aesthetic unity. But the early moments of romantic art's development attend too avidly to the determinate universals of Christian religion to be of much help. As with symbolic art, only the final moments of the romantic trajectory will best model a properly sublime reflection.[19]

As noted before, romantic art focuses at first on the pure inwardness of subjectivity. It contemplates "the withdrawal of the inner into itself, the spiritual consciousness of God in the individual" (LFA 520; 14:131).[20] As an exploration of subjectivity in its *individual* richness, though, romantic art soon turns to those particularities that, according to Hegel, express universal spirit, namely chivalry in the forms of honor, love, and fidelity.[21] Romantic art began by cleaving apart subjectivity and sensuous externality; as this art comes to focus more and more on the individual, the dichotomy between pure inwardness and contingent, external particulars grows. All the transient subjective feelings and lived situations of the individual become "only a contingent world out of which the Absolute gathers itself together into the inner world of the spirit and only so comes to truth in its own eyes."

Romantic art is riven by an unbridgeable gap between "two worlds: a spiritual realm, complete in itself . . . ; [and a] realm of the external as such which, released from its fixidly secure unifications with the spirit, now becomes a purely empirical reality by the shape of which the soul is untroubled" (LFA 526–527; 14:139–140). The contingent particularity of the individual is as much a part of this empirical dross as the world of passing events. In the disintegration of romantic art the soul will not long remain untroubled by the mass of contingency it has sought, in its inward flight, to leave behind.

Hegel treats the destruction of romantic art in "The Formal Independence of Individual Characteristics." This art loses its mooring in absolute subjectivity and instead gives itself over to "the world of the particular, of the existent in general. . . ." It finds satisfaction in "the thirst for this present and this reality itself"; its products, *and reflection on them*, is no longer "permeated by . . . compression into the unity of the Absolute" (LFA 573; 14:195). Romantic art devolves in its final moments into a return of the oppressed: it brings to the fore the very contingent subjectivity and empirical particularity that had previously been banished from the unity of the work of art. Romantic art abandons that balance of contingency and necessity Hegel required of the classical Ideal: it gives free rein to the play of subjective contingency and the senseless multiplicity of worldly events. In the collapse of the romantic form the artist comes to mock any necessity of content or form once required for the presentation of a unified theme. Hegel writes: "[E]very independence of an objective content along with the inherently fixed connection of the form . . . is annihilated in itself, and the presentation is only a sporting with the topics, a derangement [*Verrücken*] and perversion of the material . . . , a criss-cross movement of subjective expressions, views, and attitudes whereby the author sacrifices himself and his topics alike" (LFA 601; 14:229).[22] Contingency reigns over the dissolution of art. Subjectivity revels in its particularity, refusing to present a unified theme. It alienates itself as well from the outside world, where beauty was to be made manifest. Hegel concludes that "we acquire as the culmination of the romantic in general the contingency of both inner and outer, and the separation of these two sides," whereby art sacrifices its reconciling function and betrays the Ideal of Beauty (LFA 528; 14:141).

The destruction of romantic art by a play of contingent particulars reaches its peak in the final sections of part II of Hegel's *Lectures*, "The Dissolution of the Romantic Form of Art."[23] In keeping with romantic art's cleavage between subjective and external worlds, Hegel treats this divide in terms of both "the Subjective Artistic Imitation of the Existent Present" and a phenomenon he calls "Subjective Humor." The first artistic presentation of contingency "takes for its subject-matter not the inherently necessary, the province of which is complete in itself, but contingent reality in its boundless modification of shapes and relationships" (LFA 595; 14:223). Such art—exemplified for Hegel by tales of the solace of family life and the intrigues of civil society, still-life paintings and *trompe l'oeil* trickery—celebrates the rich detail of human life, "the incalculable mutability of the external objective world," without regard for its relevance or irrelevance to the unity of the Idea (LFA 598; 14:226). Hegel thinks this late romantic art of worldly particulars shares with Protestantism the search for "a sure footing in the *prose of life*," and this aesthetic reflection on daily life is the critical feature of such art (ibid.; my emphasis). Dissolute romantic art, lacking any unified theme to present, turns to the contemplation of mundane existence. *Aesthetic reflection turns there, too.* In its presentation of daily life's contingent details, this art provides aesthetic imagination an occasion to reflect on that world in all its disorderly multiplicity. This turn to the empirical in the romantic disintegration of art will later motivate us to extend the production of aesthetic unity beyond the domain of art works and into the lived world that surrounds them.

On the subjective side of romantic art's defining dichotomy, Hegel calls the ultimate product of its dissolution "subjective humor." He regards this disruptive sporting as "the perversion and derangement [*Verrücken*] of everything objective and real by means of wit [n.b.] and the play of a subjective outlook, [ending] with the artist's personal productive mastery over every content and form" (LFA 576; 14:198). Recall again the balance between necessity and contingency maintained by a work of art. The particular aspects of the work must be allowed their independent strength even as they are integrated into the thematic of the Idea. But with the upsurge of contingency in subjective humor, the strength, in their own reality, of the diverse subjective aspects of the artist overwhelms any necessary connections among them. In subjective humor the artist sacrifices the unity of beauty for the play of a disordered thought process. Here the chief activity of the artist, writes Hegel, "by the power of subjective notions, flashes of thought, striking modes of interpretation, consists in destroying and dissolving everything that proposes to make itself objective and win a firm shape for itself in reality, or that seems to have such a shape in the external world" (LFA 600–601; 14:229). Subjective humor undermines the presentation of a conceptually organized theme, and it thus functions within Hegel's system as a place marker for caprice: "For steadily to interrupt the rational course of the thing, to begin, proceed, and end capriciously, and to throw into mutual confusion a series of witticisms [*Witzen*] and feelings, and thereby to produce fantastic caricatures [*Karikaturen der Phantasie*], is easier than to develop from oneself and round off an inherently solid whole stamped with the true Ideal" (LFA 295; 13:381). Subjective humor willfully sinks into a merely contingent play. Instead of symbolically conveying the Idea, it "deviates into indefiniteness," and seeks "often with deliberate bizarrerie [to] conjoin the most heterogeneous things" (LFA 601; 14:230).

It should be evident that subjective humor embodies precisely that "sport of vacant-minded ideation" in the association of ideas which Hegel dismisses in the *Encyclopedia*. In fact, we noted in chapter 5 that Hegel categorizes such association as a matter of caprice as early as the "Anthropology." There the associative play of the soul was relegated to the dreams of its sleeping part so that soul could awake to rational self-possession. The sleeping play of the soul became the merely associative *Einbildungskraft* of Hegel's "Psychology," and that decrepit form of association now usurps the work of imagination in subjective humor. In the dissolution of romantic art the symbolizing function of *Phantasie* has no role to play because art no longer has a theme to present, and imagination distills instead a contingent play. We saw in the case of symbolic art that mere association was taken up into the symbolizing aims of *Phantasie* to produce an aesthetic unity neither contingent nor determinately unified. The metaphorical products of comparative art brought together diverse material into relations which illuminated their significance or disclosed new avenues for interpreting them. In the case of subjective humor, Hegel criticizes the novelist Jean Paul for aiming to astonish "precisely in the baroque mustering of things objectively furthest removed from one another and in the most confused disorderly jumbling of topics related only in his own subjective imagination" (LFA 601; 14:230).[24] Subjective humor would appear to engage in an associative reflection so idiosyncratic, according to Hegel, that it cannot speak to others.[25] The question will soon be whether imagination can construct from subjective humor an aesthetic unity that surpasses this associative idiolect to present networks of relation with a communicable claim to validity.

We saw in chapter 5 that the associative play of the soul claimed, in madness, to be sublimely incomprehensible. That claim was given the lie by habit-formation, as was the "threat of sublimity" posed by the pit of images imagination faced in its production of determinate concepts. In both cases a homogenizing power to think the particular under the universal dispelled the presumption of the particular to remain sublime. But we saw that in an aesthetic context, in Hegel's symbolic form of art, the lack of any determinate theme with which to make sense of a work led imagination to respond to the sublime differently. Instead of unifying like particulars under a concept, associative *Phantasie* produced the heterogeneous relational network of an aesthetic idea. If the romantic form of art is also to involve a reflection that constructs aesthetic unity, subjective humor should again evidence an encounter with sublimity.

The associative play of subjective humor already evinces that anti-Ideal disorder and confusion that constituted the "threat of sublimity" found in the sleeping soul and its later pit of images. But it is possible to see subjective humor in greater detail as a Hegelian version of the Kantian sublime. In what follows we will note important differences between Kant's sublime and the character of subjective humor. These differences will point out a significant departure in the use to which Hegel puts the sublime in his aesthetics. Hegel himself connects his account of subjective humor to the symbolic form of art where his discussion of the sublime resides. He writes of subjective humor: "In thus drawing together and concatenating material raked up from the four corners of the earth and every sphere of reality, humour turns back, as it were, to symbolism where meaning and shape likewise lie apart from one another, except that now it is the mere subjective activity of the poet which commands material and meaning alike and strings them together in an order alien to them" (LFA 601; 14:230). The arbitrary connection between meaning and shape that limits the expressive power of symbolic art is manifested by the sublime absence of the Idea, at this stage of art, from any attempt to present it. Similarly in subjective humor, the absence of the Idea is apparent in the merely contingent association of material guided by no unity of theme or purpose. The primary difference between these Hegelian sublimes is that symbolic sublimity yearns for the Idea it lacks, while the romantic sublime revels in the very capricious play that disrupts thematic unity. We will soon see that this difference indicates subjective humor to be a special appropriation of the sublime in Hegel's thought.

I will argue that subjective humor in fact fulfills three main features of the Kantian sublime. First of all, the experience must involve an overwhelming of imagination in its effort to comprehend some multiplicity of elements as a unity. It must appear, for Kant, "incommensurate with our power of exhibition, and as it were violent to our imagination." Secondly, this experience must have a basis in feeling akin to that given in Kant's sublime, namely of undergoing "a pleasure that is possible only by means of a displeasure." Finally, this humbling of imagination must ultimately prove itself purposive for the cultivation of reason's highest potentials. In enduring the sublime, Kant writes, "this same violence that the imagination inflicts on the subject is still judged purposive for the whole vocation of the mind" (CJ 245, 260, 259).

The play of subjective humor signals the activity of a mere associative imagination exceeding the bounds of any fixed theme or concept. For Kant, the sublime escapes comprehension as a unity because imagination is overwhelmed by the sheer multiplicity of elements it must try to hold together. Similarly in Hegel's subjective humor, a capricious play of elements defies the thematic bounds of the Idea. Hegel's imagination sinks into a state in which its grasp of thematic unity is lost to a "criss-cross of subjective expressions." Hegel's symbolizing *Phantasie*, at least in the classical Ideal, comprehends and presents wholes. But in the fall of romantic art into subjective humor, imagination reverts to its capacity for mere contingent association.

Phantasie's comprehension of the sensualized Idea collapses as *Einbil-dungskraft* "deviates into indefiniteness . . . with deliberate bizarrerie." In the Kantian sublime, imagination is overwhelmed by a multiplicity of parts beyond its capacity to comprehend. In the Hegelian romantic version, *Einbildungskraft* sinks into a subjective humor that overwhelms *Phantasie*'s capacity to present beauty in a unified Idea.

There is an evident difference in the "structure of overwhelming" at work in these Kantian and Hegelian sublimes. Kant's imagination is overwhelmed by an incomprehensible object, while in subjective humor *Phantasie* is overwhelmed from within by a lawless play of association. What does the overwhelming appears to be a more internal cognitive relation in Hegel's case, while in Kant's case imagination is overwhelmed from without by the sublime object. But in fact, what initiates the slide into contingent association for Hegel is the instance of subjective humor to which imagination responds. There is as much a relation to an external force of sublimity in Hegel's account as in Kant's. And there is in Kant's account as much of an internal component to inducing an experience of sublimity, in that it is reason's demand for totality which sets imagination up for a fall. There does remain this difference, that the sublime of subjective humor *seeks to undermine* aesthetic comprehension in a manner alien to Kant's account. We will see this destructive tendency again in discussing the next criterion; we will be better positioned there to ask what this difference means.

The second criterion for a Kantian experience of the sublime was that it be based in a certain feeling, namely a displeasurable frustration which imagination suffers in its failed effort to intuit unity. Given the antisubjectivist orientation of his aesthetics, Hegel has little to say, as we know, about the affective component of aesthetic experience; he gives few clues to what feeling accompanies subjective humor. We can, however, discern from the *Encyclopedia* Hegel's suspicion of feeling as a merely subjective and capricious component of experience. His pronouncements there make it clear that subjective humor can be seen as of a piece with a reliance on mere feeling, for he who appeals to feeling "shuts himself up in his own isolated subjectivity—his private and particular self." Hegel thinks it *"suspicious* or even worse to cling to feeling" because it speaks only for the "particular subjectivity with its vanity and caprice." Subjective humor sinks to the level of mere feeling when it plays with contingencies at the expense of rational necessity. Significantly, Hegel argues that displeasure arises from a lack of agreement between one's inner determinations (feelings and desires, say) and what affects one from without.[26] Subjective humor, in its destruction of the Idea, is the essence of such disagreement between inner and outer. Though aesthetic feeling little concerns Hegel, one can discern in subjective humor a negative pleasure akin to that suffered by Kant's imagination.

The main difference at the level of feeling between the Kantian sublime and the Hegelian romantic sublime is that the subjective humorist appears to *enjoy* the masochism of destroying the presentable Idea. As with the previous criterion, subjective humor pleases in its very destructiveness, while the pleasure that ultimately issues from Kant's sublime arises rather from the respect for reason which it affords. This rather stark difference ultimately proves less problematic than it might seem, because, as we will see in considering the last criterion, Hegel takes the priority of reason's pursuits to be recovered in the transition to religion and philosophy brought on by subjective humor's destruction of art. But the delight Hegel accords subjective humor in its play with destructive contingency suggests that Hegel's sublime discloses in the contingent something of more lasting significance than mere disruptiveness. The ultimate lesson of subjective humor will become clear in the next section.

Finally, the third criterion demands that subjective humor must have some ultimate purposiveness. For Kant it is reason that demands the holistic comprehension of which imagination proves itself incapable, and the humbling of imagination awakens us to our rational vocation. In the case of subjective humor, caprice reigns over the dissolution of art. This dissolution marks the impasse beyond which art cannot go in its effort to realize the Idea. In the end of the romantic form, "art annuls itself and brings home to our minds that we must acquire higher forms for the apprehension of truth than those which art is in a position to supply." Hence subjective humor plays a role in spurring the transition from art into the domains of religion and philosophy, where the rational Idea reaches its fullest form. Subjective humor, and the influx of contingency it causes, has a subversive power "which could make every determinacy waver and dissolve and therefore make it possible for art to transcend itself" (LFA 607; 14:237). Like the Kantian sublime, subjective humor serves an important catalytic function in Hegel's narrative of human spiritual development.[27]

The experience of sublimity in subjective humor arises from the activity of a capricious imagination which destroys the presentable Idea in favor of the play of contingent associations. The unity sought by creative *Phantasie* loses out to the sport of *Einbildungskraft* as the rounded whole of beauty is overwhelmed by contingency. This dissolution brings on the demise of the romantic form of art and so occasions, in Hegel's system, the infamous end of art's role as a significant medium for articulating the Idea. The presence of sublimity at the conclusion of art's development shows the sublime to frame both ends of Hegel's account of artistic determinacy. The sublime of symbolic art emphasizes its alienation from the Idea and motivates the transition to the classical ideal. The sublime of romantic art plays out the endgame of art's effort to present the Idea. Preceding and following the unity of beauty, the unpresentable sublime both opens up and closes down the project of artistically *determining* the concrete universal. It remains to be seen whether the romantic sublime instead occasions, as did the symbolic sublime, the production of *indeterminate* unity along the lines of a Kantian aesthetics of sublimity.

Aesthetic Unity in Objective and True Humor

The contingent play of subjective humor is ultimately succeeded by higher forms of expression in religion and philosophy—richer articulations of the necessity once grasped by art. The fall of romantic art into the play of subjective humor forms the backdrop of Hegel's infamous claim that art has reached its end as a primary means of spiritual expression. This "death of art thesis" has been the main focus of commentary on his aesthetic theory, as each generation has debated whether Hegel "really meant" that art would cease to be produced, whether Hegel was a philistine for not anticipating Cubism and the like. With the exception of the authors discussed later in this section, unfortunately, scholars have generally ignored the critical role subjective humor plays in Hegel's narrative of art's demise. Nor have they given adequate attention to the phenomena of objective and true humor, which show that Hegel, I will argue below, accords a lasting value to art despite its succession by religion and philosophy.

In fact a striking departure from Hegel's usual methods marks the final pages of his general aesthetic theory, prior to his studies of the individual arts. The *Aufhebung* of art into religion is not immediate. Before the partial recovery of the Idea in revelation, art plays out a few final turns. In the demise of romantic art Hegel pursues what appears to be a detour from the passage into religion. Often in Hegel's dialectic an at first subjective phenomenon receives some objective expression; these two sides must then be reconciled in a unity that grasps the truth of both. Typically this procedure prepares the next stages of Hegel's system; but at the end of romantic art, subjective humor undergoes this dialectic apart from the lifting of art into religion. For Hegel considers an *objective humor* that surpasses the contingency of subjective caprice, and in which we will discern once more the production of aesthetic unity by an associative power of *Phantasie*. Subjective humor is the final moment from which the transition to higher forms of truth arises. But it is not the final moment of art, nor the end of art's value.

Before evaluating Hegel's remarks on objective humor, we must clarify the medium of expression romantic art favors at this late point in its development. In the extensive elaboration of the individual arts in the second half of his *Lectures,* Hegel argues that art makes use of progressively more plastic means of expression as its spiritual accomplishment grows. Though all the arts may be practiced at any time, Hegel takes architecture, for example, to be a lower form of art, in its crude symbolism and blunt materiality, than poetry, which transcends the limitations of any physical medium. In poetry, Hegel's highest romantic art, the artist adopts language as the most plastic, most spiritual means of expression, where imagination as such can shine through: poetry "is the *universal* art which can shape in any way and express any subject-matter capable at all of entering the imagination [*Phantasie*], because its proper material is the imagination itself, that universal foundation of all the particular art-forms and the individual arts" (LFA 967; 15:233).[28] Poetry, by which Hegel means the literary arts in the broad sense and not just poems, achieves the purest possible expression of creative *Phantasie.*

But in the context of romantic art *Phantasie* cannot express that complete unity of form and content indicative of the classical Ideal. The romantic schism between subjectivity and external forms requires *Phantasie* to deploy the *indirect* means of innovative uses of language to express a content that cannot be determinately conveyed. Given everything we have seen, it should come as no surprise to learn that Hegel takes romantic poetry to express itself quintessentially in metaphor: "The romantic imagination . . . gladly expresses itself metaphorically, because in it what is external for the subjective life withdrawn into itself counts only as an accessory and not as adequate reality itself. This external field, in this way as it were a metaphorical one, configured with deep feeling and detailed richness of insight or with humorous conjunctions, is the impetus which enables and stimulates romantic poetry to invent things always anew" (LFA 1004; 15:279–280). Romantic imagination will forge precisely the sort of disclosive metaphorical connections we saw also in the aesthetic unity of symbolic art. Here again the positive wit of an insight achieved through "humorous conjunctions" points to the revelatory power of an *associative Phantasie* that surpasses the mere caprice of subjective humor. In Hegel's account of romantic art's end, following the encounter with sublimity induced by subjective humor, we will see *Phantasie* once more produce aesthetic unities of affine relation.

In the closing pages of his discussion of the romantic form, Hegel introduces, all too briefly, the notion of an *objective* humor that arises from the caprice of association. In fact, Hegel draws explicit attention to the structural homology between the symbolic comparative form and the endgame of subjective humor. In the dissolution of romantic art, Hegel writes, "we have stressed principally how art falls to pieces, on the one hand, into the imitation of external objectivity in all its contingent shapes; on the other hand, however, into the liberation of subjectivity, in accordance with its inner contingency, in humour. Now, finally, . . . we may draw attention to a coalescence of these extremes in romantic art. In other words, just as in the advance from symbolic to classical art we considered the transitional forms of image, simile, epigram, etc., so here in romantic art we have to make mention of a similar transitional form" (LFA 608; 14:239).[29] What Hegel will call "objective humor" brings together the associative play of subjective humor with an attentiveness toward the surrounding external world. In subjective humor imagination loses itself in fascination with its power of association, with the destructive power of its own contingency. But in objective humor, according to Hegel, imagination begins to pay closer attention to what it brings together in its play. He writes: "[I]f this satisfaction [of subjective humor] is intensified . . . into the heart's deeper immersion in the object . . . , then we acquire thereby a growing intimacy with the object, a sort of *objective* humour" (LFA 609; 14:240). Subjective humor becomes objective when it turns its associative aesthetic reflection on what Hegel earlier called the "prose of life" (LFA 598; 14:226). What it relates in its play no longer reflects just the interior contingency of an isolated subject, but also the reality of a shared world.

Hegel derides subjective humor for succumbing to a contingent play which, as we have seen throughout his system, he attributes to an *assoziierende Einbildungskraft*. But in objective humor, as imagination comes to focus on the material it associates, *Phantasie* resurfaces as a (partially) comprehensive activity of imagination. Hegel describes objective humor as marked by "a deep feeling, *an apt wit*, an ingenious reflection, and an intelligent movement of imagination [*Phantasie*] which vivif[ies] and expand[s] the smallest detail through the way that poetry treats it" (LFA 609; 14:240).[30] In objective humor *Phantasie* savors the particularity of its objects and in this way celebrates the rich specificity of its world. The interior play of subjective humor takes on objective relevance when imagination turns to lived contexts of significance.[31] Objective humor, as Hegel indicates, displays that *positive wit* for disclosing meaningful connections which we have seen *Phantasie* exercise with the aid of its latent associative powers. The fresh view of the object that this wit provides evinces the same associative reflection that goes awry in subjective humor. But *Phantasie*'s effort to present an intelligible reading of its world shows objective humor to surpass the mere contingency of its subjective counterpart. The caprice of subjective humor lay in its indulgence of personal particularities of association; but what objective humor seeks to relate in a network of connections is a field of shared meaning.

Hegel conceives objective humor as a convergence of tendencies found in subjective humor and the "Imitation of the Existent Present."

In his few comments on it, however, Hegel formulates the notion mainly on the side of its subjectivity, but grants that it can have objective effects: he comments that if objective humor "were extended and carried through within objectivity, it would necessarily become action and event and an objective presentation of these" (LFA 609; 14:240). Albert Hofstadter has pointed to Marcel Duchamp's turn to a life of chess as an example of objective humor become action, of wit become a way of life, and he claims that the ultimate modern fruition of objective humor is the condition of "everyone doing his own thing."[32] But this exaggerates the subjective particularity involved here. If subjective humor revels in the chance associations of an isolated subject, objective humor discloses meaning-giving relations common to a larger constellation of subjects. Its objectivity lies in its surpassing the particularity of subjective association to bring together objects, ideas, and feelings in connections others make as well. Objective humor embraces the play of meanings in its world and shows itself a master of the connotative links through which we judge and act. As a kind of aesthetic reflection, it commits one to seek an awareness of the webs of significance that influence our thoughts, beliefs, and behaviors. Objective humor requires that "a rich consciousness shall be entirely absorbed in the circumstances, situation, etc., tarry there, and so make out of the object something new, beautiful, and intrinsically valuable" (LFA 610; 14:241). In disclosing the metaphorical linkages that influence our thinking, objective humor reveals not only a shared milieu of connotation. It exposes as well the lack of rational unity, the haphazard construction and the mutability of webs of meaning whose status as contingent historical encrustations is revealed by their improvisational disorder. Objective humor intervenes in those networks by presenting alternative metaphors or patterns of connotation that challenge contemporary habits of thought. This dual power of sublime reflection, to disclose intersubjectively active, (dis)unities of affine relation, and to pose creatively metaphorical alternatives which open new interpretive avenues, I call a *sublime understanding*. I will explore it further in part III.

A number of commentators have remarked on the "sad state" into which romantic art falls in objective humor. Karsten Harries argues that this final return to objectivity "lacks necessity. Why turn to this theme rather than to another? The rise of our reflective culture leaves the artist with no good answers to such questions. There is no longer a content which demands that he place himself at its service."[33] Annemarie Gethmann-Siefert claims that in objective humor's "attempt to manifest the reconciliation of subjectivity and substantiality in a (fantasy) world, romantic art engenders the bad infinity of a perpetual, never-to-succeed process of reconciliation."[34] Rüdiger Bubner expresses the aversion to objective humor most categorically. He claims that objective humor "is the name for an art without a future, an irrelevant form which has lost all force or tension and can go on forever. The artist unrestrictedly playing around with content and historical figures is unable to create anything original; there is no historical hindrance to his continuing, but there is no philosophical value in it."[35] These authors share a common allegiance to Hegel's systematic prerogatives, even if only as expositors of his system. They deride objective humor as a detour from the consummation of systematic unity sought by speculative reason. It lacks the necessity Harries expects from art, but on my account this lack reflects its responsiveness to the meaning-context of a particular historical locale. For Gethmann-Siefert, objective humor must be an "empty effort in view of the necessarily fixed objective of actualizing reason."[36] But for my aims, its antipathy to determined rational unity can only recommend it. Given my focus on sublime reflection's production of *indeterminate* unity, we can attend to what objective humor contributes to that aim, irrespective of its status in the narrative of reason's self-actualization. Doing so will allow us to notice the quite positive tone in which Hegel writes of objective humor, evident in all the passages cited above, in contrast to the scornful tone it inspires in many latter-day Hegelians.

Only Dieter Henrich has made sense of objective humor as a currently relevant mode of aesthetic reflection and production, independent of its status within Hegel's system.[37] Henrich, too, has sought a model for aesthetic presentation outside the determinacy of Hegel's Ideal of Beauty. He finds in the dissolution of romantic art starting points for an aesthetic of "partiality": "Presentation can, after all, be of a partial character, and just for this reason be combined with the openness, reflectedness, and historical constitution of the modern artist. In other words, the actuality which art brings to appearance does not have to be interpreted as a larger, universal actuality."[38] Henrich would have art seek only a partial, perspectival presentation of a world, without expecting from it the universal revelations Hegel demands. If such partiality can devolve into subjective humor, Henrich insists that it has the potential to disclose shared aspects of a historical situation: "Cutting our ties with Hegel's concept but not with presentational esthetics will mean that we interpret contemporary art as manifestation of a *particular and significant* actuality."[39] Aesthetic reflection can at best hope to grasp some particular features of the complex present and express them in a manner which surpasses subjective idiosyncrasy to strike a chord with others. Henrich takes any comprehension of the whole to be beyond the means (by now) of the reflective subject of modernity who "has as its complement not only the certainty of being based on a foundation not within its arena of control but also the knowledge that this foundation will remain inaccessible to it."[40] The modern self pursues its freedom in a complex and shifting social context that constantly exceeds its power to understand or control. We might say that the modern world *remains sublime*, beyond the efforts of its subjects to grasp determinately.

Henrich thinks aesthetic production must enact this modern dilemma as a striving for a unified mastery which never comes: "Art will, therefore, present every essent in such a way that it points above and beyond itself to a ground which [lies] beyond manifestation. . . ."[41] He thereby adopts the standpoint of Kantian aesthetic reflection, in which a search for purposive coherence issues, when faced with the unpresentable sublime, in the production of aesthetic unity. An art which points beyond itself to an unpresentable whole assumes the partial expressive form of an aesthetic idea; it only intimates a unified meaning via a loose relational unity of components (as in, e.g., a collage). Henrich sees two modifications this artistic pursuit can assume; they correspond to subjective and objective humor, released from their devalued position within Hegel's system. First, the effort to confirm the ambiguous autonomy of the self "can occur by the self confirming itself as a power over the natural order of things. The given is broken down into its elements [and new] orders are produced from them. . . ."[42] This "subjective art" corresponds to the associative play of subjective humor, though Henrich accords it a higher status than Hegel would. But second, when a more objective presentation is attempted, "things can be combined into new associations and configurations [that disclose] an order which has grown of itself. The work can show how fragments of actuality combine of themselves into new relations. They can indicate another actuality in which the essence of things does not resist the being of the self. (Technique of Collages)."[43] The art of objective humor is the *bricoleur's* art which brings together disparate materials into a revelatory juxtaposition, as in Max Ernst's collage "novels" (e.g., *A Little Girl Dreams of Taking the Veil*), or the "pop" collages of a Rauschenberg. When it transforms present configurations of meaning, such art reveals at the same time the imbeddedness of the self in the fields with which it plays. This art cannot present a conceptually determined whole, because it relies on the incongruity of its elements to express affinities that suggest more than a concept can encompass. That is, objective humor, in its reflection of current habits of association or in its provision of new metaphorical alternatives, presents the indeterminate unity of an aesthetic idea.[44]

Hegel affirms the power of objective humor to disclose indeterminate webs of shared meaning when he accords to humor the potential to rise to "truth":

True humor . . . requires great depth and wealth of spirit in order to raise the purely subjective appearance into what is actually expressive, and to make what is substantial emerge out of contingency. . . . The self-pursuit of the author in the course of his expressions must, as is the case with Sterne [n.b.] and Hippel, be an entirely naive, light, unostentatious jogging along which in its triviality affords precisely the supreme idea of depth; and since here there are just individual details which gush forth without any order, their inner connection must lie all the deeper and send forth the ray of the spirit in their disconnectedness as such. (LFA 602; 14:231)

As in the metaphors of symbolic art, true humor continues to present the indeterminate unity of all Hegel's "decrepit" aesthetic phenomena. But the relational networks of true humor can present the "inner connection" of putatively unrelated phenomena, can disclose in them the purposive unity sensed in aesthetic reflection. The truth that humor achieves is that positive wit we have seen Hegel repeatedly laud, a wit that brings apparently incongruous material into disclosive relations.[45] True humor thereby exposes the patterns of sense-making that structure our thoughts and judgments. As in the production of metaphor, objective and true humor transcend mere caprice when they construct aesthetic unities that disclose established or innovative semantic connections. These products do not enjoy the universal necessity of Hegel's Ideal. In fact, their dehabituating wit exposes the contingency, debunks the "naturalness" of associations we take for granted. But by illuminating our shared universe of meanings, intervening to critique harmful patterns of association, and inventing new metaphors to challenge self-understanding, aesthetic reflection can bolster, if not the necessity of our world, at least the cognizance of our participation in it.[46]

The fact should not be missed that Hegel points to Laurence Sterne as an exemplary practitioner of "true" humor. His *Life and Opinions of Tristram Shandy* is celebrated as a presciently premodern precursor of the postmodern novel, and with good reason: its blanked-out pages and bizarre digressions, its savaging of Locke and teasing of Shakespeare, its play with language and with narrative expectations embodies the combinatory wit of sublime reflection. Much recent cultural production pursues Sterne's strategies of ironic reversal and unsettling juxtaposition, as in the self-portraits of Cindy Sherman or the video art of Gary Hill. Sterne's own mimicking of historical styles has become the style-quotation of postmodern architecture and the sampling strategies of popular music, except that Joyce beat postmodernity to it by composing one chapter of *Ulysses* as a stylistic history of English literature (including a dead-on parody of Sterne). A host of twentieth-century artistic movements, from surrealism to pop art, from photorealism to conceptual art, can be seen to enact Hegelian objective humor, his version of the reflective wit of a sublime understanding. In all these instances and others, art displays the subjective mastery over any material, turned to revelatory effect through the exposure or cultivation of shared connotative networks, while posing the sublime indeterminacy of a meaning beyond our reach.[47] I will consider further in chapter 9 how well the aesthetics of sublimity I have drawn from Kant and have coaxed from Hegel is suited to our reflective situation at present.

We can now revisit the question raised at the end of chapter 5. We noted the "threat of sublimity" posed both by the associative disarray of the sleeping soul, and by the nocturnal pit of images in representational thought. In each case this "threat" was overcome in the formation of an imagination that subsumed its content under fixed categories. We asked whether Hegelian *aesthetic* imagination might respond differently to the sublime, and produce the indeterminate unity of Kant's aesthetic idea. By sidestepping the determinate expression of Hegel's classical Ideal, we have found that the associative and symbolizing powers of Hegelian *Phantasie* converge, at key moments in the symbolic and romantic forms of art, to generate aesthetic (dis)unities of relation. In the "decrepit" aesthetic domain that borders Hegel's classical Ideal at both ends, associative play—which was seen at its worst in the anthropological madness of the sleeping soul—is transformed into an intersubjectively valid reflective wit. This wit produces from its encounter with the limits of determinate presentation the sense-making networks of aesthetic unity. The comparative art of the symbolic form showed that sublime reflection produces metaphor. Objective and true humor in the romantic form opened the possibility of extending aesthetic reflection beyond the interpretation of works of art to reflection on shared webs of meaning. This result shows an aesthetics of sublimity at play in the production of metaphor and in our interpretive mapping and extending of shared sense. These reflective products will be at center stage as we further explore the nature and validity of a sublime understanding in part III.

Interlude: Wit and Judgment in Empiricist Aesthetics

We might look back on the results of parts I and II this way: if Kant elaborates the *formal* structure of aesthetic reflection, Hegel helps clarify the *content* or material with which aesthetic reflection plays. Kant's judgments of taste and sublimity outline the contours of aesthetic response; I have construed sublime reflection in particular as an interpretive and open-ended process of seeking expressive coherence among the diverse attributes of an object and our response to it. Hegel's elaborate theory of imagination helped specify that response, but more significantly, his philosophy of art has clarified just *what* imagination plays with in its responses. In its effort to make sense of a work, sublime reflection draws on patterns of association that constitute the shared webs of meaning in which we think and judge. Aesthetic reflection both relies on the sense-making resources of those networks and inventively poses new disclosures of meaning through its combinatory reworking of that material. We will see this most clearly in chapter 8, when we explore a claim intimated by Kant and confirmed by Hegel: the exemplary status of metaphor as a product of the aesthetic response to sublime indeterminacy. Part III as a whole will elaborate the interpretive play of sublime understanding further, both in terms of its reliance on established networks of affinity and its production of new insights.

While wrestling an aesthetics of sublimity from Hegel, we saw that his system repeatedly lauds an imaginative wit that plays at the juxtaposition of disparate ideas. This connective activity exemplifies reflective judgment's effort to disclose affinity among a manifold of elements. We have seen that the products of this reflection can make some claim to intersubjective validity in part because they draw on established webs of relation. This positive wit has a disclosive power because its connective play does not reflect mere subjective idiosyncrasies of association. What I want to suggest now is that sublime understanding as I have construed it involves an interplay between notions of wit, judgment, imagination, and association, an interplay that in fact has an old pedigree. In this Interlude I will trace it running through the aesthetic theories of the British and Scottish empiricists of the seventeenth and eighteenth centuries. As we noted in chapter 5, the associationism of the empiricists raised the sort of quandaries for the cognitive validity of our experiential judgments that motivated Kant's critical philosophy. Reviewing the role association plays in empiricist theories of imaginative wit and aesthetic judgment will clarify the differences between Kantian aesthetic reflection and his predecessors' views. Better yet, certain affinities between empiricist aesthetic theories and Hegel's own philosophy of art will highlight the unique significance of Kant's introduction of indeterminacy into the aesthetic domain.

We can begin with Thomas Hobbes, who in *Leviathan* (1651) contrasts wit and judgment as opposed but complementary powers. The former finds fanciful affinities among things while the latter soberly maintains distinctions: "Those that observe their similitudes, in case they be such as are but rarely observed by others, are sayd to have a *Good Wit*; by which, in such occasion, is meant a *Good Fancy*. But they that observe their differences, and dissimilitudes; which is called *Distinguishing*, and *Discerning*, and *Judging* between thing and thing; in case, such discerning be not easie, are said to have a *good Judgement*."[1] These two powers are merged in aesthetic reflection, as we saw in chapter 4, when a respect for difference or heterogeneity tempers the discernment of relational affinities. In fact, the indeterminate unity of aesthetic reflection relies on the maintenance of this balance. While the presentation of a network of affinities gives unity to reflective wit, its maintenance of irreducible difference assures the indeterminacy of a product that will be averse to the subsumption of elements under any determinate rule. Keeping this in mind, though, Hobbes and many of the later empiricists, as we will see, put judgment in charge of reining in the excessive play of fanciful wit that, if left to its own devices, would make everything similar. Hobbes thinks judgment is needed to keep wit oriented toward some end: "But without Steddiness, and Direction to some End, a great Fancy is one kind of Madness."[2] Here Hobbes expresses distrust for an associative play that threatens to dissolve orderly categories of thought. This problem will haunt empiricist associationism throughout the eighteenth century; suffice it for now to note that the connection Hegel made between madness and rampant association also has an old pedigree.

To rein in the excesses of wit, Hobbes requires that its play be thoroughly governed by a judgment oriented toward *definite* purposes. Of this "acquired wit," as he calls it, educated in method and science, "there is none but Reason": that is, Hobbes regards the fanciful play of wit as a threat to order that must be ruled by the rational methods of determinative judgment.[3] Unfettered fancy is madness, and one sort of madness Hobbes discusses is "absurdity in discourse." Absurdity undermines the rational bases of our claims, and Hobbes lists among the causes of absurdity the use of metaphor.[4] Metaphors violate good judgment because they "openly professe deceit; to admit them into Councell, or Reasoning, were manifest folly."[5] For Hobbes, when wit plays at the production of metaphors it makes idiosyncratic associations that violate common standards of judgment.[6] In the interplay of wit and judgment, the extent to which associative wit can be curbed by rational judgment will determine whether there will be any uniformity in people's reflections. When it comes to the question of aesthetic judgment for the empiricists, they will err on the side of demanding determinate rules and standards of taste to constrain the play of wit.

This need for constraint informs David Hume's aesthetic theory, and it reflects the centrality imaginative association has in his entire psychology. At the outset of *A Treatise of Human Nature* (1739), Hume attributes all our complex ideas to the associative work of imagination. What distinguishes it from brute sensation is *"the liberty of imagination to transpose and change its ideas,"*[7] and its liberty requires Hume to immediately rein in this power. "As all simple ideas may be separated by the imagination, and may be united again in what form it pleases, nothing wou'd be more unaccountable than the operations of that faculty, were it not guided by some universal principles, which render it, in some measure, uniform with itself in all times and places. Were ideas entirely loose and unconnected, chance alone wou'd join them; and 'tis impossible the same simple ideas would fall regularly into complex ones (as they commonly do) without some bond of union among them, some associating quality, by which one idea naturally introduces another."[8] Hume appeals to three "laws" of the association of ideas: resemblance, contiguity in time and place, and cause and effect. They secure the regularity of imagination's work and purport to give validity to the complex ideas it constructs. But the skeptical conclusions regarding causality in Hume's *Treatise* leaves the status of these "laws" highly ambiguous. Hume writes that the principle of association among ideas "is not to be consider'd as an inseparable connexion; for that has already been excluded from the imagination: . . . but we are only to regard it as a gentle force, which commonly prevails."[9] Laws that exert a gentle force do not bind their subjects very tightly, and Hume is well aware that only arbitrary customs stand between regular society and the dissolution of imagination's associative play into pure idiosyncrasy.

I argued in chapters 5 and 6 that Hegel's biting critique of the empiricist association of ideas does not keep him from appropriating it. For Hegel it becomes a function of the soul which is ultimately redeemed in the unifying symbols of artistic imagination. *Phantasie* pursues expressive purposes in art which recuperate the mere associative play of the soul, granting it a determinate coherence. The notion of a relational manifold brought by imagination to determinate unity, a unity which respects the free individuality of its parts, dominates Hegel's theory of art. But it also dominates, in fact, the British and Scottish associationist aesthetic theory of the eighteenth century. It is typical in the aesthetics of David Hume, Edmund Burke, Alexander Gerard, Archibald Alison, and others to base aesthetic pleasure on the association of ideas; but these philosophers and critics just as typically require the beautiful work of art to be unified by the aim of determinate expression. The potential for associative wit to disrupt the order of sound judgment leads Hume, for one, to insist that works of art exhibit strict unity according to ends. "In all the nobler productions of genius,"

Hume writes in "On the Standard of Taste," "there is a mutual relation and correspondence of parts; nor can either the beauties or blemishes be perceived by him, whose thought is not capacious enough to comprehend all those parts, and compare them with each other, in order to perceive the consistence and uniformity of the whole. Every work of art has also a certain end our purpose, for which it is calculated; and it is to be deemed more or less perfect, as it is more or less fitted to attain this end."[10]

Like Hegel, Hume expects a work of art to be formed to express a definite idea and that all its parts be subordinated to the uniform and consistent expression of that idea. As he indicates, aesthetic response to the work succeeds when it comprehends the determinate unity of the whole and the place of each part in it. By means of this neoclassical emphasis on strict unity and harmony, oriented toward a fixed purpose, Hume hopes to avoid the "diversitarian" implications for aesthetic judgment of the free play of association. If an audience can find pleasure in whatever subjective emotions, images, and ideas it associates with the work, there will be no basis for agreement in taste. The unity of the work constrains imagination to apply its powers to it in a definite way, and only thus are the conditions for agreement established. On this point Hume's theory is closer to Hegel's than to Kant's, for Hegel also imposes on art the neoclassical demand for strict unity and determinate expression. For both Hume and Hegel, understanding a work involves grasping the determinate purpose that sculpts all its parts into an univocally expressive whole. Hence for all of its contemporary appeal, Kant's commitment to the indeterminate unity of aesthetic reflection, and the multiple valid interpretive responses to a work which this allows, seems like an aberration between the aesthetic unitarianism of Hume and Hegel's Ideal of Beauty.[11]

As the prominence of association increased in British empiricism, its diversitarian implications for aesthetic judgment became ever harder to avoid. Edmund Burke, in *A Philosophical Enquiry into the Origin of Our Ideas of the Sublime and the Beautiful* (1757), sought to avoid arbitrary association by basing his theory of taste on "naturally," and thus universally, pleasant sensations. Commenting on the by then traditional distinction between combinatory wit and differential judgment, Burke notes that finding resemblances is more pleasurable than maintaining differences, since the former enlarges our stock of images, while the latter task is "more severe and irksome": "the most ignorant and barbarous nations have frequently excelled at similitudes, comparisons, metaphors, and allegories, who have been weak and backward in distinguishing and sorting their ideas."[12] We avidly pursue the subjective play of wit, because "the pleasure of resemblance is that which principally flatters the imagination." But Burke argues that "the principle of this knowledge is very much accidental, as it depends upon experience and observation, and not on the strength or weakness of any natural faculty; and it is from this difference in knowledge that what we commonly, though with no great exactness, call a difference in Taste proceeds."[13] Burke opposes universal pleasures of sensation to the subjective variation caused by mere association, and denies association any role in the experience of beauty.

In effect, Burke hopes to avoid entirely the tension between wit and judgment provoked by association. He does so by reverting to the most classical of positions: that beauty represents an objective relation between properties inherent in certain objects and our perception of those properties. Burke is better known for his theory of the sublime, and association does in fact play an important role in his account of sublimity. Hence darkness, for example, is considered sublimely terrible in Burke's view because of its associations with danger.[14] But his account of the relationship between association and sublimity offers little help to my aims, because he casts the relationship in terms of physiological responses to natural phenomena. Burke's sublime differs entirely from a Kant-inspired model of sublime reflection, which construes imaginative association as a process of constructing or interpreting the meaning or import of something. Burke does remind us, however, that the empiricist aesthetic theories under review here focus mostly on beauty. We will be better positioned later in this section to reorient the problematic of wit, judgment, and association to an aesthetic of the sublime.[15]

Despite Burke's reaction against the role of association in aesthetic theory, the prominence of the notion only grew in the following decades. Alexander Gerard's *Essay on Genius* (1774) provides an exemplary case of this, and of the continued pertinence of the contrast between fanciful wit and sound judgment. Gerard espouses a theory of imagination that emphasizes the connective activity at the heart of invention. True artistry is accomplished, according to Gerard, "by assembling ideas in various positions and arrangements, that we obtain uncommon views of them."[16] Genius employs in such invention an imagination marked by "comprehensiveness" (the power to extend over a great range of material) and "activity" (the facility in movement among ideas). But imagination must also be constrained by "regularity," which "arises in a great measure from such a turn of imagination as enables the associating principles, not only to introduce proper ideas, but also to connect the design of the whole with every idea that is introduced."[17] As with Hume and Hegel, Gerard expects association to be subordinated to the production of a well-designed whole, for without guidance imagination deviates into capricious play. "The imagination produces abundance of glaring, brilliant thoughts; but not being conducive to any fixt design, nor organized into one whole, they can be regarded only as an abortion of fancy, not as the legitimate progeny of genius."[18]

Gerard must seek a standard outside imagination to assure its regularity, and he follows the tradition of submitting fancy and associative wit to the guidance of judgment; for "regularity of imagination, which is of the greatest importance in genius, could never be acquired without the aid of judgment."[19] Imagination must set all the products of its associative labor "before the discerning eye of reason" for validation, though Gerard insists that imagination can submit to such "management . . . , without having its natural sprightliness in the least impaired."[20] Gerard's theory indicates the extent to which the growing centrality of an 'untrustworthy' associative imagination forced aesthetic theorists to appeal to rationalist principles of regularity, determinate unity, and sound rules to limit the play of wit. The more association threatens to undermine rational unity, as it did in Hegelian subjective humor, the greater the temptation for associationist aestheticians to temper its play with an insistence on strict rules of order in art (as Hegel himself later insisted). But it is precisely in aesthetic experience that Kant took imagination to break free from the constraint of rules; only in his case does imagination enjoy a free rein, which nevertheless results in the spontaneous production of a felt normative validity.

British empiricism finally offers a purely associative aesthetic theory only with Archibald Alison's *Essays on the Nature and Principles of Taste*, published, as was Kant's third *Critique*, in 1790. The most extreme expression of the position, in which associative wit wins out entirely over the impositions of sound judgment, appeared in 1811, when Francis, Lord Jeffrey advocated Alison's aesthetic in the *Edinburgh Review*. Jeffrey takes the theory further than even Alison would allow, for though Alison's *Essays* represent the most elaborate effort to explain every feature of beauty and sublimity, natural or artificial, in terms of the association of ideas, he still insists on the need for fixed unity in a composition to keep fanciful wit from devolving into an associative frenzy (that is, into Hegel's subjective humor). Alison writes: "If it is true that those trains of thought which attend the Emotions of Taste, are uniformly distinguished by some general principle of connection, it ought to be found, that no Composition of objects or qualities, in fact, produces such emotions, in which this Unity of character or of emotion is not preserved."[21] Like Hegel, aestheticians such as Hume, Gerard, and Alison demanded thematic unity in the play of association. Without it, they feared, the sport of a merely associative imagination would undermine any universal standards of taste. I will focus, then, on Jeffrey's review, for the purity of his commitment to thinking imaginative association as *the* basis of aesthetic reflection.[22]

Jeffrey adopts the position that aesthetic pleasure is nothing but the satisfaction some things offer by means of their associations with other things someone has previously found pleasant. This pleasure is construed altogether empirically, unlike the a priori pleasure that comes from the free interplay of cognitive powers in Kant's theory. Thus whether someone will find something beautiful is, Jeffrey claims, "entirely dependent upon the opportunities which each individual has had to associate ideas of emotion with the object to which it is ascribed; the same thing appearing beautiful to those who have been exposed to the influence of such associations, and indifferent to those who have not."[23] Jeffrey thus commits himself to a rigorous diversitarian position on questions of taste. The contingencies of circumstance, chance exposure, personal association, and "differences of instruction or education" that plague the acquisition of taste establish that "there is no such thing as absolute or intrinsic beauty."[24] Further, this complete contextualization of taste assures that multiple taste cultures will develop around the shared associations of distinct segments of society. And different nations will have incommensurable taste cultures, due to their respective "arbitrary and national associations," each lacking any claim to necessity.[25]

At the individual level, Jeffrey articulates an egalitarian view that everyone is entitled to their peculiar aesthetic pleasures. He makes an associationist's version of the argument, found as well in Kant, that no putative rules of proper taste can deny someone their felt satisfaction in any object, no matter how dismissive of it ascendant taste might be. "If things are not beautiful in themselves, but only as they serve to suggest interesting conceptions to the mind, then every thing which does in point of fact suggest such a conception to any individual, is beautiful to that individual; and it is only quite true that there is no room for disputing about tastes, but that all tastes are equally just and correct, in so far as each individual speaks only of his own emotions."[26] Kant, of course, insists that aesthetic satisfaction must have an a priori basis; on his view, Jeffrey would be defending the unique but wholly arbitrary charms of the agreeable. But for a purely associationist aesthetic, no one can demand that everyone adopt his taste, any more than anyone can demand that he abandon it. In a theory like Jeffrey's, the balance earlier writers sought to maintain between the play of associative wit and rules of sound judgment entirely breaks down. Imaginative association alone, in each person's unique response to an object, defines aesthetic pleasure. The role of judgment—to rein association in, to subordinate it to comprehension of a determinate design or end in a work—has been removed from aesthetic reflection. With its removal from an associationist aesthetic go any grounds for demanding universal agreement or validity in matters of taste.

Despite the diversity of taste entailed by his associationism, Jeffrey attributes to artists who communicate with a wide public the aim of appealing to *shared associations*. The artist "must be cautious to employ only such objects as are the natural signs, or the inseparable concomitants of emotions, of which the greater part of mankind are susceptible; and his taste will then deserve to be called bad or false, if he obtrude upon the public, as beautiful, objects that are not likely to be associated in common minds with any interesting impressions."[27] Jeffrey's appeal

to the "naturalness" of some associations should not be taken too literally, for he refuses to base his aesthetic theory on the neoclassical
notion that we directly apprehend beauty in things. He is committed
to the view that socially conditioned patterns of association govern
aesthetic response, and whatever agreement there may be on matters
of taste reflects the pervasiveness of those habits of association. I have
argued that Kantian aesthetic reflection has a transcendental basis of
validity in the a priori status of affinity, but that empirical conditions
imposed by shared webs of sense also affect the reception which a
given projection of aesthetic unity will receive. Jeffrey verges on this
claim in his appeal to a common store of association as the source of
the broad-based appeal of some works rather than others. But his core
emphasis on each individuals' unique associations leaves him with a
largely "solipsistic" account of taste.

This brief look at the empiricist aestheticians has shown their uneasy
relationship to their own associationist proclivities. They analyze pleasure in the beautiful as arising from the play of imaginative wit, but
this free play threatens to carry aesthetic judgment away into purely
personal, varied, and intersubjectively groundless ruminations. They
counter this tendency by opposing to wit a power of sound judgment
that reins in the excesses of association. This judgment imposes rules
of composition, definite purposes, and demands for harmony that
require wit to submit to the enjoyment of a determinate configuration.
In the empiricist balance of wit, judgment, and association, rule-
governed unity grounds the universal appeal of the beautiful and
constrains the associative play of imagination. Hegel derides the asso-
ciationists for basing their psychology on "vacant-minded ideation,"
but at least in the case of art they consistently submit the play of association to rules of determinate expression and unified design. They
take both the disparity of elements contributing to a work of art, as
well as imagination's masterful unification of those elements, to be
conditions of a work's success. By doing so, empiricist aestheticians
attributed to art something like the structure of Hegelian concrete
universality. However little credit Hegel gives the association of ideas
in the *Encyclopedia Philosophy of Mind*, it appears that his conception of
imaginative artistry shares many features with the associationist aesthetic theories of the eighteenth century.[28]

Empiricist aesthetic theory would have the compositional perfection of a work, and the ends for which it is meant, curb imaginative wit. But this balance cannot be maintained in this fashion for a Kant-inspired aesthetics of sublimity, where no determinate rule or concepts of perfection guide the play of imagination. In a Kantian model of sublime reflection, not even putatively "objective" features of the object can limit the "multitude of kindred presentations" brought into constructing an aesthetic idea. The interpretive richness of aesthetic ideas suggest much to the subject beyond what is present in the presentation. Imagination's effort to comprehend a whole extends beyond what it immediately apprehends: this is how its difficulties begin. The open-endedness of what can enter into aesthetic response became apparent, after a fashion, to empiricist aestheticians who embraced association to the exclusion of neoclassical rules of sound judgment. Martha Woodmansee notes the extent to which, for Alison and Jeffrey, the power of aesthetic response comes from its surpassing reflection on the immediate qualities of a work. The play of imaginative wit extends, writes Alison, to "a variety of great or pleasing images . . . beyond what the scene or description . . . can, of itself, excite. They seem often, indeed, to have but a very distant relation to the object that at first excited them; and the object itself appears only to serve as a hint to awaken the imagination, and to lead it through every analogous idea that has place in the memory."[29] This "train of associations" will differ according to each individual's biography and current social position. As Woodmansee puts it, "Our affiliations of age, income, education, occupation, nationality, and the like disperse us into distinct interpretive communities. By shaping the ideas we associate with objects, they differentiate the way in which we construe, or construct our world."[30] For associationist aestheticians this variety in association threatens the indisputable diversity of taste; if consistently maintained, it wholly undermines any intersubjective validity claim for aesthetic reflection.

But note the critical difference between the *train* of associations pursued by Jeffrey's aesthetic respondent and the Kantian construction of aesthetic *unity*. Sublime reflection seeks to comprehend a rational whole, and fails; but in that failure it realizes a possibility that the empiricist dichotomy between a mad wit and rule-bound judgment occludes. Jeffrey's diversitarian associationism falls short of the Kantian aesthetic demand to present and enjoy indeterminate unity. Jeffrey's imagination falls in fact into the merely contingent play of Hegel's *Einbildungskraft*. In both pure association and its Hegelian proxy subjective humor, a mad wit thoroughly undermines even the partial unity of Kant's aesthetic idea. But at the same time, empiricist neoclassicism oversteps the Kantian aesthetics of sublime indeterminacy. The rules imposed by Hume or Gerard require aesthetic response to conform to determinations of the work in a manner akin to Hegelian *Phantasie's* classical Ideal. Kantian aesthetic ideas, to the contrary, construct an indeterminate web of meaning-giving relations. These expressive unwholes fall short of a rational unity requiring univocal understanding, but they are more organized, and more telling, than a train of arbitrary associations.

The connective "wit" of this sublime reflection neither falls into purely subjective play, nor requires the guidance of sound judgment to properly maintain differences. The positive wit of imaginative (partial) comprehension *is* aesthetic reflective judgment, constructing a differential affinity of parts to give coherence to something in the absence of determinate understanding. In the *Anthropology*, Kant in fact contrasts judgment and wit precisely in terms of his distinction between determinative and reflective judgments: "Just as the power of finding out the particular for the universal (the rule) is *judgment,* so the power of thinking out the universal for the particular is wit [*Witz*] (*ingenium*)."[31] The ingenious wit of a sublime reflection accomplishes interpretive insight through relating the diverse, without the determining aid of prior rules, and as we have seen throughout, nor does the combinatory wit of reflective judgment issue in the production of a determinate universal. In the Kantian production of aesthetic unity, the empiricist dichotomy between associative wit and sound judgment resolves into what we might describe as a *sound wit,* which produces compelling networks of relation from the manifold of experience. It is this resolution of a shared yet nonconceptual productivity in Kant's aesthetics of sublimity that makes it unique among his contemporaries, and uniquely relevant today. As wit unfolds or transforms these florid arrays of shared meaning, "So wit is said to blossom," and Kant adds: "just as nature seems to be carrying on a game in its flowers and a serious business in its fruits, so talent in wit is thought to rank lower (in terms of reason's ends) than talent in judgment."[32] Yet for the "ends" of sublime reflection, it is the serious play of ingenious wit that brings to flower revelations of affinity, and bears the fruit of a shared yet indeterminate understanding.

In an aesthetic context, imaginative wit show its power to judge soundly without the aid of conceptual rules. The wit of this sublime understanding lies in its power to discern or invent webs of meaning; the soundness of its play comes from the fact that, when successful, it produces a shared field of social meanings that guide our thoughts and judgments. We saw this positive wit crop up also in Hegel's philosophy of art, though only on the margins of his theory where the Ideal of determinate presentation is not achieved. In the absence of conceptual determinacy, sublime understanding offers a properly aesthetic, felt sense for the whole. Partial and open-ended, its shared vision situates and orients our interpretive engagements not merely with works of art, but also with the webs of meaning we inhabit and continually rebuild.

III

Sublime Understanding

8

The Metaphorical Sublime

Hobbes distrusted the discursive absurdity of metaphors that "openly professe deceipt." He sensed in their folly a wit unbound by good judgment, but my Kantian and Hegelian extrapolations of an indeterminate sublime reflection suggest that metaphor is one of our principal aesthetic means of understanding. Metaphors tap into situated webs of shared meaning; they pave new avenues of sense-making through which we transform ourselves and our worlds. Echoing a broader feminist metaphor, a Barbara Kruger work declaims, "your body is a battleground," and when people revise their political imperatives in the light of that metaphor, the imaginative production of relational affinities helps create new shared norms and actions. The philosophical tradition has typically lodged metaphor among the devices of "merely" aesthetic play, in favor of a sober cognition governed by conceptual rules. It has ignored along the way just how deeply metaphorical structures permeate our efforts at understanding. Perhaps the key lesson of Kant's insights into aesthetic indeterminacy is that intersubjective validity does not end where the aesthetic or the indeterminate begin. The kind of understanding conveyed through metaphor offers a *different* sense, one for richly interconnected experiential wholes, than that captured in determinate concepts.

In this chapter I present metaphor in greater detail as a product of what I call a sublime understanding. I begin by relating metaphor to the structure of sublime reflection, and make a case that Kant's aesthetic idea in fact anticipates the most viable contemporary view of metaphor, known as the "interactionist" theory. In keeping with the lessons of Hegel's objective humor, we will see that metaphorical wit relies on fields of shared connection that are exploited and inventively reworked by innovative new metaphors. For both contemporary theories and my own conception of a sublime understanding, bold metaphorical thinking exceeds current habits of intelligibility to explore new sense-making alternatives. I then consider what different statuses Kant and Hegel would grant metaphor in relation to cognition. By distinguishing metaphorical expression from conceptual cognition in terms of the Kantian difference between reflective and determinative forms of judgment, I establish the sublime understanding enacted in metaphor as an interpretive competitor of conceptual understanding.

Making this case requires that I defend the notion of metaphorical meaning, as well as the very distinction between metaphor and concept, against those who would either debunk or fetishize metaphor. I resist Donald Davidson's influential critique of metaphorical meaning, but I also preserve the distinction between an indeterminate, metaphorical understanding and the schematic understanding of determinate cognition. Nietzsche and Paul de Man represent the position that all conceptual thinking belies a universal metaphoricity that destroys the claims of cognitive validity. I explore the extent to which metaphors structure our takes on our worlds, but I propose that there are benefits to be had from resisting the notion that understanding is really metaphor "all the way down." By distinguishing an indeterminately sublime understanding from conventional conceptual cognition, we gain insight into those moments when everyday concepts fail us and we struggle to make sense of the uncanny. By maintaining the distinction, we highlight the import and value of the unique *aesthetic* validity, Other than the cognitive, that issues from our responses to the sublime.

Metaphor and Sublime Reflection

We have seen that aesthetic reflection "thinks" the unfamiliar, whatever we lack definite concepts for, by relating a manifold of parts in terms of their similarities and striking differences. Productive imagination's pattern-building work in this distinctively aesthetic pursuit differs considerably from the acts of conceptual subsumption undertaken by determinative judgment. Determinate subsumption negates distinctions among particulars to emphasize their sameness as tokens of a type. Aesthetic reflection links particulars as similar and diverse, constructing a differential affinity among parts, the whole of which exceeds determination by any definite concept. This production of uncanny relations among far-flung phenomena, so central to sublime reflection in particular, is the hallmark of the metaphorical use of language.

It is typical, in fact, to contrast metaphorical projections of differential affinity with subsumption under abstract concepts, as Hans-Georg Gadamer does in *Truth and Method*: "[If] a person transfers an expression from one thing to the other, he has in mind something that is common to both of them; but this in no way needs to be generic universality. Rather, he is following his widening experience, which looks for similarities, whether in the appearance of things or in their significance for us. The genius of verbal consciousness consists in being able to express these similarities."[1] Gadamer goes on to argue that metaphor and concept are not merely opposed responses to patterns of affinity. In fact, he sees the generation of similarity in metaphor as the engine that drives the development of language. The conventional hierarchy of valuing the "proper" meanings of determinate concepts over the juxtapositional play of metaphor obscures, according to Gadamer, the origins of the former in the latter. In such a hierarchy, he writes, "the logical ideal of the ordered arrangement of concepts takes precedence over the living metaphoricity of language, on which all natural concept formation depends. . . . What originally constituted the basis of the life of language and its logical productivity, the spontaneous and inventive seeking out of similarities by means of which it is possible to order things, is now marginalized and instrumentalized into a rhetorical figure called metaphor."[2] This indicates that Gadamer sees metaphorical transference as the generative principle of concept formation. To cast this in Kantian terms, Gadamer allies himself with a view of reflective judgment that would make it the metaphorizing means by which determining concepts are produced. In such a view, metaphor creatively collocates similarities which collapse over time into the "proper" meanings of abstract universals. In such a view, the concepts deployed by determinative judgment would all be the dead metaphors of a more fundamentally aesthetic mode of "cognition."

Conceiving reflective judgment as an aesthetically metaphorizing power of concept formation would seem to expand its import dramatically; for all of conceptual cognition would then have an aesthetic base and dimension. From a Kantian perspective, there is some element of truth in this. But I have argued from chapter 1 that we must carefully distinguish the formation and determinative application of concepts from the "ingenious" production of aesthetic unity. Failing to do so obscures the distinctively pre- or nonconceptual unities produced by aesthetic reflection, and so obscures the power of aesthetic experience to establish a sphere of felt validity distinct from conceptual cognition. The affine networks of relation revealed and reworked by a specifically sublime reflection allow the sort of sustained interplay of related differences that resists the collapse into conceptual homogeneity. And it is through its play with intersubjectively valid but disunified networks of meaning that aesthetic reflection can contribute a sublime understanding of interpretive unwholes, an understanding Other than that provided by homogenizing concepts. By regarding metaphor as a tool of concept formation, Gadamer overemphasizes similarity as the dominant quality metaphors discern. He destines metaphor to a continual slide into conceptual determinacy, which would effectively prevent this dimension of aesthetic reflection from producing anything irreducibly alien to conventional cognition. If we are to understand metaphor as the product of a properly sublime reflective judgment, we need to do justice to metaphor's maintenance of irresolvable difference across the affinity it reveals. We need to think the differential affinity of metaphor in terms of the production of aesthetic unities that defy resolution into a concept, whether old or new.

Metaphor's maintenance of differential affinity comes out more clearly in Paul Ricoeur's construal of the juxtaposition of unlike terms in metaphor as a "semantic impertinence" that violates rules of standard linguistic usage. He argues that it is precisely the literal falsehood of metaphorical speech that allows it to produce relations of affinity while maintaining the balance of similarity and difference absent from conceptual determination: "Metaphor displays the work of resemblance because the literal contradiction preserves difference within the metaphorical statement; 'same' and 'different' are not just mixed together, they also remain opposed."[3] Metaphor violates subsumptive categories by juxtaposing things that cannot be resolved into any overriding unity. Whereas subsumption denies difference by construing diverse things as instances of an abstract concept, metaphor captures affinities that give meaning to related differences. Metaphor, Ricoeur argues, "presents in an *open* fashion, by means of a conflict *between* identity and difference, the process that, in a *covert* manner, generates semantic grids by fusion of differences *into* identity."[4] The possibility of metaphorical meaning that arises from this impertinence "is not the semantic clash but the new pertinence that answers its challenge. . . . What constitutes the new pertinence is the kind of semantic 'proximity' established between the terms despite their 'distance' apart. Things that until that moment were 'far apart' suddenly appear as 'closely related.'"[5] The impertinence of metaphorical speech reflects the "audacity" with which aesthetic reflection produces unfamiliar relations. The pertinence of a metaphor lies in the surprising affinity it discloses between quite disparate phenomena. Ricoeur analyses the imaginative work of metaphorical expression in just these terms: "Imagination . . . is this *ability* to produce new kinds by assimilation and to produce them not *above* the differences, as in the concept, but in spite of and through the differences."[6]

Ricoeur emphasizes the destructive and transformative power of metaphor: "Can one not say that the strategy of language at work in metaphor consists in obliterating the logical and established frontiers of language, in order to bring to light new resemblances the previous classification kept us from seeing? In other words, the power of metaphor would be to break an old categorization, in order to establish new logical frontiers on the ruins of their forerunners."[7] Sublime reflection violates given categories because its uncanny object surpasses their explanatory power. Productive imagination yet seeks purposive design in this object, and in its failure to exhibit a whole nevertheless generates relations that transform given material. Such reflection does not produce new concepts in subservience to determinative judgment, inasmuch as its products juxtapose similarity *and* difference where abstract concepts do not. Its metaphors can die away into concepts, when their meanings become so conventional over time that they lose their allusive indeterminacy. But sublime understanding at its most inventive produces in metaphor new and uncanny relations among things which resonate with each other through their strange affinity and opposition, and which, through this differential affinity, retain their sublime defiance of conceptual determination. Reflective judgment, seeking to present the manifold as a purposive whole, transgresses habitual uses of concepts to highlight the relations of similarity and difference that weave shared experience into an affine but incomplete whole.

We can further unfold the *sublimity* of metaphor by considering the account Thomas Weiskel provided before his death twenty-five years ago.[8] Weiskel sensed the connections between metaphor, wit, and association that became apparent in Hegel's symbolic form of art. He regards metaphor as "a compromise struck between the old and the new, between the overwhelming authority of language and the irrepressible anarchy of wit, or whatever principle of unprincipled association makes wit possible."[9] Weiskel views the "compromise" of metaphorical expression as a response to sublimity.[10] His concern is the interpretation of poetic texts, and he argues that readers experience sublimity when a work provokes an excess of signification too rich or ambiguous to indicate determinately what it signifies: "The signifiers cannot be grasped or understood; they overwhelm the possibility of meaning in a massive underdetermination."[11] The ambiguity of poetic language lets loose a "syntagmatic flow" that parallels the multitude of kindred presentations brought to mind in the reflection on aesthetic ideas. We have seen that sublime reflection seeks to comprehend this manifold as a whole, to give some purposive order to it. Weiskel claims that an at least partial order is regained by a metaphorical "substitution." "[The] syntagmatic flow must be halted, or at least slowed, and the chain broken up if the discourse is to become meaningful again. This can only be done through the insertion of a substituted term into the chain, i.e., through metaphor. The absence of a signified itself assumes the status of a signifier, disposing us to feel that behind this newly significant absence lurks a newly discovered presence, the latent referent, as it were, mediated by the new sign."[12] Sublime reflection, faced with the "absence of a signified," lacking a determinate concept for its object, responds to reason's demand for totality by seeking to construct the "latent referent" that would make of its object a purposive whole. If imagination could meet reason's demand, it would present its object as a systematic unity, locating every part in a structure determined by its crowning idea. Failing this, imagination fashions an aesthetic unity for its object, relating incongruous parts through metaphorical links that weave the manifold into a purposive but polysemic design. Imaginative reflection feels sublime in its doomed but productive effort to present unity, and it proposes a metaphorical meaning to intimate the determinate meaning beyond its means to grasp: "[The] affective elaborations of the reader's sublime will abound in the metaphorical associations which have rescued the possibility of meaning from the ambivalent excitement of incomprehension."[13]

We noted in chapter 4 that just *what* meaningful relations a given subject will discern within a manifold is empirically conditioned in manifold ways. The metaphorical construct that issues from an encounter with the sublime will reflect the situation and orientation of the aesthetic judge. Weiskel recognizes this, and argues that "the 'meaning' of the sublime moment cannot be derived from the signifying relations that occasion it. [At this point] an ideological component necessarily enters the sublime moment."[14] His first point reflects just the aesthetic and sublime status of the experience: no rule can determine in advance the outcome of aesthetic reflection, and sublime reflection cannot "derive" the meaning of its object in any case. The "ideological component" of sublime reflection points to the empirical bases of aesthetic validity: the effort to make some sense of the unpresentable by means of metaphorical substitution inevitably leaves the subject to appeal to connections already intelligible within her specific cultural context. Even the creative work of metaphor does not invent meanings in a vacuum. It relies on extant patterns of relation when transferring terms from a currently standard domain to an alternative one. We will see that though metaphorical expression forges new semantic relations, its claim to validity will still rest on how it exploits given conventions of association. Even at its inventive boldest, aesthetic reflection is still situated in and oriented by the empirical context from which it departs.

Ricoeur asks of metaphor's power to re-form our networks of association: "Does not the fittingness [of certain metaphors] . . . indicate that language not only has organized reality in a different way, but also made manifest a way of being of things, which is brought to language thanks to semantic innovation? It would seem that the enigma of metaphorical discourse is that it 'invents' in both senses of the word: what it creates, it discovers; and what it finds, it invents."[15] The patterns of relation that metaphor exploits, violates, and extends are themselves sediments of a history of reflection, the inherited grid of shared connection in which we judge and act. When metaphorical expression "creates" new relations to further knit the skein of meanings, it "discovers" connections that might be thought to lie in "real" similarities awaiting discovery. Indeed, the intersubjective validity of a metaphor will often be reflected in the extent to which we feel what it shows to be a discovery. But the unmined resources of meaningful relation that new metaphors "find" reflect the inexhaustible flexibility of what aesthetic reflection has previously "invented." In this ongoing process of seeking more sense in things than present concepts capture, imaginative reflection, as Ricoeur puts it, "contributes concretely to the *epoché* of ordinary reference and to the *projection* of new possibilities of redescribing the world."[16] Metaphorical ingenuity appeals to the established legitimacy of previous inventions to validate its new discoveries. The new discoveries of aesthetic reflection regularly reinvent the sublime object they strive failingly, but productively, to comprehend. In its cumulative but always partial advancements of comprehension, metaphor exemplifies the effort of sublime understanding: to extend our fields of shared meaning beyond the limit of current habits of thought.

Kant and Interactionist Theory

I have articulated a Kantian model of sublime reflection that claims metaphor as one of its distinctive forms of understanding. In this section I want to indicate the extent to which this view has affinities with contemporary theories of metaphor. We saw in chapter 3 that some commentators have detected accounts of metaphor both in Kant's theory of symbolic exhibition and in his doctrine of aesthetic ideas.

Kantian symbols appear to have a metaphorical dimension due to their analogical function; the tradition of thinking metaphors as implicit analogies runs back, of course, to Aristotle. It is worth noting that the ambiguity between invention and discovery which Ricoeur detected in metaphor also arose for us in regarding aesthetic ideas as both presentations of genius in art, put there to be found by its audience, and as "ingenious" products of the inventive interpretation of works. Ricoeur is one proponent of the most viable current school of thought on metaphor, known across variations as the "interactionist" theory. I will show that the metaphoricity of aesthetic ideas is better captured by interactionism than by the analogy tradition. Doing so will not only demonstrate the "subterranean" presence of Kantian aesthetic-theoretical structures in current ways of thinking about metaphor. It will also, over the course of the chapter, help bring to a finer point the question of the relation of metaphor to concept, which has become for us a question about the relation between the sublime understanding of an aesthetic reflection based on feeling and the objective cognition of determinative judgment.

For purposes of a brief discussion, Max Black's seminal 1962 essay "Metaphor" counts as the source of interactionism.[17] The general way of conceiving metaphor is held by Ricoeur, Nelson Goodman, George Lakoff and Mark Johnson, Eva Kittay, and others.[18] A metaphor sparks a semantic interaction when a concept is transferred from its customary domain to an alien one. Black's metaphor "people are wolves" is literally false due to its extension of the concept "wolf" to the human domain, but what gets transferred is a set of connotations that flesh out our understanding of these canines.[19] The metaphor focuses our thoughts about people by invoking the "system of associated commonplaces" or the "implication-complex" we carry around about the ravenous, skittish, pack nature of wolves.[20] The past connotations of the secondary subject "wolf" are imposed in the metaphor on a primary subject, "people," the standard connotations of which both resist and invite the transference. In this transfer, as Goodman argues, "a set of terms, of alternative labels, is transported; and the organization they effect in the alien realm is guided by their habitual use in the home realm."[21] By this means metaphor promotes the reorganization of our patterns of discrimination, extending terms into new territory by forming novel links between previously unrelated things. The process is "interactive" because the primary subject influences what connotations of the secondary subject seem relevant, those connotations in turn spark a new consideration of the primary subject, and our understanding of even the secondary subject is transformed through the invented isomorphism.[22] Assuming we find some truth in the metaphor "people are wolves" (we may well not), our perspective on both people and wolves is transformed in the process.

In the interlude we saw some empiricist aestheticians halt the slide into associative idiosyncracy in aesthetic judgment by appealing to the associations shared by similarly acculturated people. Interactionist theorists of metaphor adopt the same strategy to explain the communicative success of metaphor. Hence "people are wolves" communicates broadly only if most everyone (who has heard of them) shares roughly the same connotations about wolves. A park ranger with a special fondness for wolves might attribute a different meaning to the metaphor from the one our shared commonplaces encourage. Or she might "get" the broadly shared meaning but dispute the metaphor and substitute "jackals" for "wolves." In any case, the validity claim of a metaphor relies on its success in transferring connotations. Imagination, in producing the aesthetic unity of metaphor, appeals to conventional associations, but its play is free and productive because the new connections it presents are not determined by prior rules or categories. A metaphor like Kruger's "your body is a battleground" invents a novel connection between disparate things, discloses a troubling congruity made all the more vivid by the juxtaposition the metaphor achieves. The demand for agreement made in aesthetic reflection is seen in a speaker's conviction that the associations called forth by her metaphor warrant application in a new domain and illuminate that domain in a novel way. Whether others come to agree will decide the success of the metaphor. If disseminated widely enough, a metaphor's disclosive links may join the array of commonplaces already orienting our patterns of recognition and discrimination. Imaginative reflection crosses categories, opposes and relates them. This play succeeds—fulfills its claim to validity—when others find that its product powerfully discloses new relations, and achieves a more or less audacious reorganization of given relational structures.

Even so, this success does not require that a metaphor mean just the same thing to everyone. The array of commonplaces a metaphor calls up for me may differ somewhat from yours; you may see an implication of it that others miss. This indicates that interactionist theory maintains the openness or inexhaustibility of metaphorical meaning. Because metaphors juxtapose disjoint and complex domains of connotation, their meaning varies with the interpretive finesse of their audience, and so cannot be specified by any interpretive rule. One cannot claim that all and only these commonplaces must be transferred successfully for a metaphor to mean. Just as sublime reflection can draw on contextualist materials external to a work in the process of interpreting it, as we saw in chapter 3, here too appeal to a background of connotation admits variety into our construals. But this does not make metaphorical meaning arbitrary either, for not just any commonplace can contribute to the transfer it affects. The metaphor "people are wolves" does not usually highlight that humans have a keen sense of smell, much less that we mark our territory with certain eliminations. A successful metaphor conveys a particular range of meaning in the array of relations it transfers; but it does not determine that meaning with finality, because the transfer varies across hearers, and the set of relevant comparisons is in principle open to addition.[23] Metaphor conveys an indeterminate meaning with the allusive directedness which we have seen in aesthetic reflection's projection of purposive design, and the interactionist account of metaphor captures this open-ended yet structured invitation to sense-making.

We already know that aesthetic ideas enjoy the inexhaustibility of meaning which interactionist theory attributes to metaphor. I argued in chapter 3 that aesthetic ideas do not function as symbols in Kant's sense because they do not have an analogical structure. The determinate rule-content of an analogy is incompatible, we saw, with the inexhaustibility of aesthetic ideas. If Kant's doctrine of aesthetic ideas harbors an account of metaphor, it will not be by virtue of a reliance on analogy, as is the case for Kantian symbols. For however sensible it might be to regard his symbols as metaphors, this interpretation comes at a price. For one, Kant would get little credit for shedding light on how metaphors work if his remarks merely repeated Aristotelian doctrine. Causabon might be fascinated to learn that Kant followed Aristotle on this point, but the discovery would not gain the rest of us much. More importantly, the venerable pedigree of the metaphor-as-implicit-analogy thesis obscures the fact that interactionism rejects the Aristotelian view as inadequate. The problem with construing metaphor in analogical terms is that an analogy can be reduced to a complex simile. As we saw in chapter 3, beauty can symbolize morality because aesthetic experience is *like* moral reflection due to the disinterested and free universality *common* to both. Because the meaning of a Kantian symbol can thereby be specified by the rule-content of the analogy involved, these symbols are at odds not only with the inexhaustibility of aesthetic ideas, but also with the inexhaustibility of metaphorical meaning which most current theories uphold. A metaphor such as "Juliet is the sun" can mean all of a variety of things that no interpretive rule could encompass; no construal could establish its meaning with finality. The task now is to take a closer look at how aesthetic ideas work, in order to substantiate the claim that they function as metaphors on an interactionist view.

As we know, Kant characterizes the aesthetic idea as a presentation of the imagination which spurs an open-ended reflection on the meaning of some idea or concept. This presentation "aesthetically expands the concept in an unlimited way," and this expansion amounts to "expressing the concept's implications and its kinship with other concepts" (CJ 315). Kant calls these "implications" *aesthetic attributes*, to distinguish them from the "logical" attributes contained in the already given content of the idea. His primary example (which we have seen before) is only so helpful: "Thus Jupiter's eagle with the lightning in its claws is an attribute of the mighty king of heaven, and the peacock is an attribute of heaven's stately queen. [Through] these attributes, unlike [through] *logical attributes*, [we] do not present the content of our concepts of the sublimity and majesty of creation, but present something different, something that prompts the imagination to spread over a multitude of kindred presentations that arouse more thought than can be expressed in a concept determined by words" (ibid.). An image of an eagle grasping lightning bolts, a conventional symbol (not in Kant's sense) for Jupiter, is an aesthetic attribute attaching to the idea of creation's majesty. Such attributes "yield an *aesthetic idea*" when they prompt imagination "to spread over a multitude of kindred presentations," the whole of which "serves the mentioned rational idea as a substitute for a logical exhibition" (ibid.).

The example is confusing because it leaves unclear whether the aesthetic idea is the origin or the outcome of the expansive reflection on the original idea; once again the discovery/invention uncertainty crops up here. The aesthetic idea in this example is either the image of the lightning-wielding eagle, which prompts the aesthetic expansion of the idea of a majestic creation, or instead the aesthetic idea is *the aesthetically expanded idea of majesty* resulting from the reflection the eagle-image prompts. I suggest that the latter alternative makes better sense of an ambiguous text, especially because the eagle-image would not on its own seem to count as an *idea* at all, whereas the majestic-creation-idea-expanded-through-an-array-of-aesthetic-attributes would. On this reading, an aesthetic idea is a concept aesthetically expanded "in an unlimited way" by bringing its "implications and its kinships with other concepts" to bear on its rich meaning. It may be that the eagle-image prompts this concept-expanding reflection; that is, the eagle-image may be the original "presentation of imagination" which gets reflection on the concept going. The aesthetic idea, however, is the new, aesthetically inflected notion of an "eaglish" majesty of creation, enriched with images, associations, implications, and kinships with other features of experience and the iconographic tradition.

One could then also characterize the aesthetic idea as a *metaphorically enriched concept.* Consideration of Kant's clearest statement of what an aesthetic idea is, applied to a second example, makes this apparent. "In a word, an aesthetic idea is a presentation of the imagination which is conjoined with a given concept and is connected, when we use imagination in its freedom, with such a multiplicity of partial presentations that no expression that stands for a determinate concept can be found for it. Hence it is a presentation that makes us add to a concept the thoughts of much that is ineffable, but the feeling of which quickens our cognitive powers and connects language, which otherwise would be mere letters, with spirit" (CJ 316). Suppose the original "concept," or as Black would say, the "primary subject," is Juliet, and the presentation that imagination makes regarding it is "Juliet is the sun." This presentation spurs a free imaginative reflection on "kindred presentations" that *express* "the concept's implications and its kinship with other concepts." That is, we interpret the metaphor to mean a great variety of things: Juliet gives life to Romeo; he cannot live without her; she makes everything visible to him in a fresh light; she is the center of his universe; he is perhaps endangering himself by making her the center of his universe, since the sun is only falsely conceived as the universe's center, and you can, after all, get burned by it, which sparks its own set of metaphorical linkages, and so forth. This reflection expands the concept "in an unlimited way" because the metaphorical enrichment of it is open-ended; there is no point at which we could claim to have exhausted its meaning. The outcome of this process, the aesthetic idea "Juliet-the-sun," represents an open-ended *transference* of attributes onto Juliet from the domain of solar "commonplaces" or "entailments," or features of the "sun" semantic field, as this or that interactionist theorist of metaphor would have it.[24] In sum, the suspicion of several commentators that Kant's aesthetic ideas function as metaphors is confirmed by the fact that his very account of how they operate corresponds nicely to the contemporary interactionist perspective.

Aesthetic ideas share with metaphor as currently conceived an inexhaustibility of meaning. The expansive reflection that produces aesthetic ideas, like the unfolding of connotations in metaphor, is incompatible with the view that their meaning could be reduced to a literal paraphrase or brought to any determinate completion. This is, of course, in keeping with Kant's account of genius as the source of aesthetic ideas, as well as with my interpretation of the process of sublime reflection through which we make partial and indeterminate sense of those ideas. Genius creates in art a presentation "for which an adequate concept can never be found" (CJ 307): the artistic meanings housed in aesthetic ideas provide an open-ended locus of interpretation for a work's audience. Art shares with metaphor this invitation to an unlimited elaboration of meaning, and of course many contemporary philosophers of art theorize artistic expression as deeply metaphorical in structure.[25] A creative metaphor counts as a miniature work of art in its own right; like all art worth the name, it brings together disjoint materials to express a new perspective which transforms our understanding of ourselves and our world. Works of art have this power in Kant's aesthetic theory because they express through metaphor in the interactionist sense.

There is a another trait that aesthetic ideas share with metaphors on the interactionist view, and that is lacking in the analogical metaphoricity of the Kantian symbol. Kant's theory of the symbol differs from current thinking on the extent of *creativity* attributed to metaphorical understanding. If a metaphor merely compares entities to point out their similarity, it at best creates a new awareness of an *antecedently given* but unnoticed commonality. The metaphor would not *create a new affinity* between its relata, as interactionism maintains. In the case of Kant's symbols, the rational ideas and empirical intuitions which they relate are radically disjoint, because such ideas cannot be directly exhibited in intuition at all. Regarding his primary example of the hand mill as a symbol for despotism, Kant notes that "though there is no similarity between a despotic state and a hand mill" in terms of their appearance, "there certainly is one between the rules by which we reflect on the two," and the analogy that relates them picks out this preexisting commonality (CJ 352). The symbol is somewhat creative inasmuch as symbolic exhibition is the work of the *productive* imagination active in reflective judgment in general. Imagination's reflection *discloses* an isomorphism in our thinking on hand mills and despotic states, and forges a connection which enhances our understanding of despotism, but it works from given conceptual rules. I will contrast this "weak" creativity of analogy-making with the "strong" creativity attributed to metaphor by interactionists, for whom metaphors establish original affinities between features of the world, rather than discovering given ones.[26]

Black speaks for most interactionists when he suggests that "it would seem more illuminating in some . . . cases to say that the metaphor creates the similarity than to say that it formulates some similarity antecedently existing."[27] If metaphors *produce* new affinities between empirical entities, such as people and wolves, they in effect ascribe new qualities to the subjects related in the metaphor, in which case they transform our understanding of what those entities are. Interactionists defend the position that at least some metaphors generate cognitive insights on the "real" world around us by performatively bringing into being the affinities they "disclose." Black likens the productivity of

metaphor to the cognitive supplements provided us by new technolo-
gies. Before the invention of cinematography, the slow-motion appearance of a galloping horse did not exist. This addition to our visual
equipment altered the world around us by adding incontestably real
but previously nonexistent features to the world.[28] Metaphor-as-new-
technology is itself a metaphor for what metaphors do, and as with all
metaphors on the interactionist view, it transforms, if accepted, our
understanding of the subjects it relates. In this case the metaphor
transforms our understanding of what constitutes a world. Black is
clear that the creativity of metaphors, their contribution of new
insights on the world, makes sense so long as one understands that
"the world is necessarily a world *under a certain description*—or a world
seen from a certain perspective."[29] If Kant's aesthetic theory prefigures the interactionist view of metaphor, it will reflect in some way this
conviction.

While a Kantian symbol creates only in the weak sense of bringing
given but unnoticed commonalities to light, the aesthetic idea models
metaphor as both inexhaustible (not replaceable by a literal paraphrase, or as Kant would say, by a "concept determined by words") and
significantly creative. Aesthetic ideas are the product of an imagination
which is, as Kant writes, "very mighty when it creates, as it were,
another nature out of the material that actual nature gives it" (CJ
314). Imagination can, through the metaphorical means of aesthetic
ideas, "restructure experience," and can "process [the material that
nature lends it] into something quite different . . . that surpasses
nature" (ibid.). The *productive* imagination responsible for metaphor
is "free," Kant claims, "from the law of association (which attaches to
the empirical use of the imagination" (ibid.). Noticing antecedently
given similarities would be the work of empirical association, but
metaphor on the interactionist view invents new affinities between
domains of experience. It thereby transforms our understanding of
the features of the world which the metaphor relates; if we maintain
Black's conviction that a "world" is always a "world under a certain
description," then the creativity of metaphors (at least those we
embrace) transforms the relata themselves. In the context of Kant's
thought, a productive imagination, through the invention of a "second
nature" in aesthetic ideas, would be the agent of that transformation.

This imaginative recasting of the "given" into metaphorically expressive un-wholes is the work of sublime understanding.

Rudolf Makkreel has argued that the Kantian subject creates aesthetic ideas as an attempt to make sense of experience and the world as a coherent whole.[30] If this is right, our interpretive perspectives on the world, and the world conveyed through those perspectives, are deeply structured in metaphorical terms, as interactionist theorists would maintain. Some features of the world are made through metaphor, and so metaphor makes an indispensable cognitive (though conceptually indeterminate) contribution to a broad conception of human understanding construed, by Goodman, for one, as "world-making." In a strong sense our perspectives count as creative works of art (second nature), and the world embodied by our perspectives is a product of artistic endeavor. The generation of meaning through metaphor does not unify worlds as determinate wholes, however; the aesthetics of sublimity in which I have located metaphor renders its sense-making efforts partial and interpretively open. Sublime understanding casts a net of differential affinity over the world through metaphor, but it never catches the prey (a determinate totality of meaning) that reason pressed it to hunt. I will further explore the role of a sublime understanding in interpretive "world-making" in the next chapter.

Metaphor and Cognition in Kant and Hegel

We have seen that there are two accounts of metaphor to be gleaned from Kant's aesthetic theory. One construes metaphor analogically, harking back to Aristotle: it grants metaphor only a weakly creative dimension, and limits metaphorical meaning in accordance with an analogical rule. Metaphors of this sort play a symbolizing role in giving intuitive embodiment to reason's ideas, especially in the moral sphere. The other can be found in Kant's notion of the aesthetic idea: it grants metaphor the potential for the strong creativity and the inexhaustibility of meaning which is emphasized by contemporary interactionist views. Aesthetic ideas form the core of artistic expression and lend a metaphorizing dimension to our broader interpretive aims. Given their role in the Kantian subject's sense-making efforts to express purposive design in its world, what status does each of these kinds of metaphor have in Kant's view of cognition?

We found in chapter 4 that transcendental affinity partially grounds the validity claim of sublime reflection. When imagination plays aesthetically, it celebrates the differential, undetermined affinity it "finds" in its presentations despite the absence of ordering concepts. Imagination celebrates the connectivity of all presentations, and in metaphorical expression realizes this affinity in instances of uncanny relation. Metaphor is one way we imaginatively explore and rework the latent affinities and isomorphisms that "run through and gather together" our shared webs of semantic relation. In the process of this play imagination discloses the affinity of the manifold to be the aesthetic condition of all conceptual knowledge. Only if all the content of experience is in principle associable, only if imagination provides an affine whole to conceptual thinking, can elements of that whole be ordered in the manner specific to subsumption under concepts. This conclusion is just a restatement in first *Critique* terms of Kant's third *Critique* tenet that the free, preconceptual accord of imagination and understanding in aesthetic experience is the condition of possibility for the conceptually determinate experience in which understanding legislates to imagination. The status of affinity as a transcendental condition of even conceptual cognition reveals the sort of end-run metaphor does around concepts in order to claim its validity. For Kant, the disclosure of affinity in metaphor would gain its validity from the same preconceptual transcendental starting point as determinate knowledge.

This much is true for both kinds of Kantian metaphor, but the respective implications of their appeals to this transcendental basis differ greatly. In the case of Kantian symbols, one of the relata whose affinity is disclosed through the analogical metaphor is a rational idea. These metaphors help the Kantian subject *think* about supersensibles which cannot be directly *cognized* in experience. The analogy through which we think God as author of the world motivates the reflective search for the coherence among physical laws which nature would presumably display were it a product of intelligence. The analogy which relates the free productivity of norms in aesthetic experience to the enactment of freedom in the moral sphere helps convey the third

Critique message that mechanistic nature might have room in it for practical autonomy. These metaphors gain their normativity from the transcendental status of affinity, but also from the transcendental pedigree of the rational ideas they symbolize. Such ideas are common to the "thought-range" of all rational subjects, and as the finest fruits of reason Kant thinks they are enjoined upon us to think. Recall that the analogy in these metaphors discloses a similarity between (1) the rule under which we think some idea of reason, and (2) the conceptual rule through which we cognize a class of empirical objects or experiences. It may be that more than one object could symbolize the idea. Something other than the hand mill could symbolize despotism, but only so long as its concept shared the same isomorphic rule with our idea of despotism as our thought on the hand-mill intuition does. Hence metaphors of this kind have for Kant a secure claim to universal validity, given their reference to a transcendental relatum, although which intuition makes for the best symbol of that relatum might vary across cultural contexts.

Because Kantian symbols refer to rational ideas, they have little bearing on *cognition* of the empirical world. In keeping with this, such metaphors do not transform our understanding of the empirical intuition used as symbol, because the rule through which we think it is not altered by being compared analogously to our reflection on a rational idea. These metaphors are not creative in the strong sense, but only in the weak sense of pointing out a previously unnoticed, preexisting similarity. The stakes change dramatically when we turn to the kind of metaphor embodied in Kant's aesthetic idea, for these metaphors relate empirical particulars (people and wolves, say), and so are deprived of the universal validity assured by the symbol's supersensible reference. Given that metaphor relies on the transference of shared connotations, the connotations must first be shared before metaphors can mean, and their cognitive significance will be localized to "communities" of shared background understanding, however great or small those communities may be. Some metaphors may enjoy wide (if not global) acceptance in human discourse and practices; but on the other hand, West Coast high-technology workers who convey that they cannot expend time or attention on some issue by saying, "I don't have the disk space for that," should not expect that this will communicate their meaning effectively to everyone.[31] We will see in chapter 9 that the appeal which a sublime understanding makes to localized patterns of intelligibility effectively constrains the extent of universality which its reflective products can claim.

The key issue in assessing the cognitive status of the Kantian metaphors embodied in aesthetic ideas is their strong creativity. On the interactionist view, powerful metaphors create affinities between components of experience and the world, transform our understanding of those features, and hence transform the world sculpted through our metaphor-inflected perspectives on it. Metaphor does not merely compare the furniture of our worlds, it helps to craft it. If this is true of Kant's aesthetic ideas, it will be so because they relate disjoint empirical entities, and transform what we make of them, rather than referring an intuition to a rational idea, as his symbols do. As the philosopher of the Copernican Revolution, Kant embraced the idea that human subjectivity gives the empirical world a human shape. The world is the way we "find" it due to a productive synthesis under the categories, along with the various "axioms," "anticipations," "analogies," and "postulates," that Kant thinks attend upon that synthesis. This transcendental act of "world-making" is a far cry, however, from the artistic creation of metaphors that purport to transform the empirical world in midstream, as it were. Whether Kant would embrace the strong creativity thesis of interactionism hangs, then, on whether he would extend the transcendental *spontaneity* of the human mind into the cognition of empirical particulars. It is the productive imagination of Kant's aesthetic theory which displays the creative spontaneity in question, and so ultimately the issue comes down to whether Kant would accept an aesthetically reflective dimension to cognition of the world.

In a strict sense, we could conclude that the imaginative *aesthetic* act of inventing metaphor cannot count as cognition for Kant, which on his first *Critique* terms requires schematized rule determination under the categories. Alternatively, we might take seriously the enriched conception of the human subject Kant presents in the *Critique of Judgment*. Kant grants this aesthetically active subject new powers to imaginatively elaborate the significance of experience and the world as a whole by means of symbolization and expression, the twin routes of metaphor-making we have analyzed. Aesthetic ideas in particular, in the media of metaphor and art, allow us to interpret and recast our understandings of the world, which surely counts as a cognitive mission given a broader conception of human understanding than Kant's. In the spirit of Goodman's pragmatism, understanding involves the myriad ways we sort and compose, weigh and order the furniture of the worlds we make by those means, all of which reflects our practical engagement with those worlds, all of which deeply involves metaphor. Kant perhaps comes close to this more generous conception of cognition at one point in the *Critique of Judgment*, when he grants that it may be permissible to call a way of construing our experience cognition "if this cognition is a principle not for determining the object theoretically, as to what it is in itself, but for determining it practically, as to what the idea of the object ought to become for us and for our purposive employment of it" (CJ 353). Kant likely means this to refer to his conception of practical *moral* cognition, so we cannot make too much of the passage, but I have extrapolated a sublime understanding from his aesthetic theory in the spirit of this broader, less determinately conceptual construal of sense-making. The powers Kant grants imagination in the third *Critique*, as a maker of worlds through metaphor, suggest that the affine relations sublime understanding produces contribute as much as conceptual knowledge to the orienting reflections of concretely situated interpretive subjects.

With Hegel, as we know, all of this changes. By locating metaphor among the poor accomplishments of the symbolic form of art, Hegel minimizes its cognitive contribution. And by rejecting Kant's doctrine of aesthetic ideas, Hegel effectively vanquishes aesthetic indeterminacy, and specifically the open, differential affinity of metaphor from the terrain of shared sense-making. Hegel does of course embrace the spontaneity of human thought in its conceptualization of the world, as was evident in the first interlude regarding his development of the Kantian regulative idea of an intuitive intellect. Yet the consummated spontaneity of the spirit in Hegel's mature system is its *determinate* unfolding of the Idea in concrete reality. The open-ended expressiveness of metaphor has no place in the Hegelian Idea's achieved totality. The aesthetics of sublimity I have developed from Kant (and wrestled from Hegel) pictures a shared striving for sense "doomed" to a partial and slippery, metaphorical grasp, rather than the rational unity made literal in the world as promised by Hegel.[32]

Indeed, the conclusion that metaphor has cognitive value for the Kantian interpretive subject is reflected in a negative light in Hegel's devaluation of all that subject's finite imaginative thinking and conceptual understanding. All representational thinking, whether metaphorical or straightly conceptual, all of which Hegel takes to oppose the subject to its object of thought, is superseded in the reconciling satisfactions of the Hegelian systematic Concept. Even if metaphors have cognitive value for Kant, both metaphors and straight concepts produced by a finite imagination and understanding must be demoted a step by Hegel to make room at the top for the infinite free thinking of his systematic reason. Hegel says as much and more in a remarkable statement in the *Encyclopedia Logic*: "Presentations [*Vorstellungen*] in general can be regarded as *metaphors* of thoughts and concepts."[33] Hegel appears to mean this quite literally: by presentations he means all the feelings, beliefs, concepts, and images of the Kantian subject; these are metaphors for the thoughts and concepts to be perfected in and only in Hegel's speculative system. Kant is a metaphor for Hegel, in the sense that Hegel raises to literal and articulate unity what Kant had supposed the metaphorical unity of in the merely regulative ideality of his concept of reason. The incomplete presentations Hegel calls metaphors will gain their true and determinate meaning by their elevation into his system.

From a Hegelian perspective the cognitive claims of metaphor must pale in comparison to the systematic aims of speculative reason, while for Kant metaphor enjoys a cognitive value to rival the claims of conceptual thinking. Kant may in fact be one of the only philosophers of the modern period for whom metaphors are philosophically honorable. Even so, Hegel's caution with regard to metaphor does not keep him, as we have seen, from according it a curious status as the product of a positive wit, at least on the non-Ideal margins of his philosophy of art. Hegel's aesthetic theory, and his account of the imaginative wit at work in metaphor, highlights and preserves the striving of metaphor to make valid disclosures of affinity by virtue of its conceptual distortions. Because the kind of unity which Hegel seeks must ultimately embarrass the piddling insights of metaphorical wit, he can afford to grant them some preliminary validity. He thereby on one level confirms the insight I have attributed to Kant, that aesthetic production in the form of metaphor contributes a sublime understanding unavailable to a cognitive relation to the world that is beholden to concepts. Whether we would follow Hegel in demoting metaphor, by appeal to a higher cognition that would surpass any contribution of the aesthetic, depends on our commitments to his greater project. Until such a commitment is made, if ever, we could accept the "equiprimordial" legitimacy of sublimely reflective and conceptually determinate advancements of understanding.

Debunking or Fetishizing Metaphor

Not everyone has been sympathetic to the strain in contemporary theories of metaphor that I have shown a Kant-inspired notion of sublime understanding to favor. This tradition of thinking about metaphor preserves the distinction between literal and metaphorical meaning, which, as I have suggested, maps onto Kant's separation of determinative and reflective forms of judgment. This allows metaphor, and other products of aesthetic reflection, their own domain of validity distinct from the conceptual literal. Opponents of this tradition attack the distinction from one of two directions, depending on their proclivities: either they deny that there is any such thing as metaphorical meaning, and so collapse the distinction to the benefit of the literal, or they claim that all concepts are ultimately metaphorical, and collapse the distinction to the chagrin of the literal. I want to consider each of these charges briefly, because they will help thematize the case I want to make that the indeterminacy of sublime understanding, so present in metaphor, is a quasi-cognitive tool that counters and complements determinative conceptual understanding, rather than replacing or undermining it. Donald Davidson represents the first position, that there is no such thing as metaphorical meaning. The second position, that there are *only* metaphors, alive or dead, I will take Nietzsche (in one mood anyway) and Paul de Man to represent.

Davidson has famously argued that the literal falsehood of metaphors indicates that they have *no metaphorical* meaning.[34] The only meaning we can ascribe to a metaphor, he argues, is the meaning of the baldly false literal statement of which the metaphor consists: "metaphors mean what the words, in their literal interpretation, mean, and nothing more."[35] For the truth-conditional semantic theory Davidson espouses, a statement gets its meaning from the conditions under which it could be true. The statement "wolves are canines" can have a meaning because one can specify the condition, namely that wolves are canines, which would make the statement true. But the metaphor "people are wolves" cannot be literally true given the conventional allocations of reference in our language. Because we cannot elaborate a T-sentence that would specify the conditions under which the statement is true, it cannot have a meaning beyond its false claim that people are wolves. A truth-conditional semantics cannot allow for metaphorical meanings distinct from the literal because (1) there obviously obtain no external conditions that could make a metaphor's literal falsity literally true, and (2) the metaphorical use of words adds nothing to the elements of the literally false sentence that could alter its truth-conditions and so its meaning.

Instead of having "a cognitive content that its author wishes to convey and that the interpreter must grasp if he is to get the message," Davidson claims that metaphor offers the hearer an occasion to ruminate about whatever the metaphor brings to mind. "[What] we attempt in 'paraphrasing' a metaphor cannot be to give its meaning, for that lies on the surface; rather we attempt to evoke what the metaphor brings to our attention."[36] None of these ruminations constitute meanings of the metaphor; instead, what a metaphor manages to suggest to us derives from its *effects* upon us rather than from any content the expression possesses, which could be called its metaphorical meaning. Hence Davidson steers metaphor exclusively into the pragmatics of language, making it a tool we use to bring on an open-ended *reaction* in the hearer, but not to convey a specific meaning. "I depend on the distinction between what the words mean and what they are used to do. I think metaphor belongs exclusively to the domain of use."[37] So while Davidson wishes to deny statements anything like a metaphorical meaning, he does affirm metaphor's power to prod us into noticing things through our reaction to its literal falsity. "Metaphor does lead us to notice what might not otherwise be noticed, and there is no reason . . . not to say these visions, thoughts, and feelings inspired by the metaphor are true or false."[38] Because this response has nothing to do with comprehending a metaphorical meaning of the expression, Davidson argues that we could not provide any literal paraphrase of its meaning. I have argued for the aesthetic indeterminacy of metaphorical meaning, but for Davidson that indeterminacy is not a quality of the metaphor's meaning, which does not exist and so surely could not be paraphrased. The "indeterminacy" lies only in our varied and open-ended responses to a literally false statement's prodding.

Davidson's debunking of metaphorical meaning has been criticized at great length and, I think, persuasively. For example, Nelson Goodman argues among other things that literal language can just as easily be used to prod the hearer, and hence metaphor cannot be defined—and relegated to pragmatics—as if a prodding function were peculiar only to it.[39] Max Black argues (among other things) that just as Davidson *says something* about metaphor by calling it "the dreamwork of language" in his essay, speakers of metaphor *make claims* with the metaphors they speak.[40] That is, a metaphor does convey an intended message, though the opacity of its meaning leaves hearers to puzzle out and assess the message for themselves. David Novitz, for another, has made a case for tailoring Davidson's truth-conditional semantics to the recognition of metaphorical meanings.[41] Most significantly, I think, Eva Kittay has made a powerful case that Davidsonian semantics is simply inadequate to account for the reality of metaphorical meaning, and that we need a *relational* theory of meaning which renders all meaning context-dependent and suffused with pragmatic factors.[42]

I will not rehash all of the extensive argumentation back and forth, nor have I the space for a thorough critique of Davidson's position (and I think much of that work has already been done). Members of some philosophical schools think Davidson's debunking of metaphor is obviously right, while members of other schools think he is obviously and hopelessly wrong. The extent of disagreement suggests that very deep issues, and uncertainties, about the nature of language and meaning crop up here. I want to make just two points. First: we have seen that sublime reflection involves a *controlled* response to the uncanny. Imagination seeks to make sense of what exceeds our conceptual grasp by networking attributes of the thing—and other elements that arise in the response to it—into an expressive though incomplete "un-whole." This effort is driven by the reflective sense that a purpose undergirds what imagination plays with, though no determinate rule guides our sense-making. In the case of metaphor (and here I follow Black), a speaker's intention to express not just anything, but a plausible range of meaning, directs the hearer towards a meaning the metaphor leaves unstated. The metaphor's success hangs on its bringing the right range of things to mind which take the hearer in the right direction. Davidson claims that metaphor has only to do with the pragmatic effects of language. But if his metaphor "metaphor is the dreamwork of language" had "effectively" nudged me into thinking about filial obligations in Ming China, Davidson would be justified in insisting that I missed his point entirely and got his metaphor grossly wrong.

That is, there is more structure to the communication of meanings through metaphor than the forcing of a reaction. Through metaphor we claim to disclose startling affinities running through our semantic networks, or we create new affinities to further weave the semantic skein. Just as aesthetic ideas are as much a product of reflection on a work as a meaning already present in the work, metaphors get their meaning from *both* the richly suggestive message conveyed *in* the metaphor and the hearer's wide-ranging interpretive response *to that open message.* Not just any response will do, which is why we can evaluate one interpretation of a metaphor's meaning (or any interpretation for that matter) as better or worse than another. We would have no cause for such evaluation if forcing a reaction of any kind were all that metaphor accomplished. But neither can we dictate one proper understanding of the metaphor, for interpreting it allows the possibility of multiple plausible construals. Davidson will have truck only with meanings univocally conveyed by sentences whose truth-conditions make them mean the same thing to everyone. Metaphors will not mean the same thing to everyone, but neither will their meaning amount to an entirely arbitrary reaction different in each person. The reason lies in the structure of sublime understanding, in the way its reach for sense-making affinities, both in the production and the interpretation of metaphor, inevitably appeals to our sedimented resources of *intersubjectively shared* semantic connection.

Second, I think one can make a case that Davidson's own theory of interpretation is incompatible with his denial of metaphorical meaning. The claim warrants extensive development in another setting; here I will only briefly outline it. The core of his view is the contention that "interpreting an agent's intentions, his beliefs and his words are parts of a single project, no part of which can be assumed to be complete before the rest is."[43] The meanings of speakers' statements are dependent on the beliefs the speakers hold, and this complicates the project of interpretation. Making sense of what someone believes and means by what they say requires having some purchase on their beliefs beyond the mere words they use. Davidson famously thinks that this requires that interpretation be guided by a "principle of charity" which has interpreters ascribe many of their own beliefs to speakers. This basis of agreement in beliefs provides the common mooring of speaker and interpreter, which allows the latter to interpret the former's words. Such charity is indispensable: "we cannot take even a first step towards interpretation without knowing or assuming a great deal about the speaker's beliefs. Because knowledge of beliefs comes only with the ability to interpret words, the only possibility at the start is to assume general agreement on beliefs."[44]

If understanding a speaker's meaning requires appeal to a background of beliefs and intentions, as Davidson holds, it would seem that a speaker's beliefs and intentions about speaking metaphorically affect a change of meaning from cases in which she intends to speak literally and believes she is doing so. When someone speaks in metaphor, she does not intend her words to be taken literally. She believes she is saying something other than what her words convey literally, and we must charitably ascribe different beliefs and intentions to her in order to interpret her metaphorical speech. But if meaning depends on ascribed beliefs and intentions, then, contra Davidson's critique of metaphorical meaning, a metaphorical statement must say something other than what the literal falsehood it is couched in states, because the statement is not spoken with the same meaning-affecting constellation of beliefs and intentions which inform the literal statement (whatever that constellation would be). It would seem that when we interpret metaphorical meaning, by puzzling out what things a speaker might plausibly mean, we engage in just the sort of charity that Davidson's theory of interpretation requires of us. The indeterminacy of metaphorical meaning arises, as it has arisen for products of aesthetic reflection throughout this study, from the absence of a known intention that would decide the "proper" meaning of a metaphor. But it would be the height of uncharitability to think a speaker were idiotically claiming that people literally are wolves (werewolves maybe?), instead of searching out the altered meaning their statement purposively, though vaguely, points toward.

If Davidson would dismiss metaphorical meaning, Nietzsche and de Man would debunk *literal* meaning as the forgetful occlusion of a universal metaphoricity. Because I see metaphor as a case of sublime understanding's disclosure and reworking of the networks of meaningful relation that orient our interpretive engagements, Davidson's attack on metaphorical meaning is more threatening than a view that would valorize it. Given the aesthetic character of the kind of (un)holistic understanding I have thematized, I have more in common with a position that would reverse the hierarchy of the literal over the figurative and humble the presumptions of "proper" cognition. But as I indicated early in this chapter, I preserve Kant's distinction between determinative and reflective forms of judgment because I think we gain something through the distinction. We gain a specifically aesthetic conception of validity, distinct from conceptual validity, and in the process we gain a revised conception of understanding in which the aesthetic and the cognitive (as traditionally demarcated) intermingle. I will carry this idea into the following section, where I will indicate how far one might go in "metaphorizing" our relation to our worlds, while still maintaining a role for the literality of homogenizing and determinative concepts. So here I will only sketch the view that, to put it metaphorically, it is really metaphor "all the way down."

In the early essay "On Truth and Lying in the Extra-Moral Sense," Nietzsche advances the claim that every concept is "merely the residue of a metaphor": "the illusion which is involved in the artistic transference of a nerve stimulus into images is, if not the mother, then the grandmother of every single concept."[45] Nietzsche's argument for this universal metaphoricity of concepts is based on two observations about their formation. He first construes the entire process of taking in sensory material as itself a metaphorizing procedure: "To begin with, a nerve stimulus is transferred into an image: first metaphor. The image, in turn, is imitated in a sound: second metaphor. And each time there is a complete overleaping of one sphere, right into the middle of an entirely new and different one."[46] Nietzsche would appear to be claiming that representation as such, any act of presenting something in a medium other than its original, counts as metaphor. On this view even a photograph of a tree would be a "metaphor" for a tree; Nietzsche has in mind an extremely broad conception of metaphor, and he needs it if he is to wage an attack on representation generally.

Second, he argues that representational transference *cannot preserve* the content it presumes to re-present. Our confidence in our representational powers is delusory: "we believe that we know something about the things themselves when we speak of trees, colors, snow, and flowers; and yet we possess nothing but metaphors for things— metaphors which correspond in no way to the original entities."[47] Specifically in the case of our concepts, abstract representation proves doubly (or triply) metaphorical in that "Every concept arises from the equation of unequal things."[48] A concept such as "leaf" is a mere metaphor for actual leaves in all their specific diversity, for we arrive at the concept by "arbitrarily discarding these individual differences and by forgetting the distinguishing aspects." I have construed metaphor, and sublime reflection generally, as the relating of the affine diverse *as diverse*, while abstract concepts relate the diverse *as the same* and ignore difference. But Nietzsche makes all concept-formation metaphorical by regarding even the discernment of abstract sameness as a metaphorizing function. On his view "people are wolves" of course counts as a metaphor, but so does "this is a leaf," because it transfers onto the specific entity a representation of leafness that, according to Nietzsche, "corresponds in no way" to the original entity. He concludes that the concepts with which we presume to make valid judgments are in fact "a mobile army of metaphors" produced by an "*artistically creating* subject" who forgets that she invents a world rather than knowing it.[49]

By arguing that the abstract concept formation of determinate cognition is as metaphorical a process as the crafting of aesthetic ideas (and so really not determinative at all), Nietzsche is effectively collapsing the basic Kantian division between determinative and reflective forms of judgment into an omnipresent aesthetic expression. If all presentation is metaphorical, then all concepts are really aesthetic ideas. Following this implicit Nietzschean tradition, Paul de Man challenges Kant's division of judgments in order to make a case for the irreducible metaphoricity of all, and especially all philosophical, discourse.[50] De Man focuses on Kant's distinction between schematic and symbolic exhibition, (properly) lining up the former with determinative and the latter with reflective judgment. We have, of course, located one kind of Kantian metaphoricity in his theory of the symbol; it should be noted that de Man does not consider the expressive metaphorical potential of aesthetic ideas. He bases his case for dissolving the distinction at issue on the presence of one shattering word in Kant's discussion of the two forms of exhibition. Kant notes, as we know, that symbols involve "a transfer of our reflection on an object of intuition to an entirely different concept, to which *perhaps* no intuition can ever directly correspond" (CJ 352–353).[51] If an intuition *perhaps could* correspond to the concept, then it would not be a metaphorizing case of symbolic exhibition but rather a *schematic* presentation of the concept. De Man argues that "it has been the point of the entire argument that we know for certain whether a representation directly corresponds to a given concept or not."[52] The uncertainty expressed in Kant's "perhaps" suggests to de Man that we may not have any way of distinguishing which of our concepts are schematic and which symbolic, in which case the distinction loses its meaning. Kant also remarks in the same paragraph that the word "foundation" [*Grund*] has a symbolic dimension (CJ 352), so de Man charges that in the "grounding" of symbol and schema as two distinct forms of exhibition, Kant relies on a notion of "grounding" that he has conceded is symbolically metaphorical. If Kant's distinction between symbol and schema "can only be stated by means of metaphors that are themselves symbolic," de Man thinks that the priority of the symbol over the very distinction between symbol and schema would establish the metaphoricity of all discourse.[53]

If Nietzsche and de Man have it right, then the distinction, put in Kantian terms, between determinative schematic judgments and the sort of aesthetic reflective judgments produced by a sublime under-standing, cannot be maintained. If it is metaphor "all the way down," if we *always and in every case* face uncanny indeterminacies which we try to make sense of through metaphor, through the networking projec-tion of aesthetic unity, then an "artistically creative" sublime under-standing would be the only understanding we have. In the next section I will explore the extent to which metaphor does quite thoroughly per-vade our cognitive takes on our worlds; but I will also make a case for preserving the Kantian reflective/determinative distinction from which this study set out.

Living Metaphor from a Pragmatic Point of View

I have presented metaphor as one product of a sublime understanding that affords us a broad interpretive grasp of the indeterminately uni-fied fields of semantic relation in which we live. Some contemporary theorists of metaphor also emphasize the role metaphorical networks play in structuring shared contexts of meaning and interaction. These theorists emphasize the extent to which metaphors serve to organize experience at fundamental levels. For Wayne Booth, "The metaphors we care for most are always embedded in metaphoric structures that finally both depend on and constitute selves and societies."[54] A "metaphoric world" is constituted by the web of differential affinity an array of interlocking metaphors sustains. Such structures orient per-ception, self-understanding, and action, and so the production of new metaphors always poses a challenge to the interpretive status quo of participants in a given world. Metaphorical innovations that alter the web of meanings transforms the worlds those metaphors make mean-ingful; as Booth puts it, "to *understand* a metaphor is by its very nature to *decide* whether to join the metaphorist or reject him, and that is simultaneously to decide either to be shaped in the shape his metaphor requires or to resist."[55] Metaphors shape the network of meaning-giving relations they appeal to in their transfers. They can alter that network, and so our worlds, in remarkable ways when people find an innovation compelling enough to validate and enact it.

The critical role metaphor plays in structuring and transforming lived worlds has been explored in depth by George Lakoff and Mark

Johnson in *Metaphors We Live By*. They claim that metaphor structures much of our interpretive activity, that "our ordinary conceptual system, in terms of which we both think and act, is fundamentally metaphorical in nature."[56] They discuss a great many "structural metaphors" of the sort we have mainly considered in this chapter, metaphors which organize one domain of experience in terms of another. In the metaphor "argument is war," for example, not just the concept but the activity of argument and the way we talk about it are ordered by a transfer of commonplaces about war into the domain of disputation. The metaphorical connections between our social practices of argument and battle show up in the relations everyday language deploys:

Your claims are *indefensible*.

He *attacked every weak point* in my argument.

His criticisms were *right on target*.

I *demolished* his argument.

You disagree? Okay, *shoot!*

If you use that strategy, he'll *wipe you out*.

He *shot down* all of my arguments.[57]

Generally accepted metaphoric relations between argument and war influence people's behavior in argumentative settings, shape a world of argument for them. Such structural connections between domains of experience form empirical conditions of life within a given world. They have no transcendental necessity, beyond the weak validation provided by the transcendental status of affinity as such. Their validity as empirical conditions is tied to the histories of particular cultures and what has received intersubjective legitimation through that history. Hence when sublime understanding reworks our sense-making networks, the chances of its product being adopted as a "valid" reformation of the field of given relations depends heavily on its subtle negotiation of possibilities left open by the empirical conditions of present comprehension.

   Lakoff and Johnson reveal how deep the metaphorical structuring of worlds goes in their treatments of "orientational" and "ontological" metaphors. An orientational metaphor "organizes a whole system of concepts with respect to one another," often by spatializing whole arrays of concepts in broad coherent patterns. Thus a great variety of orientational metaphors that order judgment and action, e.g., "happy is up, sad is down;" "conscious is up, unconscious is down;" "virtue is up, depravity is down;" "rational is up, irrational is down" all cohere with the general orientation of "good is up, bad is down."[58] Broad orientational metaphors play a major role in constraining the range of admissable metaphorical invention, and so also condition opportunities for valid aesthetic reflection at an empirical level. The metaphorical expression, "He rose into a depression," stands little chance of capturing people's experience in any compelling way because it violates the given network of metaphorical relations in which sadness is spatialized as downwardly mobile. Ontological metaphors, in turn, further orient us in our worlds by having us "[view] events, activities, emotions, ideas, etc., as entities and substances." Metaphors such as "inflation is an entity":

Inflation is lowering our standard of living;

Inflation is backing us into a corner;

or "the mind is a brittle object":

Her ego is *very fragile*;

His mind *snapped*;

These relational links between disparate phenomena provide us an articulate world; they locate and motivate us within it.[59]

So much metaphorical structuring and ordering might suggest that metaphor *determines* our conceptions in systematically complete forms that would leave little room for the free play of imaginative reflection. We can highlight how some metaphors reflect the inexhaustible wealth of response to Kantian aesthetic ideas by focusing on the metaphorical relations that give content to "love." Lakoff and Johnson illustrate how a whole array of metaphors inform *some* features of loving. "Love is a physical force," "love is a patient," "love is madness," "love is magic," and "love is war": all these metaphorical relations express some facets of the rich content of the idea of love.[60] Each set of relations captures some features of loving while ignoring others, but none capture the entirety, no final network of love-relations can complete our conception of love in any determinate way. All these relations point toward and seek to articulate the same *sublime* phenomenon that defies comprehension as a whole. This array of metaphors constitutes the loose relational products of sublime reflection, seeking to make sense of experiences that surpass conceptual determination by binding far-flung materials into a differential affinity. The aesthetic (dis)unity of love-relations invites continued reflection on the matter. Its indeterminate unity orients imagination toward presentation of love's purposive design while assuring that sublime reflection will never pretend to have completed its labor of understanding.

Just as given metaphorical relations emphasize or hide certain features of a world, novel metaphors may differently organize and prioritize aspects of a world to promote a new order. Lakoff and Johnson consider the alternative metaphorical transfer "love is a collaborative work of art."[61] This nonstandard view of love appeals to a great many commonplaces associated with artistry and collaboration; it produces new relations that highlight features of loving: love is work, love cannot be achieved by formula, love creates a reality, love requires compromise, love "needs funding," and so on. Furthermore, the metaphor is itself related differentially to other love-metaphors, in that it shows what others hide and ignores some of what they show. For example, love as a collaborative work of art emphasizes that love requires work, discipline, and cooperation, while the metaphor "love is madness" occludes these features of the experience. New metaphors forge new relations in our webs of meaning; they may join and transform our shared webs if people validate and adopt their "revelations." In the process, worlds are transformed: "New metaphors have the power to create a new reality. This can begin to happen when we start to comprehend our experience in terms of a metaphor, and it becomes a deeper reality when we begin to act in terms of it. If a new metaphor enters the conceptual system that we base our actions on, it will alter that system and the perceptions and actions that the system gives rise to."[62] By this process, the "artistic" invention of new relations fulfills the potential granted productive imagination by both Kant and Hegel, to produce a "second nature" from the material "actual nature" gives it. The sedimentary history of our relational networks, however, shows "nature" to have long since been left behind by the interpretive play of sublime understanding.

But the metaphorical dimension of much of our conceptual "system" does not imply the *omni*presence of metaphor, nor does it undermine the cognitive validity of determinate concepts. This returns us to the issue we have repeatedly encountered in this chapter, whether the sublime understanding exemplified by metaphor, and the production of aesthetic unity generally, complements or supplants the determinate judgment of conceptual cognition. The issue might also be put this way: if sublime understanding continually invents a sedimentary accumulation of "second nature" that provides historically situated subjects with broad sense-making un-wholes of shared meaning, what becomes of "actual nature" in the process? Does the inventive play of imaginative wit carry the "soul" so far from its "natural" origins that the entirety of our accumulated store of meaning counts as one vast work of art? If "argument" is a metaphorically structured notion imbedded in historically sedimented practices that shape argumentation through an affinity with war-making, is "water" also such a notion? As I put it earlier, if all concepts are truly aesthetic ideas, then all cognition is a playful aesthetic response to an omnipresent indeterminacy that we continually "fill in" with an artful weave of meanings we make and remake as we go. If we find everywhere the sort of sublime indeterminacy that sparks metaphorical sense-making or aesthetic reflection more broadly, there will be nothing left of which determinative judgment could have a "knowledgeable" cognitive grasp.

When the issue is put in these ways, it becomes clear that my extrapolation of Kant and Hegel's aesthetic theories stumbles onto huge and currently vexing, highly contested questions. At stake is the status of knowledge claims and their mode of productivity. At stake is the viability of antifoundationalist epistemologies and pragmatist or social-constructionist conceptions of knowing. At stake is the status of philosophical reflection in relation to natural-scientific versus "literary" construals of sense- and claims-making. This study will have achieved its goal if it has shown that Kant's aesthetic theory in particular, in its articulation of a sphere of felt validity "alterior" to conceptual unity, opens up these questions in one of the founding documents of modern thought. The notion of a sublime understanding conjoins indeterminate aesthetic unity with a shared insight on our worlds. Their intermingling throws into question the traditional separation of aesthetic and cognitive spheres. Reading Kant and Hegel's aesthetics as I have done confirms that current dilemmas surrounding the claims of knowledge turn on the question of whether "discovery" or "invention" provides a better metaphor for understanding. As we have seen, metaphor trades on the oscillation between these options quite explicitly. The fact that metaphor exemplifies the "serious play" of sublime understanding suggests that its "inventively disclosive" interpretive sense for our webs of meaning is the imaginative "common root" that makes possible both the play of pure aesthetic response and the work of conceptual cognition.

This conclusion warrants our preserving, *to a point*, the distinction between metaphor and concept, between indeterminate aesthetic reflection and the determinately conceptual. The warrant can be provided on what will amount to "pragmatic" grounds. If Kant's pure judgment of taste offers the aesthetic validity of a universal *feeling* entirely devoid of conceptual content, determinative judgment offers the cognitive validity of *knowing* the world through our concepts. Sublime understanding, metaphorically placed "between" them, captures the blending of aesthetic and cognitive strivings for validity. Its aesthetic sense for affinity and its intellectual striving for unified comprehension assist us in making sense of that which currently exceeds our conceptual grasp. Our determinate cognition relies on conventional, habitual categories of thought, while sublime understanding "outdoes" those habits. It reaches for a broader sense for the whole and the expanded vision that comes with discerning new relationships patterning our takes on the world and each other. We have seen that metaphorical affinities organize many of our practices and ways of talking, and Nietzsche or de Man would claim that this aesthetic dimension pervades *all* understanding and undermines its pretense to have any cognitive validity.

But even if all of our determinate concepts were really secretly nothing more than sedimented metaphors, aesthetic ideas produced by an "artistically creative subject," they still accomplish their cognitive work, or we revise them to make them work better. The concept "tea" works just fine to refer to darjeeling, assam, Earl Grey, and the rest, and whether or not its irreducible metaphoricity has been lost in the mists of time makes no practical difference to its adequate functioning. Hence from a pragmatic perspective we do not get much of anything from thinking that "darjeeling is a tea" is secretly "merely" a metaphor rather than a literal use of a determinate concept. The practical benefit we do receive from realizing that understanding has an "artistically creative" dimension is an awareness that much of our situating and orienting interpretive webs are made up of second nature rather than first. An awareness of this, as we saw at the end of chapter 7, debunks the "naturalness" of taken-for-granted associations and patterns of discrimination, but I hardly think it need lead us to distrust our concept of tea. The transformative play of sublime understanding does encourage flexibility, a preparedness to rework our categories in the light of new revelations, but this sort of flexibility is the mark of any cognitive ability worth the name. We rework our determinate concepts, when prodded to by new information, just as much as we continually revise our broader sense for the whole through the revelations of affinity that new metaphors provide. In neither case does this revisability undermine the validity of our unique aesthetic and cognitive advancements of understanding; rather, this flexibility enhances their legitimacy.

Maintaining the distinction between metaphor and concept, between aesthetic reflection and conceptual determination, allows us to appreciate the different work of each of these modes of understanding. Cognitive concepts, as we have seen throughout, subsume diversity under abstract representations of likeness, while metaphors and other products of sublime reflection relate the diverse *as diverse* into an open network of meaning-giving affinities. We "resort" to the latter when faced with densely meaningful, complex experiences or artifacts or practices whose richness overwhelms our conceptual grasp. Not everything overwhelms us in this way, not everything conceals a deep sublimity that would spark our metaphorizing efforts to pull sense out of its mystery. This is not to say that experiences or situations we think are cut and dried will remain so. We might "unearth" a sublime indeterminacy of rich meanings where we had thought we knew our way around, or others might foster a sublimity in practices we take for granted. In this sense, our determinate use of concepts contrasts with moments of dense sublimity in the way my making a cup of tea contrasts with the pregnant significances of a Japanese tea ceremony. Claiming that everyday cognitive validity belies an invalidating and universal metaphoricity is like claiming that my cup of tea always holds unfathomable and sublime multitudes. No, it only holds them in certain shared contexts of historically specific fluorescences of meaning; when those contexts do not obtain, it is just a cup of tea.[63]

Every community of meaning-makers has its "sites" of sublime indeterminacy, where metaphorical understanding comes to the fore to pose interpretive connections. However many such sites there are, and however much they may shift over time, the pragmatic prerogatives of everyday "getting by" render a great many of our experiences and practices largely determinate and unremarkable. Distinguishing those moments that engage a sublime understanding allows us to assess their import as distinctively *aesthetic* experiences in which a distinctive aesthetic form of validity takes precedent. Allowing our responses to the uncanny Other of conceptual understanding their own character and legitimacy highlights their alternative, equally valuable contributions to sense-making.

9

The Interpretive Sublime

Consideration of metaphor has suggested that the validated products of aesthetic reflection contribute to the creation of shared worlds. The vast webs of shared meaning that sublime understanding works and reworks through its metaphors provide some coherence to experience and give our worlds the appearance of purposive design. In keeping with Kant's notion of reflection as a process of accounting for one's presentations, and making sense of them as a related whole, we might conceive the primary aims of a sublime understanding this way: to gauge our situation by disclosing the network of meaning-giving connections in which we judge and act, and to revise it continually through the free imaginative production of new metaphors. This aesthetic understanding traces how things seem to cohere as a designed whole, but embraces the sublime condition that the design it seeks to exhibit always exceeds its constructive powers. The "open work" imagination seeks to interpret in piecing together its world both resists systematic determination and, by that very fact, provides continual opportunities for reflection to see how else things might cohere in designed but indeterminate ways. This chapter explores this dimension of sublime understanding further, with the aim of showing the great variety of intersections between the interpretive aesthetics of sublimity I have developed from Kant and Hegel and recent thinking on interpretation as we enact it both in and beyond the sphere of art.

I begin by revisiting the conception of aesthetic interpretation that issued from my reading of Kant in part I. By positioning this manner of responding to art in relation to some recent views of interpretation, I highlight sublime understanding's prerogative: to reach for a unified meaning by relating diverse material into a sense-making network of affinities. This emphasis brings out the open-endedness of interpretive response, and its accommodation of multiple plausible construals of a work. It also brings out the inevitable empirical specificity of interpretive reflection, and this raises deep questions about the universality of sublime understanding's claim to validity. The conclusion of the chapter will address this. Especially when considering Hegel's aesthetic theory, I have suggested ties between the kind of indeterminate aesthetic response a sublime reflection exemplifies and the sort of experiences inspired by modernist and especially postmodern impulses in the arts. I explore this connection more thoroughly here, and address the issue whether all art is sublime in the sense I have described. As a source of shared validity, sublime understanding takes on a positive significance occluded by some postmodern theorists of the sublime, and I take issue specifically with Lyotard's purely negative construal of sublimity in art.

I then turn from responses to art to a broader conception of an interpretive sublime understanding. The kind of sense-making we attempt when appreciating art exemplifies a much broader interpretive practice by which we constitute the felt experiential wholes that situate and orient us in shared worlds. Sublime understanding makes and remakes fields of meaning-giving connection, and in the process it helps shape the very worlds we inhabit. Such an understanding contributes a shared sense for the whole, however partial and incomplete, that complements our more determinate conceptual cognition. I relate this uniquely aesthetic dimension of sense-making to Nelson Goodman's pragmatistic "irrealism," and elaborate sublime understanding as a practice of interpretive "world-making." However much a sublime reflection may contribute, through metaphor and interpretation generally, to extending our sense for the whole beyond the present range of determinate cognition, my way of using Kant's judgment of sublimity as a model for an aesthetically reflective understanding ultimately limits the universality its inventive prowess can claim. In the final section I embrace this departure from Kant, yet I suggest that this deuniversalization does not keep sublime understanding from promising an ethic of vision that challenges habitual ways of thinking within specific cultural contexts.

Interpreting the "Open Work"

Part I already presented the contours of aesthetic interpretation as it is embodied in a Kantian sublime reflection. I will only summarize those results here. The interpretive response to a work of art is motivated by reflective judgment's principle of purposiveness to attempt a unification of all its features as an expressive whole. Imagination freely emulates a rational ideal of totality in seeking a unified meaning for the work, so what it finds will not be a technical unity prescribed in advance by any specified artist's intention or other determinate purpose which the work fulfills. This free interpretive play implies that imagination constitutes a meaning for the work rather than receiving it from any authority, whether critical, authorial or other. This starting point for conceiving aesthetic interpretation is at odds with, for example, E. D. Hirsch's well-known claim that the one correct interpretation of a literary work must recover the intended meaning of its author, preserved in the verbal meaning of the text, which can have no other meaning aside from this determinate one.[1] Hirsch's position shares with Hegel's classical Ideal an assumption of predetermined meaning in the object of interpretation; put more skeptically, his view turns interpreters into what Kant would call mere technicians of art, operators of a machine built to crank out a fixed meaning.

A properly Kantian response to the sublime riches of artistic meaning does not presume to catch "the" meaning "pinned and wriggling" in a work. In its interpretive production of aesthetic ideas, sublime reflection begins with the effort to make sense of a multitude of kindred presentations as a whole. It draws some of these elements directly from the work to which it responds, but other elements will come from what else beyond the work the work brings to mind, other associations and possibly telling relationships. Interpretation overflows the bounds of the work, and this excess assures the overwhelming of imagination in which it feels sublime. Imagination cannot unify this wealth of material as a totality of meaning. Its sublime reflection issues instead in the production of aesthetic unity—a network of meaning-giving relations between diverse features of the work and other features, drawn from their responses, which interpreters choose to include. This sublime understanding of art makes interpretation always a partial and open-ended insight into the plausible meaning of a work. It will not determinately constitute a meaning that would count as the only admissible reading. And because the very range of features brought into the interpretive fold will vary across persons, a variety of plausible interpretations of a work is possible.[2] Perhaps the more sublime a work of art, the more and varied partial unities of expression people will make a case for "seeing" in it. Or conversely, perhaps the more interpretations a work inspires people to construct, the more sublime we might judge it. Aesthetic interpretation offers a partial understanding of a work in which we admire how it exercises our always incomplete efforts to encompass all of its potential meaning.

Umberto Eco advocates a conception of the "open work" of art that would afford precisely the pleasures of overwhelming possibility, indeterminate unity, and multiple plausible response that sublime understanding enjoys. Eco sees a work of art as "a complete and *closed* form in its uniqueness as a balanced organic whole, while at the same time constituting an *open* product on account of its susceptibility to countless different interpretations which do not impinge on its unadulterable specificity."[3] In our constructive response to such works, seeking to organize what the work "brings to mind," Eco writes that "The free play of associations . . . becomes an integral part of the work, one of the components that the work has fused into its own unity and, with them, a source of the creative dynamism that it exudes."[4] This play can vary radically for different respondents to a work, but Eco insists that "The *possibilities* which the work's openness makes available always work within a given *field of relations*. . . . [We] may deny that there is a single prescribed point of view. But that does not mean complete chaos in its internal relations."[5] Just as Kantian imagination freely respects the demand for unity which anticipates a purposive core of meaning in a work, interpretive freedom for Eco is "constantly curtailed by the *germ of formativity*" that would make the work an integral whole. No rule governs response to the work, but this does not open up mere associative chaos. Rather, through its suggestive ordering of materials, the open work promotes a "*controlled* disorder, . . . a circumscribed *potential*," that allows variety in interpretation while orienting sublime understanding to appreciating the work as potentially whole.[6]

Recall from chapter 4 that both transcendental and empirical conditions affect the validity claim of sublime reflection. Imagination charges itself with revealing affinity in the manifold, and claims the intersubjective disclosivity of its connections. In its relating of the diverse, aesthetic reflection fulfills a transcendental reflective requirement that we anticipate purposive unity. For its play to constitute a valid interpretation, sublime understanding must attempt comprehension of a whole. A standard of internal coherence, built into the search for purposive unity in reflective judgment, guides aesthetic reflection toward construction of a relational network that does not do undue violence to the integrity of its object. The validity of an interpretation will rest in part on its success in not violating constraints placed by the content of the work. Both empiricist aestheticians and Hegel required a unity of determinate expression from *works* of art; in the case of a Kantian sublime understanding, such a requirement holds as a regulative standard for *interpretation* even when no determinate theme or artistic intention decides the "correct" meaning of a work.

The sublimity of interpretive response leaves unbounded what may contribute to an interpretation's network of relations. A reading that employs ideas and associations totally foreign to the work itself, its author or its contemporaries, is still valid so long as it "works" to illuminate what the work might be taken to mean without contradicting it. Sublime reflection follows no rule in producing interpretations, but the rational standard of internal coherence does constrain imaginative play to avoid certain outcomes. In this way the very form of aesthetic reflective judgment helps distinguish valid from abortive interpretations. As a search for a coherent unity of parts, sublime reflection must seek to unify as many features of a work as it can. The principle of specification in aesthetic unity demands that a diversity of attributes be related, and the more elements an aesthetic idea can relate while sustaining its differential affinity, the more compelling as a product of aesthetic reflection will it be. The form of aesthetic unity, and the principle of purposive unity that motivates its creation, indicate that achieving the greatest affinity across difference provides a measure of sublime understanding's interpretive prowess.

But in addition to this a priori requirement, the construction of aesthetic unity is constrained by its empirical character. When building a sense for a work as a whole, sublime reflection cannot but appeal to our common store of sense-making connections. As we saw in the case of metaphor, shared experience, patterns of acculturation, customary discursive practices and the like generate and sustain an intersubjective network of established associations through which similarly constituted subjects think and judge. When sublime understanding seeks an expressive unity of meaning in its object, when it begins to differentiate parts and relate them as a tentative whole, common cultural assumptions provide guidance to imagination's effort. Much of the multitude of kindred presentations a work brings to mind will not be peculiar to the individual, but will reflect acquired patterns of relation, conventional responses to the aesthetic situation, common assumptions about a certain artist or a kind of art. Personal associations may also inform an aesthetic response, but the communicability and appeal of an interpretation will largely depend on the success with which it exploits a store of patterned thought shared with others. The "empirical validity" of a given product of sublime reflection lies partly in its success at accessing and manipulating associative links within that shared relational network. At the level of empirical conditions, in order to find a receptive audience, sublime understanding's disclosures must meet with commonly shared expectations, even as it reworks given materials in ingenious ways.

The sheer range of empirical factors that come into play in interpeting works of art is evident in the aesthetic theory advanced by Stephen David Ross. He locates aesthetic value in precisely the sort of differential affinity I have thematized in Kant. Kantian aesthetic unities sustain a loose network of relations in which the diversity of particulars plays as central a role as whatever patterned unity may be discerned among them. Ross argues similarly that "*Similarity coupled with difference* is the artistic value," and that this quality is manifested in a work by the "intensity of contrast" sustained by its opposing features: "If contrast is unity amidst plurality, then intensity of contrast must be the heightened opposition of synthesis and plurality, realized either in the strength of the unification or the opposing polarities of the diversity."[7] For Ross the rich suggestiveness of artworks lies in the contrasting qualities they present, the play of similarity and difference they maintain; this play provides an inexhaustible opportunity for reflection on their meaning. As does Kant, Ross holds that reflection on a work's open meaning is constrained by regard for the integrity of the work as a designed whole, but within that whole the work sustains a "controlled play" of contrasting potential interpretations.[8]

Ross analyzes a great many contrasts that contribute to the sense-making play of aesthetic interpretation. They give some idea of the potential complexity of differential aesthetic unity, but they also represent empirical conditions that influence the construction of interpretive networks of relation. "Traditionary" contrasts between works and their immediate and distant predecessors, between schools and their antagonists, between artists and their colleagues deeply affect our sense-making responses to art. "Intramedial" contrasts between the different physical materials used in a composition influence our (free) assessment of an artist's aim, what the work seeks to express.[9] "Intermodal" contrasts between different ways of judging a work—morally, politically, or aesthetically, for example—affect our sense of a work's value. "Intersubjective" contrasts between the artist and the audience's relationship to a work, or between different audiences' interpretations of a work, or intergenerational contrasts in its reception, all add to our appreciation for a work as an inexhaustible locus of reflection.[10] Ross also discusses the role of other specific types of aesthetic contrast: between generality and specificity, simplicity and complexity, tokens and types, surface and depth, beauty and ugliness, and spatial and temporal contrasts within the world the work conveys.

The sheer variety of potentially relevant factors indicates how far outside the strict bounds of a work sublime reflection may rove in its marshaling of kindred presentations from which to construct its interpretation. It is for this reason that sublime reflection can be much more welcoming of the sort of contextualist and historicist considerations that Kant's formalist judgment of taste could not accommodate. Sublime understanding can rove outside the work in its effort to make sense of it. Letting in the outside is what unbinds a work's sublime meaning and also assures the diversity of interpretive response. In mapping the many affinities that we discern running through a work and giving it meaning, we judge the work's success by how well it sustains and enlivens the many relations that inform it. What is perhaps the same thing, we judge the perspicacity of interpretations by how much insight they afford into the web of networked meanings which a work is.

But more significant than this play among shared meanings, the transformative potential we value in a work of art lies in the audacity of the new relations it brings sublime understanding to invent. When works "create novel ways in which separate and diverse elements of our experience may be brought together,"[11] as was the case with metaphor, interpreting them reworks available categories to disclose alternative orientations to the understood status quo.

The empirical wealth of differential affinities that come into play in aesthetic response has considerable implications for the validity sublime reflection can claim for its interpretations. An innumerable array of relations within a work and between the work, its producer, its audience, and their histories intersect in interpretation. Seeking to make sense of the work as a unique whole, but free of rules that would determine what is relevant to "finding" this sense, imaginative reflection must make choices that limit the comprehensiveness of any single interpretation. The inexhaustible relational network which imagination seeks to grasp as a rational whole consistently defies determinate exhibition. So as Ross puts it, "No interpretation and critical analysis could tell us *all* that a great work means or might mean. It surpasses any telling, especially as the future brings new relations for it."[12] An interpretation reflects a distinctive imaginative response to an unbounded array of aesthetic attributes. Some of these attributes will be drawn directly from the work; others will be brought to bear from the culturally and historically situated orientations of the interpreter. Sublime understanding seeks to relate material from all these sources into a plausible response to the work, but as Ross argues, "[there is] no uniform fund of common experience relative to which a work of art possesses its values, . . . no all-encompassing order in which a work is *those* contrasts of *that* intensity, without qualification. The work cries out for diverse interpretations relative to different perspectives. . . . [There] is no 'description,' no 'interpretation,' that can exhaust the relevant features of any work of art."[13] In keeping with the rational demand met by sublime reflection, interpretation respects the integrity of a work as a unique whole. "The meaning of the work" serves as the regulative idea toward which imaginative comprehension gropes. This constrains imagination to present a realized unity, though what it gets instead is an interpretation, an aesthetic idea which relates as many features as possible into a network of attributions. Within this constraint, the empirical diversity of potentially relevant features allows for alternative interpretations; the alternatives result from divergent constructive responses to the overwhelming material. Each outcome of sublime understanding will reflect the distinct social, historical, and personal position of the interpreter. In this sense reflective judgment generally, in its purposive locating and relating of presentations, situates judging subjects as well within the sense-making possibilities of their worlds.

But sublime reflection does more than simply ape received habits of thought and association. If it only shored up old habits, its work would fall, as Kant indicated, to a merely reproductive imagination. It would not exhibit the dehabituating imaginative artistry Hegel praised. Productive imagination relies on given shared fields of meaning, but at its most vividly *aesthetic* it forges alternative mappings of the relational terrain and challenges conventional conceptual categories or patterns of thought. The greatest challenge to received ways of threading together the world comes from a reflection that claims validity for aesthetic unities that defy the associative status quo. As in striking new metaphors and stunning interpretive pyrotechnics, sublime understanding shows itself most clearly at play when projecting new patterns in the absence of guiding rules. Although sublime reflection pursues the rational requirement that interpretation seek unity, it does so as an imaginative wit drawn to the distinctively aesthetic prerogative of what we might call interpretive audacity. The more incongruous the attributes imagination relates, the more remarkable the interpretation that constructs a disclosive affinity among them. This peculiarly aesthetic aim reflects the fact that it is easy to construct a network of relations among already closely related things. The open work of art challenges its respondents to invent ingenious variations on its meaning. Bold new interpretations are themselves such genial open works, and they audaciously invite us to see affinities that challenge our expectations. The empirical specificity of reflecting subjects does imply that sublime understanding always relies on our common cultural store of affine networks of relation. But the most audacious interpretive responses to art (or anything else), the most revolutionary of metaphors, will exceed and extend given habits of thought. In the spirit of Hegelian aesthetic dehabituation, and tempered by Kant's embrace of aesthetic indeterminacy, the interpretive sublime reaches for an understanding not yet thought and, given the limits of sublime reflection, never to be thought completely.

Locating the Interpretive Sublime

I have advanced the view that a sublime reflection, when it responds interpretively to art *generally*, confronts an indeterminacy from which it imaginatively produces aesthetic unities short of conceptual determination. It may be, however, that some works of art, designed to maximize this encounter with indeterminacy, illuminate better than others the challenge which the interpretive sublime poses. I noted in chapter 6 that Lyotard attributes the dehabituating power of much twentieth century modernist and postmodern art to its embrace of an aesthetics of sublimity. The "stake" of this aggressively sublime recent art has been "to be witness to the fact that there is indeterminacy."[14] Such art has built into its very form and content narrative discontinuities, stylistic experiments, unnerving juxtapositions, perspectival variations, and other devices that mitigate against comprehension of the work as a determinately unified, univocally meant whole. Though all works of art, just as any object of aesthetic reflection, should invite an open-ended play, the notion of the open work reflects Eco's sense that recent artists have embraced this openness to the point of designing it into the very substance of their work. "[Though] organically completed," Eco writes, such ambivalently expressive works "are 'open' to a continuous generation of internal relations which the addressee must uncover and select in his act of perceiving the totality of incoming stimuli."[15] Such works actively defy determinate comprehension, and so vividly realize the "plight" of sublime understanding. Imagination's effort to present an interpretive whole meets in these works the very indeterminacy and disunity which inevitably mark all its own interpretive outcomes. In this sense sublime under-standing's always partial insight into our shared fields of meaning meets its match in the vigorously fragmented and dehabituating art of this century.[16]

Eco's favorite case of the open work is Joyce's *Finnegans Wake*. He treats Joyce's polyglot collage and multiply intelligible wordplay as a lit-erary representation of a "Global Semantic Network," an "encyclope-dic" structure of conventional cultural associations within which, by a kind of semiotic holism, "every item of a language must be interpreted by every other possible linguistic item which, according to some pre-vious cultural conventions, can be associated with it."[17] Eco analyzes Joyce's elaborate puns as echoes of "a form of background knowledge based on a network of previously posited cultural contiguities or psy-chological associations. But at the same time it is the text itself which, by a network of interconnected puns, makes the cultural background recognizable."[18] The Joycean pun-word "meandertale," for example, rests, Eco argues, on the basic semantic units "meander," "tale," and "Neanderthal," and an elaborate network of other words Joyce uses in his text to which they are linked in polyvalent ways.[19] Joyce's linguistic play succeeds by appealing to a common fund of historically built-up cultural associations. His highly innovative use of language "works" to the extent that it discloses unforeseen ways of plausibly linking com-ponents within this field of relations. The linguistic stew of *Finnegans Wake* disrupts and reworks given semantic networks, and presents pre-cisely the sort of expressive unwhole that any interpretation of it would also be.[20]

The high modernist Joyce perhaps turned postmodern in this final work, and much postmodern architecture, film, and literature has been most celebratory of the indeterminacy and polysemy that sub-lime understanding draws from its responses to art. Recall that we found the roots of aesthetic reflection's attention to disunified but affine fields of shared meaning in the dissolution of Hegel's romantic form. There, *Phantasie* sought to overcome the mere contingency of subjective humor's associative play by exhibiting, in objective humor, shared networks of relation. We saw in chapter 7 that collage should be a favorite technique in the art of objective humor, as this tech-nique explicitly undertakes the creation of affinity among diversity that aesthetic response itself produces. The transformative, reconfiguring power of collage comes to maturity in much modernist and postmodern cultural production, from Picasso's use of found materials in some of his paintings to Peter Greenaway's sets and camera work. One might argue that Hegel's remarkable prophetic ability shows through in the way his account of romantic dissolution, and the positive wit of objective humor, prefigures postmodern trends in the arts. The historical eclecticism of postmodern architecture, and its use of multiple layers of coding to appeal to both sidewalk and theoretically savvy admirers,[21] resist the univocity of the "one true theme" in Hegel's classical Ideal. The juxtapositional, disorienting effects of postmodern *bricolage* techniques in film and literature are reflected in the combinatory play Hegel takes to follow the end of art's effort to exhibit a rational Ideal. A film like Robert Altman's *Short Cuts*, with its interweaving of multiple Raymond Carver stories into an impressionistic evocation of California life, and Venturi and Brown's celebration of the bizarre styles of the (1960s) Vegas Strip—"Miami Moroccan," "Arte Moderne Hollywood Orgasmic," "Yamasaki Bernini cum Roman Orgiastic," "Moorish Tudor"[22]—are anticipated in Hegel's perhaps premature observation that "art does not need any longer to represent only what is absolutely at home at one of its specific stages, but everything in which man as such is capable of being at home" (LFA 607; 14:238).

The proliferation of styles and tones, of thematic incongruities, narrative disturbances, and devices to destabilize even the integrity of the text on the page make postmodern literature a site for a hyperbolic presentation of the indeterminacy of textual meaning and the dispersal of authorial intent. I noted earlier that Laurence Sterne's "pre-postmodern" *Tristram Shandy* plays all these tricks as it sports with the conventions of the English novel before the genre even quite existed. Sterne's crazy-quilt juxtaposition of the high and (very) low brow, the missing chapters, Walter Shandy's construal of everything according to the principles of scholastic rhetoric, the preface one stumbles over in the middle of the book, Uncle Toby's obsession, even when falling in love, with military fortifications—all betray what Nietzsche judged "the enjoyment of a baroque, indeed depraved imagination."[23] With stunning prescience, Hegel identified Sterne as a master of true humor, of that wit which goes on a holiday of combinatory genius in the best instances of postmodern art. There is little point to insisting on Hume's or Hegel's neoclassical unity of theme when faced with a work like *Gravity's Rainbow*, for example, in which the more or less central character, Tyrone Slothrop, simply dissolves, near the end of the novel, into the improbably flower-strewn landscape of the wartorn Zone. The final page of Pynchon's *The Crying of Lot 49* finally explains the title, but leaves both Oedipa Maas and the reader forever in suspense as to the revelation promised by the auctioneer's permanently deferred cry. Pynchon's critics of course discern overarching themes in his work, say of entropy or paranoia, but if they are good postmodernists they do not pretend to fix in their interpretations on the "one true theme" and meaning, the "round[ing] off [of] an inherently solid whole" which Hegel would expect (LFA 295; 13:381). The demand for a presented univocity of meaning, expressible in one theme that makes sense of every part, betrays a failure of taste when faced with the layered, multicoded richness of much recent art.

In the transgressive art of objective and true humor, writes Hegel, "bondage to a particular subject-matter and a mode of portrayal suitable for this material alone are for artists today something past, and art therefore has become a free instrument which the artist can wield in proportion to his subjective skill in relation to any material of whatever kind" (LFA 605; 14:235). A recent example of this artistic verve for throwing together the most diverse material, and making it work expressively, is David Foster Wallace's *Infinite Jest*. A thousand-page series of some hundred vignettes, the novel depicts a quasi-dystopian near future in which calendar years are named for commercial products ("Year of the Whopper"); in which an "aprés-garde" practitioner of "anti-confluential" cinema founds a tennis academy; in which some of the most important information for making sense of the novel's narratives appears only in the extensive footnotes one might easily skip; in which Quebeçois terrorists hunt down the filmmaker's paralyzing last work ("Infinite Jest") in order to spread it through the U.S. population as a strategy for forcing Canada to cede most of "New New England" *back* to the United States and grant Quebec independence; in which a U.S. government agent in drag and a Canadian counter-counter-agent have a conversation that surfaces every once in a while over the course of a thousand pages; in which the garbled time sequences of the narrative leave it uncertain just how, or when in the novel, or even *whether* the story ended, and so on. The novel's aggressive integration of disparate themes, images, characters, and narratives offers sublime understanding just the sort of expressive unwhole it recasts reflectively. If interpretation involves relating disparate material into a sense-making network, relying on received shared fields of meaning, but also generating new meaning through inventive connections, a postmodern work like *Infinite Jest* is delivered already in that form, flaunting its own status as an imaginative interpretation of the future.

The sort of expressive unwholes which sublime understanding discerns in its response to art seem right at home in much twentieth-century artistic production. If so, this nicely confirms that my appropriation of Kant and Hegel's aesthetic theories, and in particular my emphasis on the sublime indeterminacy of aesthetic understanding, helps raise classical German aesthetics to the challenge of recent art. But it also raises a troubling issue: if my construal of interpretation as a form of sublime understanding best suits our sense-making response to *certain kinds* of currently practiced art, is my account of aesthetic reflection not sufficiently general? Could it be that only some art holds the sublime potential to overwhelm our interpretive powers, while other art would call for a more conventional, perhaps determinate understanding? The same question could have been raised about metaphor: is all metaphorical meaning sublimely indeterminate, or do only some especially rich and powerful metaphors push the limits of comprehension? I have construed sublime understanding as a form of aesthetic reflection that, in the process of relating presentations, effectively situates the interpretive subject within the sense-making options of a concrete shared context. It may be that my focus on indeterminate aesthetic unity, and its apparent affinity with contemporary artistic impulses, also effectively situates "sublime understanding" as a currently salient notion that would not apply beyond the art that exemplifies those impulses.

It would appear that some art may not induce feelings of interpretive sublimity at all. An exceedingly conventional landscape painting of the "motel art" variety may not offer much of a site for the sort of indeterminate, open-ended connotative response I have thematized. A highly rule-bound, traditionally scripted depiction of a religious theme, say, may shut down the expansiveness of sublime reflection. Recall also that I presented Kant's judgments of taste and sublimity as moments in a broader aesthetic response. If there were a work of art that appealed only to taste through its formal qualities alone, without conveying any representational content or apparent meaning, it might not require any sublime feats of interpretive skill. Perhaps a Sousa march does not hold sublime depths, but it does offer a formal tapestry of sound for taste to enjoy. Military marches were Kant's favorite form of music, after all. On the other hand, as a historically situated expression of American patriotism, there may be much to reflect on in Sousa. And we also know that thoroughly nonrepresentational works of art, which might be the model object of a formalist taste, call for at least as much interpretive ingenuity as anything else. Some people respond to works by Pollock or Rothko, say, with almost spiritual feelings of sublime agitation and repose. So even works produced under the influence of formalist aesthetic doctrines can come to induce the more "content-rich" responses of a sublime understanding.

The hallmark of this response, recall, is that it exceeds the bounds of the work to play at relating whole manifolds of meaning-giving connection in which the work is embedded. The question, then, is not whether all art is sublime, but whether all *responses* to art enact the sublime reflective expansiveness I have elaborated from Kant and Hegel. The answer to this question is surely no. If one "gets" from a work of art what one has been told is there to get, and leaves it at that, one will miss the chance to see more. If one understands art largely according to received critical habits without exploring further, one's judgment will be legislated by external authority, and hence will not on Kant's view count as aesthetic at all. If one does not open one's understanding of a work to the myriad relations that cross through it from its context, whether physical, geographical, historical, political or personal, one does not treat the work as the sort of meaning-rich site which I have made the object of a sublime understanding.

We could say that *in principle* works of art as such invite us to reflect on them as sites of dense connectedness. A vigorously sublime modernist or postmodern work might demand this reflection more insistently, or more blatantly, but every work of art worth the name can take such attention. It is often more a question of one's willingness to be overwhelmed by complexity than a question of some quality one work has that another does not. However, if things are worth the name "art" when they encourage the indeterminate play of a sublime reflection, this indicates the evaluative dimension of "art." We honor something by calling it art in part because we find that it conveys rich webs of meaning. As an evaluative term it admits of degrees, and it may well be that some art exercises sublime understanding's agitated quest for meaning more thoroughly than does other art. The same conclusion applies to metaphor: perhaps not every metaphor draws on the richest networks of connotation, but our construals of them are, in principle, indeterminate and open-ended. They are so because the range of connotations a metaphor sparks is not fixed in advance for every hearer, and more connotations can always be added by innovative interpreters of its meaning.

If we attend to art with the free productivity of a sublime understanding, it can always to some extent induce a rich interpretive response. The indeterminacy of interpretation is the hallmark of a Kant-inspired theory, and all properly aesthetic responses to art will enjoy the sublime feeling of reaching for a meaning just beyond reach. If particular works of art or particular forms of artistic expression carry this experience to a higher pitch, so do the most striking and vision-altering metaphors, so do the most revolutionary new takes on our selves and our worlds. The common feature running through all these experiences is a certain kind of broadly encompassing but cognitively indeterminate sense-making practice. Because my aim has been to position this uniquely aesthetic mode of understanding as the legitimate Other of determinate cognition, it would not be surprising if expanding aesthetic understanding beyond responses to art favored, in the end, some works of art over others. Those works would themselves enact the very indeterminacy, polysemy, and challenge to conventional habits of thinking that sublime understanding also pursues outside works of art.

The constitutive inability of sublime understanding to unify its object explains why the sublime in particular has been so attractive to theorists of the postmodern. Postmodern culture is supposed to reject modernity's confidence in progress and rational order; it offers instead a rich but disunified eclecticism, a mess of fragmentary cultural phenomena, and labyrinthine webs of intertextual reference. We saw earlier that Umberto Eco thinks that the open work requires a free (though constrained) interpretive play that defies all determining narratives and order. He thinks that the current appeal of such play is no accident, that the rise of the open work reflects its origins in a disunified social world: "The discontinuity of phenomena has called into question the possibility of a unified, definitive image of our universe; art suggests a way for us to see the world in which we live, and, by seeing it, to accept it and integrate it into our sensibility. The open work assumes the task of giving us an image of discontinuity. It does not narrate it; it *is* it."[24] The indeterminate networks of relation that aesthetic reflection presents would then reflect our felt sense for worlds marked by disorder and uncertainty. The failure of sublime reflection to present its object as a rational whole would confirm the unintelligibility and fragmentation of the postmodern world, which reflective judgment seeks to comprehend. Hence we can locate the interpretive sublime not only in those recent works of art that most explicitly embody the indeterminacy of aesthetic experience, but also in the overwhelming complexity of the cultural context those works reflect.

Lyotard's classic statement of the postmodern condition expresses the contemporary fascination with the sublime as the negative limit of presentability. Assessing his remarks will distinguish his purely negative construal of an aesthetics of sublimity from the positive contribution sublime understanding can make to our interpretive efforts. Lyotard takes the defining mark of modernity to be that "in whatever age it appears, [it] cannot exist without a shattering of belief and without discovery of the 'lack of reality' of reality, together with the invention of other realities."[25] Modernity delegitimizes traditional belief systems and seeks to replace them with procedures for maintaining just and efficient economic and social relations. Modern life is taken to "derealize" traditional worldviews, and Lyotard sees an earlier modulation of this revelation of unreality in the Kantian theme of the sublime. The experience of sublimity "[presents] the fact that the unpresentable exists," and this visible absence reveals "the incommensurability of reality to concept which is implied in the Kantian philosophy of the sublime."[26] Sublime reflection shows that current categories fail to comprehend reality and so throws our confidence in those categories, and our sense of the real, into question. No secure agreement obtains about the world in which we move, and the presense of unpresentability in contemporary life serves to undermine even modernity's self-assurance.

Lyotard suggests that one can respond to this lack of confident reality by lamenting the powerlessness of presentation to accord itself with something determinate; or one can celebrate the "increase of being and the jubilation which result from the invention of new rules of the game, be it pictorial, artistic, or any other."[27] Sublime reflection's invention of new "rules" in the "second nature" of aesthetic ideas would provide not conceptual rules, but suggestions for ordering new realities; and we know its outcome would be no more natural than what it transforms. But Lyotard sees the distinction between his two options only as an oscillation between either lamenting the sacrifice of modern conviction and determinacy to the destabilizing effects of the unpresentable, or instead celebrating the same:

Modern aesthetics is an aesthetics of the sublime, though a nostalgic one. It allows the unpresentable to be put forward only as the missing contents; but the form, because of its recognizable consistency, continues to offer to the reader or viewer matter for solace and pleasure. . . . The postmodern would be that which, in the modern, puts forward the unpresentable in presentation itself; that which denies itself the solace of good forms, the consensus of a taste which would make it possible to share collectively the nostalgia for the unattainable; that which searches for new presentations, not in order to enjoy them but in order to impart a stronger sense of the unpresentable.[28]

The postmodern would be that moment of hesitancy within modernity that constantly awakens skepticism toward current habits of intelligibility and motivates the projection of new relational alternatives. But Lyotard would have sublime reflection contribute only a negative counterpoint to presentable reality: "it must be clear that it is our business not to supply reality but to invent allusions to the conceivable which cannot be presented."[29] In my account of sublime understanding, such allusions comprise the array of networked attributes in which we sense, and attempt to make sense of an unpresentable design. These webs of meaning situate us in and orient us toward our world: that is, they contribute to our primary sense of reality.

Lyotard recruits the sublime to the cause of resisting what he sees as the totalizing claims of rational cognition, but his dichotomy between a modern presumption of determinate reality and a postmodern, purely disruptive sublime is false. Sublime understanding helps invent our indeterminate worlds; it also violates the limits of current comprehension without pretending that its product is complete or that it now captures some given reality. Aesthetic reflection's production of indeterminate webs of shared meaning provides us constantly un-whole worlds, riven by irreducible heterogeneity, confused juxtapositions of incongruous interpretation, and multiple avenues for critique and transformation, but it helps articulate worlds for us nevertheless. Contrary to Lyotard, the postmodern sublime not only disturbs and dehabituates our secure categorial sense of reality, it also contributes to the ongoing projection of the historically sedimented, multiple and ambiguous networks of "irreality," to borrow Goodman's term, in which we all live. Sublime understanding does not destroy "determinate reality," and an aesthetics of sublimity suitable for our present self-understanding need not have the purely negative destination Lyotard directs it toward. Rather, sublime understanding as I have developed it from Kant and Hegel faces the unpresentable, uncanny Other of the conventionally understood, and fails to present any rational whole, yet it presents something else even so, however disunified and indeterminate its meaning-giving webs of relation-building might be. In the process, sublime understanding helps fashion and sustain, along with our more determinate cognitive claims, the only reality—however indeterminate, fragmented, and mongrelized—we've got.

Interpretive Worldmaking

We have seen throughout that the projection of purposive unity in aesthetic reflective judgment serves a regulative function. It motivates imagination to seek design in its object, but if its effort is to remain reflective, imagination's work will not issue in the production of any determinate conceptual unity. When reflection does "figure out" its object, it contributes to empirical concept formation and adds to the stock of categories under which determinate judgment can subsume things. But a reflectively *sublime* understanding strives to comprehend the unpresentable, and produces interpretive aesthetic unities that intimate a purposive design beyond our means to encompass. It orients us toward and intervenes in the shifting fields of affinity by which our judgment and behavior is patterned. But this reflection admits a sublime discontinuity between the object of thought and our ability to think it as a whole. A reflective imagination situated in dense and layered webs of meaning shows its finitude when it inevitably falls short of presenting them as a complete system, as a rational totality. Sublime understanding must always accept the disunity of its suggestive products, the provisional nature of its partial comprehension, the multiple perspectives it engenders, and the permanent deferral of full conceptualization. This is true not only for its takes on works of art, but also for its contributions to the shaping of shared worlds.

David Kolb offers a perspective that embraces our existence in fields of disunified multiplicity without falling into nostalgia for determinacy, or into Lyotard's version of subjective humor. Sublime understanding seeks to make sense of the riven manifold, to find some purposive design in the heterogeneity in which we live. Though Kolb does not present this interpretive sense in its distinctively aesthetic character, he acknowledges the constitutive limitations of such striving: "There is no point of view from which ["the multiplicity around us"] can be seen as a whole; we are strung out within multiple fields of possibility that do not come neatly individuated one by one or as a totality. We can be aware of our rootedness and our identification with ways of thought and life only piecemeal."[30] The rooted situation and orientation from which aesthetic reflection always sets out to make sense of or transform its world of connections does not render us powerless; it rather provides the footing world-making requires: "None of this [disunified multiplicity] prevents us from trying for various kinds of unity or totalization, as long as we realize that the results will be another element in the multiplicity. We should not confuse efforts at totalization with achieved totality."[31] The sense that determinate cognition is not always to be had motivates not (only) the escapist play Hegel derided but the effort to present purposive design and coherence without guarantees. Making sense of unthought multiplicity involves relating parts into the partial coherence of aesthetic unity without claiming to have mastered the sublime. Sublime understanding in fact exemplifies a critical perspective toward claims to reduce complex and contextually shifting phenomena to fixed structures. Subsumption under concepts may claim to determine the nature or purpose of its object. But sublime understanding always awaits the revision of its tentative claims, claims that in their very partiality spur on the search for other construals of purposive design.

Kolb articulates an attitude he calls "humble irony" that would appear to have much in common with the objective or true humor Hegel found in the dissolution of romantic art. Just as objective humor makes us aware of the shared fields of meaning in which we are empirically situated, the web of positive wit already orienting our judgment, humble irony provides "a sidelong awareness of contingency and of being always already out beyond what we can be sure of, distanced from what we are but not parted from it."[32] Such awareness hones our felt sense for the meanings we operate among, clarifying both our dependence upon them and our power to alter their sometimes arbitrary hold on us. It should come as no surprise that Kolb sees metaphor as one of the means by which our belonging to and transgression of current conditions of intelligibility is enacted. If, through the "impertinent moves [of metaphor] which extend and change our language and practices," "we create or find meanings and let them work *as* new, the sidelong awareness of contingency and fragility is signaled by the act of changing or blending the vocabulary."[33] The metaphorical wit of sublime understanding both exposes the contingent relational networks in which we are embedded, and it poses new connections that may tranform our perception, our judgment, and the very world those networked connections sustain.

If, then, contrary to Lyotard, facing the sublime does positively contribute to our vision and revision of worlds, it does so much the way Nelson Goodman would have it. Goodman has argued that worldmaking, or the production of "versions" by means of which we make sense of our worlds, proceeds along lines that we have seen an aesthetically reflective judgment follow. He especially emphasizes the processes of composition and decomposition that make world-versions: "Much but by no means all worldmaking consists of taking apart and putting together, often conjointly: on the one hand, of dividing wholes into parts and partitioning kinds into subspecies, analyzing complexes into component features, drawing distinctions; on the other hand, of composing wholes and kinds out of parts and members and subclasses, combining features into complexes, and making connections."[34] Goodman, as we saw in chapter 8, thinks that the work of conjointly maintaining distinctions while inventing connections is especially exemplified in metaphorical expression. But in addition to composition and decomposition he includes weighting, ordering, deletion and supplementation, and deformation among the methods of world-making.[35] Weighting, for example, involves making things comparatively relevant or irrelevant or differentially significant to the contours of a world. Deletion removes material from and supplementation introduces material into the making of a new world from an old one. These features of world-making emphasize again that worlds are always built from their predecessors. "Given" contexts of understanding, "given" patterns of classification always pose empirical constraints on the sorts of departures from them that are likely to be sufficiently disclosive or fitting to receive intersubjective validation: "We start, on any occasion, with some old version or world that we have on hand and that we are stuck with until we have the determination and skill to remake it into a new one. Some of the felt stubbornness of fact is the grip of habit: our firm foundation is indeed stolid. Worldmaking begins with one version and ends with another."[36] New metaphors or other vision-changing revelations of affinity loosen the grip of habit and bring on a re-formation of our worlds. Such world-building is a cumulative process, though Kolb reminds us that it is never so organically cumulative that any one world-version encompasses or reflects the entire development. But however multiple and disordered our accumulated webs of sense-making relation might be, they condition our efforts to fulfill the transcendental promise of the affinity which we always "discover" anew.

Ricoeur's account of metaphor suggested that products of aesthetic reflection have an ambiguous status: they seem to both discover and invent the connections they disclose. This ambiguity becomes a central tenet of Goodman's "ontological relativism" or "irrealism," for which world-making is as much a matter of invention as discovery. What a given world is made from, and how it is pieced together, shapes the standards of "reality" to which people are acculturated in that world:

"reality in a world, like realism in a picture, is largely a matter of habit."[37] The webs of shared meaning that situate and orient us do not just describe, but help constitute the contexts in which we perceive, judge, and act. Even the elements from which sublime understanding constructs world-versions do not proceed world-making as preformed raw material; parts are *made* parts in the process of their inclusion in a networked whole. "[We] want to distinguish between versions that do and those that do not refer, and to talk about the things and worlds, if any referred to; but these things and worlds and even the stuff they are made of . . . are themselves fashioned by and along with the versions."[38] It has seemed at times in this study that aesthetic reflection is simply given parts that need purposive ordering; but even what constitutes a relevant part only becomes clear in the process of sifting through a manifold for intimations of purposive design. Sublime understanding always makes worlds from material its situating contexts provide; but imagination's unruled productivity leaves it to recast that material, giving it a new "nature" within new contexts of relation.

I put "given" in quotes earlier because Goodman would of course reject the Given conceived as an unmediated sensible foundation for cognition, an "aboriginal world" available to us prior to our meaning-making impositions. For Goodman's conventionalism, "complete elimination of the so-called artificial world would leave us empty-minded and empty-handed."[39] Instead, the given world from which new world-making ventures depart is always already suffused with the "second nature" produced by the inventive, interpretive surpassing of first nature in aesthetic ideas. It is worth noting that John McDowell sees the spontaneous cultivation of second nature as the solution to the modern epistemological oscillation between a Myth of the Given and a "frictionless coherentism" which he associates with Davidson. Second nature would be the "*habits* [n.b.] of thought and action," the "patterns in a way of living" which provide "the framework within which meaning comes into view. . . ."[40] Second nature makes our grasp of the world always a handle on something already conceptually articulated through meaning-giving and shaping norms. Second nature accumulates in linguistic practices, as was especially evident for us in the case of metaphor, and McDowell sees language as "a repository of tradition, a store of historically accumulated wisdom about what is a reason for what."[41] We have seen the sense-making projection of second nature in Kantian aesthetic reflection constantly rely on received accomplishments of meaning, and similarly for McDowell second nature implies that "immersion in a tradition might be a respectable mode of access to the real."[42] "In the context of a full-blown pragmatism," McDowell suggests, languages and cultural traditions can be seen as "constitutive of our unproblematic openness to the world."[43]

The difference between McDowell's apparent pragmatism, Goodman's pragmatism, and Kant's "pragmatism" is that the latter two embrace an *aesthetic* contribution to the cultivation of second nature. McDowell laments the fact that Kant "does not contemplate a naturalism of second nature," and so invokes Hegel as an exemplar of the spontaneous *conceptual determination* of the world through second nature.[44] The Hegelian subtext stresses the spontaneity the Kantian subject enacts in giving conceptual *determinacy* to the world; my elaboration of Kant's aesthetic theory indicates that that subject also freely interprets the world, freely cultivates second nature through the conceptually *indeterminate* production of differential affinity in aesthetic ideas and metaphor. The elaboration of "second nature" which McDowell attributes to conceptual spontaneity may be better captured, for Kant though not for Hegel, by the free spontaneity of an interpretive aesthetic reflection. Second nature as the outcome of an indeterminate sublime understanding also reconfigures *habit* as something accumulated in language and tradition, but also constantly violated and revised in the striving for alternative meaning-making options.

If our worlds are made along with the interpreting play of sublime reflection, then whatever validity world-making claims cannot be that of an achieved correspondence to a given (or Given) standard. Sublime understanding makes its own rules by inventing new networked versions; and since no version can claim to encompass the whole, many interpretive outcomes will disclose or transform features of shared worlds in alternative legitimate ways. But Goodman emphasizes that this perspectival multiplicity does not imply a crass relativism: "Willingness to accept countless alternative true or right world-versions does not mean that everything goes . . . that truths are no longer distinguished from falsehoods, but only that truth must be otherwise conceived than as correspondence with a ready-made world. Though we make worlds by making versions, we no more make a world by putting symbols together at random than a carpenter makes a chair by putting pieces of wood together at random."[45] World-making seeks to sustain and extend our sense for purposive design and coherence; as Hegel made clear, constructing such networks of disclosure involves much more than a play of subjective association. Aesthetic reflection is constrained by the effort to present unity, and this limits the ways world-versions can be put together as intelligible though open wholes. And as we have seen, aesthetic reflection is conditioned by the empirical contexts in which it plays, always seeking to produce new unities of relation both to fit and to alter the partial world it both needs and rejects. Not just any made world will do, because only some imaginative versions extend current worlds in intelligible directions. When sublime understanding revises fields of shared meaning and so recasts the worlds they pattern, the validity of its product rests on how astutely it manipulates the current practices of sense-making, and how well it communicates a compelling disclosure to those who sufficiently share the webs of connectivity it reworks. Only on the basis of shared understanding, and among those sharing it, can sublime understanding alter worlds through the invention of communicable alternative networks of meaning-giving connection.

Extending sublime reflection to the revelation and elaboration of shared, world-making webs of meaning helps in the end to make sense of Kant's remark, considered in chapter 3, that "beauty (whether natural or artistic) [is] the *expression* of aesthetic ideas" (CJ 320). Given that aesthetic ideas are supposed to be the products of artistic genius, how could they appear in mere uncrafted nature? A parallel question can be raised for sublime understanding's discernment of meaning-webs of aesthetic unity in our worlds: must there not be an intending agency behind the appearance of expressive design? Sublime understanding may make sense of some dimension of the world by relating greatly far-flung things which are in no way *presented to it as a whole* waiting to be interpreted, so have we not left Kant's intending genius, and hence his account of aesthetic ideas far behind? Fortunately we need not hypostatize a world-spirit (nor a vast conspiracy) to credit with the meanings sublime reflection discerns. Sublime understanding seeks out meanings in related things *as if* the web of relations were designed or intended, and so can make sense of worlds without any claim that someone is responsible for the meanings "found." I have construed aesthetic ideas throughout as accomplished interpretations rather than merely as objects of interpretation provided by genius and awaiting construal. This position helps to account for the possibility of sensing their expression even in nature. We can attribute meaning to nature by regarding it through the lens of reflective judgment, by seeking purposive unity in it *as if* it were intended to mean, without imputing any underlying agency. The same is true for our discernment and revision of patterns of *second* nature. In the case of artworks we surely credit the artist with providing us something to reflect on, however little her intentions might determine what we make of her work. But when sublime understanding turns to its surrounding world, it senses design but no designer (except perhaps the cumulative course of history) in the affine networks it reveals. Moreover, sublime understanding becomes the designer when it transgresses received webs of sense to propose (as in metaphor) new meaning-giving relations, new shapings of second nature.

As a world-making interpretive practice, sublime understanding positions aesthetic experience as—along with more determinate conceptual cognition—a legitimate contributor to our ways of producing shared intelligibility. Our aesthetically indeterminate, felt sense for experiential "wholes" situates us in the contexts in which we pursue more determinate acts of understanding. Some have argued that this interpretive dimension of understanding implies that *all* understanding is really interpretation.[46] I have construed interpretation as a searching response to uncanny indeterminacy that seeks to make sense of what our established habits of thought leave untouched. We interpret when, as in reflections on art and more broadly, we do not know what to make of something, or we wish to make something *else* of it. On this view, all understanding is not interestingly interpretive, any more than all concepts are secretly metaphorical, or any more than every experience holds sublime depths.[47] Not everything poses such challenges to understanding, however responsible we must be for critically revising our conceptual store as needed. I reserve the interpretive dimension for those encounters with uncanny sublimity in which we grasp for an understanding we can only partially, perspectivally convey. Construing the rest of our workaday determinate use of concepts as also ultimately interpretive only obscures the distinctive aesthetic form of reflection that makes for our loose grasp of situating unwholes, whether those constructed aesthetic unities be interpretations of a work or of a world. Worse yet, collapsing all understanding into interpretation obscures the distinctive validity of those responses to sublimity in which we build and rebuild worlds imaginatively free from the constraint of current concepts.

The Limits and Promise of Aesthetic Autonomy

The imagination engaged in the interpretive aesthetics of sublimity I have developed from Kant and wrestled from Hegel has a dual aspect; it has both negative and positive effects. First, this imagination exposes the more or less arbitrary status of current patterns of affinity, and it shows the failure of accepted categories to encompass the uncanny beyond of present intelligibility. This is the side of sublime reflection Lyotard celebrates. Recall from chapter 5 that the associative wit of nascent imagination in Hegel's *Encyclopedia* "Anthropology" stood sublimely opposed to the normalizing unifications of habit-formation. Positive wit defied mind's habituation to predictable conceptual thinking. That wit lost out, of course, to the construction of a unified and habituated subject, but the play of wit resurfaced in the associative *Phantasie* that I recovered from Hegel's aesthetic theory. If the negative moment of aesthetic reflection amounts to an unsettling of received habits of thought, by exposing their arbitrary and mutable condition, this study has shown Kantian aesthetics to also belong to that tradition of theorizing the aesthetic as a power of dehabituation which can provide unsettling critiques of the status quo. The relevance of a Kant-inspired aesthetics of sublimity to artistic avant-gardism and the political function of aesthetic critique can only be suggested here. But given that sublime understanding in particular shakes current patterns of second nature by forging into what those patterns fail to encompass, the disorienting power of aesthetic reflection, and the post-Kantian tradition that has theorized this, warrant further study in relation to the conclusions of this book.

Sublime understanding may have a negative, disorienting, dehabituating effect, but it also produces positive results. My central claim has been that imaginative reflection on the sublime can be seen not merely to cower before reason's demand for unity. Sublime reflection fails to meet that demand, but still it produces the relational affinity of aesthetic ideas. These interpretive products of an "ingenious" imagination can contribute mightily to the "impertinent" transformation of shared webs of meaning. When products of sublime understanding receive broad validation, as in the wide adoption of profound new metaphors or new interpretive takes on things, imagination contributes to revision of ourselves and the worlds we inhabit. When its insights are adopted, their validation suggests that sublime reflection contributes as much to our self-understanding and sense of reality as more conventional forms of conceptual cognition. Throughout this study I have distinguished the inventive play of aesthetic reflective judgment from the conceptualizing labor of Kant's determinative form of judgment. Not only the latter should be seen as advancing the growth of understanding. The productive, interpretive power of a sublime understanding to build shared connectivity suggests that the modern separation of cognition and aesthetic experience continues to need rethinking and reworking. However much Kant himself sought to distinguish them, the seeds of their convergence lie in his own aesthetic theory, especially in the disclosive and inventive powers of productive imagination. Their convergence lies in a broadly pragmatist conception of an understanding in which we can continue to distinguish aesthetically reflective from conceptually determinate contributions to it, as I have distinguished them throughout this study, without committing the perennial error of belittling or "disenfranchising" the aesthetic in the process.

And in transforming aesthetic reflection into a sublime understanding, what happens to Kant's notion of aesthetic validity? It has become common as of late to debunk the universal validity claims of classical modern aesthetics. The claim of good taste to advocate a universal and necessary pleasure has come to sound like the naive and pretentious voice of bourgeois self-valorization. To take one example, Pierre Bourdieu wants to provide, according to his postscript to *Distinction,* a "vulgar" critique of "pure" critiques of taste of the Kantian variety. His primary claim is that "Kant's analysis of the judgement of taste finds its real basis in a set of aesthetic principles which are the universalization of the dispositions associated with a particular social and economic condition."[48] In the universal claims of taste Bourdieu finds the expression of social privilege and class hierarchy. Aesthetic judgment's claim to validity has no universal or necessary basis, but actually represents the pernicious efforts of privileged actors to claim the heights of human delicacy for themselves: "What is at stake in aesthetic discourse, and in the attempted imposition of a definition of the genuinely human, is nothing less than the *monopoly of humanity*."[49]

Bourdieu claims that the disinterested aesthetic attitude at the heart of Kant's theory exists with a social and historical specificity that the universalizing claims of taste serve (or seek) to obscure. "The pure thinker," he writes,

by taking as the subject of reflection his or her own experience—the experience of a cultured person from a certain social milieu—but without focusing on the historicity of that reflection and the historicity of the object to which it is applied (and by considering it a pure experience of a work of art), unwittingly establishes this singular experience as a transhistorical norm for every aesthetic perception. Now this experience, with all the aspects of singularity it appears to possess . . . , is itself an institution which is the product of historical invention and whose *raison d'être* can be reassessed only through an analysis which is itself properly historical. Such an analysis is the only one capable of accounting simultaneously for the nature of the experience and for the appearance of universality which it procures for those who live it, naïvely, beginning with the philosophers who subject it to their reflections unaware of its *social conditions of possibility*.[50]

I have argued that Kant's judgment of taste cannot adequately model the connection-making, meaning-building work of an interpretive aesthetic reflection. But I have shown that Kant's judgment of sublimity, seen as an effort to comprehend wholes of meaning, admits into aesthetic reflection the empirical and social conditions of situated and orienting communicative contexts. Sublime reflection responds to a transcendental condition when it legitimately but without conceptual guidance anticipates the aesthetic unity of purposive design. But it also exposes the empirical constraints on its own search for intelligibility. Our shared webs of meaning provide contexts in which we can seek (and fail) to fulfill a transcendental demand for univocity. But they also constrain empirically the sorts of departure we can make from our multiple configurations of our worlds.

Bourdieu claims that the "pure" pleasure of aesthetic play lies in "producing, like a kind of endless fire, its ever renewed sustenance of subtle allusions, deferent or irreverent references, expected or unusual associations." Aesthetic play spins out "whole network[s] of criss-crossing references woven around [a work]."[51] I have argued that sublime understanding, not universal taste, best models this play among networked meanings. In the process I have shown that those fields of meaning not only shape our engagement with and interpretation of works of art, but they also help fashion the substance of our shared worlds. Aesthetic reflective judgment, specifically the sublime understanding of indeterminate aesthetic disunities, has proven central to processes of making worlds, exploring, critiquing, and revising them. Bourdieu does not distinguish Kant's judgment of sublimity in his wholesale rejection of classical aesthetics, which is unfortunate. For in his efforts to make critical sense of complex fields of cultural production and contestation, Bourdieu arguably employs the sublimely reflective capacities embedded in the Kantian aesthetic theory he rejects.

Nevertheless, my elaboration of a Kant-inspired sublime understanding accepts, contra Kant, that it cannot make grandly universal claims. However transcendentally grounded reflective judgment's search for purposive design is, the patterned networks it produces reflect local, empirical conditions of commonplace intelligibility. Its products rely for their validation on specific communicative contexts of shared understanding. Like metaphors that transgress but rely on current patterns of linguistic usage, products of sublime reflection invent heretofore unseen relations, but they depend on current habits of interpretation to orient us toward their peculiar forays into the unknown. Only from such shared contexts can aesthetic revision of them embark, and only among participants in those contexts can sublime understanding hope for or expect validation of the disclosures it achieves. Not just any random associating, as in Hegelian subjective humor, makes a world, as Goodman insisted; nor does just any random selection of subjects make an interpretive community trained and primed to heed the insights of a given recasting of their world. Each new metaphor, or work of art, or construal of a world is made from materials drawn from established contexts of intelligibility and is made for the inhabitants of those contexts. People can, of course, communicate across those contexts, learn from and improve on each other, and imaginative products native to one locale can take on startling new meanings in others. But sublime understanding cannot expect its revelations to mean the same, or even mean anything, to everyone, because local conditions of acculturation affect the communicative possibilities of its products. Given its reliance on fields of shared connection, the transgressive inventions of sublime understanding could claim to speak to everyone in the same way only if everyone everywhere shared the same sedimented web of meaning. They do not.

No matter how little felt they might be in the throes of imaginative play, the empirical conditions that constrain sublime understanding deny us the opportunity to demand universal assent to our constructions. But to the extent that they are widely shared within a region, a class, a profession, a country, or a culture, patterns of meaningful connectivity are "contingent necessities" that stamp individual, situated and oriented lives. However arbitrary or fabricated our received webs of meaning may be, they shape the shared worlds and orientations to them from which aesthetic reflection takes its material, and this undermines any universality for our aesthetic claims. However far from making universal claims sublime understanding might be, it can claim to convey suggestions of affine design among participants in its own communicative contexts. Aesthetic reflection's demand that others sense the affinities it produces and validate its audacious disclosures can extend only as far as the shared context in which, in each instance, it makes its case.

Bourdieu might argue that even though I refrain from the claim of classical Kantian aesthetics to secure a universal taste, I still inflate what is a merely socially conditioned activity into a universal practice (whatever its many outcomes). Instead of "sublime understanding" being a singular experience, reflective of the play-affording social position of comfortable aesthetes, I inflate it into a transhistorical condition. Yet everyone is faced by the sublime limit of presentable understanding, however much or little they think they understand,

and however much the understood is shaped by social conditions, historical location, and geopolitical position. Everyone might attempt to reach beyond received understanding to squeeze a different take out of things. Whether everyone does or not is certainly affected by the accidents of birth and upbringing, by the drift of inertia, by the extent to which a culture encourages us to be slaves of habit. Kant himself acknowledges that uncanny sublimity will only be evident to and affect those who have cultivated a freely imaginative interest in ideas (CJ 264–265), and the limited reach of this cultivation inevitably works to delimit the universality of sublime reflection. Even so, the exercise of it is not so easily located in any particular class position. Bourdieu's critique of taste locates the socially specific development of taste in the rarefied atmosphere of high art appreciation in which only a privileged few can play. My development of a sublime understanding has led it out of the museums and into our everyday efforts to make sense of things, into our perhaps less frequent efforts to break old habits of thought. It would be the height of arrogance for a social critique to suggest that these interpretive activities are pursued only by those as privileged and as clever as the critic.

If Kant would decry the loss of universality I have embraced, even so aesthetic reflective judgment, as Kant would have it, remains an autonomous form of judgment, because the peculiar disunities of relation it constructs differ from the products of conceptual cognition. But aesthetic reflection enjoys only a circumscribed autonomy, its motivating transcendental condition always constrained in practice by the empirical conditions in which we find ourselves. The free play of aesthetic response—whether before a work of art or in the midst of the surrounding world—must make use of historical encrustations of received intelligibility, and must make its new sense from those situated materials. In this sense its autonomy is limited by its available sense-making options and practices, and its inventive play does not speak with a universal voice. It speaks, at best, with what we might call a "localized universality." Sublime understanding can claim the perspicacity of its inventions only among those who adequately share the meaning-resources it reworks, however much that circle might grow or shrink with time. It always asserts the validity of the networked relations it finds or invents within contexts that both provide and limit the possibilities of discovery and fabrication. Those shared contexts in turn weight the chances of our forays into sublimity to win broad or narrow or no validation.

If its autonomy and universality have their limits, sublime understanding still promises a reflective attitude worth cultivating and celebrating. Its unfolding of the sense-making possibilities of a work, or a metaphor, or an interpretive stance toward the world betray a peculiar regard for complexity. Sublime understanding savors the rich webs of meaning and concrete relationships in which our inventions are embedded, and it allows the overwhelming complexity of those phenomena to speak through it. A metaphor might not mean much to someone who skips the playful work of unpacking its possibilities, but it might mean volumes to a more generous and inventive respondent to its claim. A hasty critic might pigeonhole a work of art in an instant, while another explodes it into a vast array of meanings—and relationships to its original and other contexts—by practicing a responsiveness that dwells on the details. A situated human vision can see the world in ways born of habit, making its needed quantity of sense according to unquestioned conventions. But a sublime responsiveness to things embraces our rich and indeterminate options for producing meaning and insight from what Hegel called the "dark mine" of our powers of presentation.

This Other of received and determinate understanding enacts what we might call an ethic of vision. It peers into experience for complex affinities and taken for granted connections. It traces those connections in all their rich variety and divergence, just as taste, pages ago, played at relating the tendrils and blooms of a flower arrangement. Sublime understanding traces and invents meaning rather than the contours of a spatial or temporal form, but along with taste it embraces the aesthetic prerogative that we attend to the intimations of purposive design weaving together the tapestry of our worlds. It advocates a complicating way of seeing that pushes beyond received understanding to attempt a deeper insight. Its free pursuit of meaning-giving purposiveness lands it in the agitating trouble of sublime feeling, as it always seeks a more unified comprehension than it can have. But going to that trouble is what makes for the ingenious advancements of sense that keep our vision from dimming. Wrestling meaning from the sublime void beyond our habits of mind, however partial and context-specific the understanding that results, leads us to constantly question our habits, to stretch out for what has been left unthought. Spinning new extensions of our webs of meaning, and responding generously and attentively to their possible validity, train us to reflect as free and supple aesthetic beings. By doing so we incorporate the power of an aesthetically sublime understanding into our more determinate cognitive aims. We also responsibly fulfill what amounts to an aesthetico-ethical imperative: to feel in and to draw from art and world their open efflorescence of meaning.

Notes

Chapter 1

1. *Critique of Judgment*, trans. Werner S. Pluhar (Indianapolis: Hackett, 1987): 179. This and subsequent references use the Akademie (v. 5) pagination found in Pluhar's margin. All subsequent references will be provided in the body of the text, using the abbreviation "CJ." On the matter of subsumptive judgments, see also Kant's "First Introduction" to the *Critique of Judgment*, appended to Pluhar's translation of CJ; the specific passage is at Ak. 202 (using the Akademie [v. 20] pagination in Pluhar's margin). Subsequent references to the "First Introduction" will also be provided in the body of the text, using the abbreviation "FI" and the Akademie pagination.

2. *Critique of Pure Reason*, trans. Werner S. Pluhar (Indianapolis: Hackett, 1996): A132/B171. All subsequent references will be provided parenthetically in the body of the text, using the abbreviation "CPR" and the standard A/B edition pagination found in Pluhar's margin.

3. "If reason is a power to derive the particular from the universal, then there are two alternatives. Either, first, the universal is already *certain in itself* and given. On this alternative, only the *power of judgment* is required, for subsumption, and by this subsumption the particular is determined necessarily. I shall call this the apodeictic use of reason. Or, second, the universal is assumed only *problematically* and is a mere idea; i.e., the particular is certain but the universality of the rule for this consequence is still a problem" (CPR A646/B674).

4. One may also include among determinative judgments reason's legislation of the moral law to itself; on this view the categorical imperative serves as a rule of subsumption for judging the morality of maxims of action.

5. The preponderate role of the understanding here indicates that one may draw the distinction between determinative and reflective judgment in terms of the relation of faculties that pertain in each. A judgment is determinative when one faculty legislates over the others in a particular domain. The legislation of the understanding in cognition, for example, makes subsumption of empirical objects under concepts determinative. As Gilles Deleuze puts it, "Saying that a judgement determines an object is

equivalent to saying that the accord of the faculties is determined, or that one of the faculties exercises a determining or legislative function." *Kant's Critical Philosophy*, trans. Hugh Tomlinson and Barbara Habberjam (Minneapolis: University of Minnesota Press, 1984): 59–60. Reflective judgments, on the other hand, would then occur where no single faculty legislates, but instead where a "free and indeterminate accord" of faculties exists, as in the judgment of taste, for example.

6. Translation slightly altered.

7. For a schematic differentiation of the varied roles of imagination, see Carl Posy, "Imagination and Judgment in the Critical Philosophy," in *Kant's Aesthetics*, ed. Ralf Meerbote (Atascadero, Ca.: Ridgeview Publ. Co., 1991): 27–48 (the anthology is vol. 1 of the North American Kant Society's Studies in Philosophy).

8. Translation slightly altered.

9. Translation slightly altered.

10. Dieter Henrich, "Kant's Notion of a Deduction and the Methodological Background of the First *Critique*," in *Kant's Transcendental Deductions*, ed. Eckhart Förster (Stanford: Stanford University Press, 1989): 42.

11. Jean-François Lyotard, *Lessons on the Analytic of the Sublime*, trans. Elizabeth Rottenberg (Stanford: Stanford University Press, 1994): 11.

12. More specifically, to the judgment of taste: we will see that the sort of validity claim made in a judgment of sublimity is more complex. See chapter 4.

13. Lyotard, *Lessons on the Analytic of the Sublime*: 26.

14. Sarah Gibbons is right to characterize reflection as a process "through which a multiplicity of representations are compared non-subsumptively." *Kant's Theory of Imagination* (Oxford: Oxford University Press, 1994): 101.

15. Anthony Genova likens the exercise of such reflection to detective work: "when we say, 'It looks as if the killer had a knowledge of medicine,' or, 'It appears to be an inside job,' we are using reflective judgment," for in such cases we must piece together disparate clues to reveal the secret intelligibility of a scene of crime. Genova, "Kant's Complex Problem of Reflective Judgment," *Review of Metaphysics* 23 (1970): 457.

16. Hannah Ginsborg, "Reflective Judgment and Taste," *Noûs* 24 (1990): 65. See also Christel Fricke, "Explaining the Inexplicable: The Hypotheses of the Faculty of Reflective Judgement in Kant's Third Critique," *Noûs* 24 (1990): 45–62. Fricke, however, distinguishes two readings of reflective judgment, only the first of which parallels Ginsborg's account of empirical concept formation. See the final section of this chapter for further discussion.

17. Ginsborg tries to account for the aesthetic judgment of taste, in which concepts play no determining role, by means of the obscure notion of "empirical conceptualization [performed] in a completely indeterminate way, which consequently fails to bring the object under any concept" ("Reflective Judgment and Taste": 74). If reflective judgment primarily involved producing concepts under which to subsume particulars, why would an aesthetic judgment that failed to do so qualify as reflective?

Notes

18. This tenet of the *Critique of Judgment* was apparent to Kant in the first *Critique*. "The hypothetical use of reason [i.e., reflective judgment] based on ideas, as problematic concepts, is properly speaking not *constitutive*. I.e., this use of reason is not such that—if we are to judge in all strictness—there follows from it the truth of the universal rule that we have assumed as hypothesis. . . . Rather, this use of reason is only *regulative*. Through it we seek, as far as possible, to bring unity into the particular cognitions, and thereby to *bring* the rule *close* to universality" (CPR A647/B675). However, Rudolf Makkreel has argued against conflating this "hypothetical" aim of unity with reflective judgment; cf. *Imagination and Interpretation in Kant* (Chicago: The University of Chicago Press, 1990): 57.

19. Gadamer has prioritized what he takes to be the "fundamental metaphoricity" of language over the formation of and subsumption under concepts. *Truth and Method*, trans. Joel Weinsheimer and Donald Marshall (New York: Continuum, 1989), 2d ed.: 428–438. I will ultimately view metaphor as a key product of reflective judgment, but only in my reading of Hegel's aesthetic theory will this conclusion fully coalesce.

20. "[T]he subjective feature of the presentation which cannot at all become cognition is the purposiveness that precedes the cognition of an object and that we connect directly with this presentation even if we are not seeking to use the presentation of the object for cognition" (CJ 189).

21. Donald Crawford characterizes reflective judgment thus: "In my reflection on the objects of my apprehension, I shall try to find a way in which they relate such that a definite concept is applicable to them. And this is to say that I come to recognize that, when the various objects of my awareness are perceived in a certain way, a set of rules for the application of a concept is fulfilled." *Kant's Aesthetic Theory* (Madison: University of Wisconsin Press, 1974): 22. Notice that this characterization applies equally well to the earlier examples of detective work and to the features of an artifact. That is, the unity of parts may consist of the parts of a single object or the elements of a situation.

22. Gadamer has characterized a "fore-conception of completeness"—a feature of the hermeneutic circle—as a "formal condition of all understanding." This fore-conception enacts the principle that "only what really constitutes a unity of meaning is intelligible. So when we read a text we always assume its completeness" (*Truth and Method*: 293–294). In the effort to understand the obscure particular in reflective judgment, we assume a unified organization for the thing which will make sense of its parts as a whole and which our reflection seeks to articulate. For the sort of aesthetic reflection I seek to theorize here, however, this *expectation* will remain purely regulative. In chapter 3, we will find Kant's judgment of the sublime to exemplify reflection on the meaning of an aesthetic object. Because this judgment always falls short of presenting a determinate unity, the "semantic completeness" of an object will be beyond the means of reflective judgment to demonstrate. In a sense, one might regard my account as developing a "hermeneutics of the sublime" which resists Gadamer's confidence in the power of understanding to fully present the meaning of its object.

23. "Now this transcendental concept of a purposiveness of nature is neither a concept of nature nor a concept of freedom, since it attributes nothing whatsoever to the object (nature), but [through] this transcendental concept [we] only think of the one and only way in which we must proceed when reflecting on the objects of nature with the aim of having thoroughly coherent experience. Hence it is a subjective principle (maxim) of judgment" (CJ 184).

24. This point raises questions about Kant's distinction between free and dependent beauties which must be reserved until later. See chapter 2.

25. *Kant and the Claims of Taste* (Cambridge: Harvard University Press, 1979): 48–66.

26. This is the most important of the several arguments Guyer advances on this issue; his other arguments largely build on it. I have chosen only to address this main argument.

27. *Kant and the Claims of Taste*: 49.

28. Emphasis added.

29. Michael Friedman concurs that "the principle of reflective judgment prescribes a law only to itself but not to nature." *Kant and the Exact Sciences* (Cambridge, Mass.: Harvard University Press, 1992): 251. Friedman concludes from this that the notion of reflective judgment cannot provide Kant the transition from metaphysics to the empirical sciences that he sought in his final work.

30. *Kant and the Claims of Taste*: 40–41.

31. Ibid., 57.

32. Ibid., 65.

33. Fricke, "Explaining the Inexplicable": 55.

34. Cf. *Imagination and Interpretation in Kant.* Subsequent chapters and notes therein will highlight points of accord and disagreement with Makkreel's important work on Kant.

Chapter 2

1. See also CJ 225, where Kant divorces the charms of sensation from "the beauty we attribute to an object on account of its form"; charms may only contribute to beauty "when taste is still weak and unpracticed, and only insofar as they do not interfere with the beautiful form." And see the *Anthropology*, where Kant maintains that "taste is a merely regulative power of judging form in the synthesis of the manifold in imagination" *Anthropology from a Pragmatic Point of View*, trans. Mary J. Gregor (The Hague: Martinus Nijhoff, 1974): 113.

2. Translation altered.

3. *Kant and the Claims of Taste*: 219.

4. Ibid.

5. Ibid., 57.

6. CPR A86/B118. Cf. also A20/B34. Donald Crawford specifies four senses in which Kant employs a form-matter or form-content distinction in the first *Critique*. First, the logical form of a judgment provided by the table of the categories contrasts with the

experiential content of judgments. Second, the activity of the understanding gives form to the material of intuition provided by sensibility. Third, the formal element of intuitions, their spatial and temporal relations, unify particular material sensations. And fourth, sensations themselves have a formal and a material part. Crawford's second and third senses are of most relevance here. See *Kant's Aesthetic Theory*: 96–98.

7. As Theodore Uehling puts it, "[N]ot the sensations [of the object] but only the forms exhibited by those sensations could correspond with the understanding as the faculty of the forms of [cognition]." *The Notion of Form in Kant's Critique of Aesthetic Judgment* (Albany: State University of New York Press, 1971): 60.

8. It is instructive to note that Guyer resists this aesthetic formalism by deemphasizing the specific nature of the accord possible between understanding and imagination. "[It] could be contended," he argues, "that it must be an independent question whether spatial and temporal form are the only features of a manifold of imagination which can cause *what is, after all, a mere feeling of unity*, or whether, say nonspatial and nontemporal relations among colors or tones might also allow the free play of the faculties" (*Kant and the Claims of Taste*: 229–230; my emphasis). The problem here is that the harmony between these faculties is not just any old "mere feeling of unity," but is rather an expression of their specific capacities and the formal ground upon which they intersect.

9. Hence the frequently discussed question regarding Kant's theory: what keeps every judgment from being a judgment of taste, or put differently, what keeps every object of cognition from being beautiful? Patricia Matthews, for one, attempts to resolve the issue by arguing that we become aware of using principles of reflective judgment through a feeling which terminates with the application of determinate concepts, such that the pleasure of aesthetic reflection is only available reflectively, however much a relation of accord between imagination and understanding may carry over into determinate conceptual cognition. "Kant on Taste and Cognition," in *Proceedings of the Eighth International Kant Congress*, ed. Hoke Robinson (Milwaukee: Marquette University Press): v. 2, 491ff. An alternative strategy is to emphasize, as I do below, the distinctive contribution of imagination to aesthetic reflection: only in the midst of its free, productive aesthetic play, which does not obtain during determinate cognition, will objects of experience "reveal" their beauty.

10. Uehling puts the accord of imagination and the understanding this way: "The representation of the object in the imagination supplies just that form which the imagination would possess if it were determined by the rules of the understanding." *The Notion of Form in Kant's Critique of Aesthetic Judgment*: 65–66. He thereby overstates the case, for, as the example in the next section will show, the imagination need not be thought to so strictly (though freely) conform to the rules of the understanding that it merely duplicates what the understanding would determine it to produce.

11. Donald Crawford takes the same position in *Kant's Aesthetic Theory*: 98–100. Rudolf Makkreel concludes that "what is apprehended in aesthetic form is not just a perceptual shape, but a purposiveness. This purposiveness apprehended in the form of an object is the a priori element contributed by the imagination in its play with the understanding" (*Imagination and Interpretation in Kant*: 60–61).

12. *Kant and the Claims of Taste*: 233, n.63. Guyer is directly criticizing Uehling's *Notion of Form in Kant's Critique of Aesthetic Judgment*.

13. Ibid.

14. Ibid., 230.

15. *Kant and the Claims of Taste*: 222.

16. As such a claim would lead one to expect, Kant goes on to praise the superiority of the English style in gardening, presumably over the French: "That is why the English taste in gardens, or the baroque taste in furniture, carries the imagination's freedom very far, even to the verge of the grotesque, because it is precisely in this divorce from any constraint of a rule that the case is posited where taste can show its greatest perfection in designs made by the imagination" (ibid.). It would be illuminating to unpack the implications of the apparent proximity in Kant's mind of the beautiful and the grotesque.

17. For the distinction between these two types of imagination, see also A100–102. The contrast between them will become increasingly important as we proceed, especially once we turn to Hegel's theories of imagination and aesthetics in part II. Suffice it for now to say that, because reflective judgment involves the *relating* of parts in order to make sense of them as a whole, the *associative* power of imagination, which is typically construed as its most crassly empirical function, will play a special role in the account of aesthetic reflection that I will construct.

18. Translation slightly altered.

19. Paul Crowther suggests that because "the *aesthetic unity* of the object is a function of the interplay between phenomenal form and the different *possible* avenues of cognitive exploration and development which it can open up," it turns out that "[an] element of randomness in judgment . . . is partially constitutive of aesthetic unity" ("The Significance of Kant's Pure Aesthetic Judgment," *British Journal of Aesthetics* 36 [1996]: 114). This indicates that two aesthetic judges of the same object need not undergo identical experiences in their imaginative reconfiguration of its formal features in order to agree in their normative assessment of the object's beauty. The point is rarely noted, though it helps to bolster the universality claim of judgments of taste by allowing a variety of aesthetic play to issue in one judgment. For further discussion, see my consideration of Kantian aesthetic validity in chapter Four.

20. I borrow the contours of the example from Paul Crowther, substituting flowers for foliage. Cf. *The Kantian Sublime* (Oxford: Clarendon Press, 1989): 55–56.

21. "Imagination and Temporality in Kant's Theory of the Sublime," *The Journal of Aesthetics and Art Criticism* 42 (1984): 307.

22. Donald Crawford shares this conception of the judgment of taste. Cf. "Kant's Theory of Creative Imagination," in *Essays in Kant's Aesthetics*, T. Cohen and P. Guyer, eds. (Chicago: University of Chicago Press, 1982): 172.

23. Thus we should resist John Sallis's claim that the judgment of taste betrays "a certain erosion of the structure of reflective judgment in its initial, cognitively related sense." Sallis argues that "though aesthetic judgment too would consist in the subsumption of a given particular under a universal that has to be sought out for it, it turns out, almost at the beginning of the analysis, that the universal to which the particular (the apprehended form) is to be referred is not at all a universal in the usual, cognitive

Notes

sense of a universal *concept*" (*Spacings—of Reason and Imagination in Texts of Kant, Fichte, Hegel* [Chicago: University of Chicago Press, 1987]: 97). A more sustained analysis of reflective judgment shows that it has little to do with subsumption. My account indicates that it operates with a principle of purposiveness that, contrary to the erosion Sallis detects, guides the judgment of taste as a case of reflective judgment.

24. Cf., e.g., Salim Kemal, *Kant on Fine Art* (Oxford: Clarendon Press, 1986): 9–21; Kenneth Rogerson, "Art and Nature in Kant's Aesthetics," in *Akten des Siebenten Internationalen Kant-Kongresses*, ed. Gerhard Funke (Bonn: Bouvier, 1991): 735–744.

25. Gracyk, "Art, Nature and Purposiveness in Kant's Aesthetic Theory," in *Proceedings of the Eighth International Kant Congress*, ed. Hoke Robinson (Milwaukee: Marquette University Press, 1995): 503.

26. Patrick Hutchings concludes from this that aesthetic appreciation of art must be purely formalist. See "Flowers as 'Free Beauties of Nature,'" *Literature and Aesthetics: The Journal of the Sydney Society of Literature and Aesthetics* 4 (1994): 26, as well as my critical discussion of his view below.

27. Kant counts "all music not set to words" (CJ 229) as instances of free beauty (though we would presumably exclude nonlyrical program music, which does purport to represent something, albeit without the aid of words). This suggests that such music affords a purely formal appreciation of temporal sound structure. My resolution of the free/dependent dichotomy will allow wordless music the *expressive* dimension which a merely formal assessment ignores, though without making appreciation of it dependent on cognition of a determinate purpose.

28. Ruth Lorand adopts the first strategy by arguing that dependent beauty cannot be a subclass of Kant's "general notion of beauty" because the general notion does not allow presupposition of a concept of purpose. "Free and Dependent Beauty: A Puzzling Issue," *British Journal of Aesthetics* 29 (1989): 33. For objections to her position, see Robert Stecker, "Lorand and Kant on Free and Dependent Beauty," *British Journal of Aesthetics* 30 (1990): 71–74. Stecker defends the view that free and dependent beauty are two distinct kinds of beauty. He argues (p. 72) that a judgment of dependent beauty manages to be an aesthetic judgment, that is, not *determined* by a concept of its object's purpose, because the judgment is instead merely *constrained* by that concept.

29. Cf., e.g., Crawford, *Kant's Aesthetic Theory*: 113–117; and Guyer, *Kant and the Claims of Taste*: 242–244.

30. See, for example, Mary McCloskey, *Kant's Aesthetic* (Albany: State University of New York Press, 1987): 74–79; and Geoffrey Scarre, "Kant on Free and Dependent Beauty," *British Journal of Aesthetics* 21 (1981): 351–362. Scarre argues that dependent beauty adds only a consideration of "decorum" to aesthetic judgment: "when we mean to judge something aesthetically, we should look at it not only from the point of view of its free beauty, but should also ask ourselves whether it is fitting that an object of its type should possess whatever features make it beautiful" (p. 358). Thus the purpose of a church would need to be taken into account in judging depictions of pagan orgies on its walls. This suggestion, however, introduces into aesthetic judgment what is essentially a moral standard, thus violating the autonomy of the aesthetic.

31. Eva Schaper, "Free and Dependent Beauty," in *Studies in Kant's Aesthetics* (Edinburgh: Edinburgh University Press, 1979).

32. Ibid., 86.

33. Ibid.

34. Emphasis added.

35. Guyer makes this point particularly well: "Since it is not just concepts of purposes which can constrain imagination, but, in fact, any empirical concepts which furnish rules for the synthesis of the manifold, and since a multitude of empirical concepts can apply to almost any empirical object, anything less than a very broad power of abstraction will make aesthetic response a rare occurrence" (*Kant and the Claims of Taste*: 252).

36. Contrary to this conclusion, Robert Wicks argues that the beauty of art is a dependent beauty because in Kant's account "we are led to the artist's intention as the source of both the artwork's purpose and, by implication, the criteria of its perfection. . . ." ("Dependent Beauty as the Appreciation of Teleological Style," *The Journal of Aesthetics and Art Criticism* 55 [1997]: 395). This seems to assume that we have available this intention upon which to make a work's beauty depend, though later Wicks indicates: "Whether or not the artist's intention is actually known in any given case is independent of Kant's general point about the basic structure of the judgment of dependent beauty: we attribute an intention to an artist, and judge the work in light of that attribution" (p. 397). The problem here is that the basic structure of the judgment of dependent beauty requires that our judgment be determined by our *knowledge of the purpose in the producing cause* (the artist), and this knowledge is something which Wicks admits we may not possess. Without it, aesthetic judgment cannot be a matter of judging dependent beauty, because dependent beauty is determined as a technical unity under the ordering of that purpose or intention (and so is not, on my view, properly aesthetic at all). We do, of course, frequently make projections and guesses about possible artistic intentions. My view (further developed in the next chapter and truer, I think, to our practices of aesthetic evaluation) is that such attributions may contribute well or ill to the process of interpreting a work, but they have (or ought to have) no determining power over the outcomes of that interpretive play. Once again, if a (claim to) knowledge of artistic intent did play such a determinative role in aesthetic reflection, we would not have a case of autonomous imaginative play; that is, we would not be talking about aesthetic reflection after all.

37. "Flowers as 'Free Beauties of Nature'": 22.

38. Ibid., 28.

Chapter 3

1. "Imagination and Temporality in Kant's Theory of the Sublime": 313.

2. Kant confirms this possibility of sublimity in the presence of form in a key passage: "if something arouses in us, merely in apprehension and without any reasoning on our part, a feeling of the sublime, then it may indeed appear, *in its form*, contrapurposive for our power of judgment, incommensurate with our power of exhibition, and as it were violent to our imagination, and yet we judge it all the more sublime for that" (CJ 245; emphasis added).

3. Derrida, *The Truth in Painting*, trans. Geoff Bennington and Ian McLeod (Chicago: University of Chicago Press, 1987): 127.

4. At least one of Derrida's commentators follows him in this confusion. David Carroll notes that Derrida's critique of Kant's aesthetics arises from the fact that "the unbounded or unlimited characteristics of the sublime seem . . . to constitute a radical break with the aesthetic and the contradictory limitations of the frame" (*Paraesthetics* [New York: Methuen, 1987]: 141). The formal boundedness of a work corresponds to the "limitations of the frame;" but the sublime and the rest of the aesthetic are not as at odds as Derrida or Carroll would like if, as Kant suggests, even formally bounded objects can induce an experience of sublimity.

5. "For just as, when we judge the beautiful, imagination and *understanding* give rise to a subjective purposiveness of the mental powers by their *accordance*, so do imagination and reason here give rise to such a purposiveness by their *conflict*" (CJ 258).

6. Cf. also CJ 245.

7. The role that the sublime plays in arousing respect for our supersensible, moral vocation is, of course, a critical function of it in Kant's system. The complex relationship between Kant's aesthetic and moral theories, however, lies beyond the scope of this study. For some discussion of the role the feeling of respect plays in the validity claim of sublime reflection, see chapter 4.

8. Patricia Matthews argues that judging mathematical sublimity cannot be purposive for reason in its intellectual or theoretical dimension, since imagination is after all incapable of advancing reason's theoretical aims, and imagination's very attempt to "illustrate" ideas of reason amounts to an illegitimate constitutive use of such ideas ("Kant's Sublime: A Form of Pure Aesthetic Reflection Judgment," *The Journal of Aesthetics and Art Criticism* 54 [1996]: 172). But imagination's reference to ideas of reason is not constitutive of anything, and does not even attempt to constitute anything, if imagination accomplishes only an indeterminate expression of them. Furthermore, imagination's attempt to go beyond the limits of experience in an expressive relation to rational ideas embodies the respect for reason's demands which makes the judgment purposive for reason's theoretical aims.

9. Kant says relatively little about imagination's function in discerning dynamic sublimity, and what analysis he does offer is a challenge to square with the range of abilities he usually ascribes to this power. But cf. CJ 262, 268–269.

10. I will, however, suggest in chapter 4 that the respect for reason integral to the experience of sublimity is fulfilled in the mathematical sublime simply through the imaginative search for a unity of meaning in a work. That search will signify an intellectual respect for reason, apart from the moral feeling of respect.

11. Cf. CJ 251–252. The imaginative powers of apprehension and comprehension are treated in more detail below.

12. We will revisit the imaginative syntheses of the "A" edition Transcendental Deduction in chapter 4, where we will consider the role of transcendental affinity in grounding the validity of aesthetic reflection.

13. I stress complexity because the array of parts imagination seeks to comprehend as a whole may consist of physical features of a structure or an object; but in the case of reflection on the sublimity of aesthetic ideas, as I will argue, the complex with which imagination plays is one of a density of allusion and significance.

14. This "revisionist" reading of the mathematical sublime, that spares it some of the cumbersome machinery of the original, is developed in detail by Paul Crowther in *The Kantian Sublime* (Oxford: Clarendon Press, 1989). He distinguishes this "austere" thesis which I am adopting here from the "baroque" thesis involving the idea of infinity.

15. Patricia Matthews criticizes Crowther's rejection of the baroque thesis, but does not show how its appeal to infinity is required for finding sublimity in Kant's own examples of the great pyramids and St. Peter's. See "Kant's Sublime: A Form of Pure Aesthetic Reflective Judgment": 172–174. Kant's description of reflection on these examples (at CJ 252) does not make use of the idea of infinity; this is one of his only specific discussions of sublimity in art, and his account fits the austere thesis well.

16. Kant's claim that the sublime, *insofar as it belongs to fine art*, may be combined with beauty may suggest that he admits only certain cases in which the beautiful and the sublime coexist, and that a work of art may be artistic without this combination. I will consider the issue later in this chapter.

17. Kant, *Anthropology from a Pragmatic Point of View*. 109. He returns in the *Anthropology* to his example of St. Peter's: "Splendour can be joined with true, ideal taste, which is therefore compatible with something sublime that is also beautiful (such as . . . a St. Peter's Church in Rome)" (p. 113). See also CJ 245, where Kant holds that "the sublime in art is always confined to the conditions that [art] must meet to be in harmony with nature. . . ." The fundamental condition, of course, is that the purposiveness of sublimity in art not be determined by a specific purpose.

18. Hence John Sallis's concern is misplaced when he warns that a relation between ideas and the sublime threatens to undermine the conceptual indeterminacy of this form of reflection. He writes: "[I]f the ideas are to be identified as the properly sublime, then the entire structure of the reflective judgment in relation to which the sublime was to have been understood will have been violated to an even greater degree, indeed completely" (*Spacings*: 120). But involvement of the sublime in aesthetic ideas does not violate this judgment's freedom from concepts, because aesthetic ideas are not determined by rules of cognition. Sallis does not consider aesthetic ideas in his argument.

19. I take issue, then, with Derrida's claim that the sublime cannot be found in works of art. He writes: "The mastery of the human artist here operates with a view to an end, determining, defining, giving form. In deciding on contours, giving boundaries to the form and the cise, this mastery measures and dominates. But the sublime, if there is any sublime, exists only by overspilling: it exceeds cise and good measure, it is no longer proportional according to man and his determinations. There is thus no good example, no 'suitable' example in the products of human art" (*The Truth in Painting*: 122). Not only does this position contradict Kant's occasional pronouncements about the presence of the sublime in beautiful form, it also repeats Derrida's problematic assumption that the sublime can only be found in utterly formless phenomena. Furthermore, the present discussion indicates that an artist's "view to an end" in her work does not determine our reflection on the sublimity to be found in it. The inevitable gap between an artist's intentions in a work and how we interpret it precludes such determination.

Derrida ignores this quite "Derridean" point in order to maximize the disruptiveness and alterity of the sublime.

20. *Kant and the Claims of Taste*: 233.

21. Ibid.

22. Ibid., 234.

23. Ibid., 233.

24. The connection made in this section and the next between the interpretation of aesthetic ideas and the judgment of sublimity is unusual; in the next section I discuss the few commentators who have suspected it. Among those who do not consider the connection—in addition to the works cited in other notes—are: Donald Crawford, "The Place of the Sublime in Kant's Aesthetic Theory," in *The Philosophy of Immanuel Kant*, ed. Richard Kennington (Washington, D.C.: Catholic University of America Press, 1985): 161–183; Paul Guyer, "Kant's Distinction Between the Beautiful and the Sublime," *Review of Metaphysics* 35 (1982): 753–784; Salim Kemal, "Presentation and Expression in Kant's Aesthetics," *British Journal of Aesthetics* 15 (1981): 32–40; and Kenneth Rogerson, *Kant's Aesthetics: The Roles of Form and Expression* (Lanham, Md.: University Press of America, 1986).

25. Donald Crawford appeals to this passage in order to construe the aesthetic idea as a schema: "That which is created in art is not simply a particular empirical object but that which expresses an idea; and here too what is constructed allows one to generate a 'multiplicity of partial presentations' connected to the concept or idea being expressed. Thus the artist creates that which serves as a schema for thought about the idea which is expressed" ("Kant's Theory of Creative Imagination": 175). Yet a schema would establish too determinate a linkage between the sensible particular and its concept or idea. If an aesthetic idea were the schema for a rational idea, judgment of it, as we have seen throughout, would follow the rule of reason and hence would not be autonomously aesthetic.

26. For statements of the view that aesthetic ideas symbolize rational ideas, see: Francis Coleman, *The Harmony of Reason*: 161; A. T. Nuyen, "The Kantian Theory of Metaphor," *Philosophy and Rhetoric* 22 (1989): 101–103; and John Zammito, *The Genesis of Kant's Critique of Judgment* (Chicago: University of Chicago Press, 1992): 286–287. See also my "Form and Content in Kant's Aesthetics: Situating Beauty and the Sublime in the Work of Art," *Journal of the History of Philosophy* 32 (1994): 443–459. This article is an earlier statement of the view that aesthetic ideas are assessed via judgments of sublimity. The position I shall take here, that aesthetic ideas do not function as symbols of rational ideas, represents a rethinking of views presented in that article. This adjustment does not harm the broader argument of that essay, for which the claim that aesthetic ideas *express* rational ideas in fact does better than the claim that aesthetic ideas *symbolize* them.

27. *Imagination and Interpretation in Kant*: 122–128.

28. Ibid., 128.

29. Cf. also *Anthropology from a Pragmatic Point of View*: 64.

30. Translation slightly altered.

31. Cf. CJ 464n.

32. See G. Felicitas Munzel, "'The Beautiful is the Symbol of the Morally-Good': Kant's Philosophical Basis of Proof for the Idea of the Morally-Good," *Journal of the History of Philosophy* 33 (1995): 302–309. See also Pauline Kleingeld, "The Conative Character of Reason in Kant's Philosophy," *Journal of the History of Philosophy* 36 (1998): 89–91.

33. *Kant and the Claims of Taste*: 378.

34. It should be noted that Kant does mention analogy once in his discussion of aesthetic ideas (at CJ 314), but each of his several explanations of how aesthetic ideas work makes no mention of analogy and does not accord with Kant's §59 account of symbolic exhibition.

35. When Coleman argues that aesthetic ideas symbolize rational ideas, he claims that aesthetic ideas are "examples of analogical reasoning" (*The Harmony of Reason*: 161). The analogy function is at odds with Kant's construal of aesthetic ideas as indeterminately expansive in their meaning. Nuyen holds that the attributes of aesthetic ideas symbolize rational concepts ("The Kantian Theory of Metaphor": 101–103); he confuses the difference between aesthetic ideas and symbols by overlooking the central role of analogy in the latter (he does not discuss analogy at all).

36. *Imagination and Interpretation in Kant*: 125.

37. Ibid., 121.

38. All passages at CJ 314.

39. Translation altered.

40. For some discussion of Kant's notion of *ästhetische Erweiterung* in the aesthetic idea, see Rudolf Lüthe, "Kants Lehre von den ästhetischen Ideen," *Kant-Studien* 75 (1984): 65–74.

41. Crowther distinguishes three feelings of sublimity art can afford: "Either through the overwhelming perceptual scale of a work making vivid the scope of human artifice, or through a work's overwhelming personal significance making vivid the scope of artistic creation, or, finally, through the imaginatively overwhelming character of some general truth embodied in a work, making vivid the scope of artistic expression" (*The Kantian Sublime*: 161).

42. The extent of the difference here can be seen in the way Crowther links sublimity to aesthetic ideas by interpreting the aesthetic expansion they induce thus: "[If] a concept is embodied in an aesthetic idea, this can lead the imagination to try and grasp a sense of the innumerable totality of instances which form the extension of that concept. The fact that the concept is schematized in such a vivid way leads us to try and schematize its many other ways of being instantiated. Our imagination, however, is soon overwhelmed by this, and we sense the immensity of those many instances from which the concept has been abstracted" (ibid., 159). His approach deviates considerably from mine because he assumes that a work of art "schematizes" some concept "in such a vivid way" that aesthetic reflection on the work is overwhelmed by haplessly thinking

up more examples of the universal instantiated in the work. But we have seen that reflective judgment in an aesthetic context does not grasp any universal schema so vividly. Instead of thinking up more instances of the same, sublime reflection on aesthetic ideas is faced with the overwhelming challenge of understanding in the first place a complex of meaning too rich or indeterminate for it to comprehend as any schematized whole.

43. *Kant's Theory of Imagination*: 142–143.

44. Gibbons in fact shares my criticism of Crowther (in the note above); she argues against him that "[the] extension of thought motivated by the aesthetic idea does not simply suggest further instances of a determinant concept" (ibid., 141). But the main problem with Crowther's view is its appeal to the schematic function of imagination; by insisting on an imaginative schematization of works of art, and hence their aesthetic ideas, Gibbons in effect reverts to the position that she criticizes Crowther for adopting.

45. Wicks presents his view in "Kant on Fine Art: Artistic Sublimity Shaped by Beauty," *Journal of Aesthetics and Art Criticism* 53 (1995): 189–193. The piece is a response to an article by Guyer in which he essentially maintains his *Kant and the Claims of Taste* view that the judgment of taste is adequate to account for appreciation of both beauty and the expression of ideas; see "Kant's Conception of Fine Art," *Journal of Aesthetics and Art Criticism* 52 (1994): 275–285. For an earlier presentation of the view I have advocated here, see my "Form and Content in Kant's Aesthetics: Situating Beauty and the Sublime in the Work of Art."

46. For a helpful overview of the issue, see D.W. Gotschalk, "Form and Expression in Kant's Aesthetics," *British Journal of Aesthetics* 7 (1967): 250–260. Gotschalk recounts how Kant transits from a formalist to an expressionist aesthetic theory as he turns his attention to fine art, "after some delay (over the Sublime)" (p. 260). On my view, Kant's delay over the (mathematical) judgment of sublimity actually provides an account of our responses to expressive art.

47. The most important defenses of this position are Kenneth Rogerson, *Kant's Aesthetics: The Roles of Form and Expression* (Lanham, Md.: University Press of America, 1986); and Paul Guyer, "Formalism and the Theory of Expression in Kant's Aesthetics," *Kant-Studien* 68 (1977): 46–70, as well as his "Kant's Conception of Fine Art." In chapter 2 I argued that Guyer's inclusion of nonformal elements in the imaginative play of the judgment of taste threatens the basis of validity of that judgment. That argument applies as well to introducing the content of aesthetic ideas into taste judgments. We will see in chapter 4 that the somewhat different validity claim of sublime reflection can readily arise from imaginative interpretation of the artistic meanings housed in aesthetic ideas.

48. Translation altered.

49. Salim Kemal has suggested as much, though he adopts the standard position of construing reflection on aesthetic ideas as a judgment of taste rather than of sublimity. See "Expression and Idealism in Kant's Aesthetics," *British Journal of Aesthetics* 16 (1976): 72.

50. The dichotomy between invention and discovery which sublime reflection appears to straddle will surface again in the next chapter, when we explore the validity claim of aesthetic reflection's products, and once again in chapter 8.

51. *Anthropology from a Pragmatic Point of View*: 114.

52. While drawing the distinction between free and dependent beauty, Kant locates "all music not set to words" on the side of free beauties (CJ 229).

53. With the aim of undermining the perceptual formalism often attributed to Kant's judgment of taste (as I have attributed it), Kenneth Rogerson argues that the expression of aesthetic ideas is in fact *criterial* for *all* beauty. See "Beauty Without Concepts," in *Proceedings of the Eighth International Kant Congress*, ed. Hoke Robinson (Milwaukee: Marquette University Press, 1995). Rogerson thereby commits himself to the unenviable claim that even Kant's wallpaper pattern expresses aesthetic ideas. Rogerson acknowledges that "Kant clearly holds that objects can be beautiful in virtue of their perceptual form alone," but then argues that this does not make the expression of ideas "inconsistent with perceptual formalism" (p. 11). My argument in this and the previous chapter has shown that there is indeed no inconsistency between Kant's perceptual formalism and his theory of expression (because these aesthetic delights are discerned by different modes of judgment); but the lack of inconsistency does not demonstrate that expression is a "requirement for all beauty," as Rogerson maintains.

54. Imagination's production of aesthetic ideas in aesthetic response would also help to make sense of Kant's claim that "We may in general call beauty (*whether natural or artistic*) the *expression* of aesthetic ideas" (CJ 320; first emphasis mine). A genial interpretive response to either natural or artistic beauty may be inspired to "find" an expression of ideas therein, even though no actually intending artistic genius gets the credit in the former case.

55. Pauline Kleingeld notes the analogical metaphoricity of Kantian symbols in "The Conative Character of Reason": 91. A. T. Nuyen also discerns an account of metaphor in Kant's theory of the symbol, but without making any reference to the role of analogy in symbolism; see "The Kantian Theory of Metaphor."

56. Aristotle, *Poetics*, trans. Richard Janko (Indianapolis: Hackett, 1987): 28 (1457b). One of his examples: "as old age stands to life, so the evening stands to the day;" hence the analogical casting of old age as "the sunset of life."

57. Kleingeld, "The Conative Character of Reason": 91–93; Nuyen, "The Kantian Theory of Metaphor": 101–105; Mark Johnson, "Introduction: Metaphor in the Philosophical Tradition," in *Philosophical Perspectives on Metaphor* (Minneapolis: University of Minnesota Press, 1981): 14, 39–40; Robert Yanal, "Kant on Aesthetic Ideas and Beauty," in *Institutions of Art: Reconsiderations of George Dickie's Philosophy*, ed. Robert J. Yanal (University Park: Pennsylvania State University Press, 1994): 174; Brigitte Sassen, "Artistic Genius and the Question of Creativity," in *Akten des Siebenten Internationalen Kant-Kongresses*, ed. G. Funke (Bonn: Bouvier, 1991), v. 2: 763. Thomas Weiskel relates metaphor to the *sublime* in *The Romantic Sublime* (Baltimore: Johns Hopkins University Press, 1976). I will consider his work in the more elaborate treatment of metaphor in chapter 8.

58. *The Harmony of Reason*: 161.

59. Ibid., 162.

60. Coleman emphasizes this combinatory function of aesthetic ideas as metaphors: "Although the literal and lexical meanings are played upon in metaphor or in 'aes-

thetic ideas' generally, because of the newness and fecundity of the combination, indeterminate connotations of the terms are brought into play. [In the process] . . . only
certain associations and connotations of the two terms are selected for their suggestive
significance" (ibid., 164).

61. "Kant on Aesthetic Ideas and Beauty": 174. In addition to arguing the metaphoricity of aesthetic ideas, Yanal also adopts the standard position I have opposed, that
appreciation of aesthetic ideas can enter into the judgment of taste.

62. Thus we must once again resist John Sallis's claim, made as well in reference to the
judgment of taste (see chapter 2), to have detected "an erosion of the judgmental structure that Kant places initially at the center of the judgment of the sublime" (*Spacings*:
122). Sallis again restricts Kant's conception of reflective judgment to a subsumptive
function, and, not surprisingly, finds judgment of the sublime not to fulfill this model:
"Just as in the judgment of taste, the reflection that forms the center of the judgment
of the sublime proves to be an operation quite distinct from the subsumption—taken
in a strongly cognitive sense—of a particular under a sought-out universal" (ibid.). My
account indicates that a more thoroughly worked out conception of the operation of
reflective judgment shows it to be active and fulfilled in different ways in judgments of
both the beautiful and the sublime.

Chapter 4

1. Translation altered.

2. Kant in fact repeats this atypical use of the term "concept" in passages immediately
preceding and following the cited passage. One paragraph before Kant describes aesthetic ideas as trying "to approach an exhibition of rational concepts (intellectual
ideas)," and in the paragraph following the above passage he describes an aesthetic
idea as "an object whose concept is a rational idea" (ibid.).

3. We will see that Hegel takes the thematic content of ideal artworks to be amenable
to systematic articulation, which in essence means that he collapses the distinction
between aesthetic and rational ideas. In his philosophy as a whole, in contrast to Kant's,
ideas of reason can achieve exhibition. This major difference between them will surely
complicate my interpretation of Hegel's aesthetic theory and what contribution it can
make to theorizing the aesthetics of sublimity of interest here. For Hegel's view of
Kant's aesthetic idea, see the first Interlude in this volume.

4. Hannah Ginsborg highlights the role of normativity in Kant's conception of purposiveness in "Purposiveness and Normativity," in *Proceedings of the Eighth International
Kant Congress*, ed. Hoke Robinson (Milwaukee: Marquette University Press, 1995), v. 2:
453–460.

5. For a careful elucidation of the normative basis of judgments of beauty, see Robert
Pippin, "The Significance of Taste: Kant, Aesthetic and Reflective Judgment," *Journal
of the History of Philosophy* 34 (1996): 549–569. Pippin advocates a view of Kantian aesthetic reflection that shows it to involve not merely an immediate feeling of pleasure in
an object, but also a reflective activity, based on conditions of a common sense, that
gives rise to a universal pleasure. His account of Kant confirms that the reflective
search for purposive unity in an object, a somewhat "intellectual" (though not conceptual) pursuit, is compatible with the "mere" feeling in which aesthetic reflection

issues. Such a view allows Kant's notion of reflective judgment to have the sort of broad implications for our sense-making practices that I am drawing out of it, rather than reducing aesthetic judgments to mere reports of certain occurrent states of feeling unaccompanied by any more "thoughtful" interpretive response to the world.

6. Jean-François Lyotard, *Lessons on the Analytic of the Sublime*: 231. Cf. Peter Fenves's discussion of this issue in "Taking Stock of the Kantian Sublime," *Eighteenth-Century Studies* 28 (1994): 71–72.

7. Paul Guyer has emphasized that the cultivation of reason affects what expectations we can have for receptivity of the sublime: "[S]ince the response to the sublime involves the imaginative satisfaction of ideas of theoretical or . . . practical reason, the actual experience of sublimity in a particular situation may require not a mere act of abstraction but rather the considerable degree of culture and education which is necessary to develop the capacity of reason and moral feeling itself even if we suppose a predisposition to this capacity in everyone." He concludes that "the fact that reason and its ideas are involved in the explanation of our response to the sublime means that intersubjective agreement about such responses, though as well-founded as the response to beauty, cannot reasonably be expected to emerge at the same point in actual practice or at the same stage in the actual development of different individuals or cultures" ("Kant's Distinction Between the Beautiful and the Sublime": 781).

8. John Zammito stresses this function of rational ideas and characterizes them as "metaconcepts, in the sense of providing rules for the organization of concepts into systems of thought" (*The Genesis of Kant's Critique of Judgment*: 164).

9. This means of developing Kant's account of reflection on aesthetic ideas has not (to my knowledge) been explored elsewhere.

10. This point above all explains why aesthetic unity cannot assume the form of systematic unity, and thus why Christel Fricke's claim to the contrary cannot be right. See "Explaining the Inexplicable": 55, and chapter 1.

11. We can see in the third *Critique* a rare suggestion of this interpretation of imaginative reflection when Kant praises that power's constructive prowess. In the midst of his discussion of aesthetic ideas he writes: "For the imagination (as a productive cognitive power) is very mighty when it creates, as it were, another nature out of the material that actual nature gives it. We use it to entertain ourselves when experience strikes us as overly routine. We may even restructure experience; and though in doing so we continue to follow analogical laws, yet we also follow principles which reside higher up, namely, in reason" (CJ 314). Keeping in mind that Kant regards art as a key locale for the presentation of aesthetic ideas, his reference in this passage to the use of material drawn from nature should not be taken to exclude imagination's construction of aesthetic ideas out of the attributes of art works. When it does, imagination follows, to the extent it can, reason's principles of specification and affinity.

12. The following pages offer only a brief and compressed look at the "A" edition Deduction for the purpose of clarifying the transcendental basis of the work of productive imagination in an aesthetic context. I do not aim to provide a thorough consideration of Kant's arguments, their merits, or the way they evolved in the "B" Deduction. It should be noted, however, that Kant's discussion of affinity in the "A" Deduction does not appear in the later version. Given the significance that transcen-

dental affinity will grant to the creative power of productive imagination, this revision may reflect the "retreat" from transcendental imagination that Heidegger detects in Kant's "B" edition. Curiously, despite the centrality of transcendental affinity to imagination's a priori productivity, Heidegger never discusses it. Cf. *Kant and the Problem of Metaphysics*, trans. Richard Taft (Bloomington: Indiana University Press, 1990), 4th ed.: esp. §§17 and 31.

13. Sarah Gibbons shares this view of preconceptual synthesis: "imagination may be active in combining the sensible manifold—synthesizing—without this synthesis being conceptualized, that is, without a specific rule which guides the synthesis being recognized in a determinant judgement. While knowledge of an *object* and, hence, determinant judgement requires this latter step of conceptualization, reflective judgement does not" (*Kant's Theory of Imagination*: 18). The nonconceptual "synthesis" of aesthetic unity is what we have seen imagination produce, in various ways, in aesthetic reflection. Gibbons discusses the special role of affinity in imaginative synthesis at pp. 32–36.

14. "Whether near or remote": if determinative empirical concepts subsume particulars "near" to each other under abstract categories (e.g., kindred varieties of dog under the concept "dog"), metaphors relate "remote" features of the world (e.g., time and money) into a striking and uncanny affinity.

15. Paul Crowther suggests in fact that "An element of randomness in judgment . . . is partially *constitutive* of aesthetic unity," though he makes the point with reference to judging beauty ("The Significance of Kant's Pure Aesthetic Judgment": 114).

16. If reflective judgment is the anticipation of a hidden, purposive unity ordering experience, paranoia would seem to be the pathological extreme of this reflection. This may help to explain why some "postmodern" works of literature (which strive to induce the sublime feeling of grasping for meanings and intentions forever beyond reach) have made paranoid thinking a prominent theme. Consider, for example, Pynchon's *Gravity's Rainbow* or Percy's *The Thanatos Syndrome*.

17. Kant also grants the judgment of taste this freedom of imagination from empirical association: "in a judgment of taste the imagination must be considered in its freedom. This implies, first of all, that this power is not taken here as reproductive, where it is subject to the laws of association, but as productive and spontaneous (as the originator of chosen forms of possible intuitions)" (CJ 240).

18. Salim Kemal argues that Kant's theory of expression is not equipped to provide criteria for adjudicating between conflicting interpretations of a work's meaning (*Kant and Fine Art*: 265–273). He concludes that when it comes to attributing meanings to works, Kant's theory cannot explain "how audiences can establish either that there is a lack of alternative readings or that a given reading is plausible" (p. 273). The account of sublime reflection which I have advanced has suggested that Kant's theory would support an interpretive practice which allows for multiple plausible "readings" of a work. Chapter 9's more elaborate consideration of the "interpretive sublime" will pursue this extrapolation further. I will ultimately agree with Kemal's related conclusion (pp. 270–273) that this variability in interpretation weakens the universality of aesthetic reflection's claim to validity. While Kemal proposes that we need to shore up and improve Kant's theory of expression, to correct for this weakening, I will instead welcome it.

Interlude: Turning to Hegel

1. G. W. F. Hegel, *Aesthetics: Lectures on Fine Art*, trans. William Wallace and A.V. Miller (Oxford: Oxford University Press, 1971): 56; *Werke in zwanzig Bänden* (Frankfurt: Suhrkamp, 1970), b. 13: 84. All subsequent references will be provided in the body of the text using the abbreviation "LFA." Each reference will provide pagination to Knox's translation, followed by volume and page numbers for *Werke* (volumes 13 to 15). In this case, for example, "LFA 56; 13:84" would refer to page 56 of Knox and volume 13, page 84 of *Werke*.

2. *Faith and Knowledge*, trans. W. Cerf and H. S. Harris (Albany: State University of New York Press, 1977): 73.

3. Ibid., 89.

4. Klaus Düsing forcefully demonstrates the links Hegel draws in *Glauben und Wissen* between a Kantian power of intuitive intellect and the specifically aesthetic activities of Kant's imagination. See "Ästhetische Einbildungskraft und Intuitiver Verstand," *Hegel-Studien* 21 (1986): 115. Ultimately for the early Hegel of *Glauben und Wissen*, writes Düsing, "aesthetic imagination and genius in their productivity present in an immediate, intuitive-sensuous manner what intuitive understanding knows by a superior method in spontaneous, constitutive acts of intellect" (p. 126). We will see more of Hegel's early response to Kant's aesthetics below, and we will also see that the power of imagination to sensuously present the Idea becomes the defining feature of Hegel's mature aesthetic theory.

5. *Faith and Knowledge*: 85.

6. *Poetic Interaction* (Chicago: University of Chicago Press, 1989): 297; emphasis in original.

7. Robert Pippin argues that Kant's notion of reflective judgment can itself be developed in the direction Hegel takes it, so that post-Kantian appropriations of reflective judgment might constitute an inner extrapolation of Kant's view, rather than an imposition of entirely external concerns. See "Avoiding German Idealism: Kant, Hegel, and the Reflective Judgment Problem," in *Idealism as Modernism: Hegelian Variations* (Cambridge: Cambridge University Press, 1997). Pippin argues that Hegel was drawn to the potential implications of the fact that aesthetic judgment offers a locus of self-orienting, nonconceptual validity that, as a sense-making relationship between subject and world, could be construed as a kind of intuitive intellection. Pippin rightly indicates (p. 148) that a major obstacle of this interpretation is whether Kant's aesthetic judgments of beauty and sublimity can truly be regarded as cases of a *reflective* form of judgment. By thematizing reflection's principle of purposiveness, and by locating its operation in both kinds of aesthetic reflection, part I has hopefully offered one resolution of that question. Of course, my account of Kantian aesthetic reflection retains, contra Hegel, the cognitive *indeterminacy* of its products.

8. *The Encyclopedia Logic*, trans. T. F. Geraets, W. A. Suchting, and H. S. Harris (Indianapolis: Hackett, 1991): §55, p. 102; italics in original.

9. Allen Hance argues this view in "The Art of Nature: Hegel and the *Critique of Judgment*," *International Journal of Philosophical Studies* 6 (1998).

10. *The Encyclopedia Logic*: §55 (*Anmerkung*), p. 102.

11. Jacques Taminiaux has shown the continued importance for Hegel of Kantian reflective judgment between *Glauben und Wissen* and the *Lectures*. See "The *Critique of Judgment* and German Philosophy," in *Poetics, Speculation, and Judgment*, trans. and ed. Michael Gendre (Albany: State University of New York Press, 1993): 29–31.

12. *Faith and Knowledge*: 87.

13. Ibid.

14. Allen Hance rightly notes Hegel's conviction that Kant's doctrine of aesthetic ideas approaches the unification of the sensuous and the intellectual which Hegel charges not only art but systematic philosophy itself with accomplishing ("The Art of Nature: Hegel and the *Critique of Judgment*": 45–46). It should be evident, however, that Hegel must reject the doctrine, because Kantian aesthetic ideas do not really achieve this unification (because, again, rational ideas are not directly presentable for Kant). This is not made quite clear in Hance's treatment, in which he also mistakenly (I think) construes aesthetic ideas as symbols; see the discussion of symbolization in chapter 3.

15. *The Encyclopedia Logic*: §56, p. 103.

16. *Poetic Interaction*: 299.

17. Patrick Gardiner's suggestion that Hegel adopts the doctrine of aesthetic ideas must be mistaken. Gardiner indicates an affinity between the "second nature" Kant takes aesthetic ideas to produce and the purification and transmutation of material achieved by art in Hegel's case. But although both philosophers grant art the power to produce something new, Hegel's artwork completely expresses its determinate content in its sensuousness, whereas what a Kantian aesthetic idea produces is not a determinate whole, not a unified theme. Hegel's transformation of Kant's aesthetic theory would not make sense without a rejection of aesthetic ideas. See Gardiner, "Kant and Hegel on Aesthetics," in *Hegel's Critique of Kant*, ed. Stephen Priest (Oxford: Oxford University Press, 1987): 161–171.

18. Hegel does treat the sublime later in the *Lectures;* his discussion will play an important role in the argument of chapter 7.

19. We will see that an added meaning accrues to a "mining of Hegel's aesthetics": artistic imagination will for Hegel draw from a "dark mine" or "pit" of images in creating its works. This will prove quite relevant to articulating an Hegelian imaginative capacity which falls short of producing the determinate expression he expects from art, and instead pursues the sort of sublime reflection productive of Kantian aesthetic ideas. See part II.

20. It will have been evident in part I that advancing a fresh interpretation of Kant's aesthetic theory requires navigating a veritable minefield of critical commentary and alternative construal. The Hegelian texts on which I will focus in part 2 are comparatively open terrain; they have in general received much less focused attention, especially in the Anglo-American context. Though I will refer to secondary resources as necessary, the reader will note in part 2 a freer (though still steady) hand at work in the picture that I will draw.

Chapter 5

1. *Hegel's Philosophy of Mind*, trans. William Wallace and A. V. Miller (Oxford: Oxford University Press, 1971): §387, p. 25; *Werke in zwanzig Bänden* (Frankfurt: Suhrkamp, 1970): v. 10, p. 38. Subsequent references will be provided parenthetically in the body of the text using the abbreviation "PM"; each will provide *Encyclopedia* paragraph numbers, will indicate passages from *Anmerkungen* and *Zusätze* with the abbreviations "An" and "Zu," and will provide English and German pagination. In this case, e.g., "PM §387, 25/38" would refer to page 25 of Wallace and Miller and page 38 of *Werke* volume 10.

2. Translation altered.

3. Translation slightly altered.

4. Translation slightly altered.

5. Cf. *A Treatise of Human Nature*, ed. Ernest Mossner (London: Penguin, 1969): 56–60, 132–142; and *An Enquiry Concerning Human Understanding*, ed. Eric Steinberg (Indianapolis: Hackett, 1993): 9–31.

6. As expected, the workings of aesthetic imagination will prove essential. We can note in advance that, in his account of the sleeping soul, Hegel anticipates a key moment of his aesthetic theory with remarkable precision. He will term *subjective humor* a certain descent of imagination into a merely capricious play of association. In that state, Hegel writes in the *Lectures on Aesthetics*, "[E]very independence of an objective content along with the inherently fixed connection of the form . . . is annihilated in itself, and the presentation is only a sporting with the topics, a derangement and perversion of the material . . . a criss-cross movement of subjective expressions, views, and attitudes whereby the author sacrifices himself and his topics alike" (LFA 601; 14:229). Meanwhile, the *Zusatz* that accompanies paragraph 398 of the "Anthropology" characterizes the dreams of the sleeping soul thus: "In dreams it is only our picture-thinking that comes into play and its products are not governed by the categories of intellect. But mere picture-thinking wrests things completely out of their concrete context, isolates them. That is why in dreams everything drifts apart, criss-crosses in the wildest disorder, objects lose all necessary, objective, rational connection and are associated only in an extremely superficial, contingent and subjective manner" (PM §398 Zu, 70/93–94). The implications of this apparent connection between the sleeping soul and subjective humor will become clear as we proceed.

7. Cf. PM §§405–407, 94–122/124–160. About these phenomena see Murray Greene, *Hegel on the Soul: A Speculative Anthropology* (The Hague: Martinus Nijhoff, 1972): 106–120. On the subject of Hegel and hypnotism, see also Jean-Luc Nancy, "Identity and Trembling," trans. Brian Holmes, in *The Birth to Presence* (Stanford: Stanford University Press, 1993).

8. This does not, of course, imply that Hegel thinks every individual must suffer madness on the way to becoming a full subject. Neither does my interpretation suggest this. Alan Olson discusses madness as developmentally prior to sanity in Hegel's system; see *Hegel and the Spirit* (Princeton: Princeton University Press, 1992): 88. But if, as Olson claims, Hegel is concerned with "how it is the case that people ever become what we call sane in the first place," his concern is surely not that we all "become" sane after first being mad.

9. My analysis must rely almost entirely on the long *Zusatz* accompanying §408 (124–139/163–182). It contains most of Hegel's account of insanity, and it follows the cues of his main paragraph even in perpetuating the interpretive difficulties discussed above. The conclusions it suggests, however, will be confirmed by Hegel's subsequent paragraphs and *Zusätze* on habit-formation (PM §§409–410).

10. Just as we noted earlier that the phenomenon of subjective humor in Hegel's aesthetic theory is prefigured by the associative play of the sleeping soul, it will be in subjective humor that the "particularity of the subject" will again "manifest itself unchecked." See chapter 7.

11. For example, Hegel recommends a playground therapy: "Of the remedies acting primarily on the body, the see-saw has especially proved efficacious, particularly with raving lunatics. The see-saw movement induces giddiness in the patient and loosens his fixed idea" (PM §408 Zu, 138/181).

12. Murray Greene and John McCumber have pointed out that Hegel mentions habit at the end of his *Philosophy of Nature*, part two of the *Encyclopedia*, where the death of the natural organism is described as its succumbing to "*habituation* without process" ["prozeßlosen *Gewohnheit*"] (§375). Greene simply notes this anticipation without worrying about it (*Hegel on the Soul*: 74). That Hegel appeals to the *spiritual* phenomenon of habit thirty-five paragraphs before its introduction into the system, and outside the realm of spirit, that is, in nature, should cause some concern. McCumber has argued, however, that Hegel presents the death of habit in the final moments of the *Philosophy of Nature* as in fact a spiritual phenomenon implicated in the immediate transition from nature to spirit which Hegel is making at that point in the *Encyclopedia*. Cf. "Hegel on Habit," *The Owl of Minerva* 21 (1990): 161. It is also likely that the dead habit of §375 represents a more rudimentary appearance of this phenomenon than the process of habituation Hegel presents in §410, which, after all, helps produce the conscious subject.

13. *Sicheinbilden*, of course, etymologically links the construction of habits to the work of imagination, *Einbildungskraft* (in one formulation), as we will see more clearly below.

14. One should not, however, overestimate the power of habit formation to complete the production of a spirit imbued with rational necessity. As John McCumber has pointed out, Hegel takes habit to provide only "subjective necessity" rather than universal validity; habituation can offer a basic structure for the soul in the form of its *finite* mediations, but can far from manage the infinite mediation Hegel attributes to rational mind ("Hegel on Habit": 156). Habits provide a foundation of order on which the whole edifice of mind can be built, but habituation cannot by itself give systematic arrangement to habits.

15. Murray Greene has suggested that the universals developed in habit formation assume a form akin to what Hegel calls the "universal of reflection" in the *Encyclopedia Logic*. This is a universal that "appears," Greene writes, "as secondary to the particulars and imposed by our subjective doing, rather than as the immanent truth of the particulars in which they are sublated as vanishing moments" (*Hegel on the Soul*: 139, n.108). Hegel describes the universal of reflection as an "external bond that embraces all the singular instances which subsist on their own account and are indifferent to one another" (*The Encyclopedia Logic*: §175 Zu, p. 253). In such a judgment a group of individuals is gathered together as instances of a given category; that is, this judgment of "allness" (ibid.) collects particulars according to their likeness (e.g., "all candy is

sweet"). The "external fastening" undertaken in the universals of habit formation relates feelings taken to be similar; the fastening of disparate phenomena in Kantian reflective judgment does not appear to occur in habituation or in Hegelian universals of reflection.

16. In §415 of the "Phenomenology" Hegel claims that "The Kantian philosophy may be most accurately described as having viewed the mind as consciousness, and as containing the propositions only of a *phenomenology* (not of a *philosophy*) of mind" (An, 156/202).

17. Errol Harris emphasizes the sense in which habit transforms the soul's *embodiment* "into the instrument, or medium (the sign), of its own self-manifestation" ("Hegel's Anthropology," *The Owl of Minerva* 25 [1993]: 8). The soul makes its body its own through the regulative ordering of habits, giving determinate unification (even if only so far to a merely subjectively necessary extent) to conceptuality and its material realization. The habituated subject is the soul's work of art in that it prefigures the synthesis of theme and ideal sensuous means of expression which artistic imagination will later accomplish.

18. My emphases.

19. If the "self-possessed and healthy subject" is the "*dominant genius*" over its particularities (PM §408 An, 123/162), Hegel marks the disordered play of the sleeping soul, by contrast, as "the evil genius of man which gains the upper hand in insanity" (PM §408 An, 124/162). For discussion of these contrasts, see Jeffrey Powell, "The Encyclopedia of Madness," *International Studies in Philosophy* 30 (1998): 97, 103–106.

20. *A Treatise of Human Nature*: 57–58.

21. The *Encyclopedia* (1830) "Phenomenology" should not, of course, be confused with Hegel's 1807 *Phenomenology of Spirit*, though the former does take up, in greatly compressed form, many themes of the latter. Considering the *Phenomenology of Spirit* lies beyond the scope of this study, which takes Hegel's encyclopedic system to represent his mature views on imagination.

22. The progress from this pit of recollection to imagination's production of linguistic signs is analyzed by Jacques Derrida in "The Pit and the Pyramid: Introduction to Hegel's Semiology," in *Margins of Philosophy*, trans. Alan Bass (Chicago: University of Chicago Press, 1982). Derrida develops there a critique of Hegel's privileging of spoken over written language.

23. Paragraph 459 and its *Anmerkung* provide a discussion of alphabetic and hieroglyphic languages that lies beyond the scope of the present inquiry. Hegel's discussion of language issues from his account of the signs produced by "sign-making imagination," the form of imagination that succeeds Hegel's penultimate form, symbolic imagination, upon which we will need to focus. Thus my reading of Hegel will concentrate on paragraphs 455 through 458 alone. For a critical analysis of §459 see Derrida, "The Pit and the Pyramid."

24. John Sallis hopes to make these textual problems as troubling as possible. He claims with regard to §455 that "the confusion introduced by the apparent disorder in the *Zusatz* is a matter of serious concern" (*Spacings*: 147). He argues that the disorder of the text indicates a fundamental instability in Hegel's account of imagination and so

also in the speculative reason which succeeds it. The resolution of the textual problems that I offer below suggests that the disorder is not as disruptive as Sallis would like.

25. De Vries, *Hegel's Theory of Mental Activity* (Ithaca, N.Y.: Cornell University Press, 1988): 135.

26. Iring Fetscher follows roughly this division of the subject-matter, using the *Zusätze* as liberally as I will. See *Hegels Lehre vom Menschen* (Stuttgart: Fromann, 1970): 162–169.

27. John McCumber has pointed out that "the only general category which is said to govern the process of working up universals at *Encyclopedia* §§453–456 is resemblance— the selective (that is, abstract) similarity of intuitions to one another and to the universals under which they eventually come" (*The Company of Words* [Evanston, Ill.: Northwestern University Press, 1993]: 227). McCumber takes imagination to work these representations up into a complex vocabulary he calls "expert discourse." He thus takes imagination's organization of likeness to define it well past §456, in fact all the way to the production of linguistic signs. I will ultimately argue that the artistic prerogatives of symbolic imagination lead it in a direction away from the conceptual satisfaction with homogeneity.

28. *Spacings*: 155–156.

29. Ibid., 153–154. Sallis links Hegel's "Anthropology" account of insanity to his "Psychology" account of imagination, but he bases the connection on Hegel's description in the (*Zusatz* to §408) of mad persons as imagining they are someone else, Hegel's mention of imagined illnesses, and so on. Sallis does not draw the detailed comparisons offered here between (1) the associative activity of the sleeping soul and the imagination's association of ideas, and between (2) the homogenizing activity of habit-formation and generalizing imagination. Sallis's claim that Hegel diminishes the transgressive power of imagination by labeling it merely anthropological misses the point that imagination also finds its first generalizing incarnation in the "Anthropology"'s habit-formative cure for insanity. That is, even in the "Anthropology" imagination's apparent moment of transgression is contained by the universalizing formation of habits.

Chapter 6

1. Hegel's demotion of beauty in nature in favor of the Ideal of Beauty realized in art is in keeping with his view of nature as the dispersal of the logical Idea into material contingency, which Idea can only be recuperated in its full determinacy in the highest products of human culture, that is, art, religion, and philosophy. For Hegel's analysis and critique of beauty in nature, see LFA 116–152; 13:157–202.

2. *Beauty and Truth: A Study of Hegel's Aesthetics* (Oxford: Oxford University Press, 1984): 16.

3. For a useful attempt to articulate a Hegelian account of aesthetic judgment, by drawing on Hegel's *Science of Logic* theory of judgment, see Robert Wicks, *Hegel's Theory of Aesthetic Judgment* (New York: Peter Lang, 1994).

4. *Poetic Interaction*: 72.

5. Ibid., 73.

6. Ibid., 83.

7. McCumber: "viewing a work of art as a reconciled whole means seeing *all* of its details as conveying a single guiding conception. Once that has been achieved the work of interpretation terminates. The standard for judging competing interpretations of the work is thus the completeness of the coherence they attribute to it" (ibid., 85).

8. Translation slightly altered.

9. He writes: "[From] the genuine subject-matter which inspires the artist, nothing is to be held back in his subjective inner heart; everything must be completely unfolded and indeed in a way in which the universal soul and substance of the chosen subject-matter appears emphasized just as much as its individual configuration appears completely polished in itself and permeated by that soul and substance in accord with the whole representation. For what is supreme and most excellent is not, as may be supposed, the inexpressible—for if so the poet would be still far deeper than his work discloses. On the contrary, his works are the best part and the truth of the artist; what he is in them, that he *is*; but what remains buried in his heart, that *is* he not" (LFA 290–291; 13: 375–376).

10. Stephen Bungay's formulation of the distinction between artistic and philosophical truth clouds their separation: "Truth is the complete articulation of reality by thought, in thought; Beauty is the complete articulation of reality by thought, in reality. . . . [A] true Concept gives the exhaustive determination of its object, and a beautiful object is one which is exhaustively determined by thought" (*Beauty and Truth*: 43). But Hegel insists that thought cannot completely articulate reality in the sensuous mode of Beauty. Art provides a sensuous point of access to truths which only philosophy can express in their entirety.

11. Translation slightly altered.

12. *The Encyclopedia Logic*: §133 Zu, 203.

13. Cf. *Languages of Art* (Indianapolis: Hackett, 1976): 50–57, 85–95.

14. Dieter Henrich, "The Contemporary Relevance of Hegel's Aesthetics," in *Hegel*, ed. Michael Inwood (Oxford: Oxford University Press, 1985): 203. In the *Encyclopedia Logic* Hegel establishes a logical correlation of form and content in which "'content' is nothing but the *overturning of form* into content, and 'form' nothing but *overturning of content* into form" (§133 An, 202). "Content" that does not assume the form of sensuous Beauty cannot be aesthetic content. Hegel goes on to state that "The only genuine works of art are precisely the ones whose content and form show themselves to be completely identical" (§133 Zu, 203). In contrast to this position, Charles Karelis discusses the content orientation of Hegel's theory of aesthetic merit in a way that separates out form and content, without recognizing the extent to which, for Hegel, the form of the Concept restricts the range of acceptable aesthetic content. See "Hegel's Concept of Art: An Interpretive Essay," in *Hegel's Introduction to Aesthetics*, trans. T. M. Knox (Oxford: Oxford University Press, 1979): xxxvi–xxxvii. Robert Wicks provides a useful discussion of the way Hegel's philosophy of art manages the form/content distinction in *Hegel's Theory of Aesthetic Judgment*: 95–99.

15. See "Art, Philosophy and Concreteness in Hegel," *The Owl of Minerva* 16 (1985): 131–146, and *Art and the Absolute* (Albany: State University of New York Press, 1986): 70–71.

16. *Art and the Absolute*: 170, n.13.

17. If we look closer at some of Desmond's arguments, we will not find justification for his claim that Hegel favors the inexhaustibility of aesthetic ideas. Desmond argues, for example, that the perfection of expression Hegel expects from fine art "displays . . . an open-ended side," in that "its realization is open to a plurality of possible actualizations. The perfection of this work, or even of that artistic movement, does not pre-empt the possibility of other future instances of perfection" (ibid., 68). An artistic theme is thus "open" because it can be expressed perfectly in various ways. Aside from questioning whether Hegel would agree with this, this sense of "openness" side-steps the evident determinacy of content, for Hegel, in *individual* works, regardless of other attempts to express the same theme. Or again, Desmond maintains the resistance of aesthetic content to finite analysis: "Every . . . assertion which tries to fix the significance of the art work to finite predicates may indeed get at one important meaning about it, but only to find itself missing another" (ibid., 71). In analyzing a complex unity of parts, discussion of how some part relates to and illuminates the whole will surely leave out discussion of other parts. This does not obviate the fact that, for Hegel, all analysis and reflection on a work finds its point of reference in the one, fixed and unifying theme which organizes every part and is itself, far from being "inexhaustible," determinable in conceptual form.

18. Vittorio Hösle describes Hegelian aesthetic unity this way: "The inner unity of individual moments of a work of art should not be as immediately knowable as what is determined absolutely, such as is the case in a philosophical system, where the individual parts have interest solely in their [systematic] connection. This connectedness must indeed exist in art as well, but it may only be hinted at, it must make itself only gradually apparent. This means the parts must have an independence and freedom which makes them interesting in themselves, even though they gain their ultimate meaning only within the totality of the work" (*Hegels System*: v. 2, p. 603).

19. Paul Guyer underestimates the role of contingency in Hegel's conception of artistic beauty when he writes of the elements related in a beautiful object that "the contingency of their connection is just an appearance, or perhaps even an illusion (*Schein*)" ("Hegel on Kant's Aesthetics: Necessity and Contingency in Beauty and Art," in *Kant and the Experience of Freedom: Essays on Aesthetics and Morality* [Cambridge: Cambridge University Press, 1993]: 172). The final sentence of the paragraph just cited indicates that for Hegel the contingency in the work cannot be a mere illusion, but is an essential component of its reality and of its realization of the Idea; the *Concept* may have a "purely ideal unity," but a sensuous appearance of the Idea must also present "the aspect of independent reality." Without the enduring presence of contingency in the work, the particular parts would suffer under an abstract subordination to the whole. The contingency inherent in the concrete world requires that contingency inhabit the essence of the sensuous manifestation of beauty.

20. *The Encyclopedia Logic*: §145 Zu, 219.

21. Dieter Henrich made the classic statement of the essential role of contingency in Hegel's systematic philosophy in "Hegels Theorie über den Zufall," *Kant-Studien* 50 (1958–59): "Hegel's speculative idealism maintains of course the necessity of the whole of being; however, it so little claims to be able to deduce every individual, that it is rather the only philosophical theory which comprehends the concept of absolute contingency" (p. 132). Henrich shows that necessity and contingency are for Hegel analytically joined; that is, the necessity Hegel so often attributes to moments of his system can arise only against a backdrop of absolute contingency (p. 135). See also Stephen

Houlgate, "Necessity and Contingency in Hegel's *Science of Logic,*" *The Owl of Minerva* 27 (1995): 37–49.

22. In fact, the presentation of beauty requires a dual cleansing from contingency, since the sensuous exterior in which beauty is to appear must also be freed from the distortions of worldly accident: "since art brings back into this harmony with its true Concept what is contaminated in other existents by chance and externality, it casts aside everything in appearance which does not correspond with the Concept and only by this purification does it produce the Ideal" (LFA 155; 13:206). "Art" that portrays mere accidents of nature fails to present the unity of a perfected theme. So, for example, in the case of portrait painting the artist must cleanse the subject of unsightly warts and scars in order to present her in her most favorable essence (ibid.).

23. Translation slightly altered.

24. See J. M. Bernstein's deft study of this trajectory in aesthetic theory, *The Fate of Art: Aesthetic Alienation from Kant to Derrida and Adorno* (University Park: Pennsylvania State University Press, 1992).

25. Lyotard, "The Sublime and the Avant-Garde," trans. Lisa Liebmann, in *The Inhuman* (Stanford: Stanford University Press, 1991): 91. In chapter 9 I will qualify Lyotard's claims regarding the "postmodern sublime."

26. "The Unpresentable," in *The Subject of Philosophy*, ed. Thomas Trezise (Minneapolis: University of Minnesota Press, 1993): 151.

27. Ibid., 155.

28. *Lessons on the Analytic of the Sublime*: 130–131.

29. Emphasis added.

30. Richard Dean Winfield considers the problems this poses for Hegel's conception of artistic creativity in the classical form; see "Hegel on Classical Art: A Re-Examination," *Clio* 24 (1995): 155–156. Hegel claims that the classical artist "does not simply *copy* or adhere to one fixed type, but is at the same time *creative* for the whole," yet he seems to indicate that this creativity is limited to "unnoticeably and unostentatiously develop[ing]" the content received through tradition (LFA 440; 14:29).

31. Winfield observes that the audience of classical art is freed "from having to unravel symbolic allusions. Once the audience recognizes a work to be classical, it will cease searching for the answers to puzzles . . ." ("Hegel on Classical Art": 160–161). This nicely contrasts the determinacy of theme in Hegel's classical art with the interpretive striving of a sublime reflection.

32. *After the End of Art: Contemporary Art and the Pale of History* (Princeton: Princeton University Press, 1997).

Chapter 7

1. Note that if Hegel's accounts of symbolic and romantic art provide what we need here, we will have confirmed William Desmond's thought that reflection on indeter-

minate content plays an important role in Hegel's aesthetic theory. However, we will have located that reflection on what Hegel sees, and must see, as the peripheries of his theory, rather than at its center, in his account of ideal (classical) art, where Desmond claims to find it.

2. Curtis Carter discusses the "dual role for the term symbol" in Hegel's aesthetic theory. See "Hegel and Whitehead on Aesthetic Symbols," in *Hegel and Whitehead*, ed. George R. Lucas (Albany: State University of New York Press, 1986): 239–256.

3. Stephen Houlgate observes that, to the extent that symbolic art is marked by "the absence of any harmony between a clearly articulated meaning and the form of expression," then modern art can be considered "symbolic in a Hegelian sense whenever it intimates that meaning is indeterminate or not wholly articulable" (*Freedom, Truth and History: An Introduction to Hegel's Philosophy* [London: Routledge, 1991]: 161). This feature of the symbolic arises for Hegel only in the symbolic form of art, not in the perfected symbolism of his aesthetic Ideal. But the connection does suggest the potential relevance of Kantian aesthetic ideas and Hegelian symbolic art for contemporary (modernist and postmodern) art.

4. Curtis Carter notes that "The problem of interpreting aesthetic symbols is further complicated by ambiguities that must be resolved or at least acknowledged. Since a work may include properties that can be organized conceptually according to more than one frame of reference, a judgment is required as to how the properties must be read" ("Hegel and Whitehead on Aesthetic Symbols": 243). He does not indicate, however, that for Hegel the ambiguities of interpretation appear much more vividly in the symbolic form of art than in his Ideal of Beauty. In the Ideal case the definite theme of a work makes sense of its every part, leaving room for scant ambiguity in its expression. It is in symbolic art, which lacks a content determinable as a whole, that ambiguities of meaning come to the fore.

5. Hegel's positioning of Kant's aesthetics under the symbolic form reflects his general disfavor for the critical philosophy. As was the case in the *Encyclopedia Philosophy of Mind*, where Hegel located Kant's account of cognition in the mid-level "Phenomenology," Hegel here positions Kant at a point in art's development prior to the realization of art's (as with cognition's) "true" significance. It will come as no surprise, then, to find that Hegel also locates the *sublime* at this decrepit beginning of art's unfolding, as we will soon see. It should be noted that Hegel positions Kantian aesthetics not only here, in the symbolic form, but in his discussion of "The Beauty of Nature," as well, which for Hegel can only offer an even "less Ideal" manifestation of beauty. Cf. LFA 116–152; 13:157–202.

6. As Stephen Bungay puts it, in symbolic art "The relationship between the form (signifier) of a symbol and its content (signified) is indeterminate, because it is not apparent exactly what the content is from the form, for they do not exhaust each other's determinacy. Symbolic art will therefore be enigmatic, for its meaning is indeterminate, the form and content in only partial unity" (*Beauty and Truth*: 57).

7. "Hegel on the Sublime," in *Displacement: Derrida and After*, ed. Mark Krupnick (Bloomington: Indiana University Press, 1983): 144.

8. Ibid.

9. Emphases added.

10. Hegel writes that in such products of *Phantasie* "picture and meaning are contrasted with one another instead of being moulded into one another. . . . [Works] of art which make this form their foundation remain therefore of a subordinate kind, and their content cannot be the Absolute itself but some different and restricted situation or occurrence" (LFA 321; 13:417).

11. In his account of "Comparisons Which Start from the Meaning," Hegel discusses riddle, allegory, metaphor, image, and simile, the last three of which he considers "comparison proper." For reasons of economy, I will pass over his brief discussions of allegory and image. But there are other reasons: Hegelian allegory reflects too great a dependence on abstract determinations, and his remarks on the image too derivative a relation to metaphor, to advance the discussion much.

12. As we saw in chapter 5, Hegel remarks that in association, "Wit connects ideas which, although remote from one another, none the less have in fact an inner connection" (PM §455 Zu).

13. Note that Hegel opposes the inventive connections of metaphor to what is *habitual,* given over to fixed rules. The opposition repeats the anthropological contrast between the associative play of the sleeping soul and the habit-forming activity of nascent generalizing imagination.

14. Gary Shapiro emphasizes the indeterminacy of metaphorical meaning as an Hegelian symbolic form: "A metaphor has both primary and secondary subjects which are juxtaposed in such a way as to create a novel spectrum of possible meanings which could not be expressed by a literal comparison. Such forms however testify to their own incompleteness, for they point to a fulfilled meaning which, by hypothesis, can never be made present" ("Hegel on Implicit and Dialectical Meanings of Poetry," in *Art and Logic in Hegel's Philosophy,* W. E. Steinkraus and K. Schmitz, eds. [Atlantic Highlands, N.J.: Humanities Press, 1980]: 38).

15. When discussing poetry in his "System of the Individual Arts," Hegel notes that the extensive use of metaphor in symbolic poetry indicates that "its symbolic procedure necessitates a wide search for kinships, and to accompany its universal meanings it provides a great multitude of concrete and comparable phenomena" (LFA 1004; 15:279). The passage begs comparison to the "multitude of kindred presentations" produced, according to Kant, by an aesthetic idea.

16. *Kunst und Subjektivität in Hegels Ästhetik* (Kronberg: Scriptor Verlag, 1976): 58. Hartwig Zander also considers the anthropological subjectivity of symbolic art; see *Hegels Kunstphilosophie* (Wuppertal: Aloys Henn Verlag, 1970): 94.

17. "Art: Death and Transfiguration," *Review of National Literatures* 1 (1970): 154. Robert Wicks makes the point that the value of romantic art will be judged differently from the points of view of art and philosophy. While romantic art represents, for Hegel, a decline from the classical Ideal, it makes progress toward the realization of philosophical ideals, which classical art cannot: "In relation to the purpose of art, classical art has a greater capacity for beauty than romantic art; in relation to the purpose of spiritual development, romantic art has a greater capacity for spirituality than classical art" (*Hegel's Theory of Aesthetic Judgment*: 125). I will be considering romantic art from the perspective of an aesthetics of indeterminacy for which this art form's decline in relation to Hegel's conception of the purpose of art will be a virtue.

18. "Art: Death and Transfiguration": 157.

19. As an historical phenomenon, Hegel understands "romantic art" to stretch from early Church spiritual art to his own romantic present. It will be in the late phenomena he takes to characterize the artistic condition of romanticism in his own time that we will find another articulation of reflective judgment's production of aesthetic unity.

20. Hegel treats "The Religious Domain of Romantic Art" at LFA 530–551; 14:142–169.

21. Hegel treats "Chivalry" at LFA 552–572; 14:169–194. He is clearly straining to have "romantic art" encompass many centuries of cultural production.

22. In this passage from Hegel's discussion of "subjective humor," note the connection between the derangement [*Verrücken*] of its sporting and the associative play that led to madness [*Verrücktheit*] in the *Encyclopedia* "Anthropology." The connection is developed further below.

23. Part Two as a whole is Hegel's "Development of the Ideal into the Particular Forms of Art," namely the symbolic, classical, and the romantic. The "Dissolution of the Romantic Form of Art" (LFA 593–611; 14:220–242) is the last of three sections comprising the chapter "The Formal Independence of Individual Characteristics." The first two sections, "The Independence of the Individual Character" and "Adventures" trace the fall of romantic art into an ever greater satisfaction in crass particularity and contingency, in both the subjective and exterior spheres. I will focus on the final section, where romantic art breaks down into reveling in the total contingency of subjective caprice and external chance.

24. Commenting on this passage, Stephen Houlgate identifies subjective humor with the "romantic irony" Hegel castigates in his introduction to the *Lectures*. Cf. *Freedom, Truth and History*: 171, and LFA 64–69; 13:93–99. Hegel thinks that this irony, embraced by Friedrich von Schlegel, originates in the Fichtean standpoint, which valorizes the arbitrary creative potential of the subjective ego on which everything is made to depend for its existence. Houlgate continues Hegel's castigation of romantic irony in "Hegel and the 'End' of Art," *The Owl of Minerva* 29 (1997): 1–21.

25. This observation recalls the chapter 4 example of paranoia, which shows that associations between far-flung phenomena are all too easily had. The remarkable internal consistency of Hegel's system is evidenced by the fact that the derangement of subjective humor is an aesthetic outgrowth of the very contingent play of the sleeping soul that led to madness.

26. Cf. PM §447 An, 194/247–248; §471 An, 231/291–292; §472 Zu, 232/293.

27. This result differs with Jean-Luc Nancy's conclusion that the sublime provides our best ammunition for opposing the Hegelian sublation of art by philosophy. Nancy has argued that the sublime "forms the exact reverse of the sublation of art" because it concerns the "presentation of liberty" rather than the end of philosophical truth. "The Sublime Offering," in *Of the Sublime: Presence in Question*, trans. Jeffrey S. Librett (Albany: State University of New York Press, 1993): 27–28. The recognition of subjective humor as a sublime moment, on the contrary, indicates that Hegel requires the sublime precisely to achieve that sublation. The destruction of the Idea of beauty by Hegel's sublime brings on the effort to recuperate the Idea in religion and philosophy.

28. In the unfolding of the symbolic, classical, and romantic forms of art into the "system of the individual arts," Hegel treats painting, music, and finally poetry as the three romantic arts. Hegel does not mean to say that these arts may not appear in the guise

of the other forms, but that they achieve their fullest expression when shaped by the prerogatives of the romantic form.

29. Recall that metaphor falls within the series of transitional forms that Hegel enumerates in this passage.

30. Translation slightly altered; emphasis added. Hegel also describes objective humor as an "ingenious freedom of imagination [*Phantasie*]," which evinces "a pure delight in the topics, an inexhaustible self-yielding of imagination [*Phantasie*]" (LFA 610–611; 14:241). Hegel treats objective humor as a product of *Phantasie* (rather than *Einbildungskraft*) throughout his brief discussion of it.

31. David Kolb writes, objective humor "does not show off the subjective facility of the author so much as the play inherent in the subject matter." *Postmodern Sophistications* (Chicago: University of Chicago Press, 1990): 193, n.6.

32. "Art: Death and Transfiguration": 162–163.

33. "Hegel on the Future of Art," *Review of Metaphysics* 27 (1974): 692.

34. "Hegels These vom Ende der Kunst und der 'Klassizismus' der Ästhetik," *Hegel-Studien* 19 (1984): 237. Gethmann-Siefert does not mention objective humor by name, but in the context it is clear that she is referring to it.

35. "Hegel's Aesthetics: Yesterday and Today," in *Art and Logic in Hegel's Philosophy*, eds. Warren Steinkraus and Kenneth Schmitz (New Jersey: Humanities Press, 1980): 30.

36. "Hegels These vom Ende der Kunst und der 'Klassizismus' der Ästhetik": 237.

37. "Art and Philosophy of Art Today: Reflections with Reference to Hegel," in *New Perspectives in German Literary Criticism*, eds. Richard Amacher and Victor Lange (Princeton: Princeton University Press, 1979). Bubner criticizes Henrich's attempt here to interpret current features of cultural production in terms of objective humor. Bubner argues that the notion should not be taken seriously because Hegel mentions it only once or twice in the hundreds of pages of his aesthetic theory, and it represents a very late and undeveloped addition to Hegel's ideas, first appearing in a published work in his Hamann review of 1828. Indeed, there we find Hegel adding little to our understanding of objective humor: he only contrasts the "self-complacency, subjective particularities, and trivial content" of Hamann's humor with the objective humor of a Hippel, in whom "humor blooms into ingenious form, into a talent for emphasizing the most individuated figures, the finest and deepest emotions, philosophically considered ideas, original characters, situations, and outcomes" ("Hamanns Schriften," in *Werke* [Frankfurt: Suhrkamp, 1970]: v. 11, p. 336). But since my aim is to articulate the reflective production of aesthetic unity, rather than to maintain a firm allegiance to Hegel's speculative system, Henrich's reflections on objective humor will be of considerable help.

38. Ibid., 115.

39. Ibid.

40. Ibid., 117.

41. Ibid., 123–124.

42. Ibid., 126.

43. Ibid.

44. Hence I question Paul de Man's conclusion that the sublime "is self-destroying in a manner without precedent at any other stages of the dialectic" and that in it "there is nothing left to lift up or to uplift" ("Hegel on the Sublime": 151). De Man is referring to Hegel's symbolic-form account of the sublime. Its role there in the production of metaphor, and the recognition that Hegel's sublime participates in the positive romantic outcome of objective humor, as well, reveals an essential constructive role for the sublime.

45. In "The Unpresentable," Philippe Lacoue-Labarthe points to wit as one locus where heterogeneity and "insubordination to the spiritual" defy inclusion in a rational totality (cf. p. 157; p. 187, n. 21; p. 192, n. 71). The insubordination of wit consists, Lacoue-Labarthe argues, in its demand to be considered an end in itself: "The speculative cannot bear that anything nonspiritual be considered an 'end in itself'—be, if you will, *cut off* from the spiritual" (p. 157). Whatever the merit of Lacoue-Labarthe's position, my approach can be taken to resist the obsession with whether wit (or anything else) can cause Hegel's system to unwind. Instead, my reading has sought from Hegel aid in articulating an aesthetics of sublimity for purposes external to Hegel's systematic philosophy.

46. David Kolb discusses a "humble irony" that resembles true humor. It allows us to "enact our inhabitation in ways that convey our awareness of its fragility" (*Postmodern Sophistications*: 141). Kolb blunts the potential critical edge of recognizing contingency by insisting that "humble irony puts no directed pressure on beliefs or practices. A wry acknowledgement of the contingency and fragility of our world does not challenge it in any particular way" (pp. 141–142). I would argue that Hegel recognized the subversive power of humor to question necessity, as, for example, in the Roman satirists whose disdain for the pantheon of gods forms the final moment of the classical ideal (cf. LFA 512–516; 14:120–126). For further discussion of Kolb, see chapter 9.

47. Hence I offer a more positive interpretation of the art of romanticism's (now perpetual) end than does Stephen Houlgate, who launches a rear-guard assault on the irresponsibility of "modern ironists;" see "Hegel on the 'End' of Art." Richard Dean Winfield also discusses anticipations of a variety of recent artistic movements in Hegel's account of the demise of romantic art; see "Hegel, Romanticism, and Modernity," *The Owl of Minerva* 27 (1995): 14–15. He observes that the audience for romantic art, faced with the proliferation of artistic methods and practices, "cannot avoid confronting the problem of judging how to identify art"; the demise of romantic art gives rise to a circumstance in which "each act of reception may well involve a renewed judgment of where lie the limits of art" (p. 16). This continual reevaluation of what counts as art is of a piece with the free exercise of imagination embodied in a (sublime) aesthetic reflection unmoored from easy conceptual certainties.

Interlude: Wit and Judgment in Empiricist Aesthetics

1. Thomas Hobbes, *Leviathan*, ed. C. B. Macpherson (London: Penguin, 1968): 135.

2. Ibid., 136.

3. Ibid., 138.

4. Ibid., 115.

5. Ibid., 137.

6. See also Locke's famous condemnation of figurative language in Book 3, ch. 10 of his *Essay Concerning Human Understanding*, ed. Peter Nidditch (Oxford: Oxford University Press, 1975).

7. *A Treatise of Human Nature* (London: Penguin, 1969): 57; emphasis in original.

8. Ibid., 57–58.

9. Ibid., 58.

10. "On the Standard of Taste," in *Art and Its Significance*, ed. Stephen David Ross (Albany: State University of New York Press, 1994), 3d. ed: 86–87. Martin Kallich indicates that Hume expands on this position in his *Enquiry Concerning Human Understanding* by orienting the laws of association toward maintaining the unity of a work. Kallich writes: "To avoid chaos, each of the parts in a work of art must be connected and so 'form a kind of *Unity*, which may bring them under one plan or view'" (*The Association of Ideas and Critical Theory in Eighteenth-Century England* [The Hague: Mouton, 1970]: 89). I cite Kallich rather than Hume because Hume's comments on aesthetics and association in section three of the *Enquiry*, "Of the Connexion of Ideas," which originally comprised the bulk of the section, have been excluded from all editions that have appeared after 1770.

11. The fact that the French rationalist aestheticians also demanded strict unity and harmony in a work, though for different reasons, further indicates the uniqueness of Kant's position.

12. *A Philosophical Enquiry into the Origin of Our Ideas of the Sublime and the Beautiful*, ed. Adam Phillips (Oxford: Oxford University Press, 1990): 18.

13. Ibid.

14. Ibid., cf. Parts Two and Four. Martin Kallich confirms the role of association in Burke's theory of sublimity in *The Association of Ideas and Critical Theory in Eighteenth-Century England*: 145. And cf. Samuel Monk, *The Sublime: A Study of Critical Theories in XVIII-Century England* (New York: Modern Language Association, 1935): 93.

15. Samuel Monk argues that the growth of interest in the sublime in the late eighteenth century undermined the neoclassical aesthetic of strict unity and fixed purposes. Empiricist aestheticians favored that aesthetic despite their commitment to an associationism which would destroy neoclassicism (*The Sublime*: 103).

16. Gerard, *Essay on Genius* (London, 1774): 27.

17. Ibid., 46.

18. Ibid., 49–50.

19. Ibid., 81.

20. Ibid., 77, 71.

21. Cited in Kallich, *The Association of Ideas and Critical Theory in Eighteenth-Century England*: 260–261.

22. Both Jeffrey's *Essay on Beauty* and Alison's *Essays on the Nature and Principles of Taste* may be found in the volume *Essays on Beauty and Taste* (London: Ward, Lock and Co., 1925).

23. *Essay on Beauty*: 34.

24. Ibid., 35–36.

25. Such national differences explain why "white is thought a gay color in Europe, where it is used at weddings, and a dismal colour in China, where it is used for mourning; that we think yew trees gloomy, because they are planted in church-yards, and large masses of powdered horsehair majestic, because we see them on the heads of judges and bishops" (ibid., 36).

26. Ibid., 59–60.

27. Ibid., 61.

28. Despite the similarities, of course, the unification of the diverse, which artistic *Phantasie* accomplishes in the context of Hegel's system, is supposed to enjoy a greater justification and warrant than an empiricist philosopher could offer. Namely, imaginative artistry shares in the progressive comprehension and articulation of the Idea. Speculative reason completes that Idea with the help of art's efforts to lend spiritual depth to the sensuous. It is largely this Absolute justification Hegel grants art which makes all the difference between his philosophy of art and the aesthetics of his associationist predecessors.

29. Quoted in Martha Woodmansee, *The Author, Art, and the Market: Rereading the History of Aesthetics* (New York: Columbia University Press, 1994): 130–131. In the essay "The Uses of Kant in England," Woodmansee aims to show that Samuel Coleridge imported the Kantian aesthetic of disinterested taste into England to oppose the diversitarian implications of a purely associationist aesthetic. She makes a case that he was motivated by his poor sales and disappointment with his audience to oppose a theory that reduced aesthetic pleasure to whatever associative enjoyment each individual happens to gain from whatever entertainment happens to please them.

30. Ibid., 131–32.

31. *Anthropology from a Pragmatic Point of View*: 73.

32. Ibid.

Chapter 8

1. *Truth and Method*: 429.

2. Ibid., 432.

3. *The Rule of Metaphor*, trans. Robert Czerny (Toronto: University of Toronto Press, 1977): 196.

4. Ibid., 198.

5. Ibid., 194.

6. "The Metaphorical Process as Cognition, Imagination and Feeling," in *On Metaphor*, ed. Sheldon Sacks (Chicago, University of Chicago Press, 1979): 146.

7. *The Rule of Metaphor*. 197.

8. *The Romantic Sublime: Studies in the Structure and Psychology of Transcendence* (Baltimore: Johns Hopkins University Press, 1976).

9. Ibid., 4.

10. He in fact develops two varieties of sublimity, a "negative" one involved in the production of metaphor, and a "positive," "egotistical," or "metonymical" sublime. The distinction between the two forms relies on Roman Jakobson's famous differentiation of the metaphorical and metonymical functions of language. I will consider only Weiskel's "negative" sublime here.

11. Ibid., 26.

12. Ibid., 28.

13. Ibid., 31. Paul Crowther criticizes Weiskel's account of the metaphoricity of the sublime by arguing that one is overwhelmed in literature by narrative content, rather than by any profusion of underdetermined signifiers: "[If] we are overwhelmed, it is surely not by the profusion of signifiers, but rather by the narrative contents—for example, overwhelming images of power, desolation, endlessness, etc. which the signifiers evoke. This means, in other words, that in literature the dimension of excess occurs at the level of the signified. In fact, the only way that textual signifiers might fail to relate to a determinate signified is if (for whatever reason) we fail to understand the semantic code in which they are inscribed" (*Critical Aesthetics and Postmodernism* [Oxford: Oxford University Press, 1993]: 142). Crowther's argument reveals that he remains tied to the notion of an artistic sublime residing in archetypally sublime phenomena, such as the windswept mountainscape from which chapter 3 sought to relieve the artistic encounter with sublimity. I have argued that sublimity is felt at the level of signification in all cases where interpretation of a work, whatever its content, leaves imagination groping for a meaning it cannot determine from its rich and varied response to its object. When understood as a process of interpretation, imaginative reflection can fail to *determine* the meaning of a work no matter how well it grasps the "semantic code" from which it is composed.

14. *The Romantic Sublime*: 28.

15. *The Rule of Metaphor*: 239.

16. "The Metaphorical Process as Cognition, Imagination and Feeling": 152.

17. *Models and Metaphors* (Ithaca: Cornell University Press, 1962): 25–47. Black refined his view in "More About Metaphor," in *Metaphor and Thought*, ed. Andrew Ortony (Cambridge: Cambridge University Press, 1981).

18. Goodman, *Languages of Art* (Indianapolis: Hackett, 1976); Lakoff and Johnson, *Metaphors We Live By* (Chicago: University of Chicago Press, 1980); Eva Kittay, *Metaphor: Its Cognitive Force and Linguistic Structure* (Oxford: Oxford University Press, 1987). See also Carl Hausman, *Metaphor and Art* (Cambridge: Cambridge University Press, 1989) for a thorough defense of interactionism and its ontological implications.

19. *Models and Metaphors*: 40. I have taken the liberty of pluralizing Black's metaphor "man is a wolf."

20. More recent theorists such as Lakoff and Johnson or Kittay replace talk of "associated commonplaces" with more elaborate accounts of transferred "entailments," "semantic fields," or other devices. See Lakoff and Johnson, *Metaphors We Live By*: chaps. 2–3, 15–18; Kittay, *Metaphor*. chaps. 6 and 7.

21. *Languages of Art*: 74.

22. Black, "More About Metaphor": 29.

23. I include "in principle" because vivid and striking metaphors will likely provide a more open-ended interpretive exercise than a tired metaphor such as "men are pigs." I will return to this issue in the next chapter, where casting it in terms of interpretation will better position me to raise a set of related concerns.

24. I owe the "Juliet-the-sun" locution to Hausman; see *Metaphor and Art*, chap. 3.

25. See, for example, Goodman, *Languages of Art*: chap. 2; and Arthur Danto, *The Transfiguration of the Commonplace* (Cambridge: Harvard University Press, 1981): chap. 7. Hausman proposes a theory of art as metaphor, in the interactionist vein, in *Metaphor and Art*: chaps. 4 and 5.

26. Nuyen argues that a Kantian symbol creates in the strong sense rather than the weak ("The Kantian Theory of Metaphor": 99). I do not think this is compatible with the analogical, comparison-making form of Kant's symbol. As was noted in chapter 3, Nuyen neglects to mention analogy in his interpretation of Kant.

27. *Models and Metaphors*: 37. Recall Ricoeur's remark: "the enigma of metaphorical discourse is that it 'invents' in both senses of the word: what it creates, it discovers; and what it finds, it invents" (*The Rule of Metaphor*. 239). Lakoff and Johnson discuss "metaphor-induced similarity" arising out of both conventional and new metaphors; see *Metaphors We Live By*: 147–155.

28. Black, "More About Metaphor": 39.

29. Ibid., 39–40.

30. *Imagination and Interpretation in Kant*: 118–129.

31. I owe the example to Amy Binder and Tim Self.

32. John McDowell's *Mind and World* (Cambridge: Harvard University Press, 1996) interprets Kant as the philosopher in which conceptual spontaneity and empirical intuition meld, though it becomes clear that it is ultimately a Hegelian image which

McDowell has in mind. The Hegelian subtext stresses the spontaneity the Kantian subject enacts in giving conceptual *determinacy* to the world; my elaboration of Kant's aesthetic theory indicates that that subject also freely interprets the world through the conceptually *indeterminate* production of aesthetic ideas and metaphor. See the further discussion in chapter 9.

33. *The Encyclopedia Logic*: §3 Zu, pp. 26–27; translation altered.

34. "What Metaphors Mean," in *Inquiries into Truth and Interpretation* (Oxford: Basil Blaskwell, 1984).

35. Ibid., 245.

36. Ibid., 262.

37. Ibid., 247. In "A Nice Derangement of Epitaphs," Davidson seems more willing to countenance a more mutual influence of semantic and pragmatic features of language. See *Truth and Interpretation*, ed. Ernest LePore (Oxford: Basil Blackwell, 1986): 433–446.

38. "What Metaphors Mean": 257.

39. Goodman, "Metaphor as Moonlighting," in *On Metaphor*: 178.

40. Black, "How Metaphors Work: A Reply to Davidson," in *On Metaphor*: 181–192.

41. Novitz, *Knowledge, Fiction, and Imagination* (Philadelphia: Temple University Press, 1987): chaps. 7–8. In the process Novitz effectively denies the open-endedness of metaphorical meaning, since specifying the T-sentence for a metaphor entails listing the bounded set of conditions which would make its claim true.

42. Kittay, *Metaphor*: chap. 3. A detailed consideration of her theory of semantic fields and metaphor's role in forging new linkages through and across those fields would show her approach to metaphor to have much in common with the broad conception of sublime understanding I have sought to advance.

43. "Radical Interpretation," in *Inquiries into Truth and Interpretation*: 127.

44. "On the Very Idea of a Conceptual Scheme," in *Inquiries into Truth and Interpretation*: 196.

45. In *Philosophy and Truth: Selections from Nietzsche's Notebooks of the Early 1870s*, trans. and ed. Daniel Breazeale (Atlantic Highlands, N.J.: Humanities Press, 1979): 85.

46. Ibid., 82.

47. Ibid., 83.

48. Ibid.

49. Ibid., 84, 86.

50. "The Epistemology of Metaphor," in *On Metaphor*. Samuel Wheeler has claimed that de Man and Davidson's conceptions of metaphor actually converge on the propo-

sition that all predication is essentially figuration. See "Metaphor According to Davidson and deMan," in *Redrawing the Lines: Analytic Philosophy, Deconstruction, and Literary
Theory,* ed. Reed Way Dasenbrock (Minneapolis: University of Minnesota Press, 1989):
116–139.

51. I have presented Pluhar's translation rather than de Man's; the emphasis, however,
is de Man's.

52. "The Epistemology of Metaphor": 25.

53. Ibid., 26. Derrida makes a similar argument in "White Mythology: Metaphor in the
Text of Philosophy," in *Margins of Philosophy.* He does not present the argument as a critique of Kant, but he makes a case that the very distinction between the metaphorical
and the conceptual literal is itself based on a kind of metaphoricity. Contrary to de
Man's aim, however, Derrida does not seek to collapse the literal into the metaphori-
cal, but rather to destabilize the distinction to such an extent that *neither* pole can
offer a founding precedent. I cannot undertake here a thorough consideration of
Derrida's complex position; for an excellent discussion, see Rodolphe Gasché, *The
Tain of the Mirror: Derrida and the Philosophy of Reflection* (Cambridge: Harvard University
Press, 1986): 293–318.

54. "Metaphor as Rhetoric: The Problem of Evaluation" in *On Metaphor*: 61.

55. Ibid., 63.

56. *Metaphors We Live By*: 3.

57. Ibid., 4.

58. For numerous examples of these metaphors see *Metaphors We Live By*: 14–17.

59. Ibid., 25–28.

60. Ibid., 49.

61. Ibid., 139–141.

62. Ibid., 141.

63. Put another way: not every tea-soaked madeleine evokes an infinite remembrance.

Chapter 9

1. See *Validity in Interpretation* (New Haven: Yale University Press, 1967).

2. Compare Hirsch: "It may be asserted as a general rule that whenever a reader confronts two interpretations which impose different emphases on similar meaning components, at least one of the interpretations must be wrong" (*Validity in Interpretation*:
230).

3. Eco, *The Open Work,* trans. Anna Cancogni (Cambridge: Harvard University Press,
1989): 4.

Notes

4. Ibid., 103.

5. Ibid., 19.

6. Ibid., 65.

7. *A Theory of Art: Inexhaustibility by Contrast* (Albany: State University of New York Press, 1982): 19, 4.

8. Ibid., 63, 195. Despite these similarities between their views, it should be noted that Ross explicitly rejects Kant's aesthetic transcendentalism, most importantly for the reason that "[The] theory of contrast emphasizes the fecundity, inexhaustibility, and novelty of contrasts in a historical and lived context as Kant's theory of the pure aesthetic judgment cannot" (p. 8). My own Kant-inspired model of sublime reflection is compatible with Ross's emphasis on historical situatedness, however distant this may be from the strictures of Kant's pure judgment of taste.

9. Ross treats metaphor as an intramedial contrast in which opposed terms are juxtaposed to revelatory effect: "In a metaphor . . . two obviously unlike terms are brought into identity, and the force of the connection either produces a remarkable intensity of contrast or dissipates itself entirely" (p. 127).

10. Ross discusses these types of contrast at pp. 117–147.

11. *A Theory of Art*: 38.

12. Ibid., 62.

13. Ibid., 84–85.

14. Lyotard, "The Sublime and the Avant-Garde," in *The Inhuman*: 91.

15. *The Open Work*: 21.

16. Albrecht Wellmer considers the challenge to rational unity posed by postmodern cultural forms in "The Dialectic of Modernism and Postmodernism: The Critique of Reason Since Adorno," in *The Persistence of Modernity: Essays on Aesthetics, Ethics, and Postmodernism*, trans. David Midgley (Cambridge, Mass.: MIT Press, 1991).

17. Eco, "Joyce, Semiosis, and Semiotics," in *The Limits of Interpretation* (Bloomington: Indiana University Press, 1990): 143.

18. Ibid., 140.

19. See Eco's "mapping" of these links as a net of connections: ibid., 141.

20. See also Wellmer's discussion of *Finnegan's Wake* in "The Dialectic of Modernism and Postmodernism": 54–55.

21. See Charles Jencks, *The Language of Post-Modern Architecture* (New York: Rizzoli, 1981).

Notes

22. See Robert Venturi, Denise Scott Brown, and Steven Izenour, *Learning from Las Vegas* (Cambridge, Mass.: MIT Press, 1977).

23. Nietzsche, *Human, All Too Human*, trans. R. J. Hollingdale (Cambridge: Cambridge University Press, 1988): 239.

24. *The Open Work*: 90.

25. Lyotard, "Answering the Question: What is Postmodernism?" trans. Régis Durand, in *The Postmodern Condition*, trans. Geoff Bennington and Brian Massumi (Minneapolis: University of Minnesota Press, 1984): 77.

26. Ibid., 78, 79.

27. Ibid., 79.

28. Ibid., 81.

29. Ibid.

30. David Kolb, *The Critique of Pure Modernity* (Chicago: University of Chicago Press, 1986): 268.

31. Ibid., 249.

32. Ibid., 270.

33. Ibid., 141–142.

34. *Ways of Worldmaking* (Indianapolis: Hackett, 1978): 7.

35. Ibid., 7–17. Goodman does not claim this to be an exhaustive list of worldmaking methods.

36. Ibid., 97.

37. Ibid., 20.

38. Ibid., 97.

39. Ibid., 100.

40. *Mind and World*: 84 (emphasis added), 78, 88.

41. Ibid., 126.

42. Ibid., 98. Read in context, it is clear that McDowell wants to claim that immersion in a tradition *is* a respectable mode of access to the real.

43. Ibid., 155.

44. Ibid., 98. McDowell's passing appeals to Hegel are found on pp. 43, 83, 111.

45. *Ways of Worldmaking*: 94.

46. In addition to Nietzsche, of course, Gadamer claims that "all understanding is interpretation" in *Truth and Method*: 389. Stanley Fish poses the challenge that "interpretation is the only game in town" in *Is There a Text in This Class?* (Cambridge, Mass.: Harvard University Press, 1980): 355.

47. Richard Shusterman argues against interpretation going "all the way down." See "Beneath Interpretation," in *The Interpretive Turn: Philosophy, Science, Culture*, David R. Hiley, James F. Bohman, and Richard Shusterman, eds. (Ithaca, N.Y.: Cornell University Press, 1991).

48. Bourdieu, *Distinction: A Social Critique of the Judgment of Taste*, trans. Richard Nice (Cambridge: Harvard University Press, 1984): 493. For a Bourdieu-inspired critique of "taste" in Hume and Kant, see Richard Shusterman, "Of the Scandal of Taste: Social Privilege as Nature in the Aesthetic Theories of Hume and Kant," *Philosophical Forum* 20 (1989): 211–229.

49. Ibid., 491.

50. Bourdieu, "The Historical Genesis of a Pure Aesthetic," trans. Charles Newman, in *The Field of Cultural Production*, ed. Randal Johnson (New York: Columbia University Press, 1993): 255–256.

51. *Distinction*: 498, 499.

Bibliography

Alison, Archibald. *Essays on the Nature and Principles of Taste*. In *Essays on Beauty and Taste*. 5th edition. London: Ward, Lock and Co., 1925.

Aristotle. *Poetics*. Translated by Richard Janko. Indianapolis: Hackett, 1987.

Bernstein, J. M. *The Fate of Art: Aesthetic Alienation from Kant to Derrida and Adorno*. University Park: Pennsylvania State University Press, 1992.

Berthold-Bond, Daniel. *Hegel's Theory of Madness*. Albany: State University of New York Press, 1995.

Black, Max. "How Metaphors Work: A Reply to Davidson." In *On Metaphor*. Edited by Sheldon Sacks. Chicago: University of Chicago Press, 1979.

Black, Max. *Models and Metaphors*. Ithaca, N.Y.: Cornell University Press, 1962.

Black, Max. "More About Metaphor." In *Metaphor and Thought*. Edited by Andrew Ortony. Cambridge: Cambridge University Press, 1981.

Booth, Wayne. "Metaphor as Rhetoric: The Problem of Evaluation." In *On Metaphor*. Edited by Sheldon Sacks. Chicago: University of Chicago Press, 1979.

Bourdieu, Pierre. *Distinction: A Social Critique of the Judgment of Taste*. Translated by Richard Nice. Cambridge: Harvard University Press, 1984.

Bourdieu, Pierre. *The Field of Cultural Production*. Edited by Randal Johnson. New York: Columbia University Press, 1993.

Bubner, Rüdiger. "Hegel's Aesthetics: Yesterday and Today." In *Art and Logic in Hegel's Philosophy*. Edited by Warren Steinkraus and Kenneth Schmitz. Atlantic Highlands, N.J.: Humanities Press, 1980.

Bungay, Stephen. *Beauty and Truth: A Study of Hegel's Aesthetics*. Oxford: Oxford University Press, 1984.

Burke, Edmund. *A Philosophical Enquiry into the Origin of Our Ideas of the Sublime and the Beautiful.* Edited by Adam Phillips. Oxford: Oxford University Press, 1990.

Carroll, David. *Paraesthetics.* New York: Methuen, 1987.

Carter, Curtis. "Hegel and Whitehead on Aesthetic Symbols." In *Hegel and Whitehead.* Edited by George R. Lucas. Albany: State University of New York Press, 1986.

Carter, Curtis. "A Re-examination of the 'Death of Art' Interpretation of Hegel's Aesthetics." In *Art and Logic in Hegel's Philosophy.* Edited by Warren Steinkraus and Kenneth Schmitz. Atlantic Highlands, N.J.: Humanities Press, 1980.

Caygill, Howard. *Art of Judgment.* Oxford: Basil Blackwell, 1989.

Cohen, Ted and Paul Guyer (eds.). *Essays in Kant's Aesthetics.* Chicago: University of Chicago Press, 1982.

Coleman, Francis. *The Harmony of Reason: A Study in Kant's Aesthetics.* Pittsburgh: University of Pittsburgh Press, 1974.

Crawford, Donald. *Kant's Aesthetic Theory.* Madison: University of Wisconsin Press, 1974.

Crawford, Donald. "Kant's Theory of Creative Imagination." In *Essays in Kant's Aesthetics.* Edited by Ted Cohen and Paul Guyer. Chicago: University of Chicago Press, 1982.

Crawford, Donald. "The Place of the Sublime in Kant's Aesthetic Theory." In *The Philosophy of Immanuel Kant.* Edited by Richard Kennington. Washington, D.C.: Catholic University of America Press, 1985.

Crowther, Paul. "The Aesthetic Domain: Locating the Sublime." *British Journal of Aesthetics* 29 (1989): 21-31.

Crowther, Paul. *Critical Aesthetics and Postmodernism.* Oxford: Oxford University Press, 1993.

Crowther, Paul. *The Kantian Sublime.* Oxford: Oxford University Press, 1989.

Crowther, Paul. "The Significance of Kant's Pure Aesthetic Judgment." *British Journal of Aesthetics* 36 (1996): 109–121.

Danto, Arthur. *After the End of Art: Contemporary Art and the Pale of History.* Princeton, N.J.: Princeton University Press, 1997.

Danto, Arthur. *The Philosophical Disenfranchisement of Art.* New York: Columbia University Press, 1986.

Danto, Arthur. *The Transfiguration of the Commonplace.* Cambridge, Mass.: Harvard University Press, 1981.

Davidson, Donald. *Inquiries into Truth and Interpretation.* Oxford: Basil Blackwell, 1984.

Bibliography

Davidson, Donald. "A Nice Derangement of Epitaphs." In *Truth and Interpretation*. Edited by Ernest LePore. Oxford: Basil Blackwell, 1986.

Deleuze, Gilles. *Kant's Critical Philosophy*. Translated by Hugh Tomlinson and Barbara Habberjam. Minneapolis: University of Minnesota Press, 1984.

de Man, Paul. "The Epistemology of Metaphor." In *On Metaphor*. Edited by Sheldon Sacks. Chicago: University of Chicago Press, 1979.

de Man, Paul. "Hegel on the Sublime." In *Displacement: Derrida and After*. Edited by Mark Krupnick. Bloomington: Indiana University Press, 1983.

de Man, Paul. "Reply to Raymond Geuss." *Critical Inquiry* 10 (December 1983): 383–390.

de Man, Paul. "Sign and Symbol in Hegel's Aesthetics." *Critical Inquiry* 8 (Summer 1982): 761–775.

Derrida, Jacques. "The Pit and the Pyramid: Introduction to Hegel's Semiology." In *Margins of Philosophy*. Translated by Alan Bass. Chicago: University of Chicago Press, 1982.

Derrida, Jacques. "The *Retrait* of Metaphor." *Enclitic* 2 (1978): 5–33.

Derrida, Jacques. *The Truth in Painting*. Translated by Geoff Bennington and Ian McLeod. Chicago: University of Chicago Press, 1987.

Derrida, Jacques. "White Mythology: Metaphor in the Text of Philosophy." In *Margins of Philosophy*. Translated by Alan Bass. Chicago: University of Chicago Press, 1982.

Desmond, William. *Art and the Absolute*. Albany: State University of New York Press, 1986.

Desmond, William. "Art, Philosophy and Concreteness in Hegel." *The Owl of Minerva* 16 (Spring 1985): 131–146.

de Vries, Willem. *Hegel's Theory of Mental Activity*. Ithaca: Cornell University Press, 1988.

Dickie, George. *The Century of Taste: The Philosophical Odyssey of Taste in the Eighteenth Century*. Oxford: Oxford University Press, 1996.

D'Oro, Giuseppina. "Beauties of Nature and Beauties of Art: On Kant and Hegel's Aesthetics." *Bulletin of the Hegel Society of Great Britain* 33 (1996): 70–86.

Düsing, Klaus. "Ästhetische Einbildungskraft und Intuitiver Verstand." *Hegel-Studien* 21 (1986): 87–128.

Eagleton, Terry. *The Ideology of the Aesthetic*. Oxford: Basil Blackwell, 1990.

Eco, Umberto. *Interpretation and Overinterpretation*. Edited by Stefan Collini. Cambridge: Cambridge University Press, 1992.

Eco, Umberto. *The Limits of Interpretation*. Bloomington: Indiana University Press, 1990.

Eco, Umberto. *The Open Work*. Translated by Anna Cancogni. Cambridge, Mass.: Harvard University Press, 1989.

Engell, James. *The Creative Imagination*. Cambridge, Mass.: Harvard University Press, 1981.

Fenves, Peter. "Taking Stock of the Kantian Sublime." *Eighteenth-Century Studies* 28 (1994): 65–82.

Ferry, Luc. *Homo Aestheticus*. Chicago: University of Chicago Press, 1993.

Fetscher, Iring. *Hegels Lehre vom Menschen*. Stuttgart: Fromann, 1970.

Fish, Stanley. *Is There a Text in This Class?* Cambridge, Mass.: Harvard University Press, 1980.

Fricke, Christel. "Explaining the Inexplicable: The Hypotheses of the Faculty of Reflective Judgement in Kant's Third Critique." *Noûs* 24 (1990): 45–62.

Friedman, Michael. *Kant and the Exact Sciences*. Cambridge, Mass.: Harvard University Press, 1992.

Gadamer, Hans Georg. *Truth and Method*. Translated by Joel Weinsheimer and Donald G. Marshall. 2nd edition. New York: Crossroads, 1989.

Gardiner, Patrick. "Kant and Hegel on Aesthetics." In *Hegel's Critique of Kant*. Edited by Stephen Priest. Oxford: Oxford University Press, 1987.

Gasché, Rodolphe. *The Tain of the Mirror: Derrida and the Philosophy of Reflection*. Cambridge, Mass.: Harvard University Press, 1986.

Genova, Anthony C. "Kant's Complex Problem of Reflective Judgment." *Review of Metaphysics* 23 (1970): 452–480.

Gerard, Alexander. *Essay on Genius*. London, 1774.

Gethmann-Siefert, Annemarie. "Hegels These vom Ende der Kunst und der 'Klassizismus' der Ästhetik." *Hegel-Studien* 19 (1984): 205–258.

Geuss, Raymond. "A Response to Paul de Man." *Critical Inquiry* 10 (983): 375–382.

Gibbons, Sarah. *Kant's Theory of Imagination*. Oxford: Oxford University Press, 1994.

Ginsborg, Hannah. "Purposiveness and Normativity." In *Proceedings of the Eighth International Kant Congress*, v. 2, pt. 1. Edited by Hoke Robinson. Milwaukee: Marquette University Press, 1995.

Ginsborg, Hannah. "Reflective Judgment and Taste." *Noûs* 24 (1990): 63–78.

Goodman, Nelson. *Languages of Art*. Indianapolis: Hackett, 1976.

Goodman, Nelson. "Metaphor as Moonlighting." In *On Metaphor*. Edited by Sheldon Sacks. Chicago: University of Chicago Press, 1979.

363

Bibliography

Goodman, Nelson. *Ways of Worldmaking*. Indianapolis: Hackett, 1978.

Gotschalk, D.W. "Form and Expression in Kant's Aesthetics." *The British Journal of Aesthetics* 7 (1967): 250–260.

Gracyk, Theodore. "Art, Nature and Purposiveness in Kant's Aesthetic Theory." In *Proceedings of the Eighth International Kant Congress*, v. 2, pt. 2. Edited by Hoke Robinson. Milwaukee: Marquette University Press, 1995.

Greene, Murray. *Hegel on the Soul: A Speculative Anthropology*. The Hague: Martinus Nijhoff, 1972.

Guyer, Paul. "Beauty, Sublimity, and Expression: Reply to Wicks and Cantrick." *The Journal of Aesthetics and Art Criticism* 53 (1995): 194–195.

Guyer, Paul. "Formalism and the Theory of Expression in Kant's Aesthetics." *Kant-Studien* 68 (1977): 46–70.

Guyer, Paul. "Hegel on Kant's Aesthetics: Necessity and Contingency in Beauty and Art." In *Kant and the Experience of Freedom: Essays on Aesthetics and Morality*. Cambridge: Cambridge University Press, 1993.

Guyer, Paul. *Kant and the Claims of Taste*. Cambridge, Mass.: Harvard University Press, 1979.

Guyer, Paul. "Kant's Conception of Fine Art." *The Journal of Aesthetics and Art Criticism* 52 (1994): 275–285.

Guyer, Paul. "Kant's Distinction between the Beautiful and the Sublime." *Review of Metaphysics* 35 (1982): 753–784.

Hance, Allen. "The Art of Nature: Hegel and the *Critique of Judgment*." *International Journal of Philosophical Studies* 6 (1998): 37–65.

Harries, Karsten. "Hegel on the Future of Art." *Review of Metaphysics* 27 (1973–1974): 677–696.

Harris, Errol. "Hegel's Anthropology." *The Owl of Minerva* 25 (1993): 5–14.

Harris, H.S. "The Resurrection of Art." *The Owl of Minerva* 16 (1984): 5–20.

Hartley, David. *Observations on Man, His Frame, His Duty, and His Expectations*. 5th edition. London: Wilkie and Robinson, 1810.

Hausman, Carl. *Metaphor and Art*. Cambridge: Cambridge University Press, 1989.

Hegel, G. W. F. *The Encyclopedia Logic*. Translated by T. F. Geraets, W. A. Suchting, and H. S. Harris. Indianapolis: Hackett, 1991.

Hegel, G. W. F. *Enzyklopädie der philosophischen Wissenschaften im Grundrisse (1830)*. Vols. 8–10 in *Werke in zwanzig Bänden*. Edited by E. Moldenhauer and K. M. Michel. Frankfurt: Suhrkamp, 1970.

Bibliography

Hegel, G. W. F. *Faith and Knowledge*. Translated by Walter Cerf and H. S. Harris. Albany: State University of New York Press, 1977.

Hegel, G. W. F. *Glauben und Wissen*. Hamburg: Felix Meiner Verlag, 1986.

Hegel, G. W. F. "Hamanns Schriften." In *Werke in zwanzig Bänden*, vol. 11: *Berliner Schriften, 1818–1831*. Edited by E. Moldenhauer and K. M. Michel. Frankfurt: Suhrkamp, 1970.

Hegel, G. W. F. *Hegel's Aesthetics: Lectures on Fine Art*. Translated by T. M. Knox. 2 vols. Oxford: Oxford University Press, 1975.

Hegel, G. W. F. *Hegel's Philosophy of Mind: Being Part Three of the Encyclopedia of the Philosophical Sciences*. Translated by William Wallace. Oxford: Oxford University Press, 1971.

Hegel, G. W. F. *Vorlesungen über die Ästhetik*. Vols. 13–15 in *Werke in zwanzig Bänden*. Edited by E. Moldenhauer and K. M. Michel. Frankfurt: Suhrkamp, 1970.

Heidegger, Martin. *Kant and the Problem of Metaphysics*. Translated by Richard Taft. 4th edition. Bloomington: Indiana University Press, 1990.

Helferich, Christoph. *Kunst und Subjektivität in Hegels Ästhetik*. Kronberg: Scriptor Verlag, 1976.

Henrich, Dieter. "Art and Philosophy of Art Today: Reflections with Reference to Hegel." In *New Perspectives in German Literary Criticism*. Edited by Richard Amacher and Victor Lange. Princeton: Princeton University Press, 1979.

Henrich, Dieter. "The Contemporary Relevance of Hegel's Aesthetics." In *Hegel*. Edited by Michael Inwood. Oxford: Oxford University Press, 1985.

Henrich, Dieter. "Hegels Theorie über den Zufall." *Kant-Studien* 50 (1958–59): 131–148.

Henrich, Dieter. "Kant's Notion of a Deduction and the Methodological Background of the First *Critique*." In *Kant's Transcendental Deductions*. Edited by Eckhardt Förster. Stanford: Stanford University Press, 1989.

Henrich, Dieter. "Zur Aktualität von Hegels Ästhetik." *Hegel-Studien* supp. 11 (1974): 295–301.

Hirsch, E. D. *Validity in Interpretation*. New Haven: Yale University Press, 1967.

Hobbes, Thomas. *Leviathan*. Edited by C. B. Macpherson. London: Penguin, 1968.

Hofstadter, Albert. "Art: Death and Transfiguration." *Review of National Literatures* 1 (1970): 149–164.

Hösle, Vittorio. *Hegels System*. 2 vols. Hamburg: Felix Meiner Verlag, 1988.

Houlgate, Stephen. *Freedom, Truth and History: An Introduction to Hegel's Philosophy*. London: Routledge, 1991.

Houlgate, Stephen. "Hegel and the 'End' of Art." *The Owl of Minerva* 29 (1997): 1–21.

Houlgate, Stephen. "Necessity and Contingency in Hegel's *Science of Logic.*" *The Owl of Minerva* 27 (1995): 37–49.

Hume, David. *An Enquiry Concerning Human Understanding.* Edited by Eric Steinberg. Indianapolis: Hackett, 1993.

Hume, David. "On the Standard of Taste." In *Art and its Significance.* Edited by Stephen David Ross. 3rd edition. Albany: State University of New York Press, 1994.

Hume, David. *A Treatise of Human Nature.* Edited by Ernest Mossner. London: Penguin, 1969.

Hutchings, Patrick. "Flowers as 'Free Beauties of Nature.'" *Literature and Aesthetics* 4 (1994): 30.

Jeffrey, Francis. *Essay on Beauty.* In *Essays on Beauty and Taste.* 5th edition. London: Ward, Lock and Co., 1925.

Jencks, Charles. *The Language of Post-Modern Architecture.* New York: Rizzoli, 1981.

Johnson, Mark (ed.). *Philosophical Perspectives on Metaphor.* Minneapolis: University of Minnesota Press, 1981.

Kallich, Martin. *The Association of Ideas and Critical Theory in Eighteenth-Century England.* The Hague: Mouton, 1970.

Kant, Immanuel. *Anthropologie in pragmatische Hinsicht.* Vol. 6 in *Werke in sechs Bänden.* Wiesbaden: Insel Verlag, 1964.

Kant, Immanuel. *Anthropology from a Pragmatic Point of View.* Translated by Mary J. Gregor. The Hague: Martinus Nijhoff, 1974.

Kant, Immanuel. *Critique of Judgment.* Translated by Werner S. Pluhar. Indianapolis: Hackett, 1987.

Kant, Immanuel. *Critique of Pure Reason.* Translated by Werner S. Pluhar. Indianapolis: Hackett, 1996.

Kant, Immanuel. *Erste Fassung der Einleitung in die Kritik der Urteilskraft.* Vol. 5 in *Werke in sechs Bänden.* Wiesbaden: Insel Verlag, 1964.

Kant, Immanuel. *Kritik der Urteilskraft.* Vol. 5 in *Kants gesammelte Schriften.* Berlin: Walter de Gruyter, 1902–1983.

Kant, Immanuel. *Observations on the Feeling of the Beautiful and Sublime.* Translated by John T. Goldthwait. Berkeley: University of California Press, 1960.

Karelis, Charles. "Hegel's Concept of Art: An Interpretative Essay." In *Hegel's Introduction to Aesthetics.* Edited by T. M. Knox. Oxford: Oxford University Press, 1979.

Kearney, Richard. *Poetics of Imagining.* London: HarperCollins, 1991.

Kearney, Richard. *The Wake of Imagination*. Minneapolis: University of Minnesota Press, 1988.

Kemal, Salim. "Expression and Idealism in Kant's Aesthetics." *British Journal of Aesthetics* 16 (1976): 68–79.

Kemal, Salim. "The Importance of Artistic Beauty." *Kant-Studien* 71 (1980): 488–507.

Kemal, Salim. *Kant and Fine Art*. Oxford: Clarendon Press, 1986.

Kemal, Salim. "Presentation and Expression in Kant's Aesthetics." *British Journal of Aesthetics* 15 (1975): 144–158.

Kittay, Eva Feder. *Metaphor: Its Cognitive Force and Linguistic Structure*. Oxford: Clarendon Press, 1987.

Kleingeld, Pauline. "The Conative Character of Reason in Kant's Philosophy." *Journal of the History of Philosophy* 36 (1998): 77–97.

Kolb, David. *The Critique of Pure Modernity*. Chicago: University of Chicago Press, 1986.

Kolb, David. *Postmodern Sophistications*. Chicago: University of Chicago Press, 1990.

Kuhn, Helmut. "Die Gegenwärtigkeit der Kunst nach Hegels Vorlesungen über Ästhetik." *Hegel-Studien* supp. no. 11 (1974): 251–269.

Lacoue-Labarthe, Philippe. "Sublime Truth." In *Of the Sublime: Presence in Question*. Translated by Jeffrey S. Librett. Albany: State University of New York Press, 1993.

Lacoue-Labarthe, Philippe. "The Unpresentable." In *The Subject of Philosophy*. Edited by Thomas Trezise. Minneapolis: University of Minnesota Press, 1993.

Lakoff, George and Mark Johnson. *Metaphors We Live By*. Chicago: University of Chicago Press, 1980.

Librett, Jeffrey S. (ed.). *Of the Sublime: Presence in Question*. Albany: State University of New York Press, 1993.

Locke, John. *Essay Concerning Human Understanding*. Edited by Peter Nidditch. Oxford: Oxford University Press, 1975.

Longinus. *On Great Writing (On the Sublime)*. Translated by G. M. A. Grube. Indianapolis: Hackett, 1991.

Lorand, Ruth. "Free and Dependent Beauty: A Puzzling Issue." *British Journal of Aesthetics* 29 (1981): 32–40.

Lüthe, Rudolf. "Kants Lehre von den ästhetische Ideen." *Kant-Studien* 75 (1984): 65–74.

Lyotard, Jean-François. *Lessons on the Analytic of the Sublime*. Translated by Elizabeth Rottenberg. Stanford: Stanford University Press, 1994.

Bibliography

Lyotard, Jean-François. *The Postmodern Condition.* Translated by Geoff Bennington and Brian Massumi. Minneapolis: University of Minnesota Press, 1984.

Lyotard, Jean-François. "The Sublime and the Avant-Garde." In *The Inhuman.* Translated by Lisa Liebmann. Stanford: Stanford University Press, 1991.

Makkreel, Rudolf. *Imagination and Interpretation in Kant.* Chicago: University of Chicago Press, 1990.

Makkreel, Rudolf. "Imagination and Temporality in Kant's Theory of the Sublime." *The Journal of Aesthetics and Art Criticism* 42 (1984): 303–315.

Makkreel, Rudolf. "On Sublimity, Genius, and the Explication of Kant's Aesthetic Ideas." In *Kant's Aesthetics/Kants Ästhetik.* Edited by Herman Parret. Berlin: Walter de Gruyter, 1997.

Makkreel, Rudolf. "Regulative and Reflective Uses of Purposiveness in Kant." *The Southern Journal of Philosophy* 30 supp. (1991): 49–63.

Matthews, Patricia. "Kant on Taste and Cognition." In *Proceedings of the Eighth International Kant Congress*, v. 2, pt. 2. Edited by Hoke Robinson. Milwaukee: Marquette University Press, 1995.

Matthews, Patricia. "Kant's Sublime: A Form of Pure Aesthetic Reflective Judgment." *The Journal of Aesthetics and Art Criticism* 54 (1996): 165–180.

Mattick, Paul, Jr. (ed.). *Eighteenth-Century Aesthetics and the Reconstruction of Art.* Cambridge: Cambridge University Press, 1993.

McCloskey, Mary. *Kant's Aesthetic.* Albany: State University of New York Press, 1987.

McCumber, John. *The Company of Words.* Evanston, Ill.: Northwestern University Press, 1993.

McCumber, John. "Hegel on Habit." *The Owl of Minerva* 21 (1990): 155–165.

McCumber, John. *Poetic Interaction.* Chicago: University of Chicago Press, 1989.

McDowell, John. *Mind and World.* Cambridge, Mass.: Harvard University Press, 1996.

Meerbote, Ralf. "Reflection on Beauty." In *Essays in Kant's Aesthetics.* Edited by Ted Cohen and Paul Guyer. Chicago: University of Chicago Press, 1982.

Monk, Samuel. *The Sublime: A Study of Critical Theories in XVIII-Century England.* New York: Modern Language Association, 1935.

Moran, Michael. "On the Continuing Significance of Hegel's *Aesthetics.*" *British Journal of Aesthetics* 21 (1981): 214–239.

Munzel, G. Felicitas. "'The Beautiful is the Symbol of the Morally-Good': Kant's Philosophical Basis of Proof for the Idea of the Morally-Good." *Journal of the History of Philosophy* 33 (1995): 301–330.

Murray, Patrick. *Hegel's Philosophy of Mind and Will.* Lewiston, N.Y.: Edwin Mellen Press, 1991.

Nancy, Jean-Luc. "Identity and Trembling." In *The Birth to Presence.* Translated by Brian Holmes. Stanford: Stanford University Press, 1993.

Nancy, Jean-Luc. "The Sublime Offering." In *Of the Sublime: Presence in Question.* Edited by Jeffrey S. Librett. Albany: State University of New York Press, 1993.

Nietzsche, Friedrich. *Philosophy and Truth: Selections from Nietzsche's Notebooks of the Early 1870's.* Translated and edited by Daniel Breazeale. Atlantic Highlands, N.J.: Humanities Press, 1979.

Novitz, David. *Knowledge, Fiction and Imagination.* Philadelphia: Temple University Press, 1987.

Nuyen, A. T. "The Kantian Theory of Metaphor." *Philosophy and Rhetoric* 22 (1989): 95–109.

Olson, Alan. *Hegel and the Spirit.* Princeton, N.J.: Princeton University Press, 1992.

Ortony, Andrew (ed.). *Metaphor and Thought.* 2nd edition. Cambridge: Cambridge University Press, 1993.

Pillow, Kirk. "Form and Content in Kant's Aesthetics: Situating Beauty and the Sublime in the Work of Art." *Journal of the History of Philosophy* 32 (1994): 443–459.

Pillow, Kirk. "Habituating Madness and Phantasying Art in Hegel's *Encyclopedia.*" *The Owl of Minerva* 28 (1997): 183–215.

Pippin, Robert. *Hegel's Idealism: The Satisfactions of Self-Consciousness.* Cambridge: Cambridge University Press, 1989.

Pippin, Robert. *Idealism as Modernism: Hegelian Variations.* Cambridge: Cambridge University Press, 1997.

Pippin, Robert. "The Significance of Taste: Kant, Aesthetic and Reflective Judgment." *Journal of the History of Philosophy* 34 (1996): 549–569.

Posy, Carl. "Imagination and Judgment in the Critical Philosophy." In *Kant's Aesthetics.* Edited by Ralf Meerbote. Atascadero, Calif.: Ridgeview, 1991.

Powell, Jeffrey. "The Encyclopedia of Madness." *International Studies in Philosophy* 30 (1998): 93–108.

Ricoeur, Paul. "The Metaphorical Process as Cognition, Imagination and Feeling." In *On Metaphor.* Edited by Sheldon Sacks. Chicago: University of Chicago Press, 1979.

Ricoeur, Paul. *The Rule of Metaphor.* Translated by Robert Czerny. Toronto: University of Toronto Press, 1977.

Rogerson, Kenneth. "Art and Nature in Kant's Aesthetics." In *Akten des Siebenten Internationalen Kant-Kongresses,* vol. 2. Edited by Gerhard Funke. Bonn: Bouvier, 1991.

Rogerson, Kenneth. *Kant's Aesthetics: The Roles of Form and Expression*. Lanham, Md.: University Press of America, 1986.

Ross, Stephen David. *A Theory of Art: Inexhaustibility by Contrast*. Albany: State University of New York Press, 1982.

Sacks, Sheldon (ed.). *On Metaphor*. Chicago: University of Chicago Press, 1979.

Sallis, John. *Spacings—of Reason and Imagination in Texts of Kant, Fichte, Hegel*. Chicago: University of Chicago Press, 1987.

Savile, Anthony. *Kantian Aesthetics Pursued*. Edinburgh: Edinburgh University Press, 1993.

Scarre, Geoffrey. "Kant on Free and Dependent Beauty." *British Journal of Aesthetics* 21 (1981): 351–362.

Schaper, Eva. *Studies in Kant's Aesthetics*. Edinburgh: Edinburgh University Press, 1979.

Shapiro, Gary. "Hegel on Implicit and Dialectical Meanings of Poetry." In *Art and Logic in Hegel's Philosophy*. Edited by Warren Steinkraus and Kenneth Schmitz. Atlantic Highlands, N.J.: Humanities Press, 1980.

Shusterman, Richard. "Beneath Interpretation." In *The Interpretive Turn: Philosophy, Science, Culture*. Edited by David R. Hiley, James F. Bohman, and Richard Shusterman. Ithaca, N.Y.: Cornell University Press, 1991.

Shusterman, Richard. "Of the Scandal of Taste: Social Privilege as Nature in the Aesthetic Theories of Hume and Kant." *Philosophical Forum* 20 (Spring 1989): 211–229.

Shusterman, Richard. "Organic Unity: Analysis and Deconstruction." In *Redrawing the Lines: Analytic Philosophy, Deconstruction, and Literary Theory*. Edited by Reed Way Dasenbrock. Minneapolis: University of Minnesota Press, 1989.

Stecker, Robert. "Lorand and Kant on Free and Dependent Beauty." *British Journal of Aesthetics* 30 (1990): 71–74.

Steinkraus, Warren and Kenneth Schmitz (eds.). *Art and Logic in Hegel's Philosophy*. Atlantic Highlands, N.J.: Humanities Press, 1980.

Taminiaux, Jacques. "The *Critique of Judgment* and German Philosophy." In *Poetics, Speculation, and Judgment*. Translated and edited by Michael Gendre. Albany: State University of New York Press, 1993.

Uehling, Theodore E. *The Notion of Form in Kant's Critique of Aesthetic Judgment*. The Hague: Mouton, 1971.

Vaught, Carl. *The Quest for Wholeness*. Albany: State University of New York Press, 1982.

Venturi, Robert, Denise Scott Brown, and Steven Izenour. *Learning from Las Vegas*. Cambridge, Mass.: MIT Press, 1977.

Warnock, Mary. *Imagination*. Berkeley: University of California Press, 1976.

Weiskel, Thomas. *The Romantic Sublime: Studies in the Structure and Psychology of Transcendence.* Baltimore: Johns Hopkins University Press, 1976.

Wellmer, Albrecht. "The Dialectic of Modernism and Postmodernism: The Critique of Reason since Adorno." In *The Persistence of Modernity: Essays on Aesthetics, Ethics, and Postmodernism.* Translated by David Midgley. Cambridge, Mass.: MIT Press, 1991.

Wheeler, Samuel. "Metaphor According to Davidson and Derrida." In *Redrawing the Lines: Analytic Philosophy, Deconstruction, and Literary Theory.* Edited by Reed Way Dasenbrock. Minneapolis: University of Minnesota Press, 1989.

Wicks, Robert. "Dependent Beauty as the Appreciation of Teleological Style." *The Journal of Aesthetics and Art Criticism* 55 (1997): 387–400.

Wicks, Robert. *Hegel's Theory of Aesthetic Judgment.* New York: Peter Lang, 1994.

Wicks, Robert. "Kant on Fine Art: Artistic Sublimity Shaped by Beauty." *The Journal of Aesthetics and Art Criticism* 53 (1995): 189–193.

Winfield, Richard Dien. "Hegel on Classical Art: A Reexamination." *Clio* 24 (1995): 147–167.

Winfield, Richard Dien. "Hegel, Romanticism, and Modernity." *The Owl of Minerva* 27 (1995): 3–18.

Woodmansee, Martha. *The Author, Art, and the Market: Rereading the History of Aesthetics.* New York: Columbia University Press, 1994.

Yanal, Robert J. "Kant on Aesthetic Ideas and Beauty." In *Institutions of Art: Reconsiderations of George Dickie's Philosophy.* Edited by Robert J. Yanal. University Park: Pennsylvania State University Press, 1994.

Young, J. M. "Kant's View of Imagination" *Kant-Studien* 79 (1988): 140–164.

Zammito, John. *The Genesis of Kant's Critique of Judgment.* Chicago: University of Chicago Press, 1992.

Zander, Hartwig. *Hegels Kunstphilosophie.* Wuppertal: Aloys Henn Verlag, 1970.

Index

Index